D0402770

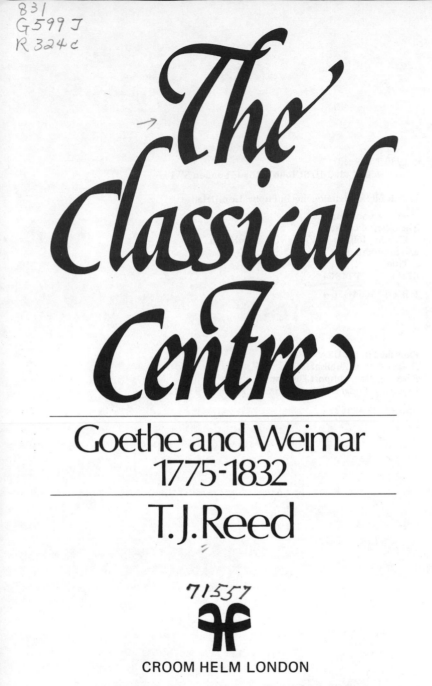

The Classical Centre

Goethe and Weimar
1775-1832

T. J. Reed

CROOM HELM LONDON

BARNES & NOBLE BOOKS - NEW YORK

(a division of Harper & Row Publishers, Inc.)

© 1980 T.J. Reed
Croom Helm Ltd. 2-10 St John's Road, London SW11

British Library Cataloguing in Publication Data

Reed, Terence James
The classical centre.
1. Goethe, Johann Wolfgang von — Criticism
and interpretation
I. Title
831'.6   PT1904

ISBN 0-85664-356-4

Published in the USA 1980 by
Harper & Row Publishers, Inc.
Barnes & Noble Import Division
Library of Congress Cataloging Card Number: 79-54252

ISBN 0-06-495825-6

Printed and bound in Great Britain

CONTENTS

For my MOTHER and FATHER

ACKNOWLEDGEMENTS

I am indebted to St John's College, St Catherine's College and the University of Oxford for two terms of leave in the course of writing this book; to the Taylorian Library and Modern Languages Faculty Office for their resources and service; to some fifteen generations of students for driving me to think about this period; and to my friend and colleague Francis Lamport for critically reading each chapter as it was finished. Responsibility for opinion and for any error is wholly mine.

Oxford, January 1979   T.J.R.

REFERENCES

Wherever possible, I refer to easily located sections of works – act and scene, or book and chapter – and to letters by recipient and date only. Page references in footnotes are to the following editions of the major authors discussed:

Goethe: Hamburger Ausgabe, ed. Trunz (= HA). For texts not contained in that selective edition, I quote from the Weimarer Ausgabe (= WA).

Schiller: *Sämtliche Werke*, ed. Fricke, Göpfert and Stubenrauch, Hanser Verlag, Munich 1958ff.

Wieland: *Werke*, ed. Martini and Seiffert, Hanser Verlag, Munich 1964ff.

Lichtenberg: *Schriften und Briefe*, ed. Promies, Hanser Verlag, Munich 1967ff.

Lessing: *Sämtliche Schriften*, ed. Lachmann and Muncker, Berlin 1886ff.

Hölderlin: *Sämtliche Werke*, Kleine Stuttgarter Ausgabe ed. Beissner, Stuttgart 1944ff.

Kant: *Werke*, ed. Cassirer, Berlin 1912ff.

F. Schlegel: *Kritische Schriften*, ed. Rasch, Munich, 1964.

1 INTRODUCTION

I

Goethe is the centre of German literature, in more than one sense. Obviously there is the sheer stature of his poetic achievement: in volume, range, quality and organic development it established a norm that is unlikely ever to be fulfilled again. Later writers have acknowledged this with varying degrees of admiration or ruefulness. Hofmannsthal put it most succinctly when he said that German literature had Goethe and rudimentary beginnings – 'Goethe und Ansätze'.

But the simple contrast between one great and many lesser achievements is not all. Goethe's work would have stood out whenever he had lived. His decisive importance for German literature lies in the timing of his contribution, and in the contrast between its richness and the relative dearth which preceded him. By 1770 Germany still had little to set beside the flourishing literary traditions of France, Spain, England. Goethe's work thus came as a fulfilment of the need – the conscious expectation, even – felt by a culture which lacked the essentials of literary tradition: native masterpieces and agreed criteria.

Germans had long been aware of these deficiencies. Eminent poet-critics – Opitz in the seventeenth century, Lessing and Wieland in the eighteenth – strove to make them good by precept and example. All three were versed in the literatures to be rivalled, classical and modern. Lessing's dramas capitalised a thorough knowledge of literary motifs and techniques to create provisional masterpieces: plays with all the workmanlike qualities that can come of applying critical insights, though lacking (or so Lessing said, with a modesty that was to damage his reputation for good) the fire of original genius. Similarly, Wieland's novels might reasonably be compared with those of his European contemporaries, though he hardly equalled them. Wieland and Lessing did what was possible in this 'Zeit der deutschen Nichtliteratur', as it was later called.[1] Wieland practised a gentle criticism and a gradual inculcation of stylistic elegance. Lessing was more uncompromising. With his clear-sighted critical campaigns and robust creativity he had the largest part in initiating what is usually called the 'literary revival' in eighteenth-century Germany.

The term is apt for a thing that inspires only limited confidence. How much promise of life is there in a revival? The look of German literature and the plans for reviving it varied between 1730 and 1770 according to whether it was Gottsched, or his Swiss opponents Bodmer and Breitinger, or Lessing who applied the artificial respiration. But with Goethe's work of the early 1770s – the novel *Werther*, the drama *Götz von Berlichingen*, the lyrical poetry and dramatic fragments which only became known later – revival yielded to renaissance. A quality was present which Germany had not seen since the middle ages. 'Genius' may not be an adequate term of explanation, but it remains a necessary point of reference in literature. It indicates that something has been created whose specific nature could not be prescribed.

Lessing's criticism had implicitly looked forward to the coming of genius. He had used his critical acuity and literary experience to create work of value while waiting. Genius, he thought, would add something unpredictable and indefinable, albeit ultimately in accord with the laws governing literature, as Shakespeare in Lessing's interpretation had turned out to accord with the *Poetics* of Aristotle and the practice of the great Greek tragedians. Genius was above mere rules and conventions, but intuitively in touch with the permanent laws.

Wieland similarly was prepared to put up with such verse-drama as Germany had only until an equal to Racine should appear, an expectation he states in the words of Corinthians I, xiii 'Wenn das Vollkommne gekommen sein wird, so wird das Stückwerk aufhören' to suggest the coming of a literary millennium.[2]

It matters little that in the event Lessing was grudging towards Goethe's early work – he was temperamentally disinclined to hail what was already a sensation. (Wieland, less pugnacious and more tolerant, recognised Goethe's stature from the first.) For with Goethe's arrival on the literary scene, an end was in sight to the controversies over literary propriety which had dominated German literature for much of the eighteenth century.

This is not to say that Goethe himself was from the first above the mêlée of controversy. He was to some extent (and to a greater extent was taken by others to be) one of the 'Germanicising' party which challenged French cultural hegemony with a programme of emphatically German themes and forms. Their ideal was the Germanic bard, who came nearest to realisation in the person of Klopstock (with the aid of a Danish pension). Goethe's *Götz*, with its German subject and its defiance of French convention, was a powerful object lesson. 'Deutschheit emergierend' was the phrase in which Goethe later summed up this phase in his work. Yet he was never really a cultural chauvinist. Even while writing *Götz*, he was studying the Greeks. And if *Götz* was a Germanic work, *Werther* was a European one, modelled in part on Rousseau's *Nouvelle Héloïse*. It became a European sensation. Similarly, Goethe was not to be limited by the aspirations of that other group with which his early work is often linked, the 'Sturm und Drang'. Conscious of being 'geniuses', these young men flouted conventions, so energetically that the flouting (violence of language and event, violation of the unities) became the main interest of their work. It is not, once the point has been taken, an absorbing interest.

If Goethe was not to be imprisoned by these different forms of liberation, national and artistic, what direction would he take? The answer is, towards classicism: a lengthy process set going by his move to Weimar in 1775 and fully realised in 1786 by his journey to Italy for a nearly two-year stay, much of it in 'time's central city', Rome. It is arguably the decisive process in Goethe's life, and it is the main topic of this book both for its own sake and for its effects beyond his individual career on German literature at large. For it is a further reason to see Goethe as the centre of German literature that he was the principal creator of Germany's classicism.

Putting it in this way — 'Germany's classicism' — is meant to suggest how important it is for a nation to have, and to have had, a classicism of its own. Classicism may be called the psychological centre of a national literature. To understand why this is so, we must enquire into the meanings and implications of the term 'classicism'.

II

The core of the word is the Latin adjective 'classicus', as used for the first and only time with literary connotations in a text from late antiquity, the *Noctes Atticae* of Aulus Gellius. In a discussion of grammatical proprieties, Gellius recommends following the usage of a major author — 'e cohorte illa dumtaxat antiquiore vel oratorum aliquis vel poetarum, id est classicus adsiduusque scriptor, non proletarius' (any one of the orators or poets, at least of the older group, a first-class taxpaying writer, not a proletarian one).[3] The metaphor is drawn from the Servian constitution of Rome which had five tax classes and the untaxed proletarians below them. A member of the top class was called simply 'classicus'. By transporting the term to questions of literary status, Gellius gave later critics, theorists and historians a name to conjure with, even if (or perhaps, as Curtius suggests, because) the exact meaning of the word in its original context was not understood. Just how it came down to modern times and acquired on the way the prestige it has, is not clear: the first modern use Curtius records is a

French one of 1548. But more important is the idea Gellius was putting forward, which remains prominent among the associations added in later times: the idea of literary status and authority.

What are those other associations? In his essay 'Qu'est-ce qu'un classique?' Sainte-Beuve said of classical ages that they are 'the only ones that offer perfected talent a propitious climate and shelter. We know that only too well, living as we do in disjointed times [*époques sans lien*] in which talents, perhaps the equal of those earlier ones, have got lost and dissipated through the uncertainties and inclemencies of the age'. Looking back over a period which had known so much upheaval – political, intellectual, artistic – Sainte-Beuve emphasises and envies the cohesion and settledness which make a favouring climate for the production of literary works. His is more an elegiac than an analytical statement; just how society shelters and fosters literature is not clear. But the central idea is important; classical ages are ages of cohesion and stability.

This is reaffirmed and elaborated in T.S. Eliot's essay 'What is a Classic?' Eliot stresses the idea of agreed stylistic norms which in turn depend on social order:

> the age in which we find a common style will be an age when society
> has reached a moment of order and stability, of equilibrium and
> harmony; as the age which manifests the greatest extremes of
> individual style will be an age of immaturity or an age of senility.
> Maturity of language may naturally be expected to accompany
> maturity of mind and manners. We may expect the language to
> approach maturity at the moment when men have a critical sense
> of the past, a confidence in the present, and no conscious doubt of
> the future.

Like Sainte-Beuve's metaphors of mild climate and inclement weather, Eliot's too contain a value-judgement: societies and cultures are represented as organic things, having youth and old age, ideally productive only at the mid-point between immaturity and senile decay. And Eliot links such maturity with men's attitudes to past, present and future.

This link is examined with immensely more penetration in Sartre's account of French classicism:

> in the seventeenth century . . . since the artist accepts the ideology
> of the elite without criticising it, he becomes the accomplice of his
> public . . . . There is no *poète maudit*, much less a prose-writer.

Writers do not have to decide with every work they write what is the meaning and value of literature, since these things are fixed by tradition; firmly integrated in a hierarchical society, they know neither the anguish nor the pride of the outsider; in a word, they are *classical* writers. For one can speak of classicism when a society has assumed a fairly stable form and is imbued with the myth of its own permanence, . . . when every reader is, for the writer, a qualified critic and a censor, when the power of religious and political ideology is so great and taboos are so rigorous that there is no question of ever discovering new realms for thought, but only of giving form to the commonplaces adopted by the elite, so that reading . . . may be a ceremony of recognition analogous to a greeting, that is to say a ceremonious affirmation that writer and reader belong to the same world and have the identical opinions about all matters.[4]

Here a new note is struck. Against the outsider status (*singularité*) of later writers, Sartre sets cultural community, shared beliefs, social integration, but he is not nostalgic about them as Sainte-Beuve was. If the age can shelter a writer, 'sheltered' can also be a pejorative term. If society in a classical age has reached a state of equilibrium and harmony, as Eliot said, harmony may spell conformism: conventions within society may be enforced conventions, equilibrium may become stagnation, confidence in the future can also be described as a belief in the eternal and exclusive rightness of the way things are now. The writer may express magnificently the agreed views of his age, but he is unlikely to disturb or advance them, to dissent or explore beyond fixed limits. He is more of a craftsman than a creator, certainly not a critic of his age. In Sartre's metaphor he is its accomplice. Nowhere is the problematic nature of classical ages so well brought out.

III

These four texts have furnished us with guiding concepts: literary status and authority; social stability; cultural maturity; intellectual community and conformity. But one obvious element is still missing. European classicisms have always drawn on 'classical' antiquity — Greece and Rome — for their forms, themes and ideals. How does this external feature relate to the concepts discussed so far? Need there be any relation at all? What we have been concerned with is the production of literary classics, i.e., great canonical works; the 'classical ages' sketched by Sainte-Beuve, Eliot and Sartre were simply those which gave rise to such works. That is something quite distinct from the use of ancient metres, the adaptation of stories from Greek and Roman history, mythology and literature, the emulation of a grand manner discerned in ancient epic or tragedy.[5] Are the ages which imitate antiquity in these respects necessarily also the stable, mature ages in which the great works of a national culture are created?

Clearly there is no logical necessity that they should be. Yet in practice connections do exist. The great works of Greek and Latin literature arose in stable, mature and powerful societies, whose religious, social and ethical attitudes they reflected. Forms derived from antiquity have in fact proved congenial to the rulers and elites of stable and powerful societies in modern Europe — the France of Louis XIV, the England of Queen Anne. Napoleon too, in his imperial phase, fostered classical forms in painting, sculpture and architecture. It may be that rulers and their arbiters of taste merely associated such forms historically with past imperial greatness. But there may also be some essential affinity between social order and the formal order first achieved by the art of Greece and Rome.

In practice, again, ages which emulated antiquity have also created some of the classics of national literatures. A classic is, precisely, a work that can claim equal status with the Latin and Greek works which for so long dominated European writing. This explains the paradox that the vernacular classics were both imitating and also rivalling the authoritative works of antiquity: only works in the same mode could hope to achieve the same status. Hence the European vernacular literatures and their classics make up a sequence of rivalries, initially with Greece and Rome, then with each other as well. First the literature of Italy established itself against the prestige of the ancients and the borrowed prestige of neo-Latin writing. Then the Pléiade poets in sixteenth-century France competed with the ancient literatures, but also now with the Italians, especially Petrarch. (Sainte-Beuve called the Pléiade France's 'first but abortive classic poetry'.) Similarly, it was with a French literary culture now long established, with a hegemony of French language and taste in Europe backed by the power of France in international politics, that Germany had to compete in the eighteenth century; and behind the prestige of French writing lay the older prestige of the Greek and Latin sources which, with whatever violence to the originals, French classical literature had adopted. This double authority is illustrated, to the point of caricature, by Frederick the Great's *De la littérature allemande* (1780), which proposed to form German taste by a grand programme of translations from French and the classical languages. It dismissed meanwhile the stirrings of life in native German writing such as Goethe's *Götz* because they broke the rules. 'The rules of the theatre', wrote the King, 'are not arbitrary. They are in Aristotle's *Poetics*'.

IV

The state of dearth in eighteenth-century German literature is now set in European perspective. The desirability of German classics, even of a German classicism, is plain. But neither could be conjured out of thin air. Gottsched's and Frederick the Great's programmes of translation and imitation presupposed that literary quality was transplantable. Lessing's campaign to raise critical standards and to offset French influence by the example of English literature was more sophisticated, more realistic even, but not different in kind: even if he was right in thinking that English literature, and Shakespeare in particular, were more congenial to the German mind than Racine and Corneille, he too was proposing to make literature from literature, awaken genius with genius. He was thus operating within a world of literature distinct from the social reality which (if the views examined above are right) is the soil from which a great and coherent literature grows. But precisely this is the problem for the critic who faces such large issues: he cannot legislate direct for the forms of society which would nurture literary production. Powerless to bring into being the presumed causes, he can only describe and prescribe the hoped-for cultural effects.

So the question arises, in what ways the condition of eighteenth-century Germany hindered the rise of great literature. One document answers this question very directly. In March 1795, the Berlin journal *Archiv der Zeit und ihres Geschmacks* printed an essay complaining at the lack of classic prose works in Germany. Goethe answered it with a piece entitled *Literarischer Sansculottismus*.[6] He argues that the charge is unfair, that the present standard of German prose writing is high, and that now is not the time for niggling criticism. True, no German author would presume to call himself a classic; but then 'classics' only arise in certain conditions, not obtaining in Germany's recent past or present.

Goethe's account of these conditions agrees strikingly with the picture we have formed of classicism and society. A classic author, he says, will appear when he finds great events in his nation's history resulting in a happy unity; when there is greatness in his compatriots' mode of thinking, depth in their feelings, strength and consistency in their actions; when he himself is imbued with a national spirit and his genius can sympathise with past and present; when he finds his nation at an advanced stage of culture, so that his own process of cultivation is made easy; when he can view an assemblage of literary materials and the perfect and imperfect efforts of his predecessors, so that there is no need to pay dearly for his apprenticeship but he is enabled to conceive and execute major work while still in his prime. All this is obviously beyond the individual's control; it is a matter of the development of a national society: 'einen vortrefflichen Nationalschriftsteller kann man nur von der Nation fordern.'

But, Goethe asks, what was and is the German case? Nowhere in Germany is there one centre of social and cultural life where writers might come together and develop in their different genres but still in a common direction ('nach einer Art, in einem Sinne').[7] Born in scattered corners, with widely different upbringing, left for the most part to themselves and the impressions of quite disparate conditions; carried away by a predilection for this or that example of native or foreign literature; forced for want of guidance into all sorts of experiment and botched work to try out their talents; only gradually persuaded by reflection what they ought to do and taught by practice what they are capable of doing; led astray again and again by a large public so lacking in taste that it consumes with equal pleasure the good and the bad . . . (Here Goethe interrupts his lament with a few mitigating circumstances) . . . then again encouraged by acquaintance with the large cultivated class, which however is scattered through every part of the Holy Roman Empire, and strengthened by the similar strivings of contemporaries . . . (But these still do not set things to rights, for when the German writer has at last served his apprenticeship and found some support, it is late) . . . he thus finds himself come to manhood and is compelled by need to support himself with hack work if he is to produce the things which alone his mind is intent on.

Almost certainly Goethe had Schiller in mind here. But it is, he says, a situation any German writer will recognise. Which of them has not sighed for a national culture to which he might subordinate his genius? A *native* culture, that is, for the undoubted cultivation of the upper classes was always of foreign origin and has on balance been more a hindrance than a help: 'die Bildung der höheren Klassen durch fremde Sitten und ausländische Literatur, so viel Vorteil sie uns auch gebracht hat, hinderte doch den Deutschen als Deutschen sich früher zu entwickeln.' In these circumstances, it is a wonder that anything was achieved at all.

The social preconditions for classicism outlined above are here restated — as lacking. And yet not only is Goethe sanguine about the present, or at least he is so when faced with an unduly sweeping rejection of its products; not only does he discern signs of Eliot's 'common style' ('eines übereinstimmenden guten Stils') in current writing; most important of all, he stands in 1795 on the threshold of major personal achievements, the creation of classic works in the mode which has come to be known as 'high classicism' (*Hochklassik*). If this was possible against all the social odds, there must be something peculiar about the German case. It is in this peculiarity, indeed abnormality, that much of the interest of German classicism for the literary historian resides.

V

Weimar Classicism, as it is also known from the minor town in Thuringia which became in a geographical sense the classical centre, was the work of two men, Goethe and Schiller. Each moved towards a classical style for his own reasons and in relative ignorance of the other. They did not make real contact until each was entering upon this new stylistic phase. They then found that, despite fundamental differences of temperament and creative method, they agreed in their ultimate aims and assumptions. They also had, in a sense, a common past. Both had come through, triumphantly if with some damage, the unfavourable conditions of their place and time. Both had shared with their contemporaries a conviction of the deficiencies of German culture and they had exercised their minds and talents on the remedies then much talked of. Examining this phase of their work will put flesh on the generalities of *Literarischer Sansculottismus*, and classical attitudes and the possibility of a classical partnership will be seen growing from the embryo.

Notes

1. Friedrich Schlegel, *Kritische Schriften* (Munich, [2]1964), p.401.
2. Wieland, *Briefe an einen jungen Dichter*, 2 (1782), *Werke* (Munich, 1964 ff.), III, 465.
3. Gellius, *Noctes Atticae* XIX, 8, 15. Quoted by Ernst Robert Curtius, *Europäische Literatur und lateinisches Mittelalter* (Berne, 1948), p.253.
4. Jean-Paul Sartre, *Qu'est-ce que la littérature?* (reprinted Paris, 1964), pp.116f. (My translation).
5. Only English among the European languages distinguishes firmly between 'classics' and 'classical' works. It is true that German uses 'Klassizismus' and 'klassizistisch' to refer to classical externals; but, like the English word 'classicistic', these suggest *mere* externals, and would not normally be used of literary works whose substantial qualities bear out the connection with antiquity. Cf. Friedrich Sengle, *Wieland* (Stuttgart, 1949), p.321: 'Zweifellos ist das antike Gewand kein Kriterium für Klassik. Die deutsche Literatur zumal,

welche einen Gottsched und Ayrenhoff mit dem Anspruch klassischer Leistung auftreten sah, ist gezwungen, zwischen Klassik und Klassizismus zu unterscheiden'.
6. HA 12, 239ff.
7. The point is the lack of a single centre. There were certainly cultural centres in the German-speaking world in the eighteenth century, but they were in competition with each other over matters of literary propriety (Leipzig and Zurich) and even linguistic usage (Meissen and Vienna). Such multicentricity inevitably hinders the growth of a unified culture. As Madame de Staël wrote: 'On ne juge pas, on ne critique pas avec sévérité, lorsque chaque ville veut avoir des hommes supérieurs dans son sein . . . et ce qui semble de l'abondance, amène la confusion'. *De la littérature considérée dans ses rapports avec les institutions sociales*, I xvii, 'De la littérature allemande'. Some of the many centres were in any case simply dominated by French taste − Frederick the Great's Berlin, or Leipzig, which when Goethe went there to study in 1765 was known as 'Klein-Paris'.

2 THEATRE AND NATION

I

In 1768 the project for a Hamburg National Theatre failed. It had arisen when a travelling company typical of eighteenth-century theatrical life set up a permanent theatre in Hamburg in 1765, fell into financial difficulties and was rescued by a group of Hamburg citizens. They began with high intentions, but internal disagreement and poor public support foiled them. In the final article of his *Hamburgische Dramaturgie*, Lessing put this failure down to the lack of a German nation: 'Über den gutherzigen Einfall, den Deutschen ein Nationaltheater zu verschaffen, da wir Deutsche noch keine Nation sind!' For German national character seemed to consist in having no character at all.

Disillusioned by the failure of a promising plan, Lessing has decided that to begin with cultural works before there is a society to support them is to put the cart before the horse, that is, he agrees with the view of literature's relation to society sketched in Chapter 1. But for a time at least he must have held the opposite view, namely that a national theatre might be created first and be the means to shape society and create a nation. This view was a commonplace of critical discussion in the 1770s and 1780s[1] and in the response to it of the young Schiller and the young Goethe there are the seeds of their mature literary programme.

Schiller, it is true, begins sceptical. In *Über das gegenwärtige teutsche Theater* (1782) he recognises that the theatre, which mirrors life in sensuous form, must be a more effective means to form morality than abstract preaching. But sensuousness is a two-edged quality. The moral of *Emilia Galotti* may be lost on a princely spectator who has eyes only for the actress playing that victim of princely despotism. The theatre (and here no doubt Schiller has Rousseau in mind, whose *Lettre à M. D'Alembert* had reawakened all the ancient prejudices against sensuous representation) risks becoming a procuress. In the end, the attitude people bring with them to the theatre is decisive. If this is frivolous and vicious, the dramatist cannot hope to be the 'Lehrer des Volks'. 'Bevor das Publikum für seine Bühne gebildet ist, dürfte wohl schwerlich die Bühne das Publikum bilden'.[2] The problem is of the same – circular – kind as the one Lessing posed;[3] and it has much the same content: in both cases we are concerned with the patriotic ambition to form the character of the dramatist's nation. But two years later, Schiller gives a very different account. He is in some respects a different Schiller, having escaped the control of the Duke of Württemberg, set up as a free writer, and had three plays acted in major centres – Berlin, Frankfurt, Mannheim. His situation as theatre-poet in the last-named is precarious, but he knows the theatrical effect of his own work, which has had considerable success. The title of his Mannheim address, 'Was kann eine gute stehende Schaubühne eigentlich wirken?', perhaps claims he knows the real truth about a much-discussed topic. This time he is wholly positive about sensuous realisation. It gives the theatre the same power as the images of popular religious belief have to reinforce doctrine. Theatre can thereby supplement the law, punish vice, pillory foolishness. It innoculates us against misfortune by showing tragic events. It is a means of enlightenment, indeed an ally of *the* Enlightenment:

> Die Schaubühne ist der gemeinschaftliche Kanal, in welchen von dem denkenden besseren Teil des Volks das Licht der Weisheit herunterströmt und von da aus in milderen Strahlen durch den ganzen Staat sich verbreitet. Richtigere Begriffe, geläuterte Grundsätze, reinere Gefühle fliessen von hier durch alle Adern des Volks; der Nebel der Barbarei, des finstern Aberglaubens verschwindet, die Nacht weicht dem siegenden Licht . . .[4]

These images, together with the examples that follow – the growth of religious toleration fostered by Lessing's *Nathan der Weise* and by the actions of Joseph II, or the possibility of showing right and wrong methods of education on the stage – place Schiller's argument firmly in the eighteenth century's rational tradition.

And he also now believes that the theatre can influence the nation, strengthening or even establishing a 'Nationalgeist', which he defines as a community of outlook on matters which another nation views otherwise. Since the theatre gathers different classes in one place and takes the direct emotive way to influence their thoughts, it only needs the appropriate choice of subject and treatment to cement society and give it an identity:

> Wenn in allen Stücken *ein* Hauptzug herrschte, wenn unsre Dichter unter sich einig werden und einen festen Bund zu diesem Endzweck errichten wollten – wenn strenge Auswahl ihre Arbeiten leitete, ihr Pinsel nur Volksgegenständen sich weihte – mit einem Wort, wenn

wir es erlebten, eine Nationalbühne zu haben, so würden wir auch eine Nation.⁵

Was this not how Greek theatre unified a scattered nation, by the patriotic content of its dramas and by the spirit, both national and humane, which breathed in them?

These are brave words spoken in the teeth of insuperable difficulties. Like Lessing in the *Hamburgische Dramaturgie*, Schiller is using the term 'nation' in a cultural, at most social, not a political sense. Yet it is the political condition of Germany, its fragmentation into countless sovereignties — principalities, dukedoms, bishoprics and city-states only loosely linked as the Holy Roman Empire 'of the German Nation' — which almost necessarily doomed any initiative to remain merely local. The Hamburg venture had failed. Vienna could have had cultural authority as capital of the Empire, but its 'Nationalbühne' (so-called from 1776) was constrained by censorship and narrow taste. Attempts were made to secure Lessing's services for Vienna, but he saw at once these fatal limitations. Mannheim too at about this time tried to attract him to its new 'Nationaltheater', and ever-hopeful he went to prospect. But he found the conception small, the word of the Elector Karl Theodor and his ministers unreliable, the outlook for dramatic writing unfavourable. He concluded: 'Mit einem deutschen Nationaltheater ist es lauter Wind'.⁶ And Lessing's friend Nicolai commented:

das, was die Fürsten für die Literatur tun sollen, sei nicht wert, dass man die Hand danach umwende . . . die deutsche Literatur ist bei den Grossen ein Ding, das durch nichts als durch eine armselige Hofintrige befördert oder verstossen wird.⁷

The Mannheim theatre was to make its name a little later through the acting of Iffland, but the technique of communicating was not matched by drama of value. Its literary glory was to be Schiller's brief stay and the production of his early works; but him it cast out as uncomfortably radical and superfluous to practical needs.

Thus literature was denied even the single pivoting-point which it required in order to take effect without the support of a coherent society. Schiller's early plays were written and produced in an insecure, hand-to-mouth situation. Yet they are positive, even sanguine in mood: they respond to what he saw as the higher needs of the time and the envisaged nation. The mood was shared by Goethe, who left the richest and most precise record of the German theatre, its aspirations and its relations with actual German society in these same years.

II

Aside from the plays they both wrote, Goethe's response to the challenge of the theatre takes a different form from Schiller's; indeed, it .typifies the difference between their natures. Where Schiller treated the question analytically and in rhetorical language, Goethe grasps its elements concretely and renders them immediately. He portrays contemporary society and the world of the theatre in a novel, *Wilhelm Meisters theatralische Sendung.*

Wilhelm Meister's passion for the theatre begins in childhood with puppet-plays at home. From early on he writes. Later, a love-affair with an actress strengthens and mixes his motivation. Travelling to collect debts for his family firm, he falls in with a company of actors on the road, lends them money, gives them a play of his own to act, even in emergency takes a major role in it, and finally throws in his lot with them. This is the end of the fragment, six books which Goethe wrote between 1777 and 1785 (though the conception probably goes back as far as 1773); a further six books were planned but never written. We thus have only the process which brings Wilhelm to his fateful decision: we do not see how his 'mission' is fulfilled.

What we do see is fascinating enough. Goethe gives us an intimate picture of actors and actresses, their professional shortcomings and difficulties, their status and the state of German literature at the time of Gottsched's supremacy, the hopes that were cherished for the theatre as a national institution and influence, the reactions of different levels of society to drama and to the acting companies as a social group. In all this, things of value mingle with things of no value, talent jostles charlatanry, ideals and ambitions are harnessed with plain gain-seeking and even swindling. It is a mixture which Wilhelm finally accepts.

From the first, his personal experience parallels and represents that larger phenomenon, the state of the theatre. The individual is rendered as an undiminished reality, but in addition he carries a general meaning. Thus, the children's theatrical games which developed from the first interest in puppets are described, and in particular the loss of spontaneity and immediate appeal when childhood gives way to adolescence. They now bite off more than they can chew, they try too hard, they lose the charm of innocence but have nothing yet to replace it:

Das Knabenalter ist, glaub' ich, darum weniger liebenswürdig als die Kindheit, weil es ein mittler, halber Zustand ist. Das Kindische klebt ihnen noch an, sie noch am Kindischen, allein sie haben mit der ersten Beschränktheit die liebevolle Behaglichkeit verloren, ihr Sinn steht vorwärts, sie sehen den Jüngling, den Mann vor sich, und weil auch ihr Weg dahin geht, eilt die Einbildung voraus, ihre Wünsche überfliegen ihren Kreis, sie ahmen nach, sie stellen vor, was sie nicht sein können noch sollen.

This is true, the narrator says, of the inner and outer development of the young person, and it was true of their acting:

Je länger sie spielten, je mehr Mühe sie sich gaben . . . wurd' ihr Spiel immer langweiliger, das Drollige ihrer ersten Unbefangenheit fiel weg . . . es ward eine steife einbildische Mittelmässigkeit draus, die um desto fataler war, weil sie sich's selbst sagen konnten und oft gar von ihren Zuschauern hörten, dass sie sich um vieles gebessert hätten.

Most harm of all was done by the chance visit of a company of players to the town, whose acting was itself affected and untrue to nature and for just that reason most easy to imitate. And this baneful influence allows a remark on the state of the German theatre, which can be understood in just the terms of growth and development that were used to describe the children:

Die deutsche Bühne war damals in eben der Krise; man warf die Kinderschuhe weg, ehe sie ausgetreten waren, und musste indess barfuss laufen.

(Book I, chapter II)[8]

The parallel is not expanded further, but the historical meaning can be inferred from what has gone before. It is spelled out later in the novel when Wilhelm meets the Principal of a travelling company. Her name, Madame de Retti, masks the historical identity of Karoline Neuber ('die Neuberin'), famous as the practical collaborator in Gottsched's schemes for 'regularising' the theatre, that is, for raising it from a common popular entertainment to an artistic institution.

This programme involved abolishing two popular elements, extemporization on-stage, and the popular comic figures Harlekin and Hanswurst. The 'literarizing' of the stage, in practice its Frenchification, demanded the snobbish removal of low-brow amusement. But Madame de Retti now has doubts and regrets:

> Wie leid ist es mir, sagte sie, dass wir um das Extemporieren gebracht sind, es hat mich hundertmal gereut, dass ich selbst mit Schuld daran gewesen; . . . denn das Extemporieren war die Schule und der Probierstein des Acteurs . . . der Schauspieler war durch die Not gezwungen, sich mit allen Ressourcen, die das Theater anbietet, bekannt zu machen, er wurde darauf recht einheimisch, wie der Fisch im Wasser, und ein Dichter, der Gabe genug gehabt hätte, diese Werkzeuge zu gebrauchen, würde auch auf das Publikum einen grossen Effekt gemacht haben.
>
> (III, 8)

Extemporising, then, was a theatrical strength, not a thing to be scorned. We know from contemporary accounts something of the unique effects which were produced by the actor skilled at improvising.[9] But, equally important, the live communication of impromptu speech and the rapport between actor and audience might have been turned to good effect by a skilful writer, as they were to be in the nineteenth-century Viennese comedies of Nestroy and Raimund.

Much the same applies to the comic figures. Carried away by 'the critics' (i.e. Gottsched), and herself too serious to enjoy farce, Madame de Retti disdained merely to entertain the crowd:

> Ich verbannte den Hanswurst, begrub den Harlekin . . . Und welcher deutsche Schriftsteller hat uns bisher für das, was wir hingegeben, entschädigt?

She would have been ruined but for the German versions of Molière, because the best German writers were 'nicht theatralisch'.

It is revealing that Molière filled the bill. His comedies are basically good entertainment, even if they also rise to the level of great art — indeed, the greatness of the art lies above all in the mastery of theatrical entertainment. In other words, Molière gives an object-lesson in the growth of literary quality out of popular conventions. (Meister himself reflects that comedy is the more refined daughter of farce, II, 5.). Such developments were precluded for Germany by Gottsched's prohibitions and prescriptions. He was digging up the roots of a native art, as some perceived. The historian Justus Möser wrote a defence of Harlekin

(1761) and argued in a letter that such character-types were a kind of common language, comprehensible everywhere in a culturally un-unified country.[10] These were the 'children's shoes' which German culture had been made to throw out, and it now went barefoot for want of any others.

It is true that Harlekin was not an original German figure, but one left behind by a much earlier foreign influence, the *commedia dell' arte*. He was not so much a national as a natural figure, so natural, in fact, that his banishment proved more apparent than real: characters with other names performed the same comic function, as Lessing gleefully pointed out. Indeed, when his own *Miss Sara Sampson* was performed in Vienna in 1763, one of the servant-roles was turned into a 'Hanswurst'.[11] Nature, driven out with a pitchfork, had come back. It is indeed nothing less than Nature which is at stake, seen in one perspective (Gottsched's) as unworthy to intrude into art, in another perspective (the repentant Madame de Retti's, Möser's, Goethe's) as the vital base on which art arises. It is apt that Wilhelm, who had once accepted Gottsched's authority and modelled his verse-plays on Gottsched's as 'klassische Muster' (II, 3), uses a homely natural image to cast doubt on the rightness of 'regularising' the theatre, saying:

dass, je mehr das Theater gereinigt wird, es zwar verständigen und geschmackvollen Menschen angenehmer werden muss, allein von seiner ursprünglichen Wirkung und Bestimmung immer mehr verliert. Es scheint mir . . . wie ein Teich zu sein, der nicht allein klares Wasser, sondern auch eine gewisse Portion von Schlamm, Seegras und Insekten enthalten muss, wenn Fische und Wasservögel sich darin wohl befinden sollen.

(II, 5)

If only Gottsched had not cleaned out the pond, if the acting troupes had had the commonsense and good fortune to encourage natural growth, then, Madame de Retti believes, they might have given Germans the materials for — a national theatre:

ein treffliches Geschenk, das der Grund eines National-Theaters geworden wäre und von den besten Köpfen hätte benutzt und verfeinert werden können.

(III, 8)

The idea of nature is central to the *Theatralische Sendung*, both as the basis from which a new art may grow and more generally as a human ideal. Indeed, it is the frustration of this ideal that leads the generation of which Wilhelm Meister is the symbolic representative to concern themselves so intensely with the theatre. The novel repeatedly asks how man can lead a natural life in society as it is constituted in eighteenth-century Germany. Neither bourgeois life, narrow and constricting, nor the life of the nobility, artificial and out of touch with fundamental human values, comes very well out of Goethe's depiction. Specifically, Wilhelm is not suited to commerce which is compared to pitch on the wings of his spirit, strings preventing the growth of his soul. Feeling, imagination, ambition are all confined:

> Sein Gefühl, das wärmer und stärker ward, seine Einbildung, die
> sich erhöhte, waren unverrückt gegen das Theater gewendet, und
> was Wunder? In eine Stadt gesperrt, in's bürgerliche Leben
> gefangen, im Häuslichen gedrückt, ohne Aussicht auf Natur, ohne
> Freiheit des Herzens . . . die alberne Langeweile der Sonn- und
> Festtage machte ihn nur unruhiger, und was er etwa auf einem
> Spaziergange von freier Welt sah, ging nie in ihn hinüber, er war
> zum Besuch in der herrlichen Natur und sie behandelte ihn als
> Besuch. Und mit der Fülle von Liebe, von Freundschaft, von
> Ahndung grosser Thaten, wo sollte er damit hin?

(I, 12)

The stage is seen as the only possible 'Heilort'. But if the theatre is the only escape – and only an escape – from the realities of bourgeois existence, its status is doubtful. However fruitful the theatromania of Wilhelm's contemporaries was to prove, it has its problematic side as (in Nietzsche's terms) a 'reactive' feeling, something Goethe intimates when he describes it as an 'unnatürliches Naturgefühl'.

How typical Wilhelm Meister was is clear, right down to fine details, from the story of another theatre-struck young man. Karl Philipp Moritz's *Anton Reiser*, sub-titled 'Ein psychologischer Roman' appeared in four parts between 1785 and 1790. If the *Theatralische Sendung* is fictional transmutation of personal experience, Moritz's novel is more directly autobiographical. It is a pathetic record. Where Wilhelm Meister suffered from the restrictiveness of easy bourgeois life, Reiser suffers grinding poverty. Throughout his school life he depends on acts of charity which repeatedly turn sour – it is his fate 'Wohltaten zu seiner Qual zu empfangen' (p.177).[12] Incident after incident undermines his standing with his teachers and schoolfellows, breaks his self-esteem, and intensifies a melancholy born of the pietist excesses of his earliest childhood. Chances of circumstance and quirks of character turn him into a total outsider: 'er wurde ganz aus der Reihe herausgedrängt − er stand einsam und verlassen da' (p.173). Inevitably he seeks compensations in an imaginary world. Like Meister, he has aspirations to write and act; in him their roots go back to a fascination with sermons and preachers. He takes every chance to act in school-plays and to see visiting companies. This theatre-mania lowers his reputation yet further, which in turn drives him deeper into his refuges of the imagination. A brilliant performer of *Emilia Galotti* makes him forget all thoughts but the theatre; Wieland's translation of Shakespeare transports him. But each time, the gap opening between Reiser and reality is stressed. His need is more desperate than Meister's, the resulting condition more pathological. He imagines himself in grand roles full of high emotion such as his everyday life cannot yield. Yet the case is akin to Meister's, down to similarities of wording:

> Dieser Wunsch war bei Reisern sehr natürlich; er hatte Gefühle für Freundschaft, für Dankbarkeit, für Grossmut, und edle Entschlossenheit, welche alle ungenutzt in ihm schlummerten; denn durch seine äussere Lage schrumpfte sein Herz zusammen. − Was Wunder, dass es sich in einer idealischen Welt wieder zu erweitern, und seinen natürlichen Empfindungen nachzuhängen suchte! − In dem Schauspiel schien er sich gleichsam wieder zu finden, nachdem er sich in seiner wirklichen Welt beinahe verloren hatte.
>
> (p.158)

This is once again an 'unnatürliches Naturgefühl' generated by the shortcomings of society and experienced as mixed frustration and aspiration.

Moritz's prime interest is psychological, as his sub-title shows. He was one of the earliest rational investigators of psychology (he founded the first German psychological journal, *Gnothi Sauton*, or 'know thyself') and Reiser's is a story of the neurosis arising from a conflict between imaginative escapism and undeniable realities. These finally prevail; Reiser's vocation is declared a false one, his illusions about his talent crumble, and we last see him with a company whose principal has absconded, leaving them a 'zerstreute Herde'. Social criticism is not a main aim for Moritz. Yet for the reader the interest is evenly divided between the two elements of Reiser's 'Widerspruch von aussen und innen' (p.340). We cannot ignore the social causes of his misery; we see how hard it was for men of talent and no means to make their way in a society whose outlook was narrowed by religion and materialism. Heine aptly called the book 'the story of a few hundred Taler which the author did not have, through which his whole life became a series of deprivations and renunciations'.[13] Formless as the book is, like so much of the autobiographical writing of this period — Jung Stilling's or Salomon Maimon's *Lebensgeschichte*, Ulrich Bräker's *Der arme Mann im Tockenburg* — its very formlessness has an effect, because it conveys the relentless monotony of small miseries and temporary, illusory hopes. And even more than Goethe's *Theatralische Sendung*, it shows the gap between a society not touched by culture, and a culture — theatre and literature — existing alongside society, living off it, avidly pursued by those whom society frustrates, but having no other, closer relationship with society.

III

Anton Reiser is doubly an outsider, thrust out by society yet unable to gain a footing in the theatre. His story accordingly lacks intimate contact with that sphere. There are literary references enough — to *Werther*, to Shakespeare, to *Emilia Galotti* — but these landmarks in German culture are seen in isolation and from the outside.

Goethe, in contrast, when he wrote the *Theatralische Sendung*, was an acclaimed author, had had successful plays performed, had been a member of a group of noted young writers, had engaged in literary controversy. He was part of the literary scene. His novel breathes its atmosphere. We catch echoes of the ideas current, perhaps already commonplace, in the sixties and seventies. They amount almost to a history of taste in that period. There is Wilhelm's original belief in Gottsched's authority — inexperience made him take Gottsched for a classic (II, 3). There is his rejection of finery and rank as a source of majesty, in favour of what is natural: 'dass das Grosse und Erhabene nur das Reinste und Wahrste des Natürlichen ist' (I, 16) — a sentiment which combines Lessing's critique of the high tragic conventions with the 'Nature' axiom of the *Sturm und Drang*. There is a questioning of the Unities, not for being too restrictive, but for being too few: 'Ja wenn denn am Ende Einheiten sein sollen, warum nur drei und nicht ein Dutzend? Die Einheit der Sitten, des Tons, der Sprache . . .' and so on, (II, 2) echoing a famous passage of Lenz's *Anmerkungen übers Theater*.[14] Then surprisingly there is praise for Corneille, Lessing's butt in the *Hamburgische Dramaturgie*, and hardly *Sturm und Drang* taste, for being 'einfach and schön', 'gross und . . . natürlich' (II, 2), which suggests that positions the historian sees as clearcut may not have been quite so hard and fast at the time. And then inevitably there is Wilhelm's discovery of Shakespeare, greeted ecstatically with images of storm-winds and great oceans and the tides of fate (V, 10).

Again, we hear actors discussing their social functions, invariably ending with 'der grosse wichtige Einfluss des Theaters auf die Bildung einer Nation und der Welt' (I, 16). We see them still struggling against the public's adverse view of the profession; and when Wilhelm protests against this he uses a familiar comparison, with the preacher — 'der Prediger, der die Worte Gottes verkündigt . . . der Schauspieler, der uns die Stimme der Natur ans Herz legt' (I, 15). He is here close to Lessing who, when forbidden to write theological polemic, put it in the form of the drama *Nathan der Weise* for his 'old pulpit', the theatre;[15] close to Schiller, whose first ambition was to preach and who saw the effects of the stage as an extension of the effects of religion; close to Reiser, whose desire to act grew out of an earlier ambition to preach; close to Iffland, who wavered similarly between the two professions and spoke of the theatre as a temple and the actor as a priest of Nature.[16]

But there is one subject of overriding importance which Goethe presents not through snippets of conversation and interwoven comment, but by a full-blown episode. That is the question of patronage. At the end of Book Four, the company is invited to a count's castle to perform for a visiting prince, whose favourite entertainment is theatre — but French theatre, so that from the first Meister's friends are a stopgap ('wenn diese Leute nicht ganz ungeschickt sind, so wäre es doch immer etwas' IV, 14). The secretary's remark that his masters are lovers of literature, especially German literature, and 'lassen ihr alle Gerechtigkeit widerfahren' (V, 2) suggests that they are not enthusiastic, but at most prepared to make allowances. These unfavourable omens are borne out. The company arrives in high hopes and pouring rain. Nobody receives them, no accommodation is ready. They finally make do with an abandoned wing, unheated and unfurnished. Only the attractive Philine is whisked away to the new castle, whose brilliant lights and busy kitchen outhouses had looked so welcoming as they arrived. They settle in, but the Principal's efforts to establish order and get rehearsals going are foiled by a swarm of young officer guests who besiege the actresses (V, 4).

Wilhelm is soon asked to read one of his plays to the Countess and her circle. He feels it is a serious test to appear before such 'practised connoisseurs'. He appears, but never reads his play — the connoisseurs are busy with a hairdresser, a fancy-goods merchant; they give Wilhelm a cup of chocolate and a present ... (V, 4) Sometimes the whole company is called before the noble society after dinner. They take this as an honour, not noticing that the dogs have been called in too, and horses led up in the courtyard (V, 7). A special *Vorspiel* is demanded of Wilhelm for the Prince's visit, but it appears he must write it exactly to the Count's conception. When he does not, intrigue is necessary to distract the Count's attention and make things pass off smoothly. Yet in a few days, the piece is totally forgotten (V, 5-7). In no time the more sensible of the Count's circle no longer bother to watch the players. As a result of all these experiences, the high assessment of the 'Grossen der Erde' with which the episode began (V, 1) is overturned. Social ease and elevation had seemed to Wilhelm the basis for a 'höherer Standpunkt'; they turn out to be an obstacle. Accustomed to material wealth ('Beiwesen der Menschheit'), the rich lose touch with natural humanity ('den Begriff des Wertes einer von der Natur allein ausgestatteten Menschheit' V, 13). It is no good expecting from them true interest or discrimination in culture.

All this deftly epitomizes the problems of patronage. The eighteenth-century prince or nobleman was above all a *consumer* of culture, and only incidentally if at all did he further it. Because he consumed other luxuries too, he was not likely to give culture his whole attention. Because he simply wanted the best available — French drama, Italian opera — he was not likely to foster by deliberate policy a lagging native culture, not even to the modest extent Gellert suggested in his interview with Frederick the Great, 'dass ein jeder Herr in seinem Lande die guten Genies aufmunterte'.[17] Culture could add to a prince's prestige, but it did so as much and more if it was imported. He was certainly not aware of a specifically 'national' responsibility. Large views were not possible in small states.

A national consciousness was alive in, and preached by, writers alone — critics like Lessing, historians like Möser, poets like Schiller. Such support as they had came from the middle classes who were glad to see themselves on stage in native *bürgerliches Trauerspiel* (a narcissistic appetite that was soon to lead drama into a slough of banality); and, at the highest, from individuals of the minor gentry like the officer Herr von C. in the *Theatralische Sendung*, a 'true patriot' who, with a European breadth of reading, still gives a special preference to German literature and knows it well (III, 11). Nor did this commitment to a 'national' idea become nationalism. The national interest writers pursued was not political. They did not aspire to a dominance of German culture in Europe, only to a belated harvest of native works. The national note in their programme did not conflict with the ideal of humanity as the Enlightenment understood it. Schiller could speak of drama's function to foster 'das grosse überwältigende Interesse des Staats, der besseren Menschheit',[18] equating the two terms with no sense of a necessary conflict between them. He was not asking for a narrow, exclusive German-ness, a deliberately national 'originality' to assert against European norms. (Noticeably, despite the appeal for 'patriotic' subjects in his Mannheim speech, his own next work was the Enlightened-cosmopolitan *Don Carlos*, and none of his later works is on a purely German subject.) Where cultural nationalism does stir, among the lesser followers of Klopstock's 'bardic' ideal, it is disowned and incisively criticised by Wieland.[19]

IV

Where does this leave Wilhelm Meister and Goethe? We have seen the ideal of noble patronage crumble, and likewise the ideal of the actor as a preacher of nature, ennobled by the literary texts he interprets. Yet in the end Wilhelm is not wholly disillusioned. He has lost individual illusions, and he has known moods of despair in which he pities himself, the theatre, poetry, and calls the theatre a will o' the wisp and a siren (IV, 7). But he also knows theatrical excitement and effect and achieves a success as an actor. He becomes realistic; though some ideals are gone, something of value is left. In a striking image, his whole theatrical experience is compared to a taffeta shot with pleasant and unpleasant colours, as if woven from silk and crude hemp; the two are inseparable and can only be accepted together or cut through together (IV, 16). Wilhelm accepts. His own talent, unlike Anton Reiser's, is not disproved. On the contrary, his Hamburg acquaintance Serlo (based on the real actor-manager F.L. Schröder) offers to take on the company when it is down on its luck solely because he values and wants Wilhelm. All their fortunes thus depend on whether he will finally become an actor and not return to bourgeois life.

Wilhelm at the end feels his mission is real. The hand of chance has led the way he wanted to go and thus confirmed his wishes:

Ja, wenn ein Beruf, eine Sendung deutlich und ausdrücklich war, so ist es diese. Alles geschieht gleichsam zufällig und ohne mein Zutun,

und doch alles, wie ich mir es ehemals ausgedacht, wie ich mir's
vorgesetzt . . .

(VI, 14)

Whether it was love of art that inspired him or love for an actress, the
impulse to escape from the bourgeois world or some purer, worthier
motive, Wilhelm's commitment is real and he goes through with it: 'Ein
kleines Ja, sagte Philine schmeichelnd. – Ja denn, versetzte Wilhelm.'
    And Goethe? For a full answer, we should have to know what the
unwritten half of his novel would have contained. But the direction
seems clear. He has pictured German society and theatre, translating
into real figures and incidents the ideas, experiences and moods we
find in other writers who were concerned at this time with the theatre
as a means to a national culture; and at the end he has confirmed the
mission of his hero. There is no evident reason for reading the fragment's title as ironic. Goethe wrote the novel substantially in his first
decade at Weimar when it may well have appeared to him, at least
spasmodically, that art was achieving a fruitful relationship with society
and might hope to have some effect. He was working in exceptionally
favourable conditions; he was aware (his poetry of the early Weimar
years – 'Seefahrt', 'Dem Schicksal' – makes plain) of being guided by
fate; there was room for a continuing belief in a cultural mission.
    The period of high classicism still holds this belief. Goethe and
Schiller may feel embattled, but they remain active and undaunted.
An unbroken line runs, in this respect, from their youth to the mature
work of their partnership. Indeed, a discernible line connects all the
major elements in the eighteenth-century rise of literature in Germany.
Literary history usually tells of the conflicts between them: Gottsched
overthrown by Lessing, the *Sturm und Drang* a rebellion against the
Enlightenment, Classicism a revulsion against *Sturm und Drang* crudities,
and all this has some truth. But it must not be allowed to obscure an
underlying agreement; the concern in the broadest sense to improve
society through the agency of art. Gottsched was set on 'the correction
of coarse behaviour, foolish habits and low literary taste';[20] Lessing
proposed the moral and hence social education of audiences through
the experience of tragic pity ('der mitleidigste Mensch ist der beste
Mensch, zu allen gesellschaftlichen Tugenden . . . der aufgelegteste')[21];
the young Goethe and Schiller saw in the theatre the means to propagate morality, as well as to create a national spirit; finally, the mature
Goethe and Schiller believed that art could mould, not now society
directly, the mass audience in the theatre, much less the 'nation', but

the individual who must go to make up any conceivable society — the arguments of Schiller's *Ästhetische Briefe* are a refinement of that vision of a restored humanity which ends his 'Schaubühne' speech of 1784. All these owe a similar allegiance to the principles of the Enlightenment. Of course there are differences. They lie in the subtlety with which the educative conception is worked out. There is bald didacticism and a deficient sense of what art is in Gottsched; rugged commonsense and artistic craftsmanship in Lessing; enthusiasm correcting itself through experience in the young Goethe and Schiller; and finally, in the two partners of Weimar Classicism, a depth of understanding of art, its inner principles and their relation to nature, man and society which results in a unique effort to marry realistic grasp with idealistic intent.

Notes

1. For a fuller discussion and documentation, see my essay 'Theatre, Enlightenment and Nation: a German Problem', *Forum for Modern Language Studies*, XIV (1978).
2. Schiller, *Werke* V, 812-14.
3. It thus anticipates the crucial issue of Schiller's mature thought as found in the *Ästhetische Briefe*, where the crisis of revolutionary society in France has raised the question how art is affected by and can affect political man.
4. Schiller, *Werke* V, 828-30. The later, more common but less dynamic title of the piece is 'Die Schaubühne als eine moralische Anstalt betrachtet'.
5. Ibid.
6. Lessing to his brother Karl, 25 May 1777.
7. Nicolai to Lessing, 5 June 1777.
8. References henceforth are by Book and chapter.
9. See W.H. Bruford, *Theatre, Drama and Audience in Goethe's Germany*, (London, [2]1957), pp.64f.
10. See Möser, *Harlekin oder Verteidigung des Groteske-Komischen*, reprint of the second (1777) edition, ed. Henning Boetius (Bad Homburg, 1968), esp. p.62.
11. See Erich Schmidt, *Lessing* (Berlin, 1899), I, 292, quoting a Viennese advertisement of 1763 for 'Missara und Sirsampson. Mit Hannswurst des Mellefont getreuen Bedienten . . .' Hanswurst also turns up in Frankfurt in 1764 as servant to Don Juan. See M. Sommerfeld, *Goethe in Umwelt und Folgezeit* (Leiden, 1935), p.109.
12. References are to the edition in the *Deutsche Litteraturdenkmale des 18. und 19. Jahrhunderts* (DLD) (Heilbronn, 1886).
13. Heine, *Sämtliche Werke*, ed. Walzel (Leipzig, 1910ff.), 4, 97.
14. *Sturm und Drang. Kritische Schriften* (Heidelberg, 1963), p.730.
15. Lessing to Elise Reimarus, 6 September 1778.
16. Iffland, *Über meine theatralische Laufbahn*, DLD (Heilbronn, 1886), pp.11f., 94.
17. The interview is reprinted in the excellent anthology *Deutsche Dichtung*

im 18. Jahrhundert, ed. Adalbert Elschenbroich (Munich, 1960), pp.186-90.

18. Schiller, *Werke* V, 830.

19. See the essay on 'Der Eifer, unsrer Dichtkunst einen National-
Charakter zu geben', *Deutscher Merkur* (May, 1773), in Wieland, *Werke* III,
267ff. Wieland deplores the deliberate revival of national differences as mere
primitivism, productive of caricature and failing in men's first duty 'sich einander
zu nähern, sich miteinander zu verbinden, und als Glieder einer grossen von der
Natur gestifteten Gesellschaft mit zusammengesetzten Kräften an ihrer
gemeinschaftlichen Vervollkommnung zu arbeiten' – a classic statement of
Enlightenment ideals.

20. Bruford, *Theatre, Drama and Audience in Goethe's Germany*, p.48.

21. Lessing to Nicolai, 13 November 1756.

3 DRAMA AND SOCIETY

I

How could playwrights in the last quarter of the eighteenth century fulfil the great expectations people had of a 'national theatre'? What means were available to them, and what did these allow and imply? Questions of artistic form interweave here with questions of politics and society.

First, there still existed the French-oriented taste originally set by the courts and Gottsched. In 1784 Schiller, with three very un-French plays behind him, writes offering to translate Corneille, Racine and Crébillon for the Mannheim stage.[1] But there had meantime been a change; Lessing had broken the monopoly of French principles and set up English models. It was now possible to think of a synthesis, and to see the French style afresh as one usable element. Setting to work on *Don Carlos*, Schiller speaks in the same letter of striking a balance between the extremes of French and English taste.

Besides the national, Lessing's campaign had had a social aspect. By relocating tragedy among the bourgeoisie, he was challenging the dominance of a style inextricably linked with the social class it portrayed and was patronised by. To be sure, his primary aim was to create tragedy, and bourgeois settings were required because he held that tragic sympathy is evoked most strongly by social equals.[2] But there were implications and consequences beyond what he intended. For a class to be written about seriously is a form of social recognition which implies eventual more substantial claims and hence ultimately the idea of social change; while the choice of bourgeois subjects and settings opened the way for realistic social observation and social criticism, which may serve as means to promote change.

The beginnings, in *Miss Sara Sampson* (1755) are unimpressive, the characters bourgeois largely in name. The action is very markedly structured on the Medea myth, as Marwood reveals with her words 'Sieh in mir eine neue Medea!' (II, 7). It is as if mere bourgeois experience is insufficient by itself to be tragic. *Emilia Galotti* (1772) is an immense advance. It too rests on and alludes to a classical story, Livy's account of the Roman tribune Virginius who killed his daughter to save her from being abducted by a tyrant. But the unobtrusive reference to this source at the climax of the play (V, 7) suggests the constancy of social injustice throughout history. The play is close to the quick of class relations in eighteenth-century Germany (the Italian setting is a transparent disguise) where small-state absolutism did take such forms. In theory it was benevolent, the prince the father of his people; in practice it was often oppressive, the paternity not just metaphorical: Wekhrlin wrote a satire about a prince who fathered his own civil service.[3] Lessing had no overt political aim — he said his play was free of 'Staatsinteresse'[4] — but it remains a classic statement on absolutism, not just its abuses but its essence. The Prince's subjects are shown to be mere objects of his will, wares to be bought.[5] He grants petitions and signs death-warrants on a whim. True, it is the whim of a man absorbed by sexual passion; but precisely this points the moral. Total power in the hands of one man with feelings to sway him holds out little hope of justice. A standard Enlightenment argument[6] comes dramatically to life. In establishing that bourgeois experience can be tragic, Lessing indicts the class that made it so.

Lessing had introduced a new artistic genre and gone far, whatever his intentions, towards realising its social potential. His were important innovations of content. The younger writers of the 'Sturm und Drang' preached and practised innovations in form. For them, the reign of rule was superseded by genius, Aristotle by Shakespeare. Shakespeare was the example of powerful and totally free expression and the authority for an 'open' drama which dispensed with the unities and all formal coherence. A number of 'Sturm und Drang' plays have social content, treating the seduction of bourgeois girls by aristocratic officers (Lenz's *Soldaten*), or the girl who kills her illegitimate child (Wagner's *Kindermörderin*). Lenz has been called a 'born sociologist'[7] and he proposes bizarre reforms, like an army of officers' women to keep the military off the bourgeois daughters. But there is in all this less grasp of politics and society than in *Emilia Galotti*. It is the formal innovation that really matters. The open form, freed from the conventional pressure to move an individual fate by connected steps to its doom, could range widely, observe conditions, portray episodic action, become in a word 'epic'.

The first German work in this mode shows its strengths. The hero of Goethe's *Götz* has elbow-room to act; for much of the play the initiative lies with him, he fights hard for principles which are in no sense a 'tragic flaw'. Lenz's enthusiastic review seized on this: heroes must act, whereas tragedy portrays passivity. This is clear from *Emilia Galotti* where Lessing has Odoardo kill his daughter rather than the Prince not so much to avoid a subversive ending as to create a conventional tragic one. The free will on which Emilia insists (V, 7) can only act back on herself as the tragic heroine.[8] *Götz* is not, in contrast, a revolutionary play, despite its cry of 'freedom' and the hero's antipathy for princes and bishops. But it shows a man actively engaging the forces of society. It left a legacy which was not fully taken up until much later. All this is the background to Schiller's early work. He begins writing when the 'Sturm und Drang' has tailed off into silence; he is influenced by it but not of it. He was born ten years after Goethe, time enough, as Goethe says in the preface to *Dichtung und Wahrheit*, to make all the difference to a man's development and effect on the world. He found artistic and social alternatives prepared for him, as well as some dormant in his character and formed by his experience.

II

From the start Schiller's mode of thought is dramatic and his talent theatrical. He conceives situations, relations between characters, even philosophical problems, in terms of conflict and tension, which are the essence of drama. He handles stage-effects with a mastery which was unprecedented in Germany then and is still striking today. If he was not already a consummate dramatist, he had the formal endowment to become one. What he lacked at first was the knowledge of men and affairs which would allow a surer grasp of the world the dramatist has to take issue with. His early plays are often theatrical in the bad sense, the characters near to caricature, their situations, emotions and imagery melodramatic. There are influences here of the 'Sturm und Drang', the literary avant-garde a young enthusiast devoured in the seventies. The hostile brothers in *Die Räuber* recall those in Leisewitz's *Julius von Tarent* or Klinger's *Die Zwillinge*, the tower where old Moor nearly starves recalls Gerstenberg's *Ugolino*. Yet there are already signs of a talent far superior to his predecessors. For example, one can compare Lenz's scene-switching, which self-consciously flouts the unities but also bewilders the spectator, with the changes of place in *Die Räuber*, which create maximum contrast and suspense yet also cohesion. We move back and forth from the Moor castle where Franz has got his brother disgraced and then reported his death, to the outcast Karl in the Bohemian forests. Act II ends with his band about to fight a desperate action, and Schiller cuts to Amalia in the castle garden. At the moment she learns that 'Karl lebt noch!' Schiller cuts to Karl musing by the Danube. The unities are here not defied but outgrown; drama is richer without them, but no less controlled.

Again, Schiller's violence of tone and action recalls the 'Sturm und

Drang'. But again there is a difference. His effects are not arbitrary. The starkly antithetical characters spring from a consistent vision to which melodramatic gesture is a heroic response. The violent language has constant underlying patterns of imagery and rhetoric.[9] Schiller is not just out to shock. Where much of the 'Sturm und Drang' seems a small voice shouting, in Schiller we hear an innate power compulsively finding outlet, and coherence underlies chaos.

What is the consistent vision? The young Schiller saw a world radically divided between senses and spirit, good and evil, idealism and materialism, the principles of justice and the practices of men. Partly this stemmed from his Christian upbringing, partly from his medical training at a time when medicine was less empirical than speculative and analysed Man in Cartesian dualistic terms; partly again from his own experience of oppression as one of the talented boys whom the Duke of Württemberg pressed into the Hohe Karlsschule to train for the professions his state needed. Karl Eugen's conception may be a faint reflection of the Enlightenment — few princes concerned themselves with their subjects' education at all — but its execution was ruthless. Discipline in the school was military. Add to all this Schiller's early reading — Plutarch on great men, Rousseau — and the literary result is understandable. *Die Räuber* (1781) is about manifest evils and radical cures. Its Hippocratic motto — what medicines cannot cure, the knife will; what the knife cannot cure, fire will cure — suggests rebellion.

But rebellion against what? Not just a political order. True, Schiller originally set the play in the German present; Karl Moor promises to make Germany a republic, protects peasants, attacks junkers and churchmen (II, 3); Kosinsky's misfortunes echo *Emilia Galotti* (III, 2); Franz Moor becomes a petty tyrant, voicing his scorn for moral scruple in the metaphor of a common feudal abuse: 'der gnädige Herr gibt seinem Rappen den Sporn und galoppiert weich über die weiland Ernte' (I, 1).[10] Yet Karl chafes at the constrictions of law and society as such, not those of a particular system. He aspires to sound the 'Horn des Aufruhrs' through the whole of Nature (I, 2). He appeals to Nature at large against the corruption of man when his father seems to have been unnaturally unforgiving. Even Kosinsky, whose ills are clearly social, is called another 'Kläger wider die Gottheit' (III, 2). By a striking escalation, a family schism becomes first a rebellion of the individual against society, with the robber a compound of Rousseau and Robin Hood, then of Man against God. And this rebellion is finally taken back when a remorseful Karl decides that Divine Justice needed no help from him and that lawlessness cannot make a better world.

He surrenders to atone for his crimes, and accepts justice divine and temporal. Like his earlier sense of a providential hand in his fate ('Lenker im Himmel' IV, 5), this is a vestige of old ways of thought, the tragic theodicy that still held good for Lessing.[11] The new impulse of the active individual yields to the old passive attitude, almost with relief. That impulse, it seems, was only incidently political. Yet political effect in literature does not depend wholly on intention, as we saw with *Emilia Galotti*. For the Mannheim premiere, Dalberg thought it prudent to shift the setting of *Die Raüber* to the Middle Ages. The title-page of the second edition bears a lion crouched to spring and the motto 'In tirannos', which must have seemed apposite to someone (it was not Schiller's doing). The play was a sensation largely through its rebellious posture: any disturbance – in manners, morals, language – tends to be felt as a vague threat by a settled society. It was threat enough for the Duke that a regimental doctor of his should write at all. Karl Eugen had a short way with writers (for ten years he kept the poet and journalist Schubart untried in prison). He forbade Schiller to write further. Schiller fled to Mannheim, with a partly completed second play and the idea for a third. Both are in different ways political.

Die Verschwörung des Fiesco (1783) treats a conspiracy to overthrow tyranny and restore a republic. That sounds subversive, but the case is not straightforward; not because the Republic of Genoa was a patrician oligarchy – a historical subject need only offer a rough analogy for the poet to speak through – but because of complexities in the hero. Under a mask of epicureanism, Fiesco plots single-handed against Doria while other nobles conspire; when he joins them, he insists on being 'sovereign' of the conspiracy (III, 5). Signs that he wants power for himself increase; the stern republican Verrina watches, set to kill a new tyrant. Fiesco wavers, reflecting that to renounce power would be more sublime than seizing it ('ein Diadem erkämpfen ist *gross*. Es wegwerfen ist *göttlich*') and feeling he could be Genoa's 'glücklichster Bürger' (II, 19); but ambition soon outbids virtue with the idea that great crimes are allowed to outstanding individuals (III, 2). Fiesco is a perfect example of Nietzsche's Will to Power, with its alternatives of dominating others or dominating self. If Nietzsche had remembered the moral ambiguity of Schiller's early plays, he might not have dismissed him as a 'Moraltrompeter'.

If the hero wavers, so does Schiller. In the printed text, Fiesco is drowned by Verrina (the historical Fiesco drowned, rather incongruously, by accident). In the Leipzig stage version, Verrina stabs him and declares, like Shakespeare's Brutus: 'Es war mein Busenfreund und mein Bruder, mein Wohltäter und der grösste Man seiner Zeit; aber das Vaterland war meine erste Pflicht'. But in the Mannheim version, Fiesco overcomes ambition, the curtain line is the 'glücklichster Bürger' speech, transposed from II, 19. Was Schiller perhaps trying different ways to put over the message of political virtue? Partly, or the sub-title would not have been 'ein republikanisches Trauerspiel'. Yet he was also, like Lessing in *Emilia Galotti*, out to achieve tragic effect. *Die Räuber* had the best of both worlds, grand crime followed by noble repentance. But the Fiesco story required a choice between immoralism and moral grandeur as objects of the spectator's awe. Schiller remained torn. His comment when *Fiesco* failed in Mannheim — 'Den "Fiesco" verstand das Publikum nicht. Republikanische Freiheit ist hierzulande ein Schall ohne Bedeutung . . . in den Adern der Pfälzer fliesst kein römisches Blut'[12] — suggests that his conscious intention, at least, was political. But it was distracted, and consequently obscured, by internal indecision.

Kabale und Liebe (1784) is more decisive. Instead of politics at a historical distance it shows the tyrannical pressures of contemporary society. An urge to speak about present ills makes Schiller turn to bourgeois tragedy. The play derives closely from his Württemberg experience; the tyrants great and small, parasitic on the people over whom they had power; the selling of troops to other nations to pay for the ruler's luxuries; the sexual depredations of the ruler and his underlings; exploitation, manipulation. Put thus, it sounds like a crude tract; and one influential critic has assumed that life under German absolutism must have been, if not better, then different and less melodramatic.[13] Yet what Auerbach finds unbelievable is documented fact; what he rejects because it seems overstated and therefore not realistic, was real. This is a serious confusion; as Brecht once remarked, realism must not be judged by other realisms, but by the reality it depicts. Where reality is marked by excess, the appearance of melodrama is not wholly the author's doing. The critic must not argue from stylistic impressions and factual ignorance.

Of course, Schiller's play has faults of execution. Tragedy is implausibly engineered when Ferdinand fails to see the truth he has frightened von Kalb into telling (IV, 3). There is falsely pitched dialogue, especially in the confrontation between Luise and Lady Milford in IV, 7 (the young Schiller was understandably at his worst when writing women's parts) and in general a rhetoric too elevated for the bourgeois genre betrays the pull of the high tragic mode. Yet despite these flaws, *Kabale und Liebe* manages to grasp much social reality, and not only its crudest features.

Just how it does so can be seen if we consider Auerbach's further criticisms. He argues that a love-affair is too narrow a basis for general social problems; that we learn nothing of the underlying situation, the causes of the rulers' moral decline, or conditions in the state; and that a genuine social element – Luise's typically bourgeois limitations – is obscured by the melodrama of Ferdinand's jealousy. On the first point, it is precisely at the borders between classes that class-consciousness and differences are clearest. Love between a demanding, impetuous aristocrat and a dutiful bourgeois girl created a situation rich in social implications. Ferdinand's jealousy is as much socially conditioned as Luise's filial piety; when socio-religious scruples ('die Fugen der Bürgerwelt . . . und die allgemeine ewige Ordnung', III, 4) forbid her to elope, it is precisely the upper-class, educated son, intellectually and emotionally emancipated, who is incapable of understanding her and her limitations. Luise as a love-partner is his ideal creation, and when this fails to respond as he wishes, his imperious will is baulked. Two distinct spiritual economies are illuminated. Their incompatibility – a class incompatibility – is both more tragic and more necessarily true than the plot contrived by the court party to break up the subversive love-affair.

And as for social problems, causes and conditions, only a botching dramatist would make extensive historical reference to the past record of luxury and corruption in Württemberg; to the programme of grandiose building, artistic patronage and more private enjoyments that made it necessary to sell soldiers; to the treaties with France that agreed the sales. Art must epitomise, not ramble. Schiller does this brilliantly in the famous scene II, 2, where the Duke's mistress learns from her footman how her jewels were paid for. If this scene (which Dalberg cut from the Mannheim production) leaves the impression, as Auerbach says, that Duke and court have no function, but only suck the people dry by their extravagance and misuse it for their vicious pleasures, this is very much how things were. The case is a crude one; there are limits to how subtle the art can be made that has to present them.

For all its faults, *Kabale und Liebe* was the most powerful attack on German absolutism to date, worthy in its very different mode to be set beside Beaumarchais' *Mariage de Figaro* which was premiered in Paris within two weeks of it. Broadening his themes and refining his technique, what might Schiller not make of social drama? Yet at this point he turns away from the bourgeois genre. The reasons are partly external. His meagre but vital Mannheim contract was due to expire in August 1784. Dalberg was under local pressure to drop this wild young writer, which was the easier because he had Iffland to provide the bourgeois dramas the public wanted (*Kabale und Liebe* had been a success) without being subversive. Schiller knew all this, and tried to sell himself to Dalberg by promising works of much greater prestige for a theatre than mere bourgeois subjects; he regrets ever trying to shine in a genre where others can do as well, and declares high tragedy his true field. He promises a 'Don Carlos', followed by a sequel to *Die Räuber* recanting its immorality.[14] Not all of this is tactics; jettisoning bourgeois tragedy and *Die Räuber* may be, but not the enthusiasm for 'Carlos' nor the confidence that high tragedy is his element. This merely reads the signs — the grand rhetoric and gesture — that were abundantly clear, despite the realistic features, in his first three plays. Embracing high tragedy was Schiller's own choice. It was crucial for the whole development of German literature. From now until the 1830s, no major work faces the tragic problems of society directly, as *Kabale und Liebe* had begun to do.

Instead *Don Carlos* brings together the whole range of possibilities eighteenth-century drama had to offer and out of them shapes something new. It is fascinating to watch this synthesis happen. Schiller first saw in the subject scope for the effects his previous plays achieved — 'starke Zeichnungen', 'erschütternde oder rührende Situationen'; Carlos was to be another 'feuriger, grosser und empfindender Jüngling'.[15] The situation has the emotional extremism of the 'Sturm und Drang': Carlos has lost his fiancée to his father Philipp II, the reluctant Queen still loves her stepson, the father-rival is jealous. Aptly, Schiller calls his play at this stage 'ein Familiengemälde in einem fürstlichen Hause'[16]: it is as if Lessing's principle, that when we sympathise with kings it is as human beings, had inspired Schiller to set up bourgeois tragedy in regal surroundings.

Despite this setting, it was not to be a political play, so Schiller reassured Dalberg. Yet he planned to include a cruel, hypocritical inquisitor and a barbaric Duke of Alba, and to avenge suffering humanity by pillorying the Inquisition.[17] This was pure Enlightenment and must surely become political: the power and abuses of the Church were inseparable from the state. Even the personal issues point into the social and ultimately political realm. The same Rousseauian faith to which Schiller appealed against society in general in *Die Räuber*, and against the class-structure in particular in *Kabale und Liebe*, underlies *Don Carlos* too. Nature is systematically set against convention, though far more subtly than before: the gardens of Aranjuez against the court apartments in Madrid; Carlos' and Elisabeth's love against the state policy that married her to Philipp ('Sie war gefasst auf Liebe, und empfing/Ein Diadem', II, 3); her maternal love against the court etiquette which says when she may visit her baby; and, at the centre of the play, love between father and son against the cold demands of kingship. All human feeling in Philipp has been sacrificed to policy. He must even kill his son if religion requires it:

> *König.* Ich frevle
> An der Natur – auch diese mächtge Stimme
> Willst du zum Schweigen bringen?
> *Grossinquisitor.* Vor dem Glauben
> Gilt keine Stimme der Natur.
>
> (V, 10)

The words 'Stimme der Natur' echo through the play (lines 581, 914, 5273), condemning an old man's passion for a young woman, a father's failure to love his son, and the ruthless claims of the Church. The antithesis Nature-unnature does not so much culminate in the antithesis freedom-tyranny, as it might have done in a merely political play, but rather *embraces* the variant freedom-tyranny as a matter of course. Precisely this gives the play immense power as political statement. Posa, expounding political liberalism to Philipp, appeals repeatedly to Nature. First in the image of kingly fatherhood familiar to the eighteenth century, but contrasted brutally with what was actually happening in the Netherlands:

> *Posa.* Ein gutes Volk – und Vater dieses Volkes!
> Das, dacht ich, das muss göttlich sein! – Da stiess
> Ich auf verbrannte menschliche Gebeine –

Then in the image of the spring which brings organic renewal where the King can only create a deathly calm:

> *Posa.* Die Ruhe eines Kirchhofs! Und Sie hoffen . . .
> Den allgemeinen Frühling aufzuhalten,
> Der die Gestalt der Welt verjüngt?

Last and most impressively, in his parallel between society as a liberal would have it and the whole economy of nature, free, yet still orderly because of God's laws which are eternal, not arbitrarily imposed:

Sehen Sie sich um
In seiner herrlichen Natur! Auf Freiheit
Ist sie gegründet – und wie reich ist sie
Durch Freiheit . . .
    Er – der Freiheit
Entzückende Erscheinung nicht zu stören –
Er lässt des Übels grauenvolles Heer
In seinem Weltall lieber toben – ihn,
Den Künstler wird man nicht gewahr, bescheiden
Verhüllt er sich in ewige Gesetze . . .

This appeal to Nature and freedom goes far beyond the crude Rousseauism of Karl Moor, the imperious demands of Ferdinand, and even the earlier scenes of *Don Carlos* itself, where the 'feuriger Jüngling' thought nothing of overturning the law to win back his love (I, 5). The treatment of a familiar theme has become more mature: *Don Carlos* is not an abrupt change, but an evolution.

Much of that evolution lay in the shifts of interest and emphasis as Schiller wrote, and these exacted a price. Contemporaries found the love-tragedy and the political drama inadequately integrated. Schiller wrote his *Briefe über Don Carlos* to defend the work, with some ingenuity but also a great deal of plausibility. The shift from the 'Familiengemälde' to the 'liberation of the Netherlands' plot, and from Carlos to Posa, takes place in a clear sequence. The scenario of spring 1783 ('Bauerbacher Entwurf') is domestic tragedy only. The first actual text, a three-act fragment Schiller began to publish in his journal *Rheinische Thalia* in March 1785, still stresses the domestic emotions rather crudely, but already suggests that Posa and the Queen may sublimate Carlos' private passion into public action. Near the end of Act III, Philipp begs providence for a human being whom he can trust, as he cannot trust courtiers, to find out the truth about the Queen and his son, the play's original subject. Posa, the free philosopher who has often deserved but never requested rewards because he will not be beholden to the King, fits the bill. This gives influence – on the outcome of the domestic plot, but more broadly on affairs of state – to the man of integrity. Nature can appeal in audience against unnature through a man the King was driven to need by vestiges of natural feeling.

So to this point the action is shaped to match Schiller's changed interest. He was free to pursue it from here, having once compressed and refined the first three acts. In Acts IV and V, Posa tries to both rescue Carlos from his father's suspicions and inspire him to be the saviour of the Netherlands. The twists and turns of intrigue become too complex for either the intriguer's or the dramatist's purpose. Yet one thing does stand out plainly, and it is a new variant on the play's theme, the true tragedy of the finished work: not the insuperable barriers to love, not the defeat of a scheme for rebellion, but the loss of integrity in Posa. He intrigues without confiding in Carlos, puzzling and hurting him; and he betrays the King's trust. Is this justifiable? Not by the play's own criteria. Posa and Alba, from opposed viewpoints, had wondered if Carlos' idealism would survive the realities of kingship (I, 9; II, 10); in the event, it is Posa whom power spoils. He manipulates men where he had believed in their 'natural' freedom. It is he who now goes against the 'Stimme der Natur'.

The tragedy of Posa's autocratic idealism implies a very special view of politics: the fighter for freedom is required to keep his hands clean in a way the oppressor never has, which inevitably limits his actions. Such purism may lead to inaction; yet at the other extreme ruthless action may end by merely replacing one intolerable regime with another. Rebellion is not a straightforward heroic act but an ethical problem, which eighteenth-century drama repeatedly returns to. Lessing's fragmentary *Samuel Henzi* (1749) had begun to probe the intricacies of the 'just rebellion': the relation of private to public motives, and of harsh means to noble ends, the difficulty of keeping violence within bounds and of preventing tyranny from fathering new tyranny. These are the problems Schiller took up, first in *Fiesco*, now in *Don Carlos*, and again in his later plays, several of which centre on legitimate power and rebellion. *Wilhelm Tell* in particular treats again the 'just rebellion' and very deliberately illustrates what Lessing, apropos *Samuel Henzi*, called 'die allervorsichtigste Gewalt'.[18] Through all these plays runs the idea that political action corrupts, a conviction strengthened in Schiller by the eighteenth century's practical experiment, the French Revolution. Yet he would not settle for inertia and reaction. As a thinker he sought ways to make men proof against the corrupting forces of their times — frankly, ways to perfect them for society; and as a dramatist he went on portraying men and women under political pressure, to see just how much purity could be retained in the stress of action and the clash of interests.

By referring all his characters and their actions to the court of Nature, Schiller achieved, by instinct or design, a fundamental thematic consistency. If we then move from structure to texture, no praise can be too high. In psychology, diction, theatrical restraint, the development from *Kabale und Liebe* via the *Thalia* fragment to the final *Don Carlos* is a steep ascent from rude power and erratic genius to mature accomplishment. Characters are not exaggerated even where they might seem to invite it: Domingo, Catholic dignitary, obscurantist, *Realpolitiker* and sexual go-between for his King, is a credible human being because drawn with restraint, not satirical ire; the King himself, potentially the classic villain, is treated not with loathing but with horrified sympathy. The stagecraft is masterly but, except for Carlos' final disguise as the ghost of his grandfather, not melodramatic. And the language – the language of *Don Carlos* is unparalleled in Schiller's work. He had never before attempted verse drama. Among Germans, only Wieland and Lessing had written iambic pentameter blank verse, and they with functional adequacy rather than artistic brilliance. Schiller takes one step from experiment to total mastery. His verse both flows with a beauty of its own and bends to every dramatic need. It can be stately and impressive in the finest Shakespearean manner, yet adapt to catch the nuances of thought and mood, the varying pace of conversation, the sharpness of interpellation, the musing movement of soliloquy. It is hard with Philipp and Alba, halting in Carlos' embarrassment with Princess Eboli, a mixture of tenderness and intellectual elevation in the scenes between Carlos and Posa. It breaks into sub-lines as unforcedly as it exceeds or stops short of the standard line-length to capture the grouping of speech and the incidence of pauses. There is never any sense of constriction. Lessing's *Nathan der Weise* was versified talk, often fine talk, and workmanlike verse. *Don Carlos* is dramatic poetry. Not by any deliberately poetic effects – there is more, and more striking, imagery in the foregoing prose plays. It is as hard to pinpoint the qualities of the style as it is easy to feel them. I take a passage at random, Carlos being freed by his father (V, 4):

> *König.*   Empfange
> Dein Schwert zurück. Man hat zu rasch verfahren.
> (*Er nähert sich ihm, reicht ihm die Hand und hilft ihm
> sich aufrichten*)
> Mein Sohn ist nicht an seinem Platz. Steh auf,
> Komm in die Arme deines Vaters.
> *Carlos.*   Dein
> Geruch ist Mord. Ich kann dich nicht umarmen.
> (*Er stösst ihn zurück, alle Granden kommen in
> Bewegung*)
> Nein! Steht nicht so betroffen da! Was hab

Ich Ungeheures denn getan? Des Himmels
Gesalbten angetastet? Fürchtet nichts.
Ich lege keine Hand an ihn. Seht ihr
Das Brandmal nicht an seiner Stirne? Gott
Hat ihn gezeichnet.

König.   Folgt mir, meine Granden.

It is an emotional highpoint, with the King at last opening the arms of
a father only to be rejected by his son. Yet the verse is unassertive. It
is sober without being dull, unadorned without being featureless,
dignified without being pompous; it allows a natural, only slightly
heightened speech. It is not self-sufficient poetry, but a transparent
medium for the dramatist's task. It is the source of that sense, stronger
in *Don Carlos* than in any other of Schiller's plays, that we are watching
real people with intense feelings and allegiances in a real human and
political situation.

Don Carlos grows from many roots, as we saw. 'Sturm und Drang';
bourgeois tragedy; Enlightenment thought; French and English style;
Racine, Shakespeare, Lessing — all can be found in the play's genesis or
text. But it fuses these elements into something new which would
henceforth be Schiller's genre; a poetic drama elevated without being
over-stylised, handling personal and general issues together and in the
same ethical terms, free of limitation to time or place. It has moved
away from immediate social realities, just as it has neglected — contra-
dicting Schiller's own Mannheim appeal — to treat a national subject.
Yet immediacy and patriotic interest are narrow conceptions; to
require them is to presuppose a short-sighted audience which cannot
apply a moral to other circumstances. *Don Carlos* is less direct than
Kabale und Liebe, but it still speaks plainly about tyranny — plainly
enough to have been a bête noire of censors.[20] Schiller consciously
worked on the principle that there were laws in history as in Nature,
with similar conditions producing similar results, so that past and
present are linked by analogy.

Significantly, he states this belief — in itself a common enough
Enlightenment assumption — in precisely his historical account of the
Carlos subject, published the year after the play.[21] This hints how
directly the play's moral was meant to be applied, and the hint is borne
out by the way Schiller the historian interprets the Dutch-Spanish
struggle. He sets against each other not just the tyrant and his subjects,
but 'Fürstengewalt' and 'bürgerliche Stärke', hoping to arouse in the
presumably bourgeois reader a 'fröhliches Gefühl seiner selbst'. That

is, he is avowedly set on creating a bourgeois political consciousness by the example of Dutch association triumphant. He commends his theme for its 'Mangel an heroischer Grösse', for it was the unheroic bourgeois virtues that decided the outcome: 'Die Schatzkammer der Republik waren Arbeitsamkeit und Handel'. Dutch trade supremacy accumulated wealth while Spain's assets wasted, indeed passed by way of trade into Dutch hands. It is as if Schiller were advocating bourgeois against high tragedy, but for a larger, more real stage. And to the celebration of bourgeois virtues is added, again, the appeal to Nature, but this time in that time-hallowed concept of political thought, Natural Law. The Dutch people dared to invoke this: 'Den Herrn beider Indien an das Naturrecht zu mahnen'. This sets *Don Carlos* and all Schiller's early work in new perspective; what seemed a Romantic revolt falls into a tradition reaching back from the Enlightenment to early Christian times and antiquity.

Originally, Schiller made the analogy between the Dutch rebellion and his own day quite explicit: 'Die Kraft . . . womit [das niederländische Volk] handelte, ist auch uns nicht versagt, wenn die Zeitläufte wiederkehren und ähnliche Anlässe uns zu ähnlichen Taten rufen'.[22] He later deleted these words when the French Revolution failed to live up to its predecessor. But the failure only intensified his concern with history. If history showed no exact repetition, and perhaps no general trend for the better such as Enlightenment thinkers tried to persuade themselves they saw,[23] it was the more necessary to see how it really worked and to show both how men did act and how they should act under its stresses. The conclusion could still – that much of the idea of analogy remained intact – have a universal message. This principle governs Schiller's mature plays.

III

Don Carlos treats the rise of the Dutch Republic from the Spanish end. Only when Carlos and Posa are defeated and the play is over does Alba march to the Netherlands, on to the stage of Goethe's *Egmont*. For Goethe – and this is the first fundamental difference between these two works, whose identical subject and appearance in successive years invites us to compare them – Goethe sets his play in the Netherlands. Where Schiller showed great principles in conflict and decisions being taken which determine what will happen far away, Goethe shows it happening on the spot. Where Schiller's court setting, though not without an atmosphere of its own, inclined to the abstraction of political typicality, Goethe's setting has a full local reality. Indeed, it is from this that he builds up the case (the Netherlanders' and his own) against Spanish oppression. The Dutch have their own character, constitution and traditions. The alien Spaniards come to rule and to grasp. The King lacks cordiality and tolerance, he is 'kein Herr für uns Niederländer' (Act I, Armbrustschiessen). The case is put by the Regent Margarete's secretary, by a popular agitator, and most fully and eloquently by Egmont himself to Alba. In place of authoritarianism, he urges a rule to match the people's character; they must be governed with sympathy and understanding as one rides a fine horse, and this is only possible if they keep their old constitution and customs and their established rulers, the local nobility. Spanish encroachment on their rights and privileges threatens their very nature. The King 'will den Kern ihrer Eigenheit verderben ... Er will sie vernichten, damit sie Etwas werden, ein ander Etwas' (Act IV, Der Culenburgische Palast). Spanish rule in the Netherlands is thus a distortion of Nature as manifested in a particular character.

Here surely is common ground with Schiller, who also appealed to Nature against Spanish tyranny. But it is a very different idea of Nature. Schiller's argument rises in a logical progression from natural behaviour and spontaneous feeling to a visionary conception of Nature as a universal order. His associated appeal to Natural Law underlines the abstract, rational character of his ideal. It is in the Enlightenment tradition of humanitarian politics. Nature for Goethe means a local order and the quite specific freedoms which are part of it. Spanish rule infringes not universal principles, but historical individuality. This, with its more tangible reality though narrower scope, is in a new tradition. Herder and Möser, the two historical thinkers who fascinated the young Goethe, insisted on the distinct character of peoples and periods, where Enlightenment thinking tended to assimilate them to a norm. This new approach, later to be called 'historicism' (*Historismus*), was an intellectual revolution. It perfectly matched the poet Goethe's feel for empirical particulars — of atmosphere, sense experience, human character. His defence of Dutch liberties against Spain was simultaneously a defence of the 'characteristic' realities which meant most to him poetically.

This makes the poetic strength of the play but also its weakness as drama and the weakness of its hero. Egmont is the local character writ large — brave, generous, spontaneous, easy-going, the kind of man the people wish to be ruled by. Yet politically he is a liability. To Spanish authority, his carefree behaviour is a provocation; to the Regent in her efforts to control a tense situation and forestall sterner measures it is an embarrassment. Egmont's eminence and popularity make him

willy-nilly a political figure. Yet he is not politic. He will not believe
Alba is approaching; he will not accept Oranien's analysis of the situation or his advice to escape. He trusts too much — in the King's favour,
and ultimately, obscurely, in his own destiny. The images are telling:
Oranien is the chess-player, always threatened, always alert, Egmont the
rider in the chariot of Fate, careering wildly on, unable to do more than
bravely hang on to the reins and steer clear of rut and stone as they
flash toward him (Act II, Egmonts Wohnung); or he is the sleepwalker,
unseeing on the edge of a drop, safe if not woken.

'Freedom' in *Egmont* means the right to live as a natural being,
untrammelled by needs of policy, borne along by life. Once more, the
contrast with Schiller is striking: the images of *Don Carlos* and the
Geschichte des Abfalls der Niederlande are of men seizing and moulding
the stuff of chance into plan and purpose.[24] And Schiller's highest
demand is for general freedom of thought, where Goethe's is merely
that the individual should be left to go his own way, to the point of
irresponsibility. For irresponsible Egmont is. True, there is much in him
that is attractive and right — his belief that a people's good-will is the
best guarantee of order, or that his free-and-easy life should be possible
in a free society. But he is foolish not to see that it is a provocation to
Spain and hence bad tactics in a politician. For a politician, the answer
to Egmont's question — must I sacrifice the enjoyment of the present
moment merely to make sure of the next? — is not the one the rhetoric
invites. Politics is not about the present moment, though it is not for
that a rejection of enjoyment; it is an attempt to make present enjoyment a continuous possibility. If the play is a study in contrasted ways
of seeing,[25] Egmont is quite simply short-sighted. He has the limited
perspective of a single piece, even if a large one, on the chess-board
over which Oranien watches.

Schiller went to the heart of the matter in his review[26]: *Egmont* is a
tragedy of character which must aim to arouse our sympathies, but the
hero's irresponsibility forfeits them. Yet this is Goethe's doing, since he
totally changed the historical character. The real Egmont was too old
for dalliance with Klärchen, he had a large family and badly needed his
revenues as stadtholder of Brussels — that was why he did not escape.
Banal, perhaps; but to keep the fact and change the motive to mere
frivolity was perverse. The dramatist can alter history, but why do it to
his and the character's disadvantage? Egmont and Goethe are caught in
the cross-fire of Schiller's historical knowledge, dramatic sense and
moral intelligence. What credit he can, he gives in glowing terms — the
crowd scenes are put on a par with Shakespeare's in *Julius Caesar* as

products of a genius beyond all deliberate art — but it is clear he regards *Egmont* as a failed drama.

We can see now that Egmont, like most of the figures in Goethe's early work (the play was conceived around 1773), was a means to self-expression. The sense of benevolent fate was Goethe's own, which is why he later set the 'charioteer' passage at the close of *Dichtung und Wahrheit* to suggest the fatedness of his move to Weimar. Yet to know this does nothing for the play as a play. Given his end — execution — Egmont's full story was not an apt medium for stating a faith in destiny. Failure in a particular genre was a price the young Goethe risked paying for his overriding expressive impulse.

If *Egmont* is a fragment of his great confession, Schiller's review is the first speech in their great dialogue. In showing up the play's flaws, he plots the expressive aesthetic responsible for them; in criticising just those qualities of Egmont's which had Goethe's sympathy,[27] he skirmishes with Goethe's temperament and moral outlook. By an apt coincidence, the review appeared within a fortnight of Schiller's first meeting with Goethe. His reports of the man parallel his criticisms of the play.[28]

Everything was against their becoming friends. They differed radically in cast of mind, in background and development, in situation. Goethe, ten years older, was an established cultural figure, Schiller still struggling to make a living and fiercely ambitious for recognition; his feelings for Goethe mingled love and hate.[29] It was to be years yet before he came to terms with Goethe as man and artist, swallowed the implied affront to his own talents, abandoned rancour for love and joined Goethe in a fruitful partnership. By then, he too had gone through a crisis as Goethe had just done when they met in 1788. As men transformed, they were ready to transform German literature.

Notes

1. To Dalberg, 24 August 1784.
2. Cf. *Hamburgische Dramaturgie*, 14. Stück: 'Die Namen von Fürsten und Helden können einem Stücke Pomp und Majestät geben; aber zur Rührung tragen sie nichts bei. Das Unglück derjenigen, deren Umstände den unsrigen am nächsten kommen, muss natürlicherweise am tiefsten in unsere Seele dringen.'
3. 'Eine schwäbische Anekdote', reprinted in Jost Hermand (ed.) *Von deutscher Republik*, vol. 1 (Frankfurt a.M., 1968), p.77. A good general picture, and a detailed account of Württemberg, is given by A. Fauchier-Magnan, *The Small German Courts in the Eighteenth Century* (1958).
4. Cf. Lessing to Nicolai, 21 January 1758; to Karl Lessing, 1 March 1772;

and to the Duke of Brunswick, early March 1772.

5. Cf. Manfred Durzak, 'Das Gesellschaftsbild in Lessings *Emilia Galotti*', in Durzak, *Poesie und Ratio* (Bad Homburg, 1970).

6. For its explicit form, see e.g. Wieland's *Agathon* Bk IX, Ch. 4, *Werke* I, 724.

7. Bruford, *Theatre, Drama and Audience in Goethe's Germany*, p.212.

8. Goethe and Schiller later distinguish in their theory the 'ausser sich wirkenden Menschen' of epic and the 'nach innen geführten Menschen' of tragedy. See *Über epische und dramatische Dichtung*, in Schiller, *Werke* V, 790.

9. Cf. H.B. Garland, *Schiller the Dramatic Writer. A Study of Style in the Plays* (Oxford, 1969).

10. Cf. Bürger's fine poem 'Der Bauer an seinen durchlauchtigen Tyrannen', with the stanza: 'Die Saat, so deine Jagd zertritt, Was Ross und Hund und du verschlingst,/Das Brot, du Fürst, ist mein!'

11. See *Hamburgische Dramaturgie*, 79. Stück.

12. To Reinwald, 5 May 1784.

13. Erich Auerbach, 'Musikus Miller', in *Mimesis. Dargestellte Wirklichkeit in der abendländischen Literatur* (Berne, 1947), p.387.

14. To Dalberg, 7 June and 24 August 1784.

15. To Reinwald, 27 March 1783.

16. To Dalberg, 7 June 1784.

17. To Reinwald, 27 March and 14 April 1783.

18. In a letter containing and commenting on passages of the play, *Werke* V, 111. For the political ethics of *Wilhelm Tell*, see Schiller's poem 'An Karl Theodor von Dalberg'.

19. To Dalberg, 3 April 1783.

20. Cf. H.H. Houben, *Verbotene Literatur* (Berlin, 1924), pp.543-7, a useful reminder that the effects drama could have on society were less than would appear from a modern uncensored printed text.

21. *Geschichte des Abfalls der vereinigten Niederlande von der spanischen Regierung*, *Werke* IV, 45. The following quotations, ibid., pp.33-9.

22. Ibid., p.1020.

23. E.g. Kant in his *Idee zu einer allgemeinen Geschichte in weltbürgerlicher Absicht* (1784) and Schiller himself in his (pre-Revolution) lecture on *Universalgeschichte*. See below, p. 180.

24. Cf. *Don Carlos* III, 9: 'Und was/Ist Zufall anders, als der rohe Stein,/Der Leben annimmt unter Bildners Hand?/Den Zufall gibt die Vorsehung — zum Zwecke/Muss ihn der Mensch gestalten'; and *Abfall der Niederlande*, *Werke* IV, 45; 'Der Mensch verarbeitet, glättet und bildet den rohen Stein, den die Zeiten herbeitragen; ihm gehört der Augenblick und der Punkt, aber die Weltgeschichte rollt der Zufall'.

25. Cf. E.M. Wilkinson, 'The Relation of Form and Meaning in Goethe's *Egmont*', in Wilkinson and Willoughby, *Goethe, Poet and Thinker* (1962).

26. See Schiller, *Werke* V, 932-42.

27. Cf. ibid., p. 934: 'in *nichts als* sein Verdienst gehüllt' (my italics) and 935: 'durch was für *gründliche* Verdienste hat sich Egmont bei uns das Recht auf . . . Teilnahme und Nachsicht erworben?' (Schiller's italics).

28. See to Körner, 12 September 1788 and 2 and 9 February 1789; to Caroline von Beulwitz, 5 and 25 February 1789.

29. See to Körner, 2 February 1789, comparing his feelings for Goethe to those of Cassius and Brutus for Caesar (in Shakespeare's *Julius Caesar* II, 1).

4

POETRY AND NATURE

Goethe's crisis came to a head when he had been in Weimar a decade. These years had stabilised and matured him. But maturity is relative to the individual's nature and potential. Goethe in 1786 was deeply dissatisfied and unfulfilled. He travelled to Italy and felt himself reborn. In many ways it was his old self restored. However we see the process, it transformed his creative life.

To understand his Italian experience means reviewing that Weimar decade. Its achievements demand attention in their own right; but the underlying question is what Weimar gave Goethe and what it took from him. He came in 1775 at the invitation of the Duke, Karl August. This was not literary patronage — Goethe was not made court poet, any more than Wieland had been when he came to Weimar in 1772 as Karl August's tutor and personal philosopher.[1] Goethe's poetic works were taken as signs of a talent which might be of use in practical affairs. Others had guessed at this. 'Goethe wäre ein herrliches handelndes Wesen bei einem Fürsten', wrote Lavater in 1774.[2] Goethe was promptly thrust into the administrative work of the Duchy. This was not so much mature policy as self-assertion by the nineteen-year-old Duke. It ruffled the aristocratic and official establishment. In that conventional world, Goethe was like a child of nature, strange and amusing to women and young people, disturbing to the old.[3] Karl August's senior minister, von Fritzsch, refused to serve with Goethe and tried to resign; Karl August urged the value of genius and the need for a man of experience to help train it.[4] This is a pre-echo of *Torquato Tasso*, the social aspect of a confrontation between poetic talent and reality which was the formative experience of this decade.

The small-mindedness of establishment and older generation was not shared by Wieland. Bewitched by the man and bowled over by his poetry, he wrote a glowing account of both in which Goethe is a magical being ('Hexenmeister', 'Geisterkönig') and an apparition of unparalleled intensity:

Wir fühlten beim ersten Blick, 's war *Er*,
Wir fühlten's mit allen unsern Sinnen,
Durch alle unsre Adern rinnen —

yet also profoundly human and benevolent and in touch with the essence of things:

Der alle Güte und alle Gewalt
Der Menschheit so in sich vereinigt! . . .
So mächtig alle Natur umfasst,
So tief in jedes Wesen sich gräbt,
Und doch so innig im Ganzen lebt!

The scenes he has heard Goethe read (the macrocosm and Erdgeist passages of *Faust*, to judge from Wieland's own phrasing) are a miraculous combination of beauty and truth – 'So schön,/Und immer ohne zu verschönen!/So wunderbarlich wahr! So neu,/Und dennoch Zug vor Zug so treu'. The created figures have a natural reality beyond any moral reflection or ideal construct.[5]

Few men, outside love-poetry, have celebrated a fellow creature so whole-heartedly, few writers another writer; and surely no writer a young colleague who had given cause for offence as Goethe had, when he satirised Wieland's *Alceste* in the skit *Götter, Helden und Wieland*. Yet vengeful polemic on Wieland's part would have destroyed the possibility of common ground. Within the decade this had appeared, Goethe's ethical standards and his style were refined, toned down, into something nearer Wieland's.

This inevitably suggests loss, for Goethe's pre-Weimar writing has a power one would not wish to see refined away, and a self-generated inner form more impressive than any literary expertise. Loss there is. The best poems of this decade are shadows of the best before 1775. The free verse of philosophical poems like 'Grenzen der Menschheit', 'Gesang der Geister über den Wassern', 'Meine Göttin', and 'Das Göttliche', is a tentative dividing-up of rational argument, very different from the rhythmic dictates of experience which shaped 'Prometheus', 'Ganymed', or 'An Schwager Kronos'. Reflection about nature and the observation of melancholy moonlit landscapes replaces the emotion that bursts out to greet spring in 'Maifest' or, in 'Herbstgefühl' and 'Auf dem See', responds to growth in nature and senses man's place in it, raising observation to symbolic statement. In his love poetry, the pulse of feeling and the acceptance of challenge from the natural world as the lover rides to his meeting ('Willkommen und Abschied') now yield to the hushed tones of 'An den Mond', with its deliberate turn away from the world, or to the metaphysical speculations of 'Warum gabst du uns die tiefen Blicke?', where recollection of a previous existence with the beloved makes the daylight of the present seem pale — 'Dämmernd ist um uns der hellste Tag'. These examples are not tendentiously chosen. Wherever one looks in Goethe's poetry of the first Weimar decade, it has lost colour, vitality, rhythmic authority and intuitive conviction. Even where it is finely moulded to a specific experience, in the celebrated 'Über allen Gipfeln', the tone is hushed, resigned, wistful. Energy has drained away. We are forced to ask: what might Goethe's writing have been if he had not come to Weimar?

But there was the snag. Could he have gone on as he was? The intense emotion which created those remarkable early poems and so impressed Wieland, and indeed all Goethe's acquaintance, had a darker side. The feeling which at times he mastered in poetry, the whole mental state in which he came to Weimar, was potentially destructive. He needed the calming influences of this new environment — even if they also reduced his responses generally.[6]

The influences were three: administrative work, new intellectual disciplines, and personal relations. Goethe from the first sat on the Supreme Conseil, and soon headed three of its Commissions: mining, roads, and the army. We must not exaggerate — Goethe did not become a statesman. Except in the sense of sovereignty, Weimar was not what we should call a state. It was about the size of a small English county and had some six thousand inhabitants. Goethe was more like a local government official. 'Mining' meant the attempt to re-open old silver mines at Ilmenau, a hopeless task which yielded only years of tedious work and worry. 'The army' meant a handful of hussars, a few hundred part-time infantry, and the business of a triennial levy. 'Roads' meant struggling to make do and mend in one tiny area of a fragmented Germany. Then in 1782 he had to untangle the affairs of the treasury.[7] All this brought him up against awkward realities at close quarters. Had he really been a 'statesman', or even just an under-secretary of state in a large nation as another man of letters, David Hume, had recently been, he would have stayed remote from detail and learned less. But riding about the country on the Duke's behalf, seeing for himself, doing things himself, provided a rough discipline for an over-exuberant mind. Creating order in practical affairs helped him to order his own chaos. Taking responsibility for others — foremost among them the Duke himself, who was still far from being a balanced, mature man and ruler[8] — sobered a wild temperament. 'Meine Geschäfte . . . bilden mich, indem ich sie bilde', Goethe wrote towards the end of this decade.[9]

From practical affairs grew an interest in subtler disciplines: in plant biology, resulting from work on the ducal forests — 'ich war vom Bedarf zur Kenntnis gelangt', he wrote later[10] — which led in turn to geology and then to other areas. 'Specialisation' was not yet dominant; a new devotee of science could put forward his views promptly. An essay in geology, 'Über den Granit', was followed by one in anatomy, declaring the presence of an intermaxillary bone in man (both 1784).

As a result of what was to be a life-long involvement in science, Goethe ceased to look at natural phenomena merely with a powerful but undifferentiating poetic gaze. A rhapsodic poem like 'Ganymed' (1774) saw nature wholly through feeling:

> Wie im Morgenglanze
> Du rings mich anglühst,
> Frühling, Geliebter!
> Mit tausendfacher Liebeswonne
> Sich an mein Herz drängt
> Deiner ewigen Wärme
> Heilig Gefühl,
> Unendliche Schöne!

Werther's feeling too was vehement and vague. His mind cannot grasp things: 'Meine vorstellende Kraft ist so schwach, alles schwimmt, schwankt vor meiner Seele, dass ich keinen Umriss packen kann'.[11] These modes of feeling and writing become impossible when nature is grasped precisely and in detail. True, Werther is not Goethe and his intense yearnings and inability to fulfil them are part of a condition which is shown to be pathological; but we see in him the young Goethe's response to nature taken to its logical conclusion. He epitomises the way much nature poetry has been produced; generalised emotion preponderates over knowledge and understanding to the point where wonder, awe or enthusiasm demand expression.

Does science then drive out poetry? That conclusion would be premature — and defeatist. Poetry would be a poor thing if it could only grow from ignorance, illusion and imprecision. And the world would be a poor thing if it could not, when profoundly understood, still arouse feeling and inspire eloquence. What is true is that few minds have achieved scientific understanding of the world and done justice to that understanding in poetry. Goethe is one of the few. His first interest in science may have had a sobering effect, but it was an investment for the poetic future.

One cannot say as much for the main personal influence of these years, Charlotte von Stein. It is true her effect was beneficial for a time: she understood, calmed and healed him in ways he celebrates in the poem 'Warum gabst du uns die tiefen Blicke?' But she did this by imposing her standards and outlook – her concern with a reflective inner life, her belief in self-improvement for the benefit of one's friends and in renunciation and restraint. Whether we see her with her detractors as essentially (despite marriage and seven children) an old maid, or with her partisans as a Beatrice to Goethe's Dante, the point remains that she inculcated withdrawal from the world, denial of its intrinsic worth, and desire for a purely spiritual realm. These values appear in the poems and letters she inspired. She weaned Goethe away from his former strength, inspiration and article of faith: nature. It was only a question of time before he felt the deprivation, set it against the decreasing benefits of the relationship, and acted.

It took surprisingly long. But by 1786 pressure had built up. Relations with Charlotte were difficult, business pressed, multiple interests fragmented his time; he had several major projects begun and no time to finish any. Meanwhile he was revising his early works for a collected edition, which stirred up old ills but also no doubt recalled the satisfactions of completed composition. It was in every way a frustrating situation. Yet he had not lost that Egmont-like sense of benevolent fate. He had lived these years at Weimar in expectation:

> eingehüllt,
> Von holder Lebenskraft erfüllt,
> In stiller Gegenwart die Zukunft zu erhoffen.[12]

At three in the morning on 3 September 1786 Goethe slipped out of Karlsbad and headed towards Italy: 'denn es war Zeit'.[13]

II

Just as these years in Weimar were a preparation, so their achievements were provisional. The major conceptions had yet to be finished (*Tasso*, *Egmont*) or revised (*Iphigenie*) or both (*Wilhelm Meister*). The reflective poems had left behind intuitive oneness *with* nature but not yet attained a comprehensive philosophy *of* nature; if Goethe was moving towards this in his science, he had barely brought it into his poetry, nor integrated it with his ethical thinking.

The most complete of the works just named is the 1779 prose *Iphigenie*. The 1790 revision adds some striking phrases – 'Das Land der Griechen mit der Seele suchend', 'Ich untersuche nicht, ich fühle nur'; and it uses the cohesive effect of verse to build up tension and climax to much greater intensity. But the drama is already complete in the prose. Its central issue is ethical. Iphigenie, dedicated to lifting the curse on her family, risks death for herself, her brother Orest and his friend, rather than commit an action which will make her impure and thus unfit for her task. There are no such scruples in the Greek original: Iphigenie obeys Apollo's oracle and helps steal the statue of his sister Artemis from the Tauricans. Orest and Pylades are the heroes, the barbarians are the villains. In return for successful theft, the god will lift the curse. The process is mechanical, not ethical.

This is crude, but it left scope for a transforming ambiguity. Iphigenie is herself a sister to be brought home from an alien shore. At the climax, this can be read as the meaning of the oracle so that the god agrees with human intention; he too can appear to have wanted a pure Iphigenie to perform the purification, not simply a stolen statue as its price. By this time, she has in any case proved her integrity: devotion to King Thoas would not allow her to deceive him. Barbarians too deserve ethical treatment, just as they too can be expected to hear the voice of truth and humanity (V, 3).

All this — the ethical purism which will risk sacrificing self (and others), the sense of universal humanity, the 'enlightened' god — is a far cry from *Götz*, *Werther*, or 'Prometheus'. It seems just the kind of Enlightenment version of an ancient theme which Goethe had mocked in *Götter, Helden und Wieland*, where he makes Euripides himself scorn 'Würde der Menschheit' as an un-Greek accretion and the virtue and loving self-sacrifice of Wieland's Alceste as unreal, 'Ein Unding . . . wie alle Phantasie, die mit dem Gang der Welt nicht bestehen kann'.[14] Now *Iphigenie* seemed open to the identical charges.

Certainly it is not Greek, in that it has refined Euripides. Is it also unreal? Comparison with Wieland's *Alceste* is illuminating. When Iphigenie resolves to be open with Thoas, she challenges the gods to prove their virtue by supporting hers: 'und wenn ihr die Wahrhaftigen seid, wie ihr gepriesen werdet, so zeigt's durch euren Beistand und verherrlicht die Wahrheit'[15]. Wieland's Admet is similarly sure that the virtue of his wife Alceste must move the gods, if indeed they are gods:

Ihr hört sie, Götter! — Und ihr könntet sie
mir rauben? Könntet so viel Tugend
der Welt entziehen? Dieses holde, schöne
liebatmende Geschöpf in seiner Blüte
dem Orkus opfern? — Nein,

Ihr seid nicht Götter, oder
Ihr könnt es nicht![16]

The parallel leads us however to vital differences between Goethe's play and Wieland's. Admet's words have no evident effect; Alceste is brought back from the dead by Hercules, Admet is told to ask no questions and humbly gives thanks. There is no link between virtue's challenge to the gods and the outcome. But in *Iphigenie* there is. The challenger herself carries the day — not through any divine intervention, but by her character and 'freundliche Worte', which fall on Thoas' anger like water on fire. But if the gods do not intervene, what was the importance of challenging them? To assert her faith and thus strengthen her in her decision. *Iphigenie*, in other words, is about the way belief determines actions and, through them, the final outcome. Orest believes in vengeful gods, Pylades in gods who help those who help themselves, Thoas in gods who demand human sacrifice (or so he will have Iphigenie think when putting pressure on her; his real beliefs and probable actions remain uncertain till the close, which maintains dramatic tension). Iphigenie's is the most elevated conception of the gods, and in acting by it she raises the others to her level. Euripides' Greeks were rescued by a *deus ex machina*, Goethe's are saved by a *deus in anima* which is as effective. What the gods are really like, or even whether they exist at all, matters less than what men believe about them.

Goethe brought this out very clearly in some words added in the second version. At the tense close of Act IV Iphigenie, fearful of relapsing into primitive beliefs and the actions this would entail, prays to the gods to save her — and thereby, in a sense, themselves:

Rettet mich,
Und rettet euer Bild in meiner Seele!

Thus the Greek original accommodates a second ambiguity: the adventure with a graven image has become a parable about the mental images man tries to live up to. So where Wieland forged no link between virtue and action, and through his Greek subject neither questioned the divine order nor found a purely human ethical solution, Goethe does all these things. He bypasses the idea of a divine order by showing that men's own values are decisive; these must be judged by an ethical ideal, i.e., not just by which values succeed (though Iphigenie's do succeed) but by which values will make man in a nobler image.[17] This is close to Lessing, who accepted Christian teachings not because they were revealed but because they seemed right to his rational mind[18] and who in *Nathan der Weise* preached a universal humanity. *Iphigenie* like *Nathan* is an Enlightenment drama, but a more convincing one; for where *Nathan* uses contrivance to avoid disaster and thereby ends as comedy, *Iphigenie* shows a virtue which can indeed 'mit dem Gang der Welt bestehen'.[19]

Its civilising effect is usually linked with Charlotte's influence. There is also a link with Goethe's science, but one which shows that his ethics and his science were not yet fully integrated. In 'Das Göttliche', Man is exhorted to be noble and good: 'Denn das allein/Unterscheidet ihn/Von allen Wesen,/Die wir kennen.' This is precisely meant: Goethe saw Man as part of the natural continuum. He had turned out to have a vestigial intermaxillary bone, formerly assumed to occur only in animals. Did this mean he was just another animal? No, because he had distinct human qualities. But it did mean that these were the only sign of his superiority. He had to exercise them to maintain it. Being part of nature thus did not lead to ethical naturalism, but obliged Man to create his own rational ethics. 'Das Göttliche' can be read as a poetic and *Iphigenie* as a dramatic version of Kant's categorical imperative, according to which men should so act that their behaviour may yield a maxim for all actions in like situations.[20]

This aim of transcending, or at least extending, Man's natural condition is unusual in Goethe. Usually his works convey the profound satisfaction of remaining within it and realising it (in both senses) to the full. He often shows natural impulse evolving or displaying a morality of its own, as in *Die Wahlverwandtschaften* or the poem 'Das Tagebuch'. His trust in fate is matched by — perhaps in the end identical with — his trust in the benevolence of nature. When he wrote *Iphigenie* and 'Das Göttliche', he had scarcely begun the scientific work on which that mature attitude rests. He already saw unity and continuity in nature, conceptions common enough in eighteenth-century science[21] but destined to acquire in his later poetry a unique power. But for that to happen, thought had to merge fully with feeling, axioms become imaginative vision.

In the years leading up to Italy, we can see this change occurring, Goethe's excitement in the face of nature increasing; not a rhapsodic emotion as of old, but a calm exhilaration as he feels for the living processes that form natural phenomena. From his first botanical study he had rejected the Linnean approach to species of classifying by stamen- and pistil-counts; the *Genera Plantarum* was Linnaeus' system, not nature's: 'Die Natur hat kein System, sie hat, sie ist Leben und

Folge aus einem unbekannten Zentrum zu einer nicht erkennbaren Grenze', as he wrote later,[22] the shift from 'hat' to 'ist' epitomising his advance beyond Linnaeus. Nature's boundaries were fluid, her variation continuous. Perhaps this view sprang ultimately from the old 'chain of being' idea, the theological notion that God must surely have given existence to every conceivable form; certainly Goethe began by seeking rock- and plant-forms intermediate between the known species.[23] But the underlying assumption of a series of separately created specimens gradually changed into that of a single great movement of phenomena, a play of forms in which any given species was, so to speak, a 'still'. To Charlotte, Goethe spoke of 'ein Gewahrwerden der wesentlichen Form, mit der die Natur gleichsam nur immer spielt und spielend das mannigfaltige Leben hervorbringt.'[24] He believed the principle could be applied not just to plants but to every part of nature. In scientific history, this marks the beginnings of morphology and one of the eighteenth century's gropings towards an evolutionary understanding of the origin of species. In literary history, it marks the return of a mind sobered by observation to an intuitive poetic grasp of nature.

Sobriety dominates as Goethe travels towards Italy. He writes not, as Werther did, of a 'liebes Tal', but of a 'fruchtbare Teller (um nicht zu sagen Kessel) Vertiefung'. He is scientist and administrator. He notes the composition of the soil and the state of the roads, the favourable site of a wealthy monastery and the necessary location of a city. He notes the watershed between Elbe and Danube and thus moves consciously across the shape of Europe.[25] For Werther, a natural scene was ineffably beautiful and impenetrably mysterious; for Goethe now it unfolds lucidly, falls into its constituent parts and shows up the underlying forces. He avowedly used this way of seeing as a means of reducing emotion and achieving an objective view.[26]

Yet when exercised on the range of experience Italy offered, it had its own emotional satisfactions. Landscape, climate, people, flora; ancient architecture and the Renaissance buildings of Palladio; the scenes of Roman history and Latin poetry; all these flooded in on the northerner as a new, exciting and somehow realer reality than the world he came from. His response is complex; he feels he is learning to see all over again, but also that what he observes, in botany or architecture, bears out what he has long thought. He is delighted and amazed at his own inner transformation, yet it also seems to fulfil an old expectation. Sometimes he is simply overwhelmed by the volume and variety of his experience. Perhaps the most important single thing is the return to 'die sinnlichen Eindrücke ... die mir kein Buch und kein Bild geben kann, dass ich wieder Interesse an der Welt nehme'.[27] It is nothing less than a new life, a rebirth, a resumption (this note is strong in his diary) of his own personal destiny: 'Ich fange nun erst an zu leben', he writes on arriving in Rome, 'und verehre meinen Genius'.[28]

Goethe spent nearly two years in Italy living as a painter among painters. He produced some fifteen hundred drawings but only two new poems. The writer seems altogether in abeyance. His revision of early works for the Göschen collected edition was an external necessity only. True, he was writing letters which are fine literature because they are eloquent accounts of a great and complex experience; many of them went into the later *Italienische Reise*. The diary of the eight weeks journey to Rome is itself a minor classic; the sense of release and revelation as Goethe's hungry mind absorbs new reality makes it one of the happiest, most zestful books ever penned. But the real point is that Goethe's Italian experience was indivisible. It affected the writer because it involved the whole man, as had the crisis that led up to it. What Italy did for him, it did for all his activities. Drawing was not an end in itself but a means to focus the eye on realities which must be the same for artist, poet or scientist.[29] The Italian diary and letters are full of references to 'Auge', 'sehen', 'erkennen', to the training of (literal) vision which is the basis for poetic and scientific insight into the way things really are. The artist begins to see works of art as products of natural laws working through men; there is nothing arbitrary about them, 'da ist Notwendigkeit, da ist Gott'.[30] The scientist makes the breakthrough to his concept of the *Urpflanze*, the typical and original form which is yet perceptible in each specimen, and to a plant morphology or *harmonia plantarum* to complement Linnaeus' *Genera plantarum*.[31] Everything he observed in Italy seemed an object-lesson in naturalness and necessity. And he himself was drawn back into this nexus. In Weimar he had merely reflected on Man's place in nature, in essays and poems which conveyed no sense of participation in nature remotely like that of the earlier 'Ganymed' or 'Auf dem See'. But from the moment he escaped to Italy, he was casting off the bonds of social duty and renewing the claim to his own destiny, obeying *his* inner necessity: 'nur die höchste Notwendigkeit konnte mich zwingen, den Entschluss zu fassen'.[32] This is not a mystical but a natural conception: the individual is a phenomenon of nature in which laws of growth assert themselves against external pressures, as Goethe was later to state in the poem 'Urworte. Orphisch'.

In Italy Goethe perceived an organic wholeness in art, nature and the Mediterranean way of life and tried to achieve a wholeness of his own.

He sensed that he had found himself again as an artist[33] and persuaded Karl August to release him from administrative work. He returned to Weimar in 1788, restored and enlightened, to digest his Italian experience and pursue poetry and science. One thing more restored him. Soon after returning, he took Christiane Vulpius, a woman of no social or cultural pretensions, as his mistress. Their sexual harmony was the more delightful for fitting his new vision of natural being; he was fully part of nature. Christiane was the inspiration for his first classical work, the *Römische Elegien*.[34] She also increased an isolation which had been marked since his return. His friends had given him a cool reception; they could not or would not understand his Italian revelation.[35] Now Christiane's residence in his house was too much for conventional Weimar. He was driven in on himself socially as well as intellectually. 'Immer stärkeres Isolement. Zurückziehen ins Innere', he noted later of this period.[36]

These biographical minutiae have a general significance. Here is the author of Germany's imminent classicism, and not only is he tucked away in a dukedom neither prominent nor especially representative in the context of a problematic nation, but he is out of harmony even with such society as it has, and derives nothing from it:

> Gute Gesellschaft hab ich gesehen, man nennt sie die gute,
> Wenn sie zum kleinsten Gedicht keine Gelegenheit gibt.[37]

The characteristics of 'normal' classicisms — agreed values, shared conventions, a sense of community — can hardly be expected.

Yet there are analogues of all these things in what Goethe now wrote; values are drawn from antiquity and his philosophy of nature; a formal convention is derived from the Latin elegiac poets; a sense of community is based on the conviction that the way he lived and loved was a return to the deeply natural life of the ancients. Goethe's classical ethos is thus a personal synthesis, a matter between the individual, history and nature. Having direct access to their permanently valid example, he can bypass mere local society altogether. The voice of the last European classicism begins to speak in lone self-sufficiency.

But the poetry is harmonious; isolation does not sour the effect. The *Roman Elegies* are poems of fulfilment and balance, of sexual fulfilment most evidently: they bid farewell to the merely spiritual intimacy of the Charlotte relationship and to that dominant tradition of European love-lyric which wrings emotion from non-fulfilment — loss, regret, yearning, the frustration of worship from afar, the quasi-religious reverence inspired by female mystery. Instead the Elegies show the natural course of mutual attraction and a mutual 'herzliche Liebe'; they describe a responsive physical woman, divested of mystery, known and possessed. Can all this still be 'poetic'? The question is, once again, can reality pure and simple retain the power to inspire? The answer in these rare, perhaps unique poems is: yes. Where so often love-poetry is a substitute for requited love, or, if written about it, falls over into complacency, salaciousness or cynical disillusionment,[38] Goethe achieves the elusive balance and celebrates the enjoyment of love as a natural norm.

As the word 'norm' suggests, a celebration so contrary to the traditions of Christian Europe must be to some degree self-conscious, with a touch of defiance or didacticism. When we read that the poet and his mistress enjoy 'die Freuden des echten nacketen Amors' (Elegy Ia), or that she 'teilt die Flammen, die sie in seinem Büsen entzündet' (II), there is an implied contrast with less natural ways of loving. It is made explicit, even programmatic, soon after: the poet's mistress is worried lest her prompt yielding should make him think ill of her, and he reassures her that promptness is the essence of love as it should be:

> Vielfach wirken die Pfeile des Amor: einige ritzen,
> Und vom schleichenden Gift kranket auf Jahre das Herz.
> Aber mächtig befiedert, mit frisch geschliffener Schärfe,
> Dringen die andern ins Mark, zünden behende das Blut.[39]

The ancient gods are his authority:

> In der heroischen Zeit, da Götter und Göttinnen liebten,
> Folgte Begierde dem Blick, folgte Genuss der Begier.

The naturalness of this sequence is in the very syntax, as it is again when Goethe quotes examples from legend: the fulfilment and consequences of desire (in one case, the consequence is the foundation of Rome itself) follow it after a simple 'und'. Promptness is as authentically classical as it is natural.

The naturalness is in the end more important. Roman myths and poets provide an example, but what matters is its viability for a modern. Can what has so long been culture again be nature? Yes, if antiquity can only be seen, free of the prestige it has had since the Renaissance, as purely human:

War das Antike doch neu, da jene Glücklichen lebten!
Lebe glücklich, und so lebe die Vorzeit in dir!

(XIII)

For all their richness of classical allusion, the Elegies are at heart products of Goethe's own new humanity, for which ancient models offered some stimulus. There is nothing in the tortured and vengefully satirical Catullus, and little in Tibullus or Propertius, to match Goethe's gentler, warmer, homelier emotion, the affection which constantly mixes with erotic pleasure.[40] What in Elegy XVIII he calls 'Aller Güter der Welt erstes und letztes' is not just satisfied desire, but emotional security. He is, in the telling phrase of Elegy II, 'endlich geborgen'.

If that is a modern element, so inevitably is the deep reverence for the Roman setting, its past and legacy, the 'sinnlich-geistige Überzeugung, dass hier das Grosse war, ist und sein wird'.[41] No Roman poet could have got from Rome quite the stimulus it gave Goethe. The recollected city absorbs him as much as love does, a division of interest which paradoxically gives each a richer, closer attention than either would have received alone. Rome and the sense of living antiquity enhance love, love opens his eyes to the art of the past. When he says that he sees statues 'mit fühlendem Aug' and caresses his mistress 'mit sehender Hand', this is not a gallant witticism but a true statement of the way each experience has genuinely enriched the other. The integration of love, art, and history makes the balance of the Elegy cycle.

Goethe called these poems 'Früchte der reinen Natur'.[42] They were not acceptable to Weimar. The Duke, no prude in his practice, advised against publishing. It is clear why. Eighteenth-century Germany had its erotica: Wieland had often sailed close to the wind, Heinse's novel *Ardinghello* (1787) portrayed conquests galore. But the *Roman Elegies* were different. They were real, they laid claim to value, they encroached on life.[43] Ardinghello, in contrast, merely enjoyed that total irresistibility in love and war which belongs to fantasy.

This again underlines Goethe's isolation. Those who had not pursued his path could not share his vision. This was embittering, even for the most self-assured and self-sufficient of poets, for poetry is a public as well as a private art. The epigrams Goethe wrote in Venice on a second visit in 1790 accordingly sound notes of discouragement and resignation. He is certain of his truths, he is happy in the private sphere (Epigrams 93, 100), but the public will not listen. Instead it is gulled by 'Schwärmer' and their false doctrines. Few love reason, and art is only for those few:

Werke des Geists und der Kunst sind für den Pöbel nicht da.

(Ep. 15)

The German language itself now seems an insuperable obstacle to poetry (Ep. 29, 77). Even Italy, revisited, disillusions him and his old enthusiasm seems a 'falscher Begriff' (Ep. 4, 6, 7).

So it was all in vain; the long training, the secular revelation of 1786, the profound insights into art and science, the clear view of man and his works within the economy of nature – it was all doomed to remain a private consolation and a public impossibility. In exploring nature through intellect and intuition, Goethe had marked out a path no one else had the talent and aspiration to follow or the experience and insight to understand. There was no-one for him to speak to; the *Venetian Epigrams* might have been a prelude to silence.

At this decisive moment Goethe acquired what he acutely needed but could not have dared expect; a practical ally, a sympathetic audience, and a perceptive analyst of his work alike in its finest detail and its broadest cultural significance. These roles were combined in one man, Schiller. He was as if made for them. He was a poet who at his best came close to equalling Goethe and might collaborate with him as a full partner. He was a more active publicist and potential conductor of literary campaigns. Above all, as critic and theorist he was peculiarly sensitive to Goethe's qualities because they related to his own crisis. This was no less profound than the one Goethe had gone through, although very different – so diametrically different, in fact, that their cases were complementary, material for an elegantly symmetrical theory. Schiller's path was identical with Goethe's but he was proceeding along it in the opposite direction. In 1794 they met.

III

Schiller's was a crisis of self-confidence. *Don Carlos* was a symptom. Successive inspirations had moved it this way and that. Schiller had always worked by inspiration, but it now became clear how much this could place dramatic composition at risk. A more objective method was needed. In any case, by the nineties inspiration seemed to Schiller a thing of the past, of his youth; he now watched himself creating and was inhibited by critical consciousness. Could criticism – the deliberate application of artistic principles – perhaps stand in for inspiration, or make art into second nature? So Schiller asked Körner in a revealing letter of May 1792, lamenting the ideal creative freedom he had lost and aspiring to regain it or some higher analogue of it.

By this time, his self-doubts had long been aggravated by Goethe. Schiller was as sure of Goethe's genius as he was unsure of his own. His letters to Körner in the late eighties are full of animus, culminating in the cry 'Dieser Mensch, dieser Goethe, ist mir einmal im Wege'.[44] But gradually a positive response grows; Körner persuades Schiller and Schiller persuades himself that the disadvantages which seemed to spring from inferiority are in fact signs of a typological divergence: Goethe has a grasp of sensuous reality, a contempt for abstract speculation, an attachment to nature; Schiller has feelings that must seek sensuous reality for their embodiment, he has a bent for speculation, he has no intuitive closeness to nature. And as artists, Goethe apparently has an easy spontaneous creativity, where Schiller can only aspire to regain spontaneity. In other words, Goethe fills the ideal role in which Schiller sometimes also sees his younger, uninhibited self.

So far Schiller had only made Goethe's acquaintance superficially; he loved-and-hated from afar. Goethe on his side disapproved of Schiller as an exponent of extremes he himself had outgrown: 'die reinsten Anschauungen suchte ich zu nähren und mitzuteilen, und nun fand ich mich zwischen Ardinghello und Franz Moor eingeklemmt'.[45] He was no better pleased with the Kantian abstractions of Schiller's first major aesthetic essay, *Über Anmut und Würde*; *Don Carlos* (which after all was a great stylistic advance) he never even mentions.

But in July 1794 mutual sympathy was established when they met at the Jena Naturforschende Gesellschaft. Schiller objected to the piecemeal ('zerstückelt') treatment of nature in a lecture they had heard; probably as a Kantian idealist he missed the organising ideas which would make observations of phenomena meaningful. Goethe agreed, on very different, wholly realistic grounds. Nature, he asserted, could be shown 'nicht gesondert und vereinzelt, sondern . . . wirkend und lebendig, aus dem Ganzen in die Teile strebend'. Schiller doubted it. Goethe explained his theory of the *Urpflanze*, that ultimate reality of the plant world present to the observation (for him at least) in every individual plant. Schiller was adamant; that could not be an experience, it must be an idea. His obstinate idealism confirmed Goethe's view that they were poles apart – 'Geistesantipoden'.[46]

But if poles are opposites, they are also complementary. Some obscure sense of this, and of the advantages they might bring each other, saved the situation. Goethe's account of the meeting ends by recognising that their alliance was established not so much despite as because of their differences – 'durch den grössten, vielleicht nie ganz zu schlichtenden Wettkampf zwischen Objekt und Subjekt'.

Object and subject, the real world and the observing mind, object-ivity and subjectivity; these terms point us back to literature and the differences between the two men as poets. In talking about science, they had been talking about the principles underlying their poetry. The way the mind perceives, understands and renders nature was a problem common to both areas. It is symptomatic that Goethe does not use the actual word 'Urpflanze', but speaks of sketching for Schiller 'eine symbolische Pflanze' – 'symbolic' because, exactly as in his theory of literary symbol, something real is held to embody a general meaning without thereby being reduced to a mere means of communication and losing its individual reality. When he formulated this view of poetic symbol years later, he recalled that the decisive observations sprang from his 'zarte Differenz mit Schiller'.[47]

Their meeting was even more decisive for Schiller's thinking. A month later he wrote Goethe a letter which is already a miniature treatise. It distinguishes the 'intuitive' from the 'speculative' mind, does homage to Goethe's intuition as already in full command of everything that analytic speculation laboriously seeks, and accepts what in their conversation Schiller seems to have doubted – the possibility of pro-ceeding from the whole of nature to the parts – as one more of the differences between their two types: 'Sie nehmen die ganze Natur zusammen, um über das Einzelne Licht zu bekommen, in der Allheit ihrer Erscheinungsarten suchen Sie den Erklärungsgrund für das Indi-viduum auf'.[48] Schiller speaks of Goethe's intuitive procedures with a respect verging on awe, perhaps because they recall that notion of an absolute, quasi-divine intellect (*intellectus archetypus*) which Kant postulated as proceeding intuitively from the whole to the parts, in contrast to the discursive approach to which the human mind (*intellec-tus ectypus*) is limited.[49] But Schiller insists that speculative and intui-tive minds have an equal potential and pursue a common aim, albeit by diametrically opposed ways. The intuitive mind, with its concentration on empirical realities, must seek their inner necessity (i.e., natural laws). The speculative mind, with its abstract *a priori* ideas, must seek experi-ence (i.e., to give them reality). If each has sufficient of its own kind of genius, then the intuitive mind will create individuals which yet are true to the general character of their species; while the speculative mind will create general types which yet have the possibility of life.

Schiller's statement turns antithesis into reciprocity. It can still stand today as a description of his and Goethe's procedures and results. It is remarkable criticism, drawing precise observations together into a cogent generalisation. If it impresses us, it must have staggered Goethe, for it retraced with uncanny accuracy more of his inner evolution than he can conceivably yet have imparted to Schiller. For example, the account of his scientific method, though put in Kantian terms, exactly corresponds to what the documents of the 1780s tell us, especially those letters in which Goethe declares his faith in Spinoza's *scientia intuitiva*, sets 'Schauen' against religious belief as the way to a knowledge of the essence of things, commits himself to a lifetime of contemplating the particulars which contain the divine, and finds he has penetrated to the inner processes informing the entire natural realm.[50]

Goethe replied gratefully that the letter had summarised his whole existence. Clearly it confirmed what their meeting had suggested; that here was the man uniquely gifted to be his literary partner. It is virtually the treaty of their alliance, which is enough to make it a historic document. But it has a further claim to the title. In it, a long theoretical development culminates and the major issue of eighteenth-century aesthetics — the issue, indeed, which was its *raison d'être* — finds a solution. And since this solution was to be the basis of Weimar Classicism, determining its theoretical statements, critical judgements and creative practice, it is worthwhile to review briefly that whole development.

IV

Eighteenth-century Germany inherited two dominant intellectual influences, the long-standing one of Christian doctrine and the more recent one of seventeenth-century rationalism. Neither set much store by men's sense experience: the Christian's eye was on a higher world, from which the senses might seduce the erring soul; while for the rationalist, the senses were not a means to clear or certain knowledge. Sensuous reality was consequently subordinated to the schemas of dogma and metaphysical speculation respectively.

Yet in any full account of man, sense experience must have a place. Though Leibniz never descended from the heights of logic and metaphysics, his follower Baumgarten did, precisely in order to complete the system. For since there were no gaps in nature, those lower perceptions must somehow be the first steps towards rational knowledge. Their lowly status is clear in his terms, 'gnoseologia inferior' and 'cognitio confusa', to which he added (from the Greek *aesthesis* meaning 'sense-perception') the coining 'aesthetica'. The new branch of philosophy, aesthetics, began very much as a poor relation.

Still, even to have given this much attention to the unclear perceptions of actual, not purely rational man was a step in an unintended direction, towards questioning the hierarchy in which reason stood far above the senses. It allowed sense-perception to be studied in its own terms as something with its own laws. Was beauty really no more than an indistinct cognition? Was it not perhaps a different kind of cognition with an independent value, at least for the creatures that perceived it as beautiful? Was aesthetic taste really a lower form of judgement? Or perhaps judgement of a different *kind*, not reducible to rational terms without destroying the nature of the phenomenon judged? In sum, was there not an alternative to the purely rational order and did not art and beauty suggest a different definition of man from the rationalist's account?[51]

The more radical questions are no more than implicit in Baumgarten's work and it was left to his successors to ask them. They are part of a broader enquiry in which, paradoxically, the most original minds of the 'age of reason' — Hume, Rousseau, Herder — were busy reducing the claims of pure reason and giving ever more authority to its untidy but undismissable opposite, experience. In epistemology, political philosophy and historiography, as in aesthetics, the uniformity of rational truth yields to the irregularity of discrete experience, and only such generalisations may stand as are supported by accumulated experience. Reality is seen to reside in the particular rather than the general, in what is natural rather than what is abstractly rational. This is the intellectual background to the cult of nature which dominates literature well into the nineteenth century.

The more moderate and subtle minds strove to synthesize new with traditional ways of thinking and to see whether the claims of the particular could not somehow be reconciled with a rational order. Lessing's idea that genius makes its own rules yet ultimately accords with rational Aristotelean principles, is an attempt to reconcile what is individual and natural in the creative process with what is uniform and objective in art. Kant's *Kritik der Urteilskraft* worries at this same problem of particular and general. Judgement itself he defines as 'das Vermögen, das Besondere als enthalten unter dem Allgemeinen zu denken'.[52] He recognises that our judgements of beauty are subjective, but they carry for him an unmistakeable flavour of necessity, universality, general validity. Yet he is clear that, whatever this 'general' is to which our experiences of beauty in nature and art refer us, it is not definite concepts. This endorses Baumgarten's first separation of sense-experience from the jurisdiction of reason. Kant's subtleties — the ideas of subjective yet universal judgement, of pleasure without interest, of purposiveness without specific purpose — grow out of the conflict between two urges; to keep aesthetic experience in its own realm of sensuous particulars and individual response, yet also to give it laws as necessary as the ones his other two critiques had elaborated for the theory of knowledge and for ethics.[53]

With the *Kritik der Urteilskraft* we have again reached 1790 and the period of Schiller's crisis; we can see now that the personal differences between him and Goethe were also historically representative. From the wild genius that marked Schiller's literary puberty, there had emerged a strongly rationalist mind seeking objective laws on which to ground a new poetic 'nature'. *Don Carlos* showed 'Sturm und Drang' impulses making way for characteristically Enlightenment ideas. Goethe stands in the other tradition, intellectually the child of Herder's doctrine of historical and cultural particularity and later drawn to Spinoza's pantheism, which he read less as an essay in metaphysics than as a programme for empirical observation. The vigorous reality of his early lyrics contrasts with Schiller's idea-generated poetry in much the same way as we saw the localised reality of *Egmont* contrast with the general principles of Posa's appeal to Philipp. These are poetic reflections of the eighteenth century's conflict between the schematism of reason and the patterns of actual experience.

The conflict is illustrated concretely by Schiller's review of Bürger's poems in 1789.[54] It is an unhappy incident – a good popular talent was damned on high principle and a man who admired Schiller was deeply wounded – but it is revealing. Schiller objected to the excess of particularity; a real individual rendering feelings and actual situations, apparently even writing his poems under the stress of emotion. All this made them 'Gelegenheitsgedichte', a term Schiller means dismissively, for he requires of poetry a permanence beyond mere occasions. He argues that, since lyric gives us the poet's individuality, this must be idealised and ennobled; composition must take place coolly 'aus der sanften und fernenden Erinnerung'.[55] Particular circumstances must yield in order to raise 'das Individuelle und Lokale zum Allgemeinen'. Bürger was puzzled: what was lyrical poetry if not a real person's real experience? Could one write about '*keines* sterblichen Menschen Empfindungen'?[56] Schiller replied that of course he was not demanding pallid abstraction, only that what was true and natural should be so far generalised that everyone could sympathise with it.[57] But the two men were still at cross-purposes; for Schiller was pursuing an 'individuality' not peculiar to the poet and scarcely what we should now call individuality at all. In his view, we are interested in the poet's self insofar as it stands for the 'Gattung' – the genus Man, the essential human being in typical situations of happiness, passion, bereavement etc.

The review is sometimes described as a statement of new classical principles; but it is more the statement of a rationalist whose view is still limited by the philosophical poetry dominant in the mid-century. This embodied general ideas in examples, the examples in verse. It could be grandiose, as in Albrecht von Haller's stern dismissal of European decadence by contrast with homespun Swiss life; or tediously drawn out, as in Friedrich von Matthisson, whose reflective landscapes Schiller later reviewed far too favourably, no doubt because they fitted so well the 'idealisation' argument. At its best, in Schiller's own poetry – 'Die Künstler' or 'Die Götter Griechenlands' – argument and exhortation are subtly transmuted into emotion by beauty of diction and rhythm and cadence. Yet even here, any particularity is verbal, stylistic; real phenomena are not rendered. Perhaps the loving detail in the poems of Brockes (who has been called the first realist and church-father of nature-description[58]) or the exquisite seasonal vignettes of von Salis come nearest to this and are the first shoots of a new poetry of particularity. Yet in Brockes the beauties which the eye sees are denied independent value by the contexts in which they appear: 'Die grösste Schönheit dieser Erden/Kann mit der himmlischen doch nicht verglichen werden'.[59] The religious world-view here limits poetic practice much as we saw rationalism limited aesthetic theory.

What Schiller urged against Bürger has point, even if it is a product of his century's orthodoxy. We do expect more from poetry than just an account of real happening or genuine feeling. But it is not clear that 'idealisation' is the right way to guarantee that extra something. The poet intent on general truths or representative feelings may fail to pass them through the medium of experience at all. Generalisation may be premature, rhetoric replace evocation. Schiller actually says that the lyrical poet is not free to stray far from 'Allgemeinheit der Gemütsbewegungen' because a poem offers so little room to expatiate on 'das Eigentümliche der Umstände', i.e., message and medium are competing for the available space (a very non-organic way of viewing the poem!) and caution dictates that the poet stick to the general, since the particular cannot be trusted to get the meaning over. In his later Matthisson review.[60] Schiller does admittedly suggest that the poet can 'symbolise' feelings through nature-description; but this turns out to be an arid seeking of analogies and translation of ideas into sensuous form ('versinnlichen'), the normal eighteenth-century procedures. For Schiller, as for Kant,[61] 'symbol' has here no special status, implies no such true fusion of meaning and substance, general and particular, as it did for Goethe and Karl Philipp Moritz.[62]

To this point, then, Schiller lacks the insight that particulars of experience may convey meaning without recourse to abstraction. Bürger's poetry, with its easy jollity, was not good enough of its kind to impress Schiller's austere mind and challenge the dominance of his 'idealisation' theory. But in Goethe, Schiller's idealism met its match, and he was forced to reconsider. At first he was repelled by Goethe's 'Sinnlichkeit' as much as by Bürger's;[63] but then came their meeting and a sudden understanding of Goethe's sense-affirming, empirical, realistic mind. And there was no gainsaying the persuasive quality of Goethe's poetry. Yet it flatly contradicted Schiller's theories − it was rooted in particular circumstances, created no 'distance', no abstraction, no 'idealisation'. It was all born of particular occasions. Indeed that same word 'Gelegenheitsgedichte', with which Schiller rejected Bürger, was later to be Goethe's way of summing up his own lyrical method.[64] This revaluation is a measure of the change in basic assumptions about poetry in the late eighteenth century.

So even though Schiller's letter to Goethe of August 1794 still speaks positively of the generic ('Gattung'), it also conceives of a new way to get poetic results, a new direction of poetic movement. Goethe's poetry and science alike are understood to have found general truths in and through empirical particulars, which they state not abstractly but concretely, in symbolic form. It is still a general meaning that the symbolic particular conveys − to that extent Schiller is able to modify his earlier theory, not jettison it. He and Goethe are about the same business by different methods. Honour is satisfied. Envy can be dissolved in cooperation and friendly emulation.

Out of Schiller's personal crisis, poetic and intellectual, and out of the two main currents of eighteenth-century thinking about the mind and experience which flow together in that fine letter, the shape of Classicism emerges. Its programme is to reconcile particular and general, sense and reason, experience and necessary truth, man's particularities and his generic character. Only literary works which do justice to both sets of factors can claim the highest rank, and this axiom governs alike the judgements Schiller and Goethe pass on their contemporaries and the goals they aspire to in their own works. True to his speculative nature, it is Schiller who provides most of the formal statements of Classical principle. His two major aesthetic essays treat the fundamental problems of eighteenth-century culture and point towards solutions. The *Ästhetische Briefe* analyses the material-cum-rational nature of Man at every level from the detail of perceptual acts, via a definition of beauty as the fusion of living matter and abstract form, to consequent

demands on artistic works and on the larger units of social organisation.
Uber naive und sentimentalische Dichtung traces the historical coming-
about of the disharmony from which modern poets (and modern Man
generally) suffer, illuminates its effect on the whole of European poetry,
and still manages to see in the plight of moderns some inherent value
and literary potential. Alongside this theoretical activity, the two poets
are intensively productive for the decade of their partnership, establishing their 'Classicism' in far more than mere theory. But before this,
they set out to clear the ground of old attitudes and poor practitioners.
Their campaign is an apt medium through which to survey this ground,
and see how the two creators of a focal culture stood to their times.

Notes

1. Cf. Karl August to Wieland, 23 July 1772.
2. Lavater to Zimmermann, 20 October 1774.
3. Cf. the sketch for an unexecuted section of autobiography, WA 53, 383.
4. Karl August to von Fritzsch, 10 May 1776.
5. Wieland, 'An Psychen', *Werke* IV, 623f.
6. On the young Goethe's psychic condition, see the early chapters of Barker
Fairley, *A Study of Goethe*, (Oxford, 1947).
7. A full account of Goethe's administrative work is given by W.H. Bruford,
Culture and Society in Classical Weimar (Cambridge, 1962).
8. Cf. Goethe's retrospect in the poem 'Ilmenau' (1783), lines 136-55.
9. To Knebel, 30 December 1785.
10. *Geschichte seiner botanischen Studien*, HA 13, 151.
11. *Die Leiden des jungen Werther*, 1. Buch, 24. Juli.
12. 'Einschränkung', originally entitled 'Dem Schicksal'.
13. *Tagebuch der italienischen Reise*, 3 September 1786. WA III, 1, 147.
14. HA 4, 208 and 213.
15. Act V, sc.6; WA 39, 393. (Note how the verse revision creates a climax by
adding 'durch mich' after 'verherrlicht'.)
16. *Alceste*, Act II; *Werke* III, 84.
17. For a fuller interpretation on these lines, see the fine chapter on *Iphigenie*
in Staiger, *Goethe*, vol. 1, which draws illuminatingly on the poem 'Das Göttliche'
to show the virtuous circle of faith-action-success-strengthened faith-action which
Goethe is presenting.
18. *Uber den Beweis des Geistes und der Kraft, Werke* XIII, 3-8.
19. Erich Heller's view that *Iphigenie* is wishful thinking because she 'would
not do what she does . . . if her vision of life really comprehended the possibility
of her having to put her brother to death' (Goethe and the Avoidance of Tragedy'
in *The Disinherited Mind*, Cambridge, [3]1971, p. 44) disregards the Parzenlied
scene at the close of Act IV which shows that she does indeed conceive that her
whole idea of the gods and their ways may be mistaken. When she acts, she calls
success 'unwahrscheinlich' (line 1897 of verse text, p. 393 of prose). True, the
risk comes home to her even more when she *has* acted (1945ff of verse, prose
p. 394); but this is a psychological truth, not a proof of her limited vision.
20. Cf. Orest's words, clearest in the prose (V, 6; p. 400): 'Seltne Taten

werden durch Jahrhunderte nachahmend zum Gesetz geheiligt'.

21. Cf. A.O. Lovejoy's classic study, *The Great Chain of Being* (Harvard, 1936), and H.B. Nisbet, *Goethe and the Scientific Tradition* (1972).

22. *Probleme* (1823), HA 13, 35.

23. Cf. to Herder, 6 September 1784.

24. 9 July 1786.

25. *Tagebuch der italienischen Reise*, 17 September 1786, WA III, 1, 148f.

26. Cf. the later *Italienische Reise*, 27 October 1786, HA 11, 122.

27. *Tagebuch*, 11 September 1786, edn cit. p. 175.

28. *Tagebuch*, 28 October 1786, edn cit. p. 331.

29. Cf. to Charlotte, 7-10 February 1787.

30. *Italienische Reise*, 6 September 1787, HA 11, 395.

31. Cf. to Knebel, 18 August 1787.

32. *Tagebuch*, 27 October 1786, edn cit., p. 326. Cf. the letter to Charlotte of 25 January 1787, where the resolve 'sich weder um rechts noch links [zu] bekümmern' echoes the charioteer passage from *Egmont*.

33. To Karl August, 17 March 1788.

34. As to whether Goethe also had a mistress in Rome, there is only circumstantial evidence. Cf. his letters to Karl August of 3 February and 29 December 1787, and Schiller to Körner, 12 September 1788.

35. Cf. e.g. to Charlotte, 1 June 1789.

36. WA 53, 386.

37. *Venetianische Epigramme*, number 75.

38. Complacency: Chamisso's cycle *Frauenliebe und-Leben*; salaciousness: Leipzig Rococo lyric of the 1760s; cynical disillusionment: Heine's Paris cycle *Verschiedene*.

39. The first two lines surely refer to the Charlotte relationship and Goethe's role as what Kommerell called a 'Märtyrer der Seelenliebe', *Gedanken über Gedichte* (Frankfurt a.M., ²1956), p. 239.

40. Kommerell nicely remarks: 'Wenn der neue Elegiker seiner Geliebten des Hexameters Mass mit fingernder Hand auf den Rücken zählt, so hat sie einen guten, beinahe deutschen Schlaf. Cynthia [Propertius's mistress] liesse sich das schwerlich gefallen'. *Gedanken über Gedichte*, p. 231.

41. *Italienische Reise*, Bericht, Rome, December 1787, HA 11, 456.

42. In the poem 'Hier ist mein Garten bestellt', a celebration of the god Priapus, WA 1, 423.

43. Cf. Charlotte von Stein to Charlotte Schiller, 27 July 1795: 'wenn Wieland üppige Schilderungen machte, so lief es doch zuletzt auf Moral aus . . . auch schrieb er diese Szenen nicht von sich selbst . . .'

44. 9 March 1789.

45. *Glückliches Ereignis*, HA 10, 539.

46. Ibid, p. 540.

47. *Maximen und Reflexionen* nr. 751, HA 12, 471. Numbers 749, 750 and 752 also elaborate the theory of symbol, in contrast to allegory, which is the term corresponding to Schiller's procedure.

48. 23 August 1794.

49. Cf. *Kritik der Urteilskraft*, 2. Teil, 2. Abteilung para. 77. *Werke* V, 486. Goethe in later years made tentative claims to this kind of understanding. See *Anschauende Urteilskraft* (?1817), HA 13, 30f.

50. See to Jacobi, 9 June 1785 and 5 May 1786; to Charlotte 9 July 1786.

51. For an excellent conspectus of this phase in eighteenth-century thought, see Ernst Cassirer, *Freiheit und Form* (Darmstadt, ³1961), Ch. 2, 'Die Entdeckung der ästhetischen Formwelt'.

52. *Kritik der Urteilskraft*, Einleitung para. 4, *Werke* V, 248.
53. The arguments for universality of aesthetic judgements come in paras. 22, 37 and 40 of the *Kritik der Urteilskraft*; the conflict between subjectivity and universality in paras. 56 and 57.
54. *Werke* V, 970ff.
55. Ibid p. 982. The phrase has sometimes been thought a source for Wordsworth's 'emotion recollected in tranquillity', in the Introduction to the *Lyrical Ballads*. But Wordsworth, contrary to common belief, was speaking of the poet's need to relive his experience, to get back into it; Schiller is insisting that he must escape from its dominance qua single experience in order to generalise.
56. Bürger, *Antikritik*, printed in Schiller, *Werke* V, 1226f.
57. Ibid., p. 986f.
58. Arno Schmidt, 'Barthold Heinrich Brockes, oder nichts ist mir zu klein', in Schmidt, *Nachrichten von Büchern und Menschen* 1 (Frankfurt a.M., 1971), p. 8.
59. Brockes, 'Kirschblüte bei Nacht'. Cf. similarly the fine poem 'Die Rose', where exact and loving description alternates with crude didacticism ('Hieraus nun nehm ich diese Lehre'). More perfunctory poets more easily dismissed earthly experience with a 'Mir ekelt vor der Erde Schätzen' (Karl Friedrich Drollinger, 'Lob der Gottheit') or a 'Mein Heim ist nicht in dieser Zeit' (Gerhard Tersteegen, 'Abendopfer'). These continue the other-worldly message of Baroque writing from which Brockes is just beginning to emancipate poetry.
60. *Werke* V, 992ff.
61. *Urteilskraft* para. 59, *Werke* V, 428f., defines 'symbolisch' as 'Vorstellung nach einer blossen Analogie'. Schiller still understands the term this way when explaining his own poetic method to Goethe: '*Mein* Verstand wirkt eigentlich mehr symbolisierend', letter of 31 August 1794.
62. See Moritz's essay *Uber die bildende Nachahmung des Schönen*, which arose from conversations with Goethe in Rome and was partially printed in the *Italienische Reise* by Goethe as evidence of his thinking at the time. Moritz speaks of grasping 'das edle, grosse Ganze der Natur in dunkler Ahndung' and of capturing the beauty of the whole in a single object which renders it 'in verjüngendem Masstabe'. In Elschenbroich, *Deutsche Dichtung im 18. Jahrhundert*, pp. 603f.
63. Cf. to Körner, 1 November 1790: 'Seine Philosophie . . . holt zu viel aus der Sinnenwelt, wo ich aus der Seele hole. Uberhaupt ist seine Vorstellungsart zu sinnlich und *betastet* mir zu viel'.
64. See *Dichtung und Wahrheit*, Bk 15, on the dependence of his poetry on 'Gelegenheit', HA 10, 48. In Bk 10 he calls the 'Gelegenheitsgedicht' 'die erste und echteste aller Dichtarten', HA 9, 397.

5 LANDSCAPE WITH WRITERS

When Schiller founded *Die Horen* in 1794 his aim was to unite the nation's best writers in a single venture and their respective followings in a single public.[1] This was both a commercial calculation – cornering the market was a necessity if first-class writers were to be adequately paid – and a cultural ambition similar to the plan for a national theatre. There were numerous literary journals in eighteenth-century Germany, but this no more made for high literary standards than the multiplicity of theatres in different places, each inhibited by social or financial pressures, made for a thriving national dramatic tradition. Less journals of higher quality, or even one great and independent literary organ, would serve literature better.

Schiller was not the first to think so. Wieland had striven to make his *Teutscher Merkur* into an influential 'Nazional-journal' inculcating 'Nazionalgeist'.[2] There were inevitable differences of scope between this and the *Mercure de France* he emulated, but he achieved a modest success. Though he compromised with public taste rather than meet it head-on, he maintained a respectable standard, edging his readers gently towards more enlightened thinking and a less crude culture.[3] The *Horen* likewise was to work at the 'stillen Bau besserer Begriffe, reinerer Grundsätze und edlerer Sitten' in the cause of 'wahre Humanität';[4] but the announcement of its programme had a high tone, and the list of intending contributors was impressive.[5] Though Schiller promised to avoid abstruseness and to convey truth through beauty, it was clear that the *Horen* was going to be a demanding journal.

It made serious demands on its initiators, too. Goethe and Schiller's letters in the first months were much concerned with filling the promised number of pages worthily. Contributors were slow to deliver and copy was short even before the first number appeared.[6] In the first year, he and Goethe wrote nearly half the journal themselves.[7] The contrast between the grandiloquent programme and this crisis was amusing to Goethe years later; nevertheless he could see that without that crusading impulse the course of German literature would have been very different.[8]

The crisis was overcome, thanks to the finished or near-finished work already available – Schiller's *Briefe über die ästhetische Erziehung des Menschen*, Goethe's *Römische Elegien* and his novel *Unterhaltungen deutscher Ausgewanderten*, August Wilhelm Schlegel's sample translations from Dante – and a high standard was kept up. But precisely this led to conflict and controversy, to a general polemical campaign by Goethe and Schiller, and to a clearer account of their principles than might have been rendered without the stimulus of opposition. The affair made what was already proving a fruitful partnership into (as Schiller said) a Church Militant.[9]

Briefly the *Horen* was not well received. The public was confused, or disappointed in its expectations, or else it found the essays Schiller published frankly too difficult.[10] Rival journals printed negative reviews, and through these and other publications Goethe and Schiller felt a general hostility to their work and aims. They saw themselves doubly baulked; by a public not yet able to value their offerings, and by a literary world intent on preserving the market for its own. As Schiller wrote, in terms that recall Goethe's account of eighteenth-century German theatre: the public had no longer the unity of childhood taste and not yet that of cultivated taste – a situation favouring bad writers out for money, but not those with higher aims.[11] The frustration of these aims and the sting of critical attack inspired the idea of a grand counter-stroke. Throughout 1796 Goethe and Schiller composed satirical epigrams on almost everyone then writing. They were published under the title *Xenien* in Schiller's *Musenalmanach* for 1797, and they were an immediate scandal.

They are now a historical document and not much more. Satire rarely keeps its savour beyond the period it is written in, when the issues are live and the personalities known. Where it does so, it is because the pointedness achieved by style or the scurrility born of anger is so immediately striking that we do not at first care who the historical target was and whether what is said is true. That is how Pope and Heine still live. Footnotes can make our understanding of them richer, and if it can be shown that their attacks were justified, moral satisfaction is added to aesthetic pleasure. But no amount of annotation can revive satires which lack that first self-sufficient effect. Most of the *Xenien* do lack it. Friedrich Nicolai was not far wrong (though he spoke as one of the victims) when he judged that, of the 400 or so epigrams, perhaps four were excellent, forty good, some passable, many unjust and mistaken, and the vast majority flat enough to have been dreamed up by any mediocre mind.[12] The fault probably lies at the very root, in the form chosen. The classical distich (dactylic hexameter followed by dactylic pentameter) served well in poems requiring no pointed effects, such as Goethe's *Römische Elegien*; but as a two-line unit to accommodate allusion, attitude and polemical point, it was weak. It was at once too easy to compose, offering little resistance to thought, and too short on the stylistic means needed to sharpen an idea into a witticism. In particular, it lacked that great ally of verse satire in modern languages, rhyme. One need only compare Xenion 246, on the trivial country idylls of F.W.A. Schmidt's *Kalender der Musen und Grazien*:

> Musen und Grazien! oft habt ihr euch schrecklich verirret,
> Doch dem Pfarrer noch nie selbst die Perücke gebracht

with Goethe's rhymed satire on the same crude 'naturalism', 'Musen und Grazien in der Mark', which includes this:

> O wie freut es mich, mein Liebchen,
> Dass du so natürlich bist;
> Unsre Mädchen, unsre Bübchen
> Spielen künftig auf dem Mist!
> Und auf unsern Promenaden
> Zeigt sich erst die Neigung stark.
> Liebes Mädchen! lass uns waden,
> Waden noch durch diesen Quark.

Sometimes a point is made through the semantic rather than formal device of a pun, as when Nicolai's shallowness is attacked via his travel-writings, which describe the Danube's source:

> Nichts kann er leiden, was gross ist und mächtig; drum, herrliche
> 　　Donau,
> Spürt dir der Häscher so lang nach, bis er seicht dich ertappt.

Better, though for some reason never published, is a jibe at the *Aufklärer* who fought side by side with greater men like Lessing and Mendelssohn:

> Zur Aufklärung der Deutschen hast du mit Lessing und Moses
> Mitgewirkt, ja, du hast ihnen die Lichter geschneuzt.

But far more of the *Xenien* are mere assertion unblessed by convincing form and plain depreciation untouched by wit. That they nevertheless caused an uproar is not hard to explain. If satire can only survive through form, it can be scandalous in its time through content alone. The *Xenien* set everyone by the ears because almost everyone was attacked apparently without discrimination. (One of the rare witty epigrams, number 155, refuses to mock a man who would welcome even this way of being named in public.) For many decent, enlightened men it was shocking that two major talents should so demean themselves, especially when many of their attacks seemed unjust. There was no agreement that Goethe and Schiller really had been surrounded by general hostility, and this made their polemic seem arbitrary and excessive.[13]

It may seem so still to the unprejudiced observer. Manso and Nicolai, for instance, those recurrent targets of the *Xenien*, had said the *Ästhetische Briefe* were obscure, contrary to the *Horen* programme of making things accessible to the non-specialist; and that the Kantian style in philosophy was all very well for Kant but a bad influence on intellectual communication generally. These are fair points and they were repeated in other reviews and in many private letters. In them we hear the voice of the Enlightenment pleading for urbane philosophical writing against a new abstruseness which threatens to hamper its influence for good in society. When Humboldt then dismisses Manso's review as an 'elendes Machwerk ohne Philosophie', or when Schiller scorns all his critics as philosophical beginners and journalistic scribblers,[14] these are not ready-made historical judgements, but the pleas of one party in a dispute. Nicolai thought Schiller obscure, Schiller thought Nicolai's clarity the product of shallowness; the jibe 'Leerkopf' echoed and answered the jibe 'Querkopf'.[15] If we see the dispute as the open one it appeared in its own day, we more truly appreciate the *Xenien* for what they were: an act of self-assertion by men who held new views; a general castigation of the culture which had not allowed itself to be moulded as they hoped by their new journal; a survey of that culture which goes far beyond the retaliatory attack on critics of *Die Horen* and implies with every jibe and accusation an aesthetic or intellectual principle. This is what makes the work a historical document: it embodies one of those arbitrary acts which alter the course of historical development. Those gentler Enlightenment spirits were right to be shocked by its incivility.[16] It had the arrogance of self-aware superiority which overrides good manners.

The issue is epitomised in this incident: the Breslau philosopher Garve, who was originally to have been of the *Horen* group, wrote Schiller a noble, humane letter in defence of his savaged friend Manso. How could the *Xenien* poets misuse their talents to attack people they knew were genuinely deserving? If his criticisms were unjust (which they were not), was there no way of answering them with more regard for truth, charity and dignity? And why draw in and ridicule Manso's poetry, when his only 'fault' was a — perfectly competent and reasonable — review? The letter is unanswerable, in these moral terms, and Schiller duly failed to answer it. He sent it on to Goethe, whose response was a ruthless assertion of the rights of poetry to be set above civility. Such a good man, he says, and so lacking in aesthetic judgement. Were we to sit with hands in laps when we were criticised, simply so that such as Manso could go on being counted as poets? The poetry of these good, civil men is not poetry at all, but rhyming rationalism — what has it to do with the full reality, the 'empirischen pathologischen Zustand des Menschen' which poetry presents? These so-called connoisseurs only praise Schiller when they can find moral propositions in his poetry, while for the higher poetic morality of his ballads they have as little understanding as they have for the artistic treatment of apparently 'immoral' subjects (like the *Römische Elegien*, which had inevitably scandalised readers).[17]

This, revived by Garve's reproaches, is the anger which fuelled the *Xenien*. Even though those epigrams have lost most of their interest as satire, they retain a good deal as criticism: they are a survey of eighteenth-century German writing, judged by new and more severe criteria than the mere cold correct sobriety,[18] or worse, that then held sway. All rights and wrongs of civility apart, it is an illuminating survey. We must remember that arrogance and anger affect its judgements, but we must also remember the profounder conceptions of poetry and man that give rise to the arrogance and anger.

II

'Halbheit', 'Mittelmässigkeit', 'Impotenz' are the terms that recur in Goethe and Schiller's letters to express their view of their literary contemporaries. The *Xenien* duly dismiss current writing as watery fare, which explains the 'hot pepper' of their satire (Xen. 365); they see the undeniable activity of literary journals, calendars, almanachs, as a heavy traffic of coaches which raise much dust but carry precious little cargo (Xen. 245). Put at its simplest, Germany lacks literary taste; in the cycle of epigrams headed 'Literary Zodiac', the sign of the scales, standing for balance, judgement, criteria, is declared to be missing (Xen. 79).

The faults observable in contemporary literature are specified. Governing all, there is the failure to bring together and fuse the concrete and abstract, real and ideal, natural and moral. Instead, there is a crude naturalism at one extreme and a crude moralism at the other. The former, mere 'gemeine Natur', is not art but a 'Speise voll Ekel' (Xen. 9). Even for comedy, to reproduce experience directly is not enough – the fools and grotesques Germany undoubtedly possesses do not make comedy by themselves (Xen. 136). And raw experience will certainly not make tragedy. The cycle 'Shakespeares Schatten', the last and one of the best sections of the *Xenien*, surveys the present German stage in an underworld conversation with the great dramatist. He has to hear that the lessons of the Greeks and of Nature as he showed it are ignored; that crude nature appears 'splitternackend'; that the taste is for 'derber Spass' and (a fine phrase for *comédie larmoyante*) 'nasser Jammer'. In place of true tragedy the theatre offers 'das Christlich-Moralische' and whatever is 'recht populär, häuslich und bürgerlich'. Why go to the theatre then, he asks, if only to find the 'erbärmliche Natur' you left at home? As one goes to an inn, the reporter answers: the poet is mine host, the last act tots up the (moral) score, and with vice having overeaten itself, virtue is left in command of the table:

Wenn sich das Laster erbricht, setzt sich die Tugend zu Tisch

(Xen. 390-412)

The popular bourgeois plays of Kotzebue would fit well into this description – indeed, his name may have suggested the repellent image just quoted. He provided the thrills of vicarious vice and the cloying sentimentality of a return to virtue in his most famous play, *Menschenhass und Reue* (1787), where the heroine, plainly a paragon of womanhood, does long penance for an act of infidelity and at the end is reconciled with the husband whom her lapse turned into a misanthropist. This has precisely the flaw which the *Xenien* pillory; what we are asked to believe in order to accept the plot and qualify for our quota of 'moral' pleasure will not square with the character we see. Yet the play was an immense success, in and beyond Germany, and Kotzebue's works generally could claim to dominate the German theatres. Thus between 1789 and 1813, the Dresden theatre gave one evening in three to a play of his, one in twenty-five to Goethe, Schiller and Lessing taken together, and scarcely any to Shakespeare.[19] It was a situation worthy of remark.

The same impure and hypocritical mixture could be found in the novel. J.T. Hermes is pilloried for cynical use of an old trick – titillating adventures followed by moral retribution (Xen. 14). But even a whole-hearted and sincere moral intention was the sign of a primitive view of art, and the Xenion 'Moralische Zwecke der Poesie' dismissed it in abrupt terms which contemporaries found particularly shocking:

"Bessern, bessern soll uns der Dichter!" So darf denn auf eurem
Rücken des Büttels Stock nicht einen Augenblick ruhn?

This did not mean that Goethe and Schiller believed in an amoral art or
in art for art's sake. Their positive conception makes a firm link
between art and ethics; but it is not immediate and superficial. It lies
in the very nature of art as a complex expression of and influence on
man's composite character; and it excludes all direct preaching.

It excludes *ipso facto* overtly Christian art. Because art is grounded
in earthly reality, and the highest ideal for art as well as for humanity is
the integration of this with the spiritual or moral realm, an art which
flatly denies the value of earthly experience (as Christian art must tend
to do) is a contradiction in terms, and unacceptable. This had been
Goethe's instinctive reaction to Christian Renaissance painting in
Italy.[20] The same principle applied to poetry, even to the once revered
Klopstock and his *Messias*:

Deine Muse besingt, wie Gott sich der Menschen erbarmte,
Aber ist das Poesie, dass er erbärmlich sie fand?

The Xenion 'Höchster Zweck der Kunst' harks back to the controversy
of 1788 in which one of the Counts Stolberg — formerly boon companions of the storming and stressing Goethe, but since turned religiose
— had deplored Schiller's 'Götter Griechenlands' because it did not
convey the (Christian) truth.[21] Hence the comment:

Schade fürs schöne Talent des herrlichen Künstlers! O hätt er
Aus dem Marmorblock doch ein Kruzifix uns gemacht!

The same distaste makes other youthful associates and allies of Goethe
like Matthias Claudius, Jung-Stilling and Lavater targets for particular
epigrams (Xen. 18, 19, 20) and there are generalised attacks on all
'Frömmler'.

Not that old-style Enlightenment reasonableness fared better.
Nicolai's common-sense empiricism was as far from the ideal as was
transcendental religion, since it ruled out all speculation and kept its
head tediously close to the ground, unable even to recognise its own
limits since they lay in an *a priori* stupidity (Xen. 190). Nicolai's thinking remained at the surface, catching intellectual herrings and scorning

those who dived deeper into the ocean of thought (Xen. 198). His
writings were all matter, no form, and for form as a value he had no
comprehension (Xen. 198). Endless repetitions of the same opinions
(Xen. 185), shapeless literary receptacles for them like his multi-volumed
Reise durch Deutschland und die Schweiz, which would never reach the
'Land der Vernunft' (Xen. 184) – these are some of the charges against
Nicolai. They show how the *Xenien* move away from the original points
of contention to an indictment of the victim's intellectual and artistic
shortcomings generally – a logical movement insofar as these proved
their owners incompetent to criticise an undertaking as sophisticated as
the *Horen*.

Was there nothing they approved of as they looked round at literary
Germany? Little enough. Kant was the sovereign philosopher, on whom
all other thinkers merely depended (Xen. 53); J.H. Voss, the translator
of Homer, was praised for hitting off the 'Töne des Altertums' in his
idyll *Luise* (Xen. 129), a judgement which looks over-generous today;
Lessing still stands out, though dead a decade and a half, a veritable
Achilles whose memory is still very much alive (Xen. 338); and there is
some praise for Wieland (Xen. 40, 259). That is about all. The *Xenien*
declare by omission how few landmarks there are worthy of note. Even
Wieland is spoken of in mixed terms – his interminable sentences are
lamented (Xen. 280) and the moodiness of the 'zierliche Jungfrau zu
Weimar' mentioned as the price of his literary grace (Xen. 76). This
is revealing. When Goethe badly needed allies in the early nineties, there
had been a rapprochement with Wieland. But that was before Goethe
met with Schiller, and with Schiller's energy, passion and commitment.
Wieland had little to offer them now as an ally. It was fifteen years
since his last major works, *Die Abderiten*, a novel satirising in Greek
disguise the small towns and small minds of provincial Germany, and
the verse fairy-tale *Oberon*. He was now intent on preparing (and
selling) a collected edition of his works, enjoying an autumnal ease
when Goethe and Schiller were coming to the prime of their creativity.
His achievement was not to be belittled; he had created a lightweight
classicism, written works of charm and elegance; his European cultivation was a valuable counterweight to excessive literary nationalism of
the Germanic-Bardic school; he had helped polish Goethe's early work
for the 1790 edition, suggested turning *Iphigenie* into verse, his *Agathon*
was to influence the revised *Wilhelm Meister*. But from the standpoint
of the new creative partnership, he appeared as part of the past, and it
was the past that the *Xenien* strove to cast off.

Above all, they had to combat the idea that there had been a 'Golden

Age' in their German past — a myth kept up by some journals as part of their Jeremiah's lament over the present[22] — so as to insist that any golden age lay yet in the future. Which, it became ever clearer, meant two names. For Lessing was dead, Wieland passé, Kant not a poet, Voss on the kindest view no productive genius, Humboldt frankly no writer, Herder turned sour and covertly hostile, the *Horen* contributors inert or, after all, second rate.[23] If there was to be great literature in Germany, Goethe and Schiller had to write it.

III

It should be evident by now why the literature of eighteenth-century Germany suggests the metaphor of a landscape. It lacks the concentration of a single literary 'scene'. Its peculiarities are spatial. Each separate capital, residence or university town stands at a different stage in the progress of thought and letters, each is subject to local influences. Berlin, Protestant and relatively cosmopolitan, is the centre of the Enlightenment. Vienna is Catholic and — after a brief flirtation with liberalism under Joseph II — reactionary, with a censorship that virtually closes it to literary innovation. Leipzig, Gotha, Breslau, are associated with the Gottschedian style and popular Enlightenment outlook, Hamburg and the Elbe region with the Christianity of Klopstock and the Stolbergs, Jena with the new Kantianism. Many smaller courts remained mere culture-consumers untouched by new developments, devoted to the classicistic French style most unbendingly represented by Ayrenhoff, the one German writer Frederick the Great praised in *De la littérature allemande*. When we look at this spread in space and in taste, and at the geographical scatter of the *Horen* contributors, and try to guess at the effectiveness of that journal from its subscription list,[24] the difficulty of focussing literary influence is clear. Where and what was the target? 'Deutschland? Aber wo liegt es? Ich weiss das Land nicht zu finden', as Xenion 95 complains. Germany was everywhere and nowhere. The *Xenien* sections on geographically scattered journals and on the German rivers, beside each of which a different kind of taste (or its absence) ruled, show how the war had to be waged on several fronts and against several kinds and degrees of anachronism.

But behind Goethe and Schiller's campaigns across this landscape lay the consciousness of a broader setting yet, a historical map of European culture which both justified their judgements and also in a way mitigated them. For the disharmony and one-sidedness which is at bottom what Goethe and Schiller criticise in their contemporaries turns out to be not random and wilful, but rooted in the nature of the modern age.

They themselves have therefore shared it; but in their case realisation has dawned and they have sought remedies.

The essential document here is *Über naive und sentimentalische Dichtung*, undoubtedly the finest and most fruitful of Schiller's theoretical works and arguably the greatest work of German criticism. We saw its origins in the contrast between his and Goethe's character. This, at first such a bitter pill to swallow, gave rise to the idea that they were poets of fundamentally different and complementary types – an intuitive and a speculative mind, proceeding from particular phenomenon to general meaning or vice versa. But this divergence was then in turn explained by a historical, or more broadly anthropological theory of an evolution from the 'state of nature' right down to modern Man, who has 'fallen' from an original unreflective oneness with Nature much as Adam fell from innocence and oneness with God. Against this background, Goethe could appear as a rarity in modern times, either a throwback to the primal state or a genius with unique power to recreate it; at all events, analogous in the effect his work produced to the great poets of the pre-lapsarian age, antiquity. A few other post-lapsarian geniuses had a sufficient natural endowment to cancel out the disadvantage of their place in history: Shakespeare, Cervantes, Molière.

Schiller calls these poets and their works 'naive'. It is a sophisticated concept. It means not just 'natural', but 'natural as perceived by someone cut off from Nature' – a valuation placed on a certain kind of object by a certain kind of observer. The term already encapsulates much of the essay's historical argument in itself, and it clearly implies another concept; that of the type of mind which makes such a value-judgement. Schiller labels this 'sentimentalisch'. Only a 'sentimentalisch' modern mind has the experience of disharmony and separation from nature, of artificiality and convention, to look thus wistfully on works which – at the time they arose – were *natural*, but could not be found *naive* because there existed no other condition to provide a contrast. The two terms are thus intimately linked, reciprocal.[25]

But the 'sentimentalisch' modern does not regard only the works of the lost past in this wistful way, he also regards Nature itself so. Inevitably this affects the poetry he writes. And because 'Nature' means not just woods and flowers but the whole of man's experience, the 'sentimentalisch' attitude deeply colours the whole of literature. The modern treatment of human psychology, relationships, social behaviour, aspirations and beliefs is radically different from what we find in the literature of antiquity. The modern writer constantly *reflects* on what he is portraying – a point Schiller splendidly brings out by comparing Homer and Ariosto — and gives us far more of himself, his attitudes and responses, than he does of the object pure and simple: 'Wir erhalten . . . nie den Gegenstand, nur, was der reflektierende Verstand des Dichters aus dem Gegenstand machte'. Even where his theme is personal feeling, it is still reflected, self-conscious feeling that we get: 'nicht seinen Zustand unmittelbar . . ., sondern . . . was er als Zuschauer seiner selbst darüber gedacht hat'.[26] This reflective consciousness brings into literature a whole world of spiritual and psychological complexity which antiquity knew nothing of. The modern has an immeasurably larger task; he can never achieve the rounded perfection of naive works. Yet he cannot cease trying; his awareness both of the ideal organic harmony of nature, and of the perfection art could once achieve, makes him strive so to treat his modern subject-matter that his work will have the balance, integration and roundedness of the naive work it emulates.[27] Not that he can properly seek to return to the original harmony which obtained before the Fall into self-consciousness; even if that were possible, it would be wrong, a mere escape from the ills — and the challenge — of the modern condition. Schiller thinks Rousseau was guilty of this.[28] The poet must carry forward all he is and knows and feels, striving to convey it, for all its infinite and problematic richness, in some finite form. Attempting this impossible task gives him moral credit, while the naive poet has the limited yet in its way infinite credit of creating rounded perfection out of the more compact materials of an earlier age.

This is a grandiose vision of cultural development which manages to settle the long-standing 'querelle des Anciens et des Modernes' with equal honour to both sides; it gives antiquity permanent value as a model while asserting the distinctive potential of the European present. Most strikingly however for so fundamental an analysis, it is also highly practical criticism.

Firstly, the idea of divergent attitudes to nature in poetry generates a set of more specific 'Empfindungsweisen' which account for poetic genres more persuasively than the conventional divisions by externals of form. Thus, from the proposition that the 'sentimentalisch' poet is always aware of the contrast between reality and the (lost natural) ideal, which in a general sense makes everything he writes elegiac, we get three possibilities of poetic tone; satirical, elegiac in a narrower sense, and idyllic. The satirical poet takes the deficiencies of reality as his main subject and either castigates or mocks them ('strafende' or 'scherzhafte Satire' respectively); the elegiac poet evokes the lost harmony of nature and the ideal it represents; and the idyllic poet portrays harmony itself, either as a past golden age, or better (and this would be the ultimate poetic achievement) in an image embodying and harmonising the spiritual complexities of modern man.

Secondly, the discussion of contemporary poets as satiric, elegiac, idyllic casts a brilliant light on the literature of the eighteenth century (not only German). Schiller's diagnosis of modern attitudes, and his prescriptions of what modern poets should aspire to, provide firm and far-sighted criteria for all kinds of creative writing. Unlike the *Xenien*, which demolish small figures, this survey centres on writers with serious claims to attention − Haller, Klopstock, Ewald von Kleist − and gives them the extended discussion which epigrams cannot accommodate. It too is highly critical: Schiller called it a 'Day of Judgement'.[29] But the stress here is different. Whereas so many *Xenien* were to attack the flatness and banal naturalism of mediocre writing, the faults Schiller finds in the accepted poets of his age are excessive abstraction, conceptuality, immateriality. Haller is too didactic, (*'lehrt* durchgängig mehr, als er *darstellt'*); Kleist too analytical ('Reflexion stört das geheime Werk der Empfindung'); Klopstock's figures are pure abstraction, 'gute Exempel zu Begriffen, aber keine Individuen, keine lebenden Gestalten', his inspiration is 'keusch, überirdisch, unkörperlich, heilig, wie seine Religion'.[30] These are practical examples of the way both rationalism and Christianity are at odds with good poetry.

For Schiller is now clear what 'good poetry' is, and it is not what was postulated in his Bürger review. When he says that Klopstock gives us 'keine Individuen', he no longer means the purified 'Individualität' which he had insisted the lyric poet should distil from his crude empirical self; he means now the real, concrete existence which art needs as a balance to ideas. Schiller has behind him the intricate enquiries of the *Ästhetische Briefe* where he analysed Man and his perceptions into sensuous and rational, material and formal components, and set up an ideal of beauty as their integration in a 'lebende Gestalt' (which phrase he now uses to indicate what Klopstock lacks). Taking those arguments for granted, he can state their practical results simply: 'Die Schönheit ist das Produkt der Zusammenstimmung zwischen dem Geist und den Sinnen'.[31]

For modern literature, in which 'spirit' predominates, the way to that ideal integration is pointed by the naive poet, whose aim was 'die möglichst vollständige *Nachahmung des Wirklichen'*.[32] To this extent, Schiller's essay is not just theory, but a programme for Classicism − the Classical has commonly been associated with the concrete, the sculptural, the objective, as against the spiritual, musical and subjective. He already proclaims Goethe as the fulfiller of this programme, the poet who of all the moderns 'sich . . . vielleicht am wenigsten von der sinnlichen Wahrheit der Dinge entfernt.'[33] And it is surely the vision of just such a classical balance that is in Schiller's mind when late in his essay he looks forward to a reconciliation between 'naive' and 'sentimentalisch': a logically impossible notion, just as it was earlier logically nonsense for him to speak of individual works in which 'naive' and 'sentimentalisch' elements mixed, for the two terms exclude each other by definition. But what is not at all impossible, and was plainly meant by such passages, is that the *literary characteristics that go with* the two types of poetry could be combined and a synthesis striven for which would amount to a new literature, both spiritually profound and formally perfect. Goethe had already created works which embodied this dream, and Schiller — at the end now of his aesthetic theorising — was set on emulating him.

It is remarkable how the simple idea of a sense-spirit balance for art and Man serves as a touchstone in practical questions. It helps to gauge the quality of poetry in general. It solves the old problem of what is decent and indecent in literature, vindicating the *Römische Elegien* and Diderot, but sacrificing Wieland — for all his grace and wit — and Heinse.[34] It tells us what effects we should expect of literature and how to hold the mean between the excessively low and high aims of 'Erholung' and 'Veredlung' respectively. For 'Erholung' (recreation) had been taken to mean relief from the demands not just of one's occupation, but of one's own higher faculties. Result: an art which merely satisfied the sensuous urge for total relaxation: 'die losgespannte Natur darf sich im seligen Genuss des Nichts auf dem weichen Polster der *Platitude* pflegen'. Conversely, 'Veredlung' (elevation) had been held to require that we reject sensuousness, as if it were not one of the necessary constituents of Man. The wrongness of both these views is obvious if beauty is the 'Zusammenstimmung' of senses and spirit, something which speaks to the whole man and can therefore only be experienced through a full and free play of all his faculties: 'seine ganze Natur muss man beisammen haben'.[35] And it also follows that beauty can — indeed, must — provide the ideal human condition; restored to himself from excess in either direction, senses or abstraction, enjoying the full potential of his composite nature, man is most fully man. He may disturb the balance of his nature to achieve a particular goal — say, a system of abstract philosophy — and this may be of value to mankind generally. But it is in art and the experience of art that his true, full self waits for him again.

Beside these conceptions, earlier eighteenth-century views of art and its social function look primitive: the ground-level naturalism, the moral didacticism of Christians and rationalists, the sugar-and-sand mixture of vice and retribution favoured by manipulators of the public. Even Kant's aesthetic theory is a bare skeleton beside the full vision Schiller worked out in the *Ästhetische Briefe* and *Über naive und sentimentalische Dichtung*. The two men's ideas are basically similar, but how differently they are conveyed! What Kant states abstractly, Schiller wherever possible states concretely, thus approaching his own ideal of balance even in abstract argument; and where Kant puts things negatively, cutting away what aesthetic perception is not in order to leave what it is, Schiller puts things positively. What for Kant is an *absence* of practical desires ('Interesselosigkeit') is for Schiller the *activity* of play. He even posits an ideal play-impulse ('Spieltrieb') to reconcile Man's actual impulses towards abstraction and reality ('Formtrieb'/ 'Stofftrieb'). Where Kant has the observer disregard the practical reality of the aesthetic object, Schiller speaks of the object's pure appearance ('Schein') as one of its attributes. Most striking of all, where Kant makes the idea of 'disinterestedness' exclude all private, personal elements from aesthetic perception, in order to establish a rather empty universality,[36] Schiller brilliantly argues for retaining them. For him, aesthetic perception is a state of rich potential precisely because in it all the individual's past experience is liberated, waiting in a condition of 'reale und aktive Bestimmbarkeit' to be deployed in response to what he now experiences through art.[37] It is not subject to any practical demands, but it is all still there, his own:

> All you lived through,
> Dancing because you
> No longer need it
> For any deed.[38]

It is this that makes art a restorer of Man, a re-creation in the fullest sense. With the whole range of his experience given back to him and its warring elements reconciled, he can make a fresh start in practical and moral activity.[39] The effect is potentially far greater than that of any direct moral preaching or constraints, because the past has been undone, dissolved, not merely met head-on by injunctions and warnings.

Clearly, this is far from being an 'art-for-art's-sake' philosophy. If some formulations make it seem so, this is because of the then situation. Fearful moralists mistrusted, as far as they understood it, the full freedom which art could restore. They associated 'Schein' not with pure appearance, but with deception. They demanded more immediate safeguards than these conceptions provided, and accordingly refused to allow art the autonomy in which alone it could work out the kind of human salvation Schiller envisaged. So he and Goethe had to insist on art's autonomy, its obligation to obey only its own inner laws, its right not to heed the clamour for orthodox doctrine and simple answers. Inevitably, such insistence can look like an 'art-for-art's-sake' argument if we forget the pressure of simplistic thinking against which it was a defence.

The principle of artistic autonomy, great advance though it was, had nevertheless its own antecedents, which for a proper historical understanding of Weimar Classicism we should recognise. They lie in the Enlightenment struggle for intellectual and religious toleration. The Weimar group may have been associated with the new Kantian philosophy which superseded the more popular manner of Enlightenment thinkers; and the *Xenien* may have dismissed old 'Aufklärer' like Nicolai as cultural fossils. But in their aesthetic outlook, Goethe and Schiller were true inheritors of the Enlightenment. For the artist's liberty to obey only the inner laws of his work is an extension of the individual's liberty to hold his own beliefs; the requirement that each individual artistic approach be appreciated in itself, regardless of how it stands to orthodox beliefs, is an application of that philosophical relativism which held that truth was no one person's or sect's monopoly but could only be the eventual sum and reconciliation of all opinions; and the idea of art as a free play of the faculties follows from the idea that we must consequently practise a 'suspension of belief' with regard to the content of other men's thinking in order to recognise the value of the common human activity of thought.

We can see these ideas developing in an aesthetic direction in the controversy over Schiller's 'Götter Griechenlands' in 1788; the orthodox Christian Stolberg's bludgeoning approach to a fine poem calls forth the standard Enlightenment arguments in favour of intellectual liberty, but also a claim that artistic works and the artist's activity have a special status. We still hear the cry 'tolerance'; but we already hear the cry 'Spiel'.[40]

The roundedness of art and the uncommitedness, in any immediate sense, of beauty are thus a new kind of answer to the claims of sectarian 'truths'. But the Weimar poets believe that beauty and ultimate Truth are one. In the year after the Stolberg affair, Schiller worked out their relation in the poem 'Die Künstler'; beauty anticipates abstract truth, conveying it concretely to man's developing mind long before he reaches rational maturity. The beauty of phenomena is thus closely related, indeed ultimately reducible, to the truth of ideas. But this is a reduction which the artist by his very nature resists. The ideal of balancing the abstract with the concrete, the rational with the sensuous, means that the naked truth is *too* naked, for composite human beings. It must ideally be given them, even when the race as a whole has reached the stage of rationality, clothed in the material substance of the world which is their reality. In the poem which marks Schiller's return from theorising to poetry, 'Poesie des Lebens', he pleads for the phenomenal world, the 'Schein' that covers the nakedness of stern truth and necessity; for without it there is neither art nor love nor joy, but only a cold knowledge of mortality and an encroaching 'Versteinerung'. And in one of the *Tabulae Votivae*, he celebrates beauty, the transient thing we actually see, above the permanent truths of reason which but for beauty would never have a local habitation or a name:

Wäre sie unverwelklich, die Schönheit, ihr könnte nichts gleichen,
   Nichts, wo die Göttliche blüht, weiss ich der Göttlichen gleich.
Ein Unendliches ahndet, ein Höchstes erschafft die Vernunft sich,
   In der schönen Gestalt lebt es dem Herzen, dem Blick.

These lines, with their title 'Das Göttliche', put plainly the priorities of an artist who has often wrongly been thought a man of abstraction and theory. He had wrestled with theory for nearly a decade, only to arrive at a vision which put theory in its place as something partial and thereby went beyond all previous eighteenth-century thinking about art, including his own earlier ideas on 'idealisation'. He thereby joined Goethe, whose poetic practice had almost from the first been a triumphant denial of eighteenth-century assumptions about what poetry was and could do. For the one decade left to Schiller they could cooperate in creating the Classical, and classic, works of German literature.

Notes

1. See the circular to contributors, *Werke* V, 867ff.
2. Letter of 7 April 1775, quoted in Sengle, *Wieland* (Stuttgart, 1949), p. 410.
3. On the achievements and limitations of the *Teutsche Merkur*, see Sengle ibid., pp. 407-22.
4. *Ankündigung der Horen, Werke* V, 871ff.

5. Schiller named Archenholz, Dalberg, Engel, Ehrhardt, Fichte, von Funk, [Garve], [Gentz], [Gleim], Goethe, Gros, Herder, Hirt, [Hufeland], Wilhelm and Alexander von Humboldt, Jacobi, Matthisson, Meyer, Pfeffel, Schiller, August Wilhelm Schlegel, [Schütz], [Schulz] and Woltmann. Those in square brackets never in fact contributed.

6. Schiller to Körner, 29 December 1794.

7. Their work occupies 630 out of 1405 pages. For factual background, see Paul Raabe's companion volume to the reprint of *Die Horen* (Darmstadt, 1959), and Günter Schulz, *Schillers Horen. Politik und Erziehung* (Heidelberg, 1960).

8. Goethe to L.Fr. Schultz, 10 January 1829.

9. To Goethe, 1 November 1795.

10. Schiller to Goethe, 15 May 1795; Humboldt to Schiller, 15 August 1795; letter from an anonymous reader to Schiller, 10 July 1795, printed in Oscar Fambach, *Schiller und sein Kreis* in *Ein Jahrhundert deutscher Literaturkritik* vol.II (Berlin, 1957), p. 221.

11. Schiller to Goethe, 15 May 1795. Cf. the passage from *Wilhelm Meisters Theatralische Sendung* quoted above, p. 24f.

12. Quoted in Friedrich Meyer, *Friedrich Nicolai* (Leipzig, 1938), p. 58.

13. See Goethe to Schiller, 31 August 1795, and Xenion 49, 'Guerre ouverte'. It is possible to put together intrinsically non- and anti-classical features of literature at that time (see A. Bettex, *Der Kampf um das klassische Weimar*, Zurich, 1935) but hard to argue that they made up a coherent campaign, if only because – as we shall see – the 'opponents' were such a mixed bunch.

14. Humboldt to Schiller, 31 August 1795; Schiller to Cotta, 30 October 1795. Early commentators naturally took the part of their recently-established classics: Eduard Boas, *Schiller und Goethe im Xenienkampf* (Stuttgart, 1851), and to some extent Schmidt and Suphan, *Xenien 1796* (Weimar, 1893). Schulz, *Schillers Horen*, p. 79, still does not question the Weimar group's judgements. But since Fambach, *Schiller und sein Kreis*, presented all the reviews and private correspondence from which to reconstruct the situation, it is no longer necessary to see things through the eyes of one party only.

15. Cf. *Xenien* 189 and 199.

16. Cf. Jacobi to Böttiger, 1 December 1796; Garve to Weisse 14 January 1797; Garve to Schiller 23 September 1797, in Fambach, *Schiller und sein Kreis*, pp. 172ff.

17. Fambach pp. 176-80. The *Elegien* naturally provoked a suggestion that *Horen* should read '*Huren*'. See Böttiger to Schulz, 27 July 1795, quoted in Schulz, as in other refs. p. 70.

18. Fambach, p. 181, quotes A.W. Schlegel on the 'Langweiligkeit der kalten, *Schillers Horen. Politik und Erziehung* nüchternen, sogenannten korrekten Geistesprodukte' which alone orthodox opinion found worthy of praise.

19. Figures from Bruford, *Theatre, Drama and Audience in Goethe's Germany*, p. 264. There are enough overt attacks on Kotzebue in Goethe's poetry (see the section of the collected poems headed 'Invektiven') to support this reading of 'Shakespeares Schatten'.

20. Cf. *Tagebuch der italienischen Reise*, 17 September, 8 and 19 October 1786. Goethe's objection is to the paradox of Christian painting as 'the sensuous expression of conceptions which unreservedly discredit the world of sense', as Walter Pater put it, *The Renaissance* (1877), p. 217.

21. Documents in Fambach, *Schiller und sein Kreis*, pp. 44ff.

22. Cf. *Xenien* 309-18, 'Jeremiaden aus dem Reichsanzeiger'. That the 'golden age' argument was common is shown by the lengths Wieland goes to to refute it in his *Briefe an einen jungen Dichter, Werke* III, 461ff.

23. Schiller placed Wieland with Pope and Voltaire as belonging to the age that

equated genius with wit (to Körner, 1 May 1797). Herder he calls 'eine ganz pathologische Natur', envious of everything good or lively, favouring mediocrity, and hence lost to the 'good cause' (same letter). Goethe thought the same of Herder (to Heinrich Meyer, 20 June 1796). As for Humboldt, *Tabulae Votivae* number 90 praises him as a critic and exhorts him not to write; Schiller told Körner that Humboldt had 'zum Schriftsteller kein Talent' (7 November 1794). On the general standard of the *Horen*, see Schiller to Humboldt, 21 August 1795, complaining of the 'Armut am Guten'. The journal ceased publication after the third year.

24. Contributors' location ranged from Hamburg and Berlin in the north to Colmar and Switzerland in the south, from Düsseldorf in the west to Dresden and Breslau in the east. The subscription-list printed in the last number of 1795 contains mostly booksellers, so it is not clear who the actual readers were. Copies subscribed range from Chemnitz and Meissen (1 and 4) to Stuttgart and Leipzig (169 and 153).

25. As is well brought out by Peter Szondi's provocatively titled essay 'Das Naive ist das Sentimentalische' in Szondi, *Lektüren und Lektionen* (Frankfurt a.M., 1973).

26. *Werke* V, 732.

27. A footnote, ibid., p. 752, defines the 'sentimentalische Stimmung' as a product of the attempt '*auch unter den Bedingungen der Reflexion* die naive Empfindung, dem Gehalte nach, wiederherzustellen' (Schiller's italics).

28. On Rousseau, ibid., p. 730f. Earlier Schiller has insisted that the original state of nature must 'ewig hinter dir liegen', serving as a model for a new harmony to be achieved in the future. Ibid., p. 707.

29. To Goethe, 23 November 1795. Though the *Xenien* have here been treated first, the prose essay was written earlier.

30. *Werke* V, 732-6.

31. Ibid., p. 765. The concept 'lebende Gestalt' is worked out in the fifteenth of the *Ästhetische Briefe*, ibid., p. 614.

32. Ibid., p. 717.

33. Ibid., p. 738.

34. Ibid., 742ff. Schiller denies *Ardinghello* truth and aesthetic dignity, it is a 'sinnliche Karikatur'; but he allows that it shows the 'beinahe poetischen Schwung, den die *blosse Begier* zu nehmen fähig war'.

35. Ibid., pp. 764-8.

36. See *Kritik der Urteilskraft* para. 6, *Werke* V, 280. Kant makes the strangely naive assumption that whatever is not a private *desire* must therefore be universal.

37. See *Ästhetische Briefe* 19 to 21, *Werke* V, 626-36, especially Letter 20, paragraph 4 and Letter 21, paragraph 2: 'die ästhetische Bestimmbarkeit . . . hat keine Schranken, weil es alle Realität vereinigt'.

38. W.H. Auden, 'Anthem for St. Cecilia's Day', in *Collected Shorter Poems* (1966), p. 174.

39. See esp. Letter 21, *Werke* V, 634ff., which elaborates the paradox that 'In dem ästhetischen Zustande ist der Mensch also *Null*, insofern man auf ein einzelnes Resultat . . . achtet', but that 'Eben dadurch ist etwas Unendliches erreicht'.

40. Documents in Fambach, *Schiller und sein Kreis*, pp. 44-73. Körner's essay *Über die Freiheit des Dichters bei der Wahl seines Stoffes* argues for 'Toleranz' as a mark of civilisation, but also for an 'ästhetischen Gehalt' independent of morality, and for the inherent value of each man's sum of 'Ideen, Fertigkeiten, Anlagen und Talenten' — an approach to the idea of aesthetic play. Huber, in a letter to Körner, argues that a 'truth' opposed to one's own view has inherent rights, since 'Jedes Spiel (!) der Seele . . . muss ihr [viz. 'der Vernunft'] ehrwürdig sein, und

keines dieser Spiele . . . wird ein wirklich unverdorbenes Gefühl jemals beleidigen können'. Forster's essay *Fragment eines Briefes* . . . *über Schillers Götter Griechenlands* moves from the relativity of 'truths' to the idea that poetry's function is 'uns mit neuen Ideenverbindungen bereichern, das Gefühl des Schönen in uns wecken, unsere Geisteskräfte üben, schärfen, stärken', all of which is called 'lehrreich' but is much nearer to Schiller's conception of play than to any simple didacticism.

6 CLASSICS: (1) THE NOVEL

Their cooperation and friendship became a national legend. Some legends are grounded in truth, and this is one. It will not do to see in the partnership a tactical alliance which lacked warmth; or a relationship which benefited Schiller but endangered Goethe's 'deeper' poetic self; or one which rested on basic misunderstandings between two admittedly different kinds of mind.[1] The documents, especially the letters, convey discreetly but eloquently the mature affection of men who have come to terms with themselves and each other; who recognise divergence but see it resolved in a common purpose; who, far from forcing their own principles on each other, actively encourage each other's characteristic approach; and who delight to learn from one another in the cause of poetic perfection.

What they believed perfection to be, has already been sketched. We must now look beyond theory and intention, which might lead us to take the wish for the deed, at the major works themselves. If we need a context within which to appreciate their stature and claim to be called classics, it is a historical one: what Goethe made of the novel as he found it; what Schiller made of tragic drama after the development traced in Chapter 3; what the two men made of poetry, whose possibilities they had already before their meeting begun to push beyond the limits the eighteenth century had set. A simple genre-approach seems apt. We begin with the novel.

I

But was the novel a genre? Only just. It becomes accepted as such in precisely the years covered by this book. It had been prominent on the publishing, if not the literary scene since the mid-century; produced in ever growing numbers for a voracious public, the novel took over more and more of that market for devotional, biographical and memoir literature from which it drew much of its own content and psychology.[2] But that was far from making it respectable. Popularity usually inspires suspicion; the novel was the television of the eighteenth century. Its name linked it with the fancifulness of baroque 'romance'; J.G. Sulzer's *Allgemeine Theorie der schönen Künste* (1774) defines the adjective 'romanhaft' (he has, significantly, no article 'Roman') as meaning exaggerated and implausible in events, behaviour and feelings. Sulzer does however admit that novels are now trying to approach reality – 'dem Charakter der wahren Geschichte' – and that the pejorative 'romanhaft' may be on the way out, especially since novelists are now modelling themselves on antiquity.

This almost certainly refers to Wieland, most of whose novels are set in (a rather cardboard) antiquity and whose *Agathon* Lessing had praised as 'der erste und einzige Roman für den denkenden Kopf, von klassischem Geschmacke'.[3] Wieland had to be taken seriously, if only because he had proved himself in the traditional genres of drama, lyric and verse epic. This status was duly built on by the first German apologist of the novel, Friedrich von Blanckenburg, in his *Versuch über den Roman* (also 1774).

Inevitably, Blanckenburg feels obliged to rescue the novel from its ill repute as entertainment for the masses – he suggests, sensibly, that it is worth raising its standard since it is bound to be a powerful influence. But he also feels able to assert its achievements, saying of Wieland and Fielding what Pope said of Homer: 'Nature and *they* were . . . the same'.[4] This was a challenging quotation to choose, given that it was classical poetics which had till now refused to recognise the novel. Blanckenburg indeed declares that the novel could be for modern times what epic was for the Greeks. As yet there are only one or two good novels – *Agathon*, Fielding's *Tom Jones*, (he finds fault with the action and psychology of such prestigious works as Richardson's *Clarissa* and Rousseau's *Nouvelle Héloïse*); hence his practical object, to raise young novelists nearer to Wieland's level. But the shortage of exemplary works does not gainsay the principle: that the novel is not a stop-gap for the epic modern times could not convincingly produce, but the form best suited to modern interests. For these were not in warring nations such as the *Iliad* portrayed, but in Man – 'die nackte Menschheit' – his emotions and behaviour and their underlying causes. Man had progressed since ancient times; in analysing humanity for the benefit and further improvement of his readers, the novelist would necessarily show that the Greeks were not a pinnacle of perfection which had been followed by a long decline, any more than their art was.[5]

This is all refreshingly no-nonsense. Blanckenburg had his limitations – he is repetitive and sometimes unsubtle, missing the humour of Sterne's playful technique – but he deserved the title Wieland gave him in the *Teutsche Merkur*, 'ein Aristoteles für die prosaischen Homere'.[6] He had grasped the essential fact that accepting the novel and its potential meant throwing off (as to form) the yoke of antiquity-orientated criticism and accepting (as to content) areas of the modern sensibility

which had no counterpart in the ancient literatures. He had also grasped
the novel's power to show us as no other form can the delicate connections between inner and outer life and the actual process of formation
of a character.[7] If we add to this J.J. Engel's essay (again of 1774)
Über Handlung, Gespräch und Erzahlung,[8] which skilfully distinguishes
what would now be called 'pictorial' and 'scenic' methods, it is clear
that the novel was acquiring a respectable basis of technical theory.

But still not yet full respectability. By the mid-nineties, the flood of
popular fiction was at its height — one bookseller put the production of
novels, German and translated, at three hundred a year in the 1790s
and at nearly six thousand for the span 1773 to 1794.[9] Not surprisingly, 'Roman' still had pejorative associations. Even as he delights in
Wilhelm Meister, Schiller can write to Goethe that there are aspects of
it which recall — the novel![10] And Schiller marks but also limits the
progress of the genre when in *Über naive und sentimentalische Dichtung*
he sees the novelist as the poet's half-brother, who fails to rise far above
mere reality — 'die Erde noch so sehr berührt'.[11] Yet by then *Wilhelm
Meister* has already proved to Schiller that the novel *can* achieve 'die
Wahrheit des Lebens' and render a 'lebendige und bis zum Greifen
treffende Natur'[12] — very different things in Goethe's and Schiller's
aesthetic from the 'naturalism' which gets bogged down in 'mere'
reality. The novel is thus not inherently inferior as a genre; it simply has
to pull itself up by its own bootstraps, prove its potential by fulfilling
it.

We shall see how *Wilhelm Meister* tried to do that. But first, having
seen the novel halfway to acceptance ('Halbbruder des Dichters') at a
rough halfway point in our period (1795), it is worth recording a
weighty opinion at its end. Hegel's *Ästhetik* accepts the novel without
question as the modern form of the epic, 'die moderne bürgerliche
Epopöe'; if the primitive world was 'poetic', the novel does what is
possible in a 'bereits zur *Prosa* geordnete Wirklichkeit'. Indeed, Hegel
sees that one of the commonest and most appropriate themes for the
novel is precisely the conflict between poetry and prosaic reality, the
'Poesie des Herzens' on the one hand, and the 'Prosa der Verhältnisse'
on the other. He accepts that, in trying to embrace the totality of his
modern world, the novelist may draw too much of its 'prose' into his
work — but he nevertheless unhesitatingly calls him a 'Dichter'.[13] A
historical watershed has been crossed; the dissonances of modern life
which Goethe and Schiller had still striven to harmonise on the model
of the ancient literatures are now accepted. Novel and novelist are for
the first time given house-room in the grand edifice of literature proper.

II

Wilhelm Meisters Lehrjahre is to the German novel what *Don Carlos* is to the drama: it brings together the disparate elements available to the genre in its time, and crystallises them in a single form which will determine later developments. Just as its subject matter makes it a history of the various kinds of culture coexisting in eighteenth-century Germany — bourgeois, noble, Enlightened, pietist, bohemian — so its treatment makes it a compendium of the literary means and motifs which were to be found in novels high and low and in other works which fed the new genre. We can watch them being integrated into a serious purpose. Thus Mignon and the Harper, with their harrowing fate, are figures straight from the wilder reaches of romance, but Mignon is also an important part of Wilhelm's sentimental education. The 'Turmgesellschaft' is a piece of fictional material typical of a period obsessed with secret societies and their alleged doings,[14] it adds a touch of mystery to the narration. But it is also a means to give coherence and a sense of direction to the history of Wilhelm's personal development. This illustrates the way subject-matter and form interweave in the novel, episodes and figures that seem part of the material help to organise its shape: capture by pirates can be used to separate characters (Heinse's *Ardinghello*) or to reunite them (*Agathon*); a storm at sea, as Wieland confesses,[15] may be uncomfortable for the characters but handy for the author, who wants them washed up on a particular shore.

Since earlier in the century the guiding purpose in such manipulations had been a religious one. Fiction had increasingly taken over the role of direct edifying literature, which had still made up the bulk of popular reading-matter before 1750. A few novels — Schnabel's *Insel Felsenburg*, Gellert's *Schwedische Gräfin* — became 'Hausbücher' which ordinary folk kept on the same shelf as their Bible. These, often classed as 'Enlightenment' works, were strongly marked by Protestant thought and feeling; there was, indeed, little direct confrontation between Enlightenment and religious orthodoxy in Germany as there was in France, but only a gradual divergence from common roots. Other novelists consciously aspired to impart religious truth through fiction.[16]

But once used as a means, the motifs of fiction easily became a self-sufficient interest of novel-readers. The shipwreck which Schnabel had borrowed from Defoe swiftly became a simple adventure motif, massively exploited for the popular market in countless 'Robinsonaden'. Having established itself by professing a religious purpose, fiction was free to go its own way.

Yet in its serious forms it took over something else from religious literature and turned it to its own purposes. Biographies and autobiographies of the saintly and the pious are an old part of the Christian tradition. Protestant, and more specifically Pietist, practice set great store by the individual's introspection of his spiritual state and by his grateful recognition of the way Providence had guided him. Pietist communities talked of these things and wrote them down, for mutual illumination. The result was a rich store of psychological observations, and indeed the beginnings of a psychopathology of religious feeling. This last feature was by no means unbeknown to the religious themselves either. Adam Bernd's *Eigene Lebensbeschreibung* (1738) declares itself an account of the 'Leibes- und Gemütsplage' which God sent upon him, and where others thought of their anxieties and sufferings in purely religious categories, Bernd suggests a less elevated kind of explanation, crediting an upset spleen with the power to sensitise the religious conscience and moral judgement: 'Der Miltz ist der schärfste Moraliste auf Erden, der kann, wenn er kränklich und verstopft ist, und Furcht, Angst und Traurigkeit verursacht, den Menschen *per accidens* die Augen auftun, dass sie von ihrer Taten Sittlichkeit, Beschaffenheit und Grösse der Sünden weit besser als in gesunden Tagen urteilen können'.[17] The conclusion is obvious: self-examination once licensed, even by a religion with its own fixed presuppositions, drifts irresistibly towards empiricism and faces the facts of human experience.

We can see this happening in those eighteenth-century autobiographies which follow this tradition but already verge on the novel. Jung Stilling in his *Lebensgeschichte*, Ulrich Bräker in *Der arme Mann im Tockenburg*, Karl Philipp Moritz in *Anton Reiser*, all describe their inner development and state of mind; but each marks a stage in the process of secularisation by which religious self-questioning becomes psychological understanding and the individual learns to live equably with himself rather than bewail his sins or vaunt the special treatment Providence has meted out to him.

In Jung Stilling we have the most 'traditional' account. The miseries of his early life are compensated by religious faith and a sense of God's purpose — 'es war etwas in ihm, das seltene Schicksale in seinem eigenen Leben ahnte' —[18] and, as his miseries yield to success, his self-satisfaction as the recipient of divine guidance becomes ever more obtrusive. Bräker's in every way more vivid and engaging autobiography shows an easy-going, less presumptuous trust in Providence (he even good-naturedly accepts its choice of a wife for him, shrew though she is); but already the power to understand and portray both himself and others is more marked than any specifically religious consciousness. He never questions orthodoxy, but he is more *content* with himself as a natural being than is proper for a believer. He accepts and rejoices in the idea of God's mercy — *'Barmherzigkeit* — welch ein beruhigendes Wort!' — but he has other, nearer sources of consolation: 'Indessen bin ich . . . freylich nicht weniger geneigt, auch etwas Tröstendes in mir selbst aufzusuchen'. He knows he is a sinner, but he has more or less paid the price in misfortunes; he can fairly size up his own good as well as bad qualities, and find that there is after all a good deal of health in him.[19] With Moritz, finally, we have an individual who suffers more deeply than either Stilling or Bräker, and whose state of mind is more nearly pathological; who can achieve neither the complacency of the first nor the mellowness of the second. Yet he delves deeper into inner experience than either of the others and, even while showing the origins of Reiser's troubles in his religious upbringing, he cuts loose from religious ways of thinking and launches into the waters of a psychology not doctrinally limited or committed. From the believer and his soul we have arrived at man and his mind.

These accounts could claim to be true because they were autobiographical records. *Anton Reiser* might bear the sub-title 'Roman', but the foreword to Part II made it clear it was no fiction. With the *Theatralische Sendung* we are across the dividing line: for all its autobiographical elements, it is a work of the imagination. But did a work need to be any the less authentic for that? If it was not a true record of something that happened, could it not still, by virtue of the author's experience of life, be true *to* life? Wieland had made this claim in 1766 when he called his novel *Geschichte des Agathon*. Though he did not expect his public to accept the fiction that he was re-narrating an old Greek source, he claimed to tell the truth inasmuch as events and characters in his book were not fantasy but 'alles mit dem Lauf der Welt übereinstimme'[20]; he contrasted the boundless possibilities open to the mere 'Romandichter' with the narrow path which he, the 'Geschichtschreiber', had to follow[21] and dismissed the easy perfection of the heroes in 'moralischen Romanen' by appealing to real experience: 'Im Leben finden wir es anders'.[22] True, Wieland had a didactic axe to grind. Agathon's adventures in love, politics and philosophy were meant from the first to lead to a humane balance in which sensuality and scepticism offset Platonic idealism and enthusiasm; to that extent *Agathon*, for all its charm and artistry, has affinities with the 'preaching' novel, since a general truth is conveyed by and gives shape to character and story. Nevertheless, the claim to truth rests on the authority of experience,

Wieland's own. 'Ich schildere darin mich selbst' he wrote, 'wie ich in den Umständen Agathons gewesen zu sein mir einbilde'.[23]

At the opposite literary extreme from Wieland, yet similarly laying claim to the truth of real life is a work by Friedrich Heinrich Jacobi, *Eduard Allwills Papiere* (1776). Jacobi presents disjointed papers, the letters written by his characters, as neither a novel nor even proper materials for one, and the characters themselves as anything but generally instructive. He will not even give a general name to the psychological condition of the first character we meet − 'er kann nur in lebendiger Darstellung gezeigt, und nur durch Sympathie begriffen werden'. And against the owner of the Allwill papers, who doubts their 'allgemeine Brauchbarkeit', he quotes Lavater: ' "Wer alles sehen will, sieht nichts . . . Sieh Eins und du siehst alles." '[24]

This is the claim to the unique truth and value of the particular in extreme form. In the foreword to the 1792 edition, Jacobi said his aim had been 'Menschheit wie sie ist, erklärlich oder unerklärlich, auf das gewissenhafteste vor Augen zu legen'.[25] But this leap from the incoherent materials of *Allwill* to the general term 'Menschheit' was questionable. As Friedrich Schlegel asked, was the alleged 'Menschheit' really anything more than 'Friedrich-Heinrich-Jacobiheit'?[26] The particular, that is, can be so merely particular, so quirky, as to carry no general interest and hence no literary potential. That certainly seems an accurate judgement on *Eduard Allwills Papiere*.

All this is in part the familiar problem of relations between general and particular which we saw in other contexts − the contrast between Goethe's and Schiller's artistic approaches and, lying behind them, the opposition between the eighteenth century's older tendency to abstraction and the more recent philosophical emphasis on the concrete. How much general meaning could be contained in a particular, and how? But in part it is also a simpler, purely literary matter: throughout the history of fiction, its practitioners have tried not just to entertain but to convince, by creating − playfully or seriously − an illusion of reality. Wieland's appeal to a Greek source, Jacobi's to the ineffable uniqueness of individual cases were merely different tactics. At a humbler level and in a cruder way, the popular novel tried similar persuasions, exploiting the feigned biography, the 'true' *Geschichte des* . . ., in short the bluff that says fact is stranger than fiction in order to get fiction accepted as fact.[27] Which brings us back to the motifs already mentioned, the figures of mystery, the secret societies, the dark intrigues, all those essentially Gothic elements which have been well called the 'poor man's Sturm und Drang'[28] but which were perhaps susceptible of higher literary use.

We can see them halfway to such use in Schiller's novel-fragment *Der Geisterseher*. True, he wrote it as a mere filler for his *Rheinische Thalia* in the late 1780s to exploit the public's known weaknesses, began it (uncharacteristically) without a plan and refused (characteristically) to continue it later, despite the success of a book edition in 1789, since by then he was dedicated to more serious things. Yet even a pot-boiler cannot hide Schiller's talent. *Der Geisterseher* is one of the most exciting things in German prose. It shows an instinctive grasp of the alternation of methods that keeps a novel gripping − terse, swift-moving narrative for mysterious events, then tense conversational exchanges as the victims of a grand machination try rationally to unravel it, then tantalisingly distant, unperceptive letter-reports from a third party through which the truth about the final stages of the story has to be discerned. As in his dramas, Schiller has a marvellous feel for build-up, suspense, and climax. There is not a wooden or meandering sentence from start to finish. It is a prose style which for sheer power to grip the interest neither Wieland nor Goethe ever equalled. Schiller is one of the eighteenth century's great lost novelists, lured away by the traditional cultural prestige of tragic drama.

And besides the style there is something to take seriously in the basic tale, thickly strewn though it is with deliberately 'thrilling' motifs − plots and plots-within-plots, violence, executions, prophecies, apparitions false and problematic, all master-minded by the Cagliostro-like Armenian with the ultimate goal of ensnaring a Protestant Prince in the Roman Church. Where Book One is all thrills, Book Two eases the pace slightly to analyse the Prince's upbringing and mental state in a way which goes far beyond the range of a normal potboiler. After the 'victory of rationality' in Book One, where the Prince with veritably Humean scepticism rejects both the wonders he can see through and those he as yet cannot, he is gradually and subtly brought low in Book Two, his outer circumstances and his inner condition contributing to his fall. It is the story of a psychological process, a development into darkness − a 'Missbildungsroman'.

Here, 'Gothic' though some of its means are, Schiller's *Geisterseher* links up with what in an age of reason was bound to be a central concern: education. It is indeed ubiquitous in practice and theory, from Basedow's ideas of 'natural' education and Pestalozzi's labours in basic education for poor Swiss children, via Schiller's own conception in *Don Carlos* of an education in justice and benevolence for the future lord of an empire,[29] to Lessing's vision in the *Erziehung des Menschengeschlechts* of the whole progress of human thought as a single education conducted by God. More specifically, education lay close at hand for the novelist, whether he was following the tradition of psychological self-portrayal — Stilling, Bräker and Moritz all portray a kind of education, be the prime educator God or experience — or whether he was following the Enlightenment tradition of teaching by example.

Our survey has brought together some pretty ill-assorted elements of novel-writing practice up to the 1790s. One thing however is markedly absent, and it is a thing which in the novels of Russia, France and England is taken for granted as the basis of all else. From Madame de Lafayette to Flaubert, Pushkin to Tolstoy, Fielding to Virginia Woolf, the fabric of the European novel is society. But what society (once more we return to a familiar problem) was available to the German novelist? We think of Stilling in his country corner and of Bräker, after his escape from Frederick the Great's army, back on his Swiss mountainside; of Moritz in his small town and held down at its lowest social level and of Wieland fuming at the provincial small-mindedness in Biberach which gave rise to his satire *Die Abderiten*; even of Goethe in the relatively limited bourgeois sphere of Frankfurt-am-Main.

What was there in this to engage the novelist's imagination? None of that scale and substance which a great and unified nation in various and often intangible ways imparts even to the socially modest characters of the European novel. No social cohesion; the aristocracy were islands of a relative culture in a sea of provinciality, and artists' contact with them — Wieland's with the circle around Graf Stadion, even Goethe's with the Weimar circle — was not easy. No great cities of the order of London and Paris to offer the challenge and sustenance of their reality. None of those varied institutions like Grubstreet, Bedlam and Tyburn whose names, as Möser and Lichtenberg agreed, make up a national language of literary allusion.[30]

Lichtenberg incidentally — it seems most apt to treat him in a digression — is the other great lost novelist of eighteenth-century Germany. His fame rests on his aphorisms, yet it is clear that those penetrating observations and subtle reflections which he stored in his 'Sudelbücher' were never meant to be self-sufficient, and he never published them as such. They read, rather, like an intended all-embracing study of human nature which never found the right receptacle. The novel might have served. Lichtenberg knew it was an age for prose — 'Die Prose ist lange genug zu Fuss gegangen (pedestris oratio) und mich dünkt es wäre nun einmal Zeit für die Poesie abzusteigen um die Prose reiten zu lassen'; he was prepared to exchange Klopstock's *Messias* twice over for a small piece of *Robinson Crusoe*.[31] He had some ambition to be a novelist.

Certain jottings are expressly 'for use in a novel' and in 1785 he formally resolved to write one and use in it all (!) his accumulated stock of
perceptions and reflections: 'alles anzuwenden'.[32] 'Ex-Jesuits and
miserable princes' were among the planned targets, psychological
observation would have been the method; as a pastor's son and a pro-
fessor of physics, Lichtenberg brought together the traditions of intro-
spective and scientific empiricism. His aim was to show up human
nature as it really was beneath its 'social mask': 'dass wir eigentlich
nicht in Gesellschaft gehen, sondern nur einen Bevollmächtigten hin-
schicken, der über den eigentlichen Zustand seines Hofes das geheimnisvollste Stillschweigen beobachten muss'.[33] Since Lichtenberg was too
proper a sceptic and too complete a man to be a mere rationalist, yet
also too critical of fashions and pretensions to yield up reason before
the onslaughts of the new 'geniuses' or the new sentimentality, the
result would have been fascinating. But he never wrote his novel and
only published samples of his observations as material for other would-
be novelists and as object-lessons in the study of human nature. For
nobody, he said, should essay a novel unless he were in a position
'jedermanns Heimlichkeiten zu sagen' — something very different from
merely revealing one's own youthful 'Heimlichkeiten' when one has
outgrown them.[34]

Since Lichtenberg more than anyone insists on the misery of
German conditions for the writer and on the lack of social material,
these may be taken as reasons why he never wrote his novel. Yet he,
almost uniquely, might have managed without much social material,
even turning the familiar drawbacks to humorous advantage. A long
note of 1775 or so, headed 'Romane', goes into the many shortcomings
of Germany in comparison with England, but it is a humorous version
of the usual plaintive account. The German way of life is so frugal,
German towns so small, everyone so naively good that a would-be
novelist could hardly put a plot together. Mothers suckle their own
children — no chance of substitutions; girls are brought up to be domestic and unadventurous — no romantic disguises; German houses are
heated by stoves — no chance of using chimneys and fireplaces for
lovers to reach each other's rooms, while German roof-tops offer no
route for any lover but a tomcat. Follows a satire on German travel-
arrangements, which are equally plot-proof; a father may discover his
daughter's elopement three days late yet still catch her up at the next
posting-station. And how could any intrigue begin in a German post-
coach, too primitive a vehicle for any lady not highly trained for the
task to enter, and so arranged inside that nobody can see or talk to

anyone else, let alone be cosily entangled in that English manner which has ensured 'dass mancher ehrliche junge Mensch der von London nach Oxford reisen wollte zum Teufel gereist ist'. From detail to whimsical detail the case is made and a whole area of the novelist's technique subverted — except for the one part of Germany which has adequate roads and coaches, Hanover. All German novels must therefore start between Harburg and Münden — except that you now cover that stretch so fast there is scarce time to do more than praise the King of Hanover, certainly not to get properly acquainted. Moreover, travellers are so shattered by the experience of passing through Hessen, Holstein etc., that they instantly collapse into slumber. The novelist is foiled again: 'Das sind fürwahr feine Gegenstände für einen Roman, 5 schlafende Kaufleute schnarchend einzuführen, oder ein Kapitel mit dem Lobe eines Königs anzufüllen.'[35] The man who could write that might have emulated Lawrence Sterne, and made a novel from nearly nothing like the *Tristam Shandy* he knew well.

But for any other than the Shandean intelligence of a Lichtenberg, the humorous play with absences and impossibilities is not enough. The novelist needs the nourishment of social reality. What may be irrelevant to lyrical poetry is vital to the novel. No major critic of the form has been able to ignore the link between it and a growing, thriving, complex society. German critics contrast the rich society of Fielding's *Tom Jones* with Agathon's adventures in the groves of vague Greek temples,[36] or the topographically and socially realised London of Defoe's *Journal of the Plague Year* with the flimsy conventional setting of Wieland's *Abderiten*.[37] It seems likely that the characteristic German novel-form, the *Bildungsroman*, is not just the product of an age concerned with education on many levels, but also makes an artistic virtue out of necessity; lacking the riches of society, the writer was driven back on the inner riches of the individual.[38] The argument is strengthened by the otherwise closely parallel ways fiction developed in eighteenth-century Germany and England. Protestantism, philosophical individualism, the primacy of personal experience which grows out of religious introspection — all this can be traced in both. But the ways part over a major element in modern society. The English novel and its characters gravitate towards the big city, whose mysteries and prizes provide substantial themes. Triumph there becomes 'the Holy Grail of the individual's secular pilgrimage'.[39] The religious metaphor here is ironic. It is apt in earnest for the goal of the German novel-hero, 'Bildung', which though secularised has traces still of the religious preoccupations it derived from. And that the ideal of 'Bildung', both in and out of novels, was a kind of *pis-aller* is hinted by number 96 of the *Xenien*, which seems frankly to offer it as a substitute:

Zur *Nation* zu bilden, ihr hoffet es, Deutsche, vergebens;
Bildet, ihr könnt es, dafür freier zu Menschen euch aus.

One further thing follows from this non-social orientation. Elsewhere the novel is usually the least formal of the genres. It has few necessary attributes, no set number of acts, no fixed level of language. Rather than pursuing a preconceived form, it moulds itself to the places, persons and events it has to deal with. Its subtleties lie in moment-to-moment perceptions and formulations, its overall power in its scope and flexibility. This might have been the direction of development in Germany too. The autobiographers kept to the line of their experience and practised no formal subtleties. Of the novelists proper, Wieland is not yet subtle in organising his means, telling us everything with the authorial voice, varying neither pace nor mode of presentation greatly. Heinse in *Ardinghello* simply takes over the fluctuations of the swashbuckling adventure-story, intersperses some aesthetic reflexions and sketches a utopian project. Jacobi positively eschewed form, and sold (as Goethe said at the time) the raw materials out of which he might have made a finished product.[40] Goethe's own *Werther* was the German novel's only real formal success to date, for there an established convention — the epistolary novel — exactly matched the young Goethe's expressive impulse which normally overrode all formal requirements of genre. It was a success born of genius and chance, neither repeatable nor imitable.

In other words, the novel was still a simple thing, as yet only cutting its teeth; with time it might have gone on to develop (as it did elsewhere) those characteristic techniques — scenic presentation, viewpoint narrative, direct reportage and reconstruction — which aim at getting closer to inter-personal and social realities. But because it is deprived from the first of a whole range of external realities to challenge it, not just the content is affected but the direction in which the form itself will evolve. Because it is left free to construct patterns of spiritual growth in a single individual on whom all attention is focussed, new formal possibilities emerge; interrelated episodes and symmetries, leitmotifs and symbolic adumbrations, work not just for a sharp observer and robust or elegant formulator, but for the cunning artificer. The least detail of *Wilhelm Meister*, Goethe later told Eckermann, contained a higher meaning.[41] Composition was a demanding task for its author, comprehension of the resulting subtleties equally so for the reader.[42]

Even while insisting on the reader's aesthetically active role, Schiller was not confident that many would be up to it.[43]

For was not the public at this very moment enjoying the first instalment of Engel's 'Charaktergemälde' *Herr Lorenz Stark* in the *Horen* (virtually the only thing the general public *did* enjoy in the *Horen*)? To Schiller, Engel's little novel was almost beneath contempt, a mere platitude.[44] To the modern reader this seems too severe. It is a well managed, often witty domestic comedy with a not too obtrusive moral about tolerance in human relations, all enlivened by the alternation of 'Handlung' and 'Gespräch' which Engel's essay had described, and centring on the character of a good-hearted merchant whom a misunderstanding sets at odds with his son. It would be foolish to pretend Engel's work is a masterpiece, but its lightness of tone, its conversation-pieces and its approach to character point down the path which leads to Fontane and *Der Stechlin*. It was a path the novel was not yet to follow.

Instead it was to essay high art and refined form, abandoning the realistic project in an effort to counter Schiller's charge that the novelist was too earth-bound. It was not of course meant to become arbitrary or fantastic; art in Schiller's and Goethe's view had to rest on the essential truth, the scientific or philosophical necessity which the artist perceived underlying 'mere' surface reality. The novel would have to contain such reality, that was unavoidable; but it would be duly deployed and controlled in an artistic pattern so as to convey — in the phrase Schiller used of *Wilhelm Meister* — 'die Wahrheit des Lebens'.

III

But deploying real observations and experience within a conscious design alters their effect, even their nature. We can see this happening in *Wilhelm Meister*. If the manuscript of the *Theatralische Sendung* had never turned up, the elements of realism in the *Lehrjahre* would have been impressive for its time; but comparing the original fragment with the completed novel makes plain just how far 'high art' parts company with simple realism, how it moulds and polishes the given materials for its purpose. Watching Goethe rework and extend his original conception, we can better appreciate his aesthetic and his craftmanship and feel the more sure of taking the novel on its own terms — of seeing, that is, what kind of artistic synthesis he was aiming at. That does not mean that his efforts leave no residue of problems.

To begin at the beginning: Book I of the *Sendung* is a wonderfully realised account of Wilhelm's childhood, a mid-eighteenth-century middle-class childhood, but also a very particular one; we see an individual grow from the puppet-theatre and improvised dramatics of his childhood to the theatrical ambitions of early manhood. The narrative method is unsophisticated and direct, from the very conventional opening — 'Es war einige Tage vor dem Christabend 174 —, als Benedikt Meister, Bürger und Handelsmann zu M —, einer mittleren Reichsstadt, aus seinem gewöhnlichen Kränzchen Abends gegen Achte nach Hause ging' — right up to Wilhelm's discovery that he shares Mariane's favours.

The *Lehrjahre* has a far finer opening, in the best epic tradition of 'in medias res': 'Das Schauspiel dauerte sehr lange. Die alte Barbara trat einigemal ans Fenster und horchte, ob die Kutschen nicht rasseln wollten.' Barbara is Mariane's servant, the love-affair with Wilhelm is already at its height. One result of his theatre-mania — in this version of the novel very definitely to be shown as an aberration — is thus put forcefully before us at the outset. Book I of the *Lehrjahre* ends with the same disillusioning discovery, but in the completed novel Wilhelm's consequent abandoning of Mariane, and the unborn child he knows nothing of, will have immensely more moral importance. Both his remorse and the rediscovered child are powerful forces in educating him, true to the novel's basic principle that error and the fruits of error have a positive value. There is also, cunningly placed in Book I of the *Lehrjahre* before Wilhelm's disillusionment, the first marker for an important new theme, that of guidance by a higher, albeit human, agency. In I, 17 Wilhelm meets a representative of the 'Turmgesellschaft' which watches over his development, and the topics of fate, chance, guidance and the art of life are raised for the first time.

A firm artistic hand is at work. But not all is gain. Wilhelm's childhood is rendered less fully than in the *Sendung*. Rendered it has to be, because it is still necessary background to his rage for the theatre; but the more leisurely, more nearly self-sufficient 'epic' interest of the first version is gone. That is a material loss, evident only when we compare the two versions. There is also an artistic loss, more evident through comparison, but obtrusive enough by itself: we now hear about Wilhelm's childhood only as he recounts it to Mariane and Barbara. This too has artistic point — it isolates his rage for the theatre more clearly as a private aberration, where the full and loving authorial treatment in the *Sendung* gave it a very different status. Yet, even though pared down to those theatrical aspects of his childhood which are all the new conception needs, there is still too much matter to make plausible speech within the still realistic outward convention Goethe maintains.

Scenic method — the spoken exchange between characters — usually enlivens a narrative. But the reverse occurs when the author makes a makeshift of this technique to tell us at length what we need to know. Tale-telling is all very well in a Boccaccio-like situation (e.g. in Goethe's own *Unterhaltungen deutscher Ausgewanderten* of 1795) where a society has chosen this way to pass the time. Elsewhere it is an embarrassment. We tolerate it in Wieland (Agathon telling Danae the story of his past, Apollonius in *Agathodämon* sketching the past and future history of Christianity) because narration takes over so fully that we can shrug and forget that it is meant to be speech within a social context. In the *Lehrjahre* we cannot. Nor can Goethe, who is torn between using and mocking his own means. He has to tell us that Mariane can hardly stay awake, yet he must also have old Barbara encourage Wilhelm to go on — ' "wer weiss, ob wir bald wieder so ruhig und zufrieden zusammen sitzen?" ' (I, 6). His embarrassment produces a delightful vignette: Mariane asleep, hugged tight by her loquacious lover, while the old woman methodically finishes off the wine. Even then, Wilhelm talks on for another chapter (I, 8). His author has made him a bore, which was no part of the new artistic necessity.

He has also incidentally left out those delicate touches and nicely integrated authorial reflections which related Wilhelm's childhood and growth to the development of the German theatre.[45] Ordering the real, he has lost some of its power to be an enforced symbol. But then Goethe is no longer interested in the theatre and its condition, as he was in the *Sendung*. That novel, as far as it went, was about the social influence theatre might have had in Germany; if it was already about Wilhelm's 'Bildung', it was more concerned with the power of his chosen medium to educate others. But in the *Lehrjahre*, the theatre is just one more sphere of experience within which the individual may learn his limitations and work out, by trial and error, his salvation. We see much less of the theatre and associated cultural questions — Madame de Retti is gone, as is Herr von C., the sympathetic connoisseur of German literature; Wilhelm's triumphal first appearance on stage is gone, and so is the fiasco of Herr Bendel's acting. Where theatrical material is actually added in the *Lehrjahre*, it is of a critical kind. The much fuller account we get of Serlo's career and artistic philosophy serves to convey the maturer Goethe's own impatience with actors' inadequacies and excesses.[46] And the new episode in which the company does a reading of one of the fashionable 'Ritterstücke' over ample drinks shows the joint inspiration of national enthusiasm and alcohol leading to crass disorder. Wilhelm is left looking gloomily at the wreckage produced by a 'wohlgemeintes Dichterwerk' (II, 7). If this is symbol once more, something very different is being symbolised from what the Goethe of *Sendung* had in mind. And even this episode is only a side-issue, thrown up because the theatre is still the material subject of the novel. It is more important that the theatre now stands for life itself; when Wilhelm inveighs against theatrical people, Jarno laughs at him and declares ' "dass Sie nicht das Theater, sondern die Welt beschrieben haben" ' (VII, 3).

Everywhere in the *Lehrjahre* there are signs that a primary reality has been in large measure abandoned for a higher standpoint. The specific is retained as a necessary medium — human error has to happen somewhere — but what now matters is the general truth that to err is human and to err repeatedly, educative. The language most obviously reflects this change. The style has become more even (one could say more monotonous). Lively detail is cut out or toned down, the paler, more general word preferred; individual characters are made to speak in a uniform, undifferentiated style,[47] which undoes the enlivening effect of increased amounts of dialogue. The narrator, though he inter-venes with reflections less than he did in the *Sendung*, is paradoxically more obtrusive in the *Lehrjahre* by the very fact of his even, distanced tone; there is already a touch of that ponderous, 'official' quality which bedevils much of Goethe's later prose and denies him, for all the brilli-ance of certain fully realised episodes and even whole stories, the rank of a consistently great prose writer.[48] Much of the *Sendung* recalls, as Gundolf suggested, seventeenth-century Dutch paintings. If one wants a pictorial analogy for the *Lehrjahre*, it is the pure lines, typical figures and graceful groupings of another classical artist who found inspiration in Rome in 1787, John Flaxman.

For classical the new style consciously is, seeking to portray the typically rather than just the individually true by means which are restrained and elegant rather than colourful and characteristic. It is a deliberate retreat from the unprogrammatic but undeniable realism of the *Sendung*, a giving up of ground which had been won in the writer's constant struggle to encompass concrete particulars in a medium — language — which by its nature is abstract and general.[49] Of course, any classical form involves purification, and accepting this principle allows us to judge *Sendung* and *Lehrjahre* tolerantly as each 'right' in its own way.[50] They need not compete, at any rate as discrete objects of aesthetic appreciation. But in the perspective of literary history, no work is such an isolated object. *Wilhelm Meisters Lehrjahre* was to determine the later development of the German novel by the way it treated personal and social reality, by the fictional patterns it arranged them in — in short, by what it said about the relationship of experience and order.

This is the crux of the *Lehrjahre*, the centre to which all the details of adaptation and stylistic renovation point. Wilhelm undergoes an education, learning in the end that he was wrong to think he had a talent for the theatre but accepting that it is of no great moment where a man makes mistakes as long as they mature him. The last page declares that he should no more be ashamed of these origins of his maturity than of his social origins. He may feel that his whole history is one of ' "Irrtümer, Verirrungen auf Verirrungen" ' (VII, 6) and that his insights always came too late and in vain (VIII, 10). Yet precisely this was the homeopathic principle — ' "seinen Irrtum aus vollen Bechern ausschlürfen" ' (VII, 9). The process is lengthy, and the cost in human suffering high. But it can also be seen as a natural process. The seeds of individual maturity grow slowly in complex interaction with the outside world. The phases of growth, though each may involve ethical choice, have a natural necessity. Goethe put it strikingly in a letter of 9 September 1788 to Jacobi, who was dissatisfied with his son: 'Ein Blatt das gross werden soll, ist voller Runzeln und Knittern eh es sich entwickelt, wenn man nun nicht Geduld hat und es gleich so glatt haben will wie ein Weidenblatt dann ists übel. Ich wünsche dir Glück zu dieser Vaterfreude' (viz., the pleasure of watching the natural process unfold.) This was not just a metaphor. Since the mid-eighties Goethe had seen Man as an integral part of the total movement of Nature. This did not mean abandoning individual ethics, but only perceiving that, all individual effort and intention apart, certain things were constant and inevitable in any life which accepts the challenge to develop.

This natural philosophy was an adequate general principle with which to order the particulars of Wilhelm's experience — Wilhelm having decidedly accepted the challenge to develop: 'Mich selbst, ganz wie ich da bin, auszubilden, das war dunkel von Jugend auf mein Wunsch und meine Absicht' (V, 3). At a late stage, when fatherhood has rounded off his education, Wilhelm himself becomes aware of the general principle, exclaiming: ' "O, der unnötigen Strenge der Moral! ... da die Natur uns auf ihre liebliche Weise zu allem bildet, was wir sein sollen" ' (VIII, 1.)

This was Goethe's great advance. Earlier writers, in autobiography or the novel, had shown Man striving to overcome one element in his nature. Stilling had to conquer those parts of his natural being which did not conform to the Christian ideal. Wieland's Agathon too abandons his original one-sided idealism by gradual correction rather than free unfolding.[51] (This negative kind of education is seen in the *Lehrjahre* only in Book VI, the 'Bekenntnisse einer schönen Seele', where a – for Goethe – amazingly sympathetic picture of the Pietist inner life still in the end shows its impoverishment beside a more comprehensive human ideal.) The new conception is however not wholly open-ended, as later views of natural evolution were to be. It remains partly normative, as witness Wilhelm's words just quoted, that Nature unaided by morality can make us 'zu allem, *was wir sein sollen*'. Nature has an underlying purpose, an 'intention' for Man; his characteristics and potential make up what eighteenth-century writers often call his 'Bestimmung', an optimistic term which inhabits a grey area between discredited Christian theology and the speculative philosophy of an age that has not grown out of Christian habits of thought. Hence the remarkable fact that 'Nature' and 'Reason', in the most obvious sense an antithesis, are commonly found by eighteenth-century thinkers to agree. Nature is assumed rational, Reason assumed to be ultimately in tune with Nature. Even a philosophical system like Schiller's which at one level does oppose the two, nevertheless harmonises them at a higher level, where the terms become virtually synonymous.[52]

Goethe might then have adequately suggested this normative core of natural processes by nothing more obtrusive than Wilhelm's praise of nature, or that sustained image in the *Sendung* (II, 2) of the 'Weisheit einer verständigen Zuchtmeisterin' with which nature restores the lover after the shock of Mariane's infidelity. But he chose to do more. He introduced a secret society to watch over and guide Wilhelm's development, the 'Turmgesellschaft'. There were other possible reasons for the choice – secret societies, we saw, were a common feature of the still small stock-in-trade of the novelist, and likely to appeal to the reader. But it is fair to assume Goethe was not merely out to tickle the public taste. He had been a Freemason himself since the early eighties. In 1784-5 he had worked at an epic entitled *Die Geheimnisse*, which was to show religious truth as the essence distilled from many religions at the respective highpoints of their history and brought together in a rosicrucian order led by a man called Humanus. Little of the poem was executed[53] but it was to tell how the newly arrived Brother Markus is first initiated and later succeeds Humanus as head of the order. Providentially guided like Humanus ('Wie wunderbar die Vorsicht ihn geführt'), Markus has come at the orders of 'higher beings'. There are important differences – the later 'Turmgesellschaft' stands for a wholly secular, not a religious humanism, and it is presented as itself a providential agent. But the motifs are similar, and used to tackle similar themes; this at least suggests that the secret society in the *Lehrjahre* had a serious intention.

Anyway, Goethe's motives are a less important question than his effects. Within an outwardly realistic convention, he was portraying a group of men who guide other men's destinies. Technically, they act as what Schiller called epic 'machinery' — i.e. they take the role of the gods in the Homeric poems. Schiller declared himself ready to accept this. Meister's apprenticeship, he says, is not the workings of blind nature but a kind of experiment, in which the 'Turmgesellschaft' guides an unsuspecting Wilhelm towards a goal he knows nothing of, 'ohne die Natur in ihrem freien Gange zu stören'.[54] This proviso reflects exactly the view of natural-cum-rational process, of growth-and-purpose, just discussed. Yet it is plain Schiller is not wholly happy with the 'Turm' motif. He admits its necessity only came home to him after two or three readings; he wonders if it is not a concession to the popular taste. And he puts his criticism in the form of a compliment: 'Wenn je eine poetische Erzählung der Hilfe des Wunderbaren entbehren konnte, so ist es Ihr Roman'. (We recall that his own impulse, in *Der Geisterseher*, was to penetrate and dissolve mystery.) What adds nothing to a work, he goes on, may actually damage it, distracting the reader's attention to mysteries and irrelevancies when he should be imbibing its 'inner spirit'.

As a good friend, Schiller was being tactful and constructive; as a perceptive critic, he was asking the essential questions. Even allowing that a rationally planning and guiding society can be used to express certain beliefs about nature and man, was it artistically necessary? Was the account of natural human development not sufficient without further 'machinery'? How would the society and its doings be taken? All interpretations since have had to face these questions.[55]

The best approach to them is to ask what the 'Turmgesellschaft' really *does*. Its representatives crop up here and there along Wilhelm's path, convey a mysterious warning to flee the stage, discuss with him the relationship of fate, chance and providential guidance. They have his complete history among their records. They speak of educational method — 'ihn seinen Irrtum aus vollen Bechern ausschlürfen zu lassen' — and they finally put him through a kind of initiation ceremony à la *Magic Flute*. But of direct guidance there is little or no sign. Wilhelm's behaviour for good and ill is his own choice. His good actions spring from his past errors at an immediate emotional level. Thus he looks after Mignon when his remorse over Mariane and his child has been stirred up: 'er sehnte sich, dieses verlassene Wesen an Kindesstatt seinem Herzen einzuverleiben' (II, 8). The thing which does him most credit, his unswerving kindness to those strange creatures, Mignon and the Harper, is simple impulse. Lessing had thought of Freemasons as setting an ethical example'; 'Sie lassen gute Männer und Jünglinge, die sie ihres nähern Umganges würdigen, ihre Thaten vermuthen, errathen — sehen, so weit sie zu sehen sind; diese finden Geschmack daran und thun ähnliche Thaten'.[56] But Wilhelm acts spontaneously, without such example.

Thus the 'Turmgesellschaft', whatever the characters may say about it,[57] is not so much an agent in the plot as an image (symbol, allegory) of order and an aid to compositional order. These two functions may seem separate, but in fact they are related. Novelists have always used chance and coincidence to help put their plots together, but in persuading us to accept these things as plausible they have also (except when using them ironically as a convenience) been persuading us to accept a certain view of the world. Indeed, the less plausible the coincidences needed to bring about the happy ending, the more vigorously it has sometimes been argued that these were no more than the stuff of everyday life, which we normally do not remark.[58] Now if such fictional means are often hard to accept within a realistic convention, how much more problematic is the 'machinery' Goethe introduces into the *Lehrjahre*? For here too the basic convention has not moved from the realistic to the fantastic, and in realistic terms the 'Turmgesellschaft' is partly implausible, partly just superfluous. Also, it must be added, partly powerless even in the story's own terms; for it can do nothing to save those 'Romantic' figures of mystery and suffering, Mignon and the Harper, from *their* fate. They fall outside the scope of the 'Turm', and indeed of the novel's central conception. Schiller, with one of his finest insights, put it in an apt image, comparing Goethe's design to a planetary system in which everything coheres and only the two Italian figures enter it as comets, dread signs of a distant and mightier system.[59]

But if the basic convention has not overtly moved away from the realistic, we have known from the start that the artistic intention had. Goethe was aiming at 'high art', at 'form' as this is understood by the aesthetically sophisticated when they contemplate other arts (painting, sculpture) and other literary genres (drama, poetry). The question is, whether form in that sense was properly an overriding aim for the novel; whether as a genre it does not have the choice of either taking close issue with raw reality, making do with a set of techniques rather than aspiring to 'form'; or of becoming sophisticated in a way which reduces its immense potential to render, as the older genres were less able to do, the full fortuitous reality of its time. Such a task may involve accepting the novel's 'roughness, . . . even coarseness of grain as compared with other arts', and the fact that it is 'the least "artistic" of genres'.[60]

Aspiring beyond this limitation, Goethe produced a strange masterpiece and a frankly unfortunate model. It is a masterpiece, because what prose narrative can achieve as 'high art', he achieves. The skill of his ordering hand is undeniable (there has been no space to do it full justice here); there is a fine psychological understanding; and there is a material richness which, if less than in the *Sendung*, is more than Wieland or any other previous eighteenth-century novelist can show. It fails on its own terms only in that it tips the balance towards abstractions[61] too far to allow that synthesis of particular and general which was Goethe's underlying intention in all his work of this period. It was an unfortunate model because Goethe's achievement and prestige diverted the novel in Germany from the course it took in the rest of Europe. *Wilhelm Meisters Lehrjahre* established a pattern which overwhelmingly influenced the Romantic novel, even when (and perhaps because) individual Romantic writers found Goethe's educational ideal wanting; and it was still influential much later when the social conditions which gave rise to the prototype had long since changed. Novelists continued to look inwards at states of soul and follow the thin thread of individual development when they could have looked outwards at states of society and portrayed that more complex weave. They continued to resolve an individual's problems in isolation from what was going on in contemporary society, as *Wilhelm Meisters Lehrjahre* does. Indeed, Goethe actually misrepresents social reality for poetic purposes by concluding with a set of marriages across class borders between bourgeois and noble characters, though earlier in the novel he had clearly recognised how real those borders were.[62] Critics in their turn continued to dismiss any less 'poetic' subject — which included most of what English, French and Russian novelists normally treated — as somehow inferior, as mere 'Literatur', not 'Dichtung'. All this meant that an important voice in the understanding and ordering of society was muted, if not silenced. It was not Goethe's fault, but it was his doing. That, among other things, is what 'classic' means.

Notes

1. Hans Pyritz, 'Der Bund zwischen Goethe und Schiller', PEGS xxi (1950-1) denies there was any real friendship, which means overlooking the cordiality of the letters, the shock of Schiller's death ('ich verliere . . . die Hälfte meines Daseins' — Goethe to Zelter, 1 June 1805), the warmth of Goethe's retrospects (cf. HA 10, 543: 'die Hälfte voneinander ausmachen', 'grosse Liebe und Zutrauen, Bedürfnis und Treue'), the poems to and on Schiller ('An Schiller, mit einer kleinen mineralogischen Sammlung', 'Epilog zu Schillers "Glocke" ', 'Im ernsten Beinhaus') and the fact that Goethe chose to be buried beside Schiller. Pyritz particularly misrepresents the letters exchanged on *Meister*, ignoring Goethe's warm appreciation of Schiller's criticism (see esp. to Schiller, 25 November 1796) in order to suggest that it endangered — whatever this may mean — Goethe's 'geheimen Lebenssinn'. Why then did Goethe actively seek Schiller's help again when he returned later to *Faust*? Emil Staiger's 'Fruchtbare Missverständnisse Goethes und Schillers' in A. Schaefer (ed.), *Goethe und seine grossen Zeitgenossen* (Munich, 1968) is subtler, but its conjectures are adequately answered by Goethe's opinion 'dass wir uns auch da verstanden, wo wir uns nicht einig waren' (HA 10, 668). Carpings at the Goethe-Schiller partnership are ultimately rooted in the German tradition of anti-intellectualism in which the mysticising of Goethe and depreciation of Schiller, first practised by the Romantics, has always been an important paradigm.

2. Cf. Albert Ward, *Book Production, Fiction and the German Reading Public 1740-1800* (Oxford, 1974).

3. *Hamburgische Dramaturgie*, 69. Stück. Lessing goes on: 'Roman? Wir wollen ihm diesen Titel nur geben, vielleicht, dass es einige Leser mehr dadurch bekommt'. This confirms the dubious status of the novel.

4. Facsimile reprint of the 1774 original, ed. Eberhard Lämmert (Stuttgart, 1965), Vorbericht, p. vii.

5. Ibid., pp. xiii-xvii.

6. Quoted in Friedrich Beissner's Nachwort to Wieland, *Romane* (Munich, 1964), p. 908.

7. Cf. ed. cit., pp. 243, 301, 319ff.

8. Facsimile reprint of the 1774 original, ed. Ernst Theodor Voss (Stuttgart, 1964).

9. Cf. Ward, *Book Production, Fiction and the German Reading Public 1740-1800*, pp. 64f.

10. Schiller to Goethe, 28 June 1796: 'Das Pathetische erinnert an den Roman.'

11. Schiller, *Werke* V, 741.

12. Schiller to Goethe, 28 June 1796 and 9 December 1794.

13. Hegel, *Ästhetik*, ed. Friedrich Bassenge (^{2}Frankfurt a.M., n.d.) II, 452, 'Das Epos als einheitsvolle Totalität'. The *Ästhetik* was published posthumously from lecture-notes dating from the late 1820s.

14. There was widespread belief in the plots of secret societies, even in their responsibility for the French Revolution. See J.M. Roberts, *The Mythology of the Secret Societies* (1972). For contemporary German evidence of these beliefs, see Lessing, *Ernst und Falk. Gespräche für Freimaurer* (1778), *Werke* XIII, esp. 361, 363ff on the delicate question whether the Masons were politically subversive. Similarly cautious is Wieland, *Geheimnisse des Kosmopolitenordens* (1788), *Werke* III, 550ff. But Schiller in the tenth of the *Briefe über Don Carlos* equates Posa's political aims with those of the Masons and Illuminati, *Werke* II, 257. And Book V of Wieland's novel *Agathodämon* (1799) describes the role of Apollonius of Tyana's Cosmopolitans in the overthrow of the Roman tyrant Domitian. In the same year, volume 2 of Hölderlin's *Hyperion* introduces the revolutionary 'Bund

der Nemesis', *Werke* III, 144.

15. *Agathon* Bk 11, Ch. 3, *Werke* I, 846.

16. E.g. J.T. Hermes (cf. above p. 84). See the letter from the theologian Arnold to Hermes on the novel as a means of preaching, quoted in Ward, *Book Production, Fiction and the German Reading Public 1740-1800*, p. 69. Jean Paul *Vorschule der Ästhetik* para. 3, duly calls Hermes a 'Romanprediger'.

17. Quoted in Theodor Klaiber, *Die deutsche Selbstbiographie* (Stuttgart, 1921), p. 68.

18. *Johann Heinrich Jungs (genannt Stilling) Lebensgeschichte* (repr. Deutsche Bibliothek, Berlin n.d.), I, 107.

19. Ulrich Bräker, *Der arme Mann im Tockenburg* (repr. Munich, 1965), Ch. 1xxix, 'Meine Geständnisse'.

20. *Agathon,* Vorbericht (1766), *Werke* I, 375.

21. Ibid., Bk 5, Ch. 8, *Werke* I, 510.

22. Wieland to Zimmermann, 5 January 1762.

23. *Agathon*, Bk 9, Ch. 5, *Werke* I, 759.

24. Vorbericht to *Eduard Allwills Papiere*, facsimile of the 1776 original, ed. Heinz Nicolai (Stuttgart, 1962), pp. 3ff.

25. Jacobi, *Werke*, vol. 1 (Leipzig, 1812), p. xii.

26. In a review of Jacobi's *Woldemar* dated 1796, in Schlegel, *Kritische Schriften*, p. 271.

27. Cf. the examples in Ward, *Book Production, Fiction and the German Reading Public 1740-1800*, pp. 43ff.

28. Ibid., p. 53.

29. Cf. *Briefe über Don Carlos*, numbers 8 and 10, *Werke* II, 251, 257.

30. Georg Christoph Lichtenberg, *Schriften und Briefe*, ed. Wolfgang Promies, (Munich, 1969ff.), I, 167f.

31. Ibid., I, 463, 471.

32. I, 163f., II, 188, 195f.

33. II, 196.

34. 'Vorschlag zu einem Orbis Pictus für deutsche dramatische Schriftsteller, Romanen-Dichter und Schauspieler', *Werke* III, 384, 379. This is probably a dig at Goethe's *Werther*.

35. *Werke* I, 373-6.

36. Sengle, *Wieland*, p. 188.

37. Volker Klotz, *Die erzählte Stadt* (Munich, 1969), p. 62.

38. Cf. Sengle, *Wieland*, p. 190, and also the essay 'Manners, Morals and the Novel' in Lionel Trilling's *The Liberal Imagination* (repr. 1964), esp. pp.121from the novelist's need for 'enough complication of [social] appearance to make the job interesting'.

39. Ian Watt, *The Rise of the Novel* (repr. Peregrine Books 1963), p. 187.

40. Reported in Wieland to Merck, 13 May 1776.

41. Eckermann, *Gespräche mit Goethe*, 25 December 1825. Goethe added dismissively: 'Andern mag das gezeichnete Leben als Leben genügen'.

42. Goethe calls *Wilhelm Meister* something to be 'überwunden' and the demands it makes on him 'unendlich' (to Schiller, 16 October 1795 and 25 June 1796). Schiller looks forward to the task 'mich des Ganzen zu bemächtigen' and expects the process to be a 'wichtige Krise meines Geistes' (to Goethe, 16 October 1795 and 2 July 1796).

43. Schiller to Goethe, 2, 3 and 9 July 1796.

44. He had accepted it for the *Horen* as 'für das Publikum sehr passend' (to Goethe, 18 September 1795). By 23 November he is plainly cross at the popular response, and on 23 December writes that 'die göttliche Platitüde . . . ist eben der Empfehlungsbrief'. Unkindest cut of all, Goethe heard that people were betting (contributions to the *Horen* being unsigned) that *Lorenz Stark* was his work (to

Schiller, 7 December 1796).
45. See above, p. 25.
46. Serlo dismisses the actors of Wilhelm's troupe as 'Naturalisten und Pfuscher' (IV, 19); he has a jaundiced view of public taste (V, 1); and he disapproves, with the narrator, when Aurelie plays Lessing's Countess Orsina naturalistically, taking her own private jealousy on to the stage: '[sie] zog . . . alle Schleusen ihres individuellen Kummers auf' (V, 16).
47. For comparisons, see Wolfdietrich Rasch, 'Die klassische Erzählkunst Goethes', in H.O. Burger, *Begriffsbestimmung der Klassik und des Klassischen* (Darmstadt, 1972). The most sensitive and elegant statement of essentials is still Hugo von Hofmannsthal's essay of 1911, ' "Wilhelm Meister" in der Urform'.
48. The 'official' influence is important because so much of Goethe's later prose was dictated, and there is a difference between dictated and written work – as Goethe recognised implicitly in his oration on Wieland, where he stresses that Wieland wrote all his works with his own hand, testing and recasting, 'das Geschriebene immer vor Augen'. *Zu brüderlichem Andenken Wielands* (1813), WA 36, 318.
49. Cf. Schiller, last of the *Kallias-Briefe*, dated 28 February 1793, *Werke* V, 431f. This insight into the problems of literary realism suggests that the language of much eighteenth-century prose (e.g. Wieland's) has a 'general' character, not from any classicising intent, but because it has not yet solved the problem of achieving particularity by what Schiller calls 'die künstliche *Zusammensetzung des Allgemeinen*' (his italics).
50. Cf. Rasch, 'Die klassische Erzählkunst Goethes', pp. 401f.
51. This contrast is well brought out by E.L. Stahl, *Die religiöse und die humanitätsphilosophische Bildungsidee und die Entstehung des deutschen Bildungsromans im 18. Jahrhundert* (Berne, 1934), pp. 148ff.
52. See E.M. Wilkinson, 'Reflections on translating Schiller's "Aesthetic Letters" ', in F. Norman (ed.), *Schiller Bicentenary Lectures*, 1960.
53. See HA 2, 271ff. Originally the poem 'Zueignung' was the introduction to this fragment. Goethe's later essay on *Die Geheimnisse* links it with the themes of *Meister* by calling the motive behind the Order 'die Begier nach höchster Ausbildung' (HA 2, 283).
54. To Goethe, 8 July 1796.
55. Most critics have found reasons for accepting things as Goethe disposed them. Melitta Gerhard, *Der deutsche Entwicklungsroman* (Halle, 1926), p. 156, quotes nineteenth-century novelists' (Freytag, Fontane) objections to the 'Turm', but dismisses them as 'rationalistic'. Gundolf, *Goethe* (Berlin, 1916), p. 516, thought the 'Turm' itself 'rationalistic', but suggests that other elements – impulse, character, fate – offset this; yet all these are meant to be controlled or subsumed by the 'Turm' and its activities. Stahl, '*Die . . . Bildungsidee und die Entstehung*', p. 159 sees guidance by the 'Turm' as 'eine Vertiefung der Bildungsidee'. Jacob Steiner, *Sprache und Stilwandel in Wilhelm Meister* (Zurich, 1959), pp. 123f., says the 'Turm' is too rationalistic to be taken seriously and (implausibly) that Goethe 'meant' it to be seen this way. A similar line is taken by Staiger, *Goethe*, 2, 152f. But it is surely invalidated by the seriousness of the ceremonial passages late in the novel. Friedrich Schlegel saw, characteristically, irony pervading the book, but took the 'Turm' seriously enough (*Kritische Schriften*, p. 470). Georg Lukács, finally, puts more forthrightly what Schiller felt: 'dass [das Wunderbare] die Toneinheit dissonierend zerreisse: es wird zu einer Geheimnistuerei ohne verborgenen Tiefsinn, zu einem stark betonten Handlungsmotiv ohne wirkliche Wichtigkeit . . .' *Theorie des Romans* (Berlin 1920), pp. 154f.
56. *Ernst und Falk, Werke* XIII, 345.
57. E.g. Werner praises the society 'da sie dich auf den rechten Weg gebracht haben' (VIII, 1); Wilhelm himself believes that they had power to intervene and

cut short his errors: ' "Wenn so viele Menschen . . . deinen Lebensweg kannten und wussten, was darauf zu tun sei, warum führten sie dich nicht strenger?' (VII, 9).

58. E.g. Goldsmith, *The Vicar of Wakefield* Ch. xxxi, which tries to equate such chances with the 'seeming accidents [which] must unite before we can be clothed or fed'.

59. To Goethe, 2 July 1796.

60. Trilling, 'Art and Fortune', in *The Liberal Imagination*, pp. 277f.

61. Erich Trunz in his commentary to *Lehrjahre* asserts that 'das Gedankliche wird überboten durch die Anschauung, durch die Gestalten' (HA 7, 681). But Schlegel surely hit it off when he said that the characters 'gleichen . . . durch die Art der Darstellung dem Porträt, ihrem Wesen nach aber sind sie mehr oder minder allgemein und allegorisch', *Kritische Schriften*, p. 468.

62. See III, 8, on Wilhelm's flirtations with the Gräfin: 'Wie über einen Fluss hinüber, der sie scheidet, zwei feindliche Vorposten sich ruhig und lustig zusammen besprechen, ohne an den Krieg zu denken, in welchem ihre beiderseitigen Parteien begriffen sind, so wechselte die Gräfin mit Wilhelm bedeutende Blicke über die ungeheure Kluft der Geburt und des Standes hinüber'. One need not read this as Marx *avant la lettre* to see that it expresses a realistic view of society which the novel's happy ending evades.

7

CLASSICS: (2) DRAMA

I

To achieve the high art of *Wilhelm Meisters Lehrjahre*, the novel-genre itself had to be adapted and legitimised. Nothing so radical was needed in drama, a genre already hallowed by tradition. Yet here too Goethe had problems, because ultimately *all* considerations of genre were secondary in his work. Self-expression had priority, both in importance – when he called his works 'fragments of a great confession'[1], he implied that the record of his experience, thought and feeling as a whole was more important than the perfecting of single works – and in time. The expressive impulse, that is, came first, seizing on a story and hero, legendary or historical – Prometheus, Caesar, Mahomet, Ganymede, the Wandering Jew, Faust, Egmont – and only as expression advanced did the conditions of the genre Goethe had chanced into begin to be felt. He then had a choice: either to rescue the expressive core, as when he took the poems 'Prometheus' and 'Mahomets Gesang' from abortive dramas; or resolutely to complete a structure, making good any omissions or damage the expressive impulse had caused, as he did in *Egmont*. There a historical figure served as a mask to speak through, but the play had to be finished long after this purpose had passed. The first impulse was lyrical, the tidying-up had to meet dramatic requirements, rounding off the action and restoring some of the character's historical substance. Egmont's eleventh-hour transformation into a symbol of political freedom is the (equally unsatisfactory) answer to both demands. The play is completed, 'mehr wie es sein konnte als wie es sein sollte'.[2]

The problem was a large one because in the years before Italy, non-completion had become a habit; after Italy, completion was a duty. So many scattered fragments – *Meister, Egmont, Tasso, Faust* – did not befit a classicist. *Iphigenie* had dramatic structure from the first, but it came straight from Euripides. *Tasso* and *Faust* were more typical, each in its way a product of the tensions between expression, material and dramatic form.

Goethe wrote two acts of *Tasso* in poetic prose, presumably like that of *Iphigenie*, in 1780-1. He recast the play in Italy in spring 1787, and more radically in the spring of the following year. His relationship to his subject had now cooled completely: 'Hätte ich [das Stück] nicht angefangen; so würde ich es jetzt nicht wählen'. Where once it concerned him closely — 'der Reiz, der mich zu diesem Gegenstande führte, [entstand] aus dem Innersten meiner Natur' — it now offers only the analogy of Tasso's final banishment from Ferrara and Goethe's own imminent departure from Rome. Since he is nevertheless set on finishing the play, the approach must be objective; he is duly reading Serassi's new biography of Tasso, with the aim 'meinen Geist mit dem Charakter und den Schicksalen dieses Dichters zu füllen'.[3] He has a firm plan to work to.[4] Completion will be a matter of poetic craftsmanship. But certain things remained unchanged. The original first two acts, he tells us later, were roughly the same in dramatic function as the text we now have: 'in Absicht auf Gang und Handlung ungefähr den gegenwärtigen gleich'.[5] That means that *Tasso* as we have it retains the deeply personal theme ('aus dem Innersten meiner Natur') but has fused it with the substance of the historical Tasso at a stage when that theme touched Goethe less closely. So it is a carefully composed text, a 'consequente Komposition' on which he lavished 'unerlaubte Sorgfalt'[6], yet still a record of earlier conflicts.

Of course, it was a historical subject from the outset; but for Goethe in 1780 Tasso's story was a medium through which to express his continuing inner turmoil. That does not mean it was a direct statement of his experience; the expressive principle sought not equivalence but affinities, exploring and expressing an aspect of the poet's self by shaping the chosen subject with a particular emphasis. The subject-matter is not merely exploited — we learn something about Ganymede from Goethe's poem, because in part he is penetrating to what it felt like to be Ganymede. But we learn more about Goethe, because the myth helps him to understand and express what it felt like to be himself.

What did Tasso help him to see and say? Not just that it was hard being a court poet. We cannot reconstruct the lost two prose acts of the early eighties, much less any conjectural, even earlier 'Ur-Tasso';[7] but we do not need to, since on Goethe's own showing the first two acts of the final text contain the original issues substantially unchanged. And these go deeper than the problems of the Poet, even if it was as a poet that Goethe had met them, and as a poet that Tasso offered the means to formulate them. They have complexity, but also unity. Tasso sets inborn talent against social standing, the 'Gemüt, das die Natur/Nicht jedem gross verleih' against 'Adel, der uns von Vätern kam' (II, 3); he evokes a Golden Age of spontaneous behaviour, and is answered by the Prinzessin's more cautious ideal of harmonious social forms; he loves the Prinzessin, and she him, but is denied any but Platonic fulfilment by social divisions; his heart-on-sleeve approach to Antonio is cruelly rebuffed as premature; he vainly hopes that natural justice will take priority over the formal law he has broken and will acquit him as his own heart does. All these skilfully interwoven themes, all broached in the first two acts, come down to a single conflict between nature and convention. Tasso's words in IV, 3 — 'Ist nicht mein ganzer Fehler ein Verdienst?' — might stand as an epitome of the play's subject; to transgress convention is to be true to a deeper law.

It is obvious how close this subject was for a young bourgeois poet, gradually gaining acceptance and falling in love in a court society which was at first suspicious of 'genius' and its associated wildness. His first impact on Weimar, we saw, was that of a 'noble savage'. He had evoked the primal Golden Age persuasively in poetry before coming there;[8] while writing his early *Tasso* he was also at work on a novel which took a jaundiced view of noble society in its relations with poetry and the theatre.[9] On the other hand, he did not reject it wholly. By 1780 he had begun to adapt, to gain others' confidence, to discipline himself. His diaries record struggles inner and outer, but some successes; frustration and doubts, but some satisfaction and a feeling that fortune was on his side.[10] He was still living through problems, but had gained some firm ground from which to survey them poetically.

The finished *Tasso* remains a tragedy of nature versus convention. Convention attempts to guide and control nature; the court 'educates' Tasso towards its norms of social behaviour. When Tasso has approached and been provoked by Antonio, efforts to set things right remain convention-bound; Tasso is confined to his room, while Antonio — who is at least equally at fault, as the Duke sees — still remains the man he consults. The Duke senses the effect his mild punishment has on Tasso, but cannot for convention's sake simply cancel it.

In this maze of conventionality, Tasso is in large measure right. The Prinzessin is mistaken to send him to Antonio, and to assume that all at court really are bound by the principle of 'was sich ziemt'. Antonio is wrong to create a scene from barely concealed personal pique. Alfons is wrong not to cut the knot of convention and restore harmony directly. Leonore Sanvitale is morally wrong to turn an unhappy situation to her personal advantage. Tasso is right to feel he has been sinned against, right to see through Sanvitale, right to believe the Duke has been deceived about the duel-scene, right to sense that there are machinations afoot. Of course, his bitter feelings go to excess, his sense of persecution exceeds the facts, and at crucial points he misreads good intentions. But it is hard for him not to do so, since he is off-stage for the last scene of Act II and the whole of Act III while his fate is settled by others.[11] This typifies the way the court treats him; as an object of their necessary care and correction, in need of a constraining kind of 'Bildung'. Tasso the lover can gladly accept the influence of the Prinzessin as a beneficent climate:

> Ihr bin ich, bildend soll sie mich besitzen . . .
>
> . . . . O Witterung des Glücks,
> Begünst'ge diese Pflanze doch einmal!
>
> (II,2)

But that he needs adjusting — normalising, socialising — is an arrogant assumption of all the other characters. The Prinzessin later regrets causing the brush with Antonio; Antonio, as the man of experience, eventually realises that Tasso's nature is different, and presses him ('Erkenne, was du bist!') to accept, not alter his poetic nature. But it is too late. For Tasso, by a finely linked chain of psychological causation, is decisively disgraced by embracing the Prinzessin; an offence to social convention and to the Platonic convention through which alone their love could be communicated.

All this is the 'tragedy of a poet', certainly; Goethe puts a real poet before us in a way no one had tried to do before and not many of the artist-stories of modern literature have succeeded in doing since. Arguably he shows us at crucial junctures the actual creative process in operation.[12] His statement of the theme as 'die Disproportion des Talents mit dem Leben'[13] fits the particular case. But it is a particular case of something more general, one possible challenge to social convention by the forces of nature which lie outside it.[14] Goethe does not isolate the poetic temperament as a peculiar cause of tragedy. It is only because we look back at *Tasso* over nearly two centuries in which writers have become ever more obsessed with their own social position that the play seems to take on something of that obsession, even to be the first document of the modern artist's social alienation.[15] *Tasso* is neither an artist's apologia nor an attack on conventional society — Goethe had reached a *modus vivendi* with Weimar and he was anxious that the play should not be read as an account of his position vis-à-vis Weimar personalities.[16] Nor on the other hand is it a rejection of the 'Sturm und Drang' in favour of moderation — *Tasso* is simply not of that stamp. In any case, it is not the nature of tragedy to take sides, preaching or rejecting. It shows the way things are, and what follows.

Tragedy *Tasso* certainly is, even though it contains no violence and ends with no bloodshed — just as certainly as it is drama even though its action is slight and its tone restrained. To find it undramatic is crudely to limit the genre's possibilities. 'Wenn man nur aufhören wollte, vom Drama im allgemeinen zu sprechen', as the Poet says in Hofmannsthal's *Unterhaltung über den Tasso von Goethe*; and he goes on: 'Eigentlich geschieht nichts. Es entschleiert sich etwas... ein unabänderliches Verhältnis'.[17] That pinpoints the play's quality and its achievement, for which there is no parallel before Chekhov.

After the 'Hügel Tasso' there was the 'Berg Faustus' to get over.[18] The Gothic subject was an odd one for a classicist, and the new scenes written in Italy bear this out: 'Hexenküche' ironises the nordic hocus-pocus, while 'Wald und Höhle' allows Faust a new, classical serenity which conflicts in tone and substance with earlier scenes. As yet this mattered little; for the time being and the purposes of his Collected Works, Goethe bade a public farewell to *Faust*, printing it in 1790 as an avowed 'Fragment'. He even chopped off the ending of the Gretchen tragedy, partly because that whole 'sub-plot' stole too much interest from Faust and the high philosophic theme, but probably also because the stark naturalism of these scenes was too strong meat for his new aesthetic.[19] Insofar as any fragment could be compatible with a classical programme, *Faust* now was.

Yet classicism or no, *Faust* had a strange fascination: for Schiller, who recognised in the 'Fragment' the richness and boldness of genius and begged to see any unpublished scenes; for Goethe himself, who did not dare untie the packet which held Faust captive, for fear it would again capture his imagination.[20] When he did return spontaneously to *Faust* in 1797, he asked Schiller what demands he would make of the whole work. They soon agreed on the necessity of organising and unifying; for all the power of the poetry, a rational idea, a philosophical theme, a 'symbolische Bedeutsamkeit' were indispensable. But Schiller felt (and it is one more sign of his critical acuity) that the existing scenes had something of this, portraying 'die Duplizität der menschlichen Natur und das verunglückte Bestreben, das Göttliche und das Physische im Menschen zu vereinigen'.[21]

What did those scenes contain? In his spontaneous expressive way, the young Goethe had explored Faust's situation, seeing himself in the legendary venturer beyond the limits of human knowledge into the magic arts; he had then[22] explored the fate of a fugitive from academic aridity who plunges into a first idyllic, then tragic love-affair. These self-recognitions and self-expressions flowed into poetry whose concentrated evocation of character and setting ranges without stylistic clash from the charm of early woodcut to the profundity of Rembrandt. But the poet had no time for the technicalities of structure and plot. There was no pact-scene to show how Faust had acquired Mephistopheles' services and on what conditions, no rejuvenation to explain how the brooding old academic could also be the loved lover of a beautiful young girl, no suggestion of how this love-affair fitted into a Faust play at all.

As ever, the legendary theme fits where it touches. Even at these points, it is diverted from its traditional meaning. Faust in the legend trades his soul for twenty-four years of power and pleasure, setting what is ephemeral and valueless higher than what is of eternal worth — so, at any rate, the choice is presented in this Christian cautionary tale, which adds to the disapproval of earthly enjoyments an equally religious suspicion of the pursuit of knowledge.

Clearly, no writer could be true to this legend if he was out of sympathy with its Christian meaning. Goethe was. He had had a short acute attack of Christianity in 1769 following an illness. From then on Christianity's radical dualism and insistence on the overriding value of the transcendent no longer limited his mind, (except briefly during Charlotte von Stein's ascendancy). For him, earthly experience and its enjoyment were not reprehensible; nature was not a disposable package for a transcendent essence; knowledge of the natural world was a proper end and, broadly understood, the basis of all philosophical and poetic truth. Nor was this mere materialism. Goethe's spiritual aspiration and sense of wonder simply needed no dogma to sustain them. As he wrote pithily many years later:

> Wer Wissenschaft und Kunst besitzt,
> Hat auch Religion;
> Wer jene beiden nicht besitzt,
> Der habe Religion.

Thus from the outset Goethe was using a legend he would have to work against the grain. How much so is shown in the most striking of his early scenes,[23] the invocation of the Erdgeist. It is remarkable enough to introduce into a play featuring Mephistopheles an earlier apparition that steals his thunder. What is more, the Erdgeist is foreign to the legend and cuts across its traditional theology of God/Devil, heaven/hell. For what is he? Nothing less than the force of creation in the phenomenal world, the continuing process of nature itself:

In Lebensfluten, im Tatensturm
Wall ich auf und ab,
Webe hin und her!
Geburt und Grab,
Ein ewiges Meer,
Ein wechselnd Weben,
Ein glühend Leben,
So schaff ich am sausenden Webstuhl der Zeit
Und wirke der Gottheit lebendiges Kleid.

(ll. 501-9)

A world informed by such a spirit — and evoked in such poetry — can hardly be the scene of a traditional Faust drama, because it is a world understood in radically un-Christian terms. The deity that wears this living garment of nature is indifferent that birth and death ebb and flow like an eternal sea; it is a deity manifesting itself not in commandment, prohibition and judgement, but in endless movement, ever-changing patterns and sheer intensity of life.

Yet, equally from the outset, Goethe had introduced Mephistopheles, used him as a mouthpiece for some light satire on university life and implicated him in the Gretchen tragedy. He was using the Faust figure, and a Mephisto necessarily came with it. Goethe tried to reconcile him with the new pantheistic conception by making him an underling of the Erdgeist, which would have meant a total remoulding of the legend. Characteristically, Goethe never developed this conception beyond brief hints,[24] which remain in the text as fossils of an abandoned plan. They could have been deleted later — as indeed the whole Erdgeist scene could — but they never were. Perhaps Goethe consciously gave priority to poetic power over plot; or perhaps the poet, when revising a work and integrating the scenes which once so deeply involved him, sees inconsistencies less readily than his critics do. And this in turn may be because he is contriving to maintain consistency at a deeper level than that of plot or of the relations between the metaphysical agents he has called up.

This can fairly be said of *Faust I*. In completing it between 1797 and 1806, Goethe conformed outwardly to the legend. He gave the whole play a pallidly Christian backdrop by writing a prologue in heaven, where a traditional Lord actually draws Mephisto's attention to Faust and gives him permission to try his worst. Goethe wrote scenes preparing and portraying a pact between Faust and Mephisto, thereby filling up the 'grosse Lücke' which had yawned between the original Erdgeist scene and the beginning of Faust's travels. This much conformity was no doubt imposed by the circumstances of composition: Goethe was returning, as the prefatory 'Zueignung' says, to an aberration ('Wahn') of his youth which only nostalgia could make acceptable to the disciplined feeling ('das strenge Herz') of a mature classicist. It was too late now for a total remoulding of the legend on the lines of the Erdgeist conception: the mythopeic power for a task of that magnitude can only spring from an enthusiastically committed imagination. By contrast, the legend in its traditional form offered a welcome framework to accommodate piecemeal poetic execution.

Yet in practice it was not easy to conform to the legend. When it came to the pact scene, which is the crux of a Faust story, Goethe did not — could not — present the issues and terms in the traditional way. He found himself remoulding the legend from within. And here lies his essential consistency, beside which his inconsistencies, undeniable as they are,[25] pale in importance. For the pact turns on the same question the Erdgeist had raised twenty-five years before, and it is as far from the Christian spirit of the legend as if this actually had been transformed into a quite new pantheistic myth.

The Faust of the opening scene turned to magic to learn 'was die Welt/Im Innersten zusammenhält'. In the sign of the macrocosm, he sees a vision of 'die wirkende Natur' in all its complexity and harmony. It gives an intense pleasure such as his word-chopping academic pursuits cannot give, but it is less than Faust has appetite for; it is still too detached, pure contemplation:

> Welch Schauspiel! Aber ach! ein Schauspiel nur!
> Wo fass' ich dich, unendliche Natur?
> Euch Brüste, wo? Ihr Quellen alles Lebens . . .

(ll.454ff)

He is left thirsting. The Erdgeist sign, in contrast, begins to invigorate the whole man in the way he longs for:

> Du, Geist der Erde, bist mir näher;
> Schon fühl' ich meine Kräfte höher,
> Schon glüh' ich wie von neuem Wein.
> Ich fühle Mut, mich in die Welt zu wagen,
> Der Erde Weh, der Erde Glück zu tragen,
> Mit Stürmen mich herumzuschlagen
> Und in des Schiffbruchs Knirschen nicht zu zagen.

(ll.461ff)

This 'mächtig Seelenflehen' calls forth the Erdgeist, but his presence overwhelms Faust, who is only just beginning to recover when the Spirit vanishes with a scornful:

Du gleichst dem Geist, den du begreifst,
Nicht mir!

So Faust has aspired beyond mere contemplation to a total involvement in earthly experience, but has been spurned. He is thus a frustrated — what? Not 'idealist', in the normal senses, since the mere vision of the world's essence did not satisfy him, nor is there anything ethically ideal about the Erdgeist. But not 'materialist' either, in the normal sense, since he yearned for the whole range of experience from happiness to disaster, not just for the traditional Faustian pleasure and power. Goethe's Faust is a realist in so insisting on experience, yet his realism aims at a comprehensiveness which will rival the intense vision afforded by the sign of the macrocosm. It is, so to speak, an agglomerative counterpart of idealism, akin to Goethe's own realism as Schiller came to understand it in 1794.

These are the threads Goethe picked up in 1797, to integrate them for the first time in a single dramatic plan.[26] Faust is still the man he was: his attraction to the Erdgeist rather than to the pure vision of the macrocosm is echoed when he translates the 'logos' passage at the opening of St. John's Gospel not by 'Im Anfang war das Wort' but by 'Im Anfang war die Tat'. The problem now was to relate this character to a conventionally pact-hungry Mephisto. Faust's humiliation by the Erdgeist certainly sets up a seller's market for the wares of a lesser spirit. Yet Faust never actually demands these wares. He doubts from the first whether Mephisto can offer anything to satisfy him. Why then does he make any arrangement at all with Mephisto? Only because there is no alternative. He is deep in despondency, oppressed by the limitations of his world and by a material existence which lacks any higher principle: 'Dem Wurme gleich' ich, der den Staub durchwühlt'. The idea that dust is Man's element recurs as a bitter leitmotif (ll.653-6, 762f, 1116; cf. also 'Prolog in Himmel', l.334). Faust contemplates suicide, ready to risk annihilation on the off-chance of an after-life worthy of a striving spirit. He proclaims a despairing yet unchecked aspiration in his famous words on the 'zwei Seelen' within him and in this same speech calls on *any* spirits that may be near to carry him away 'zu neuem, buntem Leben!'

So when Mephisto answers this call, he has to deal with a paradoxical character, quite unlike the traditional 'Faust': a man who is disillusioned with mere experience but has been rebuffed in his effort to raise it to a higher plane; a man who does not believe in a transcendent world yet cannot give up striving, blindly like the flower towards the light, in a way it is difficult not to call 'spiritual'. Mephisto from the first fails to understand these paradoxes.

Faced with Faust's profound pessimism, he glibly offers 'dir die Grillen zu verjagen'; having heard Faust curse every aspect of existence as worthless, he can say 'Hör' auf, mit deinem Gram zu spielen'; and when Faust, with cutting irony, lists the 'pleasures' of the world, each flawed by earthly imperfection, Mephisto simply offers to provide them — 'Ein solcher Auftrag schreckt mich nicht, Mit solchen Schätzen kann ich dienen' (ll.1688f.) — ignoring Faust's tone and wholly missing his crucial words:

> Ward eines Menschen Geist, in seinem hohen Streben,
> Von deinesgleichen je gefasst?

Faust and Mephisto are at cross-purposes, and they remain so. On this the whole dramatic action and its resolution are to rest.

This is exactly expressed in the pact, or rather in the wager which Faust offers Mephisto. Mephisto proposes the old-fashioned quidproquo; he is to serve Faust on earth, Faust is to do the same for him in the after-life. Faust cares nothing for that problematic state, but since his death is the condition for entering it, and must therefore be what Mephisto desires, he says, let that be my last day if ever I declare myself satisfied. To him it seems a safe offer. He will never be satisfied, since any satisfaction must be a deceit, a matter of 'belügen' and 'betrügen' (ll.1694ff); he believes the earth is the only possible source of joy and suffering, but he does not believe that any moment could ever draw from him the words 'Verweile doch! du bist so schön!' He can only conceive of earthly joys dismissively, as inactive self-indulgence, 'Selbstgefälligkeit', 'Genuss', slothful ease on a 'Faulbett'. He in contrast is active and restless. If he gives himself over to the poor adventures Mephisto can offer, it is in despair of any other escape from his narrow life, and with no expectation of pleasure:

> Du hörest ja, von Freud' ist nicht die Rede.
> Dem Taumel weih' ich mich, dem schmerzlichsten Genuss . . .

He opens his arms to the full breadth of human experience with no other positive aim, apparently, than by embracing it to destroy himself:

Mein Busen, der vom Wissensdrang geheilt ist,
Soll keinen Schmerzen künftig sich verschliessen,
Und was der ganzen Menschheit zugeteilt ist,
Will ich in meinem innern Selbst geniessen,
Mit meinem Geist das Höchst' und Tiefste greifen,
Ihr Wohl und Weh auf meinen Busen häufen,
Und so mein eigen Selbst zu ihrem Selbst erweitern,
Und, wie sie selbst, am End' auch ich zerscheitern.

(ll.1768ff)

But this is exactly the sentiment of the Erdgeist scene, the urge to go out into the world and know its 'Glück', 'Weh', and 'Schiffbruch'. Faust and Goethe have remained true to themselves.[27]

The gap in the action is filled and Mephisto happy with a traditional pact signed in blood; but there is scarcely a whiff of sulphur, and none of sin and retribution. Mephisto has made a bad bargain, for the terms are beyond his range; he will find himself cheated even when Faust does say the fateful words because they will be spoken in a sense wholly different from the one the wager specifies. He will by then have tried long and in vain to bring about what he swore would happen in his interview with the Lord: 'Staub soll er fressen, und mit Lust' (1.334). He will paradoxically have functioned only as a stimulus to Faust, providing experience through which and despite which the principle of restless striving can be asserted; a function which, as the 'Prolog im Himmel' makes plain, is intended by the Lord and is even on occasion (ll.1335f) recognised, with inappropriate clarity, by Mephisto himself.

True, there are moments when Faust is nearly his traditional self; his 'Hör, du musst mir die Dirne schaffen!' when he first sets eyes on Gretchen is more like the crude pursuit of pleasure we might expect. Yet even his lust has some human discrimination, as the preceding lines show (2609 ff); and his affair with Gretchen becomes a *love*-affair in the fullest sense. Gretchen is not, as she would have to be to fit the legend, merely one of the promised pleasures; Faust plunges deep in guilt towards a fellow-creature, not just into legendary sin. Nor is she, as she would have to be to fit Mephisto's still blithely traditional scheme for snaring Faust, a merely sensual indulgence; she inspires in Faust what the uncomprehending Mephisto can only sneer at as fits of 'hohe Intuition' (1. 3291).

The Gretchen tragedy can be seen in two ways. Taken by itself, it is a masterpiece. No social drama in German, except perhaps Büchner's *Woyzeck*, conveys suffering more rawly. None weaves beauty and delight as inextricably with guilt, terror and despair. None can match the poetry which enhances these effects — in all but the final scene, which Goethe recast from prose so as actually to reduce the terrible intensity. Taken as part of the Faust totality, on the other hand, the Gretchen action is a paradoxical mixture. At first sight it is an unwarrantable interpolation, equally at odds with a traditional Faust play and with Goethe's own design. The traditional legend had no place for so substantial an episode, certainly not for one with a depth of human understanding such that the salvation-damnation issue loses its primitive theological clearcutness. Goethe's version, for different reasons, could hardly stand the competition of an 'episode' possessing such power. In whatever strange way it first came to be part of his *Faust*, much of his effort was later aimed at restoring the balance which its impact had upset, redirecting attention to the Faustian Faust, and away from the guilty lover.

Yet there are complications and compensations. At the simplest level, there is in any Faust play the problem of finding 'adequate employment for characters ... with superhuman and supernatural powers' which shall not descend into 'poor buffoonery'.[28] Any modernisation of a legend whose magical elements were aimed at simple gawpers has to occupy Faust in some intrinsically absorbing fashion. This the Gretchen action does, with just sufficient magic business and (in the completed *Faust I*) just sufficient attachment to the philosophical theme to pass muster. It also incidentally brings in Christian motifs of faith, sin, atonement and hoped-for salvation which were foreign to Goethe's Faust action proper[29], and thus pays his dues to the legend which he was so powerfully drawing away from its 'Urquell'. But most important, the Gretchen action is an integral part of the whole because the interplay of Faust's aspiring nature and Mephisto's limited understanding, with the cross-purposes which result, contains the fundamental theme: the spiritual elevation which grows from the experience of this world.

Gretchen is neither a final satisfaction for the restless Faust nor a merely sensual gratification, as Mephisto expected. Faust is drawn beyond lust to love, and then later drawn away from Gretchen altogether. Inevitably, in the realistic terms of the sub-plot, it must seem that he 'abandons' her; yet it would be as true to say that the Faust *theme* abandons in her its first phase, a limited but wholly characteristic one. For in his later pursuits — of Greek perfection symbolised by Helen of Troy, of power and possession — Faust remains the striver nothing will stop. His striving is never specifically moral, and to the end its side-effects go on loading him with guilt. And yet he is saved, a 'salvation' purely symbolic which uses familiar Christian iconography (though a quite different one from the 'Prolog im Himmel') to make clear what, Goethe felt, a specially devised imagery might have left vague.[30] What justification is there for saving Faust? None in conventional ethical, much less Christian terms. From first to last he is amoral. But he has fulfilled the requirements of an earthly spirituality which sees in activity and aspiration the defining attributes of Man and is prepared to accept error and disaster as recurrent consequences. Indeed the Lord in the 'Prolog' speaks the words: 'Es irrt der Mensch, solang er strebt' (though the Erdgeist, surely, is his prompter); and an angelic voice in the closing 'Bergschluchten' scene answers:

> Wer immer strebend sich bemüht,
> Den können wir erlösen.

But this most unorthodox ethic left two dramatic problems to be solved: firstly, how to rescue Faust from a still traditionally-minded Mephisto, who had a pact to point to; secondly, how within the limits of a drama which cannot go on indefinitely (though Goethe's *Faust* comes nearer to this than any other European play) to show the character's commitment to never-ceasing activity. These two birds are neatly killed with one stone. In a final act rich in ironies and late new developments, Faust ends blinded and bereft of magical powers. Loss of the outer light intensifies the inner. On the very brink of the grave, he speaks the fateful words of the wager — 'Verweile doch, du bist so schön!' — but speaks them to a moment empty of all immediate gratification, 'den letzten, schlechten, leeren Augenblick', as a bemused Mephisto comments. Yet here again, and decisively, Mephisto fails to grasp Faust's nature and with it Man's nature. As Faust had scornfully asked once before:

> Was weisst du, was der Mensch begehrt?
> Dein widrig Wesen, bitter, scharf,
> Was weiss es, was der Mensch bedarf?

> (ll. 10193ff)

For the moment is far from being empty. Faust is aspiring to reclaim land which the sea will always threaten. Its inhabitants will have to struggle ceaselessly against the elements, defending a paradise within against destruction from without. This constant necessity, not the reclamation itself, much less any 'ethical' service to the community which the project would rate as, is the essence of Faust's last vision. It is a symbolic moment, in the precise sense Goethe gave to the word 'symbol': inexhaustible content in a concrete vision. The ideal of endless activity is seized in an act of contemplation, *vita activa* reconciled momentarily with *vita contemplativa*, the energy of the Erdgeist with the serene overview of the macrocosm sign. The drama need portray no more activity, though even in heaven it is to continue. Equally, so rich is Faust's vision, and so far removed from the pleasures he scorned in the pact-scene, that only Mephisto's literal mind can think that the mere enunciation of the agreed formula automatically gives him Faust's soul. Faust is 'saved'.

We have looked beyond the years of the Classical partnership to see how the aged Goethe finished the task set him by his youth. Dramatic completeness is not necessarily the most important quality of the whole *Faust*: it is a poem *sui generis*, not easily approached (much less impugned) by usual dramatic criteria. Still, complete it is, and better so than not. Its poetry alone would make it a masterpiece, and its poetry is not all. It contains a richness of experience not merely Faust's, and a range of thought and imagination which goes beyond the requirements of the dramatic theme and becomes of self-sufficient value. Nevertheless, the critical reader may be left with a doubt and a regret — paradoxically so radical that they leave untouched the work Goethe actually wrote. We have seen how the legend had to be worked against the grain from the very first; how Goethe began to transform it and yet also fell back eventually on its basic structure and conventions; and how complex is the interplay of his and its ethos. One may see the whole thing as in a way a mistake, the most grandiose, magnificent, fruitful mistake in literary history; one may regret Goethe's self-accommodation, however incomplete, to the legend; and one may reflect how much more splendid still a *Faust* might have been which had followed through the original pantheistic conception and worked out freely, not in a limiting legend and a makeshift iconography, a salvation of Man within the laws of nature.

II

'Schillers Talent war recht fürs Theater geschaffen', Goethe told Eckermann in 1825. 'Mit jedem Stück schritt er vor und ward er vollendeter'. That suggests a development without problems, and it is true the stage was Schiller's element in a way it never was Goethe's. But it was only with *Don Carlos* that the excessive melodrama of his youth abated. And

Don Carlos was still endangered as a dramatic whole by its author's changing conceptions, each dictated by a different subjective involvement; he had there still been using his characters for what Coleridge later called poetic 'ventriloquism'.[31] Schiller was resolved not to let this problem arise again. His work in systematic aesthetics, his observation of Goethe, his study of the Greeks and Shakespeare were all aimed at offsetting subjectivity. He now aspired to do what the naive poets did – 'nur den Gegenstand geben'.[32] He was thus consciously moving into Goethe's territory, seeking an overall effect ('Totalität') rather than separate intense effects ('Mehrheit des Einzelnen', 'das Einzelne recht vordringen zu lassen').[33] His new subject, Wallenstein, Austria's ambitious and treacherous general in the Thirty Years War, was not as easy to identify with as Karl Moor, or Carlos, or Posa. What was left was the 'reine Liebe des Künstlers',[34] in other words, objective treatment.

The result is an immense achievement, in every sense. *Wallenstein* is as long as three normal plays, and for Schiller to mould its mass of material into a coherent trilogy needed greater formative power than mastering any three separate subjects. The political and military situation of Europe had to be compressed into one pregnant moment; the interests of nations and of that state-within-a-state, the army, had to be reflected in one man's wavering mind; and this man, equally devoid of moral sublimity in his hesitations and in his final decision, and denied success when he does act, had to be given tragic stature. All this Schiller manages. His drama renders the complexity of events, yet is totally lucid in organisation (which *Don Carlos* was not). By a seemingly unforced scaling-down, the pressures of policy and strategy become intimate factors in Wallenstein's dilemma, subjects for brooding over as familiar and natural as the problems of family and conscience which occupy that other tragic procrastinator, Hamlet. History yields a 'rein menschliche Fabel'. And Wallenstein's downfall is tragedy unlike any Schiller had shown before: not the pathetic frustration of some noble spirit or high ideal by an evil agency, but the implacable logic by which all human action draws its consequences after it. This truth, which the Greeks expressed in the concepts of 'hubris' and 'nemesis', is obvious enough, yet it remains the most fundamental challenge to the tragic dramatist, and the most satisfying of his achievements when he realises it in a full and balanced picture of one man's fate.

Schiller had already spoken of Wallenstein in just these Greek terms in his *Geschichte des Dreissigjährigen Krieges* (1791-3): 'die rächende Nemesis wollte, dass der *Undankbare* unter den Streichen des *Undanks* erliegen sollte'[35] (i.e., Wallenstein's ingratitude to the Emperor made it apt that he should be killed by men to whom he himself had been generous). This is not a mere figure of rhetoric, for a little further on Schiller says Wallenstein was 'unübertrefflich, wenn er Mass gehalten hätte', and failing to keep the bounds of 'measure' was precisely the Greek definition of hubris. Hubris was the immoderate ambition which made this greatest general of his day dictate the terms on which he would serve the Emperor, intrigue with the Emperor's enemies in order to take vengeance for having once been deposed, and aspire to the crown of Bohemia. Schiller the historian is unequivocal about Wallenstein's character, motives and intentions. The suddenness of Wallenstein's deposition at Regensburg prevented him rebelling then, so 'von der Zukunft erwartete er Genugtuung'.[36] Reinstated because he was indispensable, 'brütete er still die schreckliche Geburt der Rachbegierde und Ehrsucht zur Reife'; though the first negotiations with Gustav Adolf failed, 'fest stand der Vorsatz'.[37] Nothing could be more clearcut.

And yet, in his final verdict on Wallenstein at the end of Book Four, Schiller suddenly contradicts his own account. The historical point that monkish intrigues first set the Emperor against Wallenstein leads on to the historiographical point that it was monkish accounts which later established the story of Wallenstein as a traitor. Yet his treachery and ambitions rest only on probable suppositions; there is no document giving reliable insight into his motives and no authenticated action that may not have had a quite innocent cause. His undoubted act of rebellion can be explained by 'Not und Verzweiflung' – he was forced to play the role he was already believed to be playing: 'So fiel Wallenstein, nicht weil er Rebell war, sondern er rebellierte, weil er fiel.' And his fall was made complete when the enemies who survived him wrote the history books.[38]

Schiller's volte-face is the natural reflex of a historian criticising his sources, and of an Enlightenment historian polemicising against the Catholic church. But deeper down it is the reaction of an artist who senses complexities and ambiguities which historiography cannot get at. Even as a historian, Schiller was drawn towards the analysis of character – not a normal feature of the narrative history of his time. But duty to his sources and to the idea of factual truth set limits to a psychological approach. To recreate the human situation fully needed the imagination of the artist. Schiller duly grows impatient with his history, which in its later stages becomes markedly summary, and itches to write drama: 'mir juckt die Feder nach dem Wallenstein'.[39]

The idea of nemesis remains: Schiller planned to put a vignette of the goddess Nemesis on the title-page of the printed text,[40] and the Prologue calls Wallenstein a victim of 'unbezähmte Ehrsucht', which echoes the original firm historical judgement. But thè Prologue also echoes the revised historical verdict and promises the richer vision art can give:

> Von der Parteien Hass und Gunst verwirrt,
> Schwankt sein Charakterbild in der Geschichte.
> Doch euren Augen soll ihn jetzt die Kunst,
> Auch eurem Herzen, menschlich näherbringen.
> Denn jedes Äusserste führt *sie*, die alles
> Begrenzt und bindet, zur Natur zurück,
> Sie sieht den Menschen in des Lebens Drang
> Und wälzt die grössre Hälfte seiner Schuld
> Den unglückseligen Gestirnen zu.

This epitomises the mature Schiller's aesthetic. Art transcends partisan views, harmonising extremes by recreating the full natural reality – in this case, a man caught in the toils of life, victim of chance as well as of his own transgressions. Art can make us feel what it is like to be a Wallenstein, drifting into a situation with less and less options, till at last there is only one, and that fatal. Such sympathetic insight[41] – something quite distinct from that identification with a character which Schiller was now avoiding – is an essential of objective art; we come to understand Macbeth and Othello because we know their experience from within (which is not to say that we condone ambitious regicide or jealous murder). Hence the tracing of nemesis in the drama of Wallenstein is subtler, less morally emphatic, than in Schiller's first historical judgement.

This does not mean that nemesis becomes a mysterious or metaphysical agency, as has sometimes been thought.[42] 'Nemesis' and 'fate' are merely summary terms to describe the interlockings of event, character and motive which Schiller puts before us in all their complexity. Is rebellion forced on Wallenstein because the Court suspects him – 'Oh! sie zwingen mich, sie stossen/Gewaltsam, wider meinen Willen, mich hinein' (*Die Piccolomini*, II,2)? Or has he lost favour by his own acts and intentions? It is a classic political situation, as Goethe pointed out: each side takes precautions against a threatened danger, and thereby brings about what each fears.[43] On Wallenstein's side, 'precautions' meant negotiating with the Swedes. Yet he hesitates to take the final step. Is this an appraisal of the situation as not yet ripe? or residual scruple? or indecisiveness? All these motives appear. He trusts in the stars to tell him when to act, a weakness he has only shown since the Regensburg dismissal broke his old confidence in himself.[44] Illo urges him to make his own fate — 'In deiner Brust sind deines Schicksals Sterne' (*Picc.*, II,6) — but to no effect. Wallenstein vacillates on, till the capture of his go-between Sesina forces his hand. But by now it is too late for success: the intrigues of Octavio Piccolomini (whom, again, the stars bade him trust) have already begun to dissolve the army on which Wallenstein's power and freedom of action rested. Max Piccolomini's loyalty to his Emperor, and the spite with which Buttler avenges an earlier slight, do the rest.

This is a tangled skein, but Schiller's presentation is clarity itself. He shows how the catastrophe grows from Wallenstein's hesitation, but also that there is no such thing as total abstention from acting: to try and stand still in the stream of events is to be carried irreversibly with it. Besides, Wallenstein does act, not enough to catch his opportunity but enough to doom himself. It may sometimes seem to him that his mere rumination on possibilities has been transformed into implacable realities:

> Wie? Sollt ich's nun im Ernst erfüllen müssen,
> Weil ich zu frei gescherzt mit dem Gedanken?
>
> (*Tod* I,3)

and that he never went beyond a kind of aesthetic play with treason — 'Die Freiheit reizte mich und das Vermögen' (*Tod* I,4). But in fact what he sees blocking his retreat is his own acts:

> Bahnlos liegt's hinter mir, und eine Mauer
> Aus meinen eignen Werken baut sich auf,
> Die mir die Umkehr türmend hemmt!
>
> (ibid.)

The deeds he *has* performed, tentative and partly defensive negotiations (for so they are shown in the drama) cannot now be made to appear innocent, such is the 'Doppelsinn des Lebens' (ibid.).

The last phrase epitomises the shift from the historian's point of view to the dramatist's. In place of the single plain 'Sinn' of a man's acts judged from without, we have a recreation of their more complex inner 'Sinn'. There is nemesis nonetheless — it is his own acts that hem him in; but these were not evil from the start. The nemesis is complex and tragic, not a clear-cut sequence of moral guilt and retribution.

Indeed, morality is not obtrusive in *Wallenstein*. The theme offered no great moral issue like the liberation of the Netherlands. Wallenstein himself could not plausibly be turned into an idealist (though it is left just conceivable that 'peace in his time' was part of his mixed motivation). His defeat was therefore not, like Posa's and Carlos's, an Enlightenment martyrdom, but simply a defeat. There was no nobility to be wrung from his personal situation.

This was perfect for Schiller's self-correcting purpose — for the first time he could render the way things are, instead of declaring how they should be. The reality of history pervades the trilogy, guiding and containing the poetic imagination even while the dramatic understanding disposes the historical mass; and the reality of Goethe's work also plays its part,[45] as did Shakespeare's. *Wallensteins Lager* bears comparison with the crowd scenes in *Egmont*, which in turn yield little to those of *Julius Caesar*; it shows us the army on which all depends, amply realising the central figure and his power before ever he appears on stage. In the conspiring generals and the Lady Macbeth figure of Gräfin Terzky, in Wallenstein's negotiations with Wrangel (*Tod* I,5) and in his cajoling of the soldiers (*Tod* III,15) where his true character is rendered through his deliberate role-playing — in all this and much more, we are in a more real world than Schiller had previously achieved, a world 'wo hart im Raume sich die Sachen stossen'.

Wallenstein thus rescued Schiller from his youthful manner, but also (as he saw) contradicted his mature theory. For he had not abandoned moral notions when he gave up their direct 'subjective' expression. He found moral absolutes in Kant's ethics, to which the study of Kant's aesthetics had naturally led. On the principles Schiller developed in the 1790s, tragedy must show moral grandeur in response to suffering, reason must rise victorious over the life of the senses. So the tragic hero had to be morally reflective, an 'Idealist' rather than a 'Realist'. But the historical Wallenstein was plainly a 'Realist' — and Schiller's new aesthetic set some store by historical truth. He was thus as much at odds with his subject as Goethe was in *Faust*, an ironic affinity linking the two greatest works of this decade.

With *Wallenstein*, however, the result is wholly gain. We can appreciate it regardless of Schiller's theory because the fall of a great man has a timeless fascination. The sub-plot provides a tragic issue in line with the theory, and a character — Max Piccolomini — who must struggle to follow the path of duty in a night of uncertainty:

In mir ist Nacht, ich weiss das Rechte nicht zu wählen

(*Tod* III,21)

But Wallenstein suffers no such inner doubt. His hesitations are practical or superstitious, for him 'night' can only mean the outward calamity which is a challenge and a foil to his powers of generalship:

Nacht muss es sein, wo Friedlands Sterne strahlen

(*Tod* III,10)

This downfall of a Realist transcends its author's theory and takes its place in the universal tradition of grand tragedy.

In the half-decade he worked at *Wallenstein*, Schiller finally learned his trade. The play is a masterpiece in the precise sense that it ends the apprentice and journeyman stages of Schiller's work. From now till his death he completed a play a year without the difficulties that had dogged virtually all his previous works. The man who could shape *Wallenstein* could manage any dramatic subject. Not that he simply went on applying a set technique – each of his subsequent plays tries out new formal means; but there was no longer any disharmony between the poet and the dramatic mode.

Equally important is the play's historical position. It represents that synthesis of the French and English forms which Schiller had striven towards since early in the writing of *Don Carlos*. The formal elegance and structural control which recall Racine are matched by a historical mass and a range of character-types from high to low which recall Shakespeare. The succeeding works vary the mixture: *Maria Stuart* and *Die Braut von Messina* incline to a French concentration and formal purity, *Die Jungfrau von Orleans* and *Wilhelm Tell* to a broader canvas, though they never quite essay the grand episodic manner of Shakespeare's histories. *Demetrius*, the play Schiller was working on when he died, looks as if it would have rivalled *Wallenstein* in historical scope and dramatic tautness.

Schiller's mature work is concerned preeminently with history and moral action – with the home spheres of Realist and Idealist, and their relation to each other. All his later plays except *Die Braut von Messina* have a basis in history and explore the more complex dilemmas which arise on the border between private and public existence. Those early idealists, Karl Moor and Ferdinand Walter, each inhabited a self-sufficient moral world which came into violent collision with an established order. For all their grandiose reflections on Man, Nature, Society, they were not fully self-aware until the very end – they could not be, if they were to act out their role in the melodramatic stories Schiller devised. Historical situations, in contrast, challenge the individual's self-sufficiency. He is one factor in a larger nexus, his psychological and moral situation relates and ramifies and he must take account of this. Can he maintain independence of action? Can he (in the imagery of *Wallenstein*) keep to 'grade Wege' when all about him are following 'krumme Wege'? Can private morality be an adequate basis for political action (*Tell*) or a meaningful refuge from political entanglement (*Maria Stuart*)? And what if the private motives of public action become mixed, as in *Die Jungfrau* (Johanna) and *Wallenstein* (Max)? In the context of history, that is, individual morality and psychology are more severely tested and more realistically seen.

This realism partly grew from Schiller's work as an actual historian; where *Don Carlos* was written before his study of the Dutch revolt, *Wallenstein* came after his work on the Thirty Years War. Though the play catches a human reality that slips through the larger meshes of a historical account, a sense of external pressures and of tides in the affairs of men also disciplined the play. The dramas that followed benefit too. Personal conflicts are set convincingly in the hard political world, where Burleigh intrigues against Shrewsbury to dominate Elisabeth, and responsibility for Maria's death is foisted on the insignificant Davidson; where Johanna is easily abandoned when she has served the French purpose; where Demetrius's belief in his claim to the Russian throne is exploited by the Polish nobles, out for plunder, and by the Polish king, out to weaken his nobles. Though Schiller occasionally tired of history's dusty museum, and on one occasion lapsed grossly by inventing a death on the battlefield for Joan of Arc, history served him well. In it he earthed his 'speculative' mind and tried to achieve the balance of abstract and concrete which was his and Goethe's common goal.

Some have denied that he achieved it. His detractors see in him not just a moralist (which he is) but a moraliser who takes too little account of human nature, preaches an easy idealism and dramatises foregone conclusions. Nothing could be less true. Schiller is not morally facile. His theoretical essays may lay down the law uncompromisingly ('alle andere Dinge müssen. Der Mensch ist das Wesen, welches will')[46] but this is an austere requirement, not a facile assumption. The trouble is perhaps that the theoretical statements and the dramatic moments of triumph have stuck in many minds while the torments and struggles that precede moral victory in the plays have not. No wonder; for to mark his splendidly engineered highpoints, Schiller created memorable phrases: 'Gott würdigt mich durch diesen unverdienten Tod, Die frühe, schwere Blutschuld abzubüssen'; 'Kurz ist der Schmerz und ewig ist die Freude'; 'Der freie Tod nur bricht die Kette des Geschicks'. These have long had an existence outside their context as part of the standard equipment of the cultivated. They compose by themselves an all too simple picture of Schiller's work. This is another problematic aspect of being a classic: the simple formula (it may even come to appear a no longer acceptable cliché) replaces the complex action and the real conflict which it epitomises. But in context, against Maria Stuart's final serenity must be set her long struggle with the temptation to escape into her old world of sensuality and power; against Johanna's joyful certainty, her painful expiation of a moral fault; against Don Cesar's noble sentiment the difficulty — still to come — of living, or rather dying, up to it.[47]

Max Piccolomini too is sometimes remembered for an all too prompt nobility. He does act morally, but not with ease. His loyalty to the Emperor costs him a struggle. He sees his duty clearly, but he needs Thekla's emotional support to help him renounce her:

.Sag, Thekla, dass du Mitleid mit mir hast,
Dich selber überzeugst, ich kann nicht anders

(Tod III,18)

The last four words are Luther's formula of spiritual conviction; but they are set, aptly, in a dependent clause which makes them anything but firm. As the moment of abandoning Wallenstein, and thereby losing his daughter, approaches, they recur less firm still in the form of a question:

O Gott! Wie kann ich anders? Muss ich nicht?
Mein Eid — die Pflicht —

(ibid.)

It is here that Max suffers his dark night of the moral conscience. He actually leaves the final decision to Thekla — and begs her, touchingly, not to demand too much:

Nicht
Das Grosse, nur das Menschliche geschehe.

(Tod III,21)

This is not the style of a 'Tugendheld'. Nor does moral high-mindedness inspire Thekla's decision for him, but rather the practical insight one lover has into the other's nature, the knowledge that he could never be happy with an act of betrayal on his conscience:

> Reue soll
> Nicht deiner Seele schönen Frieden stören
>
> (ibid.)

That Max consequently chooses to die only shows that the friendship and love he sacrificed meant as much to him as the duty he followed. Otto Ludwig's celebrated sneer that the Schillerian hero could not die without a regiment of cavalry to help him actually points up Schiller's right dramatic instinct. His picture of the hard world had space for some nobility − 'Um die gemeine Wirklichkeit der Dinge/Den goldnen Duft der Morgenröte webend', as Wallenstein says in his epitaph for Max − but not space for much. Max's death in battle returns us to the surrounding reality of war. Its undoubted moral impact is only implicit in the Greek-style report of real events (*Tod* IV,10). The technical alternative was to be *ex*plicit: a pre-suicidal soliloquy, say, with the action marking time while moral grandeur stood in the limelight. That is the kind of thing associated popularly with Schiller, but it is not what he did.

The moral idealism of Max and Thekla is thus both touchingly human and artistically integrated. This last requirement, vital to a dramatist who knew that morality by itself was 'empty',[48] is met equally in *Maria Stuart*. Maria's acceptance of past guilt and regeneration before death is very evidently a moral theme. Yet it is part of a dramatic interplay between the incompatible characters of the two queens and their worlds. Far from being self-sufficient, Maria's purification balances and sets off the corruption and ruthlessness of the political sphere from which she belatedly opts out. The dramatist's moral idea is as much part of the structure as is the contrast between the two characters, or the elegant symmetry of acts which alternately focuses on Maria and Elisabeth in a sequence a-b-a-b-a, with a coda to show the hollowness of Elisabeth's political victory. As in all good art, it is not the single figure or episode, much less any one resounding declaration, that carries the import of the work, but an overall balance and design. Maria's self-overcoming would not monopolise attention if one came to the play without presuppositions derived from Schiller's essays or his critics. Much more striking is his picture of political life, especially of the sacrifices it can require: not just the life of the vanquished, but the humanity of the victor.

To remember Schiller's heroic moments, then, and forget the very human complexities they arise from is to go against the rules of balanced reading. Yet it may still be asked why moral freedom was so central to his conception of tragedy. The answer is rooted in the period: his theory met a challenge which faced his age, and did so with materials the age laid to hand.

The challenge was tragedy itself. It was (and is) a paradox that something so primitive should enjoy such prestige. Why should we assemble to watch chance and men's own faults bring suffering and destruction on them? In what sense can we *enjoy* a type of work which is defined by disaster and, as a normal thing, recounts or shows us despair, madness, murder, incest, suicide? And if we do not enjoy it, why do we watch it and why do we think it not just permissible but a mark of culture to do so? The problem was especially teasing for a self-styled reasonable age, far removed from the ritual roots of drama. It could have rejected tragedy altogether as indecent, but this would have needed a radicalism few ages possess. In practice, tragedy's status was unshakeable; some accommodation with it, some apologia for it, was called for.

Lessing had offered two sorts of argument: the practical social one that the sight of suffering made men more compassionate; and the higher philosophical one that tragedy shows us how suffering fits into the larger plan of the divine 'Weisheit und Güte'.[49] This was unsatisfactory because it disallowed any play that did not offer metaphysical reassurance and also because it explained the mystery of tragedy by the even more impenetrable mystery of providence.

Schiller's approach is at first sight similar, since he explains the puzzle of tragedy by the paradox of the Sublime. But he was perceiving a link which bears examination; if there was to be a rational theory of tragedy, this was a plausible model.

The Sublime was a familiar term in eighteenth-century aesthetics. It was used to distinguish from Beauty (which meant anything pleasant, harmonious, easily and undisturbingly appealing) those objects which produced more mixed sensations — the vastness of the starry heavens, desert expanses, stormy seas, mountain crags, moonlit ruins, in short the stuff of the Gothic novel of the period. The paradox is plain in Burke's *Philosophical Enquiry* (1757), which speaks of the *'delightful horror* which is . . . the truest test of the sublime', and declines to call this pleasure 'because it turns on pain, and because it is different enough from any idea of positive pleasure.[50] But Burke does little to explain the paradox. Nor does Kant in his first essay on the problem.[51] But his mature *Kritik der Urteilskraft* has a full 'Analytik des Erhabenen', which contains the decisive insight that our rational response is what makes the strangely mixed experience pleasurable. Sublime objects make us aware of our physical powerlessness to resist, but also of 'ein Vermögen zu widerstehen von ganz anderer Art', i.e., a moral capacity, a rational self 'die nicht Natur ist'.[52] We can feel that no physical threat, no destruction of the things we are concerned for, need matter if it is a question of our highest principles.

This was a happy solution for rational men. They were not after all enjoying the pain element in 'sublime' experiences, but their own rational reflex which followed it so closely as to have been indistinguishable from it by minds less acute than Kant's. And this analysis offered a key to tragedy; for it would be quite proper to enjoy tragedy if its pleasure was likewise located not in the suffering portrayed but in the moral response which this inspired.

There is however an ambiguity: whose was the response? With the sublime, one and the same person felt the threat to his physical being and asserted a higher, rational principle. But in tragedy the pain is the hero's, the spectator only 'suffers' it at one remove, aesthetically mediated. It hardly justifies the spectacle of suffering to say that it makes the − substantially unharmed − spectator withdraw into his rational citadel. That would be a more superficial and more selfish reaction than the traditional 'pity and fear' of Aristotle, however interpreted. To justify tragedy on the 'sublime' model, the rational response had to be located where the physical suffering was, in the drama itself, in the hero. The spectator could then tolerate the sight of pain and take pleasure in the hero's capacity to rise above it. This would also incidentally be a lesson in how to act himself, an innoculation with adverse fate.

That in brief is Schiller's theory. It recognises the full reality of pain; when he says 'Je furchtbarer der Gegner, desto glorreicher der Sieg',[53] he means both halves equally. But it allows no doubt about the final result, for reason is 'eine Kraft, die jedem Widerstand überlegen ist'.[54] The protagonist must be morally self-aware, an Idealist as defined in the last section of *Über naive und sentimentalische Dichtung*, so as to meet the threat to his immediate interests (love, happiness, life − everything Schiller subsumes under 'Sinnlichkeit') by asserting his ultimate commitments (loyalty, integrity, purity − everything Schiller subsumes under 'Sittlichkeit'). Equally, the spectators must be morally educated, lest acts of sacrifice should seem to them merely foolish. Schiller's is thus, like Lessing's, an exclusive theory: it excludes a good many dramas, *Wallenstein* and many of Shakespeare's among them; and it consciously excludes from the enjoyment of tragedy the 'grosse Haufen' who will be blind to moral heroism.[55]

It is also surely blind itself, to the potential tragedy of moral help-lessness. Hence perhaps the unease of later generations with Schiller. For him, men are so necessarily moral beings, at least in potential, that he cannot conceive of a mere victim as the object of tragic pity: we turn away, he says, from unrelieved suffering and an absolute inactivity of reason 'mit Unwillen und Abscheu'.[56] One thinks of Büchner's Woyzeck who is so exclusively suffering Man, who has no reserves of reason when nature moves him to urinate or to murder, and who calls morality something only the rich can afford. It is clear why Büchner cried out against the idealist portrayal of man as 'die schmählichste Verachtung der menschlichen Natur'.[57] Woyzeck's total misery, or the relative passivity of other nineteenth-century dramatic figures in the grip of circumstances or character, may raise doubts whether Schiller's plays are properly tragic at all. Despite the suffering they portray and the reality of the struggle, can the atmosphere be tragic if the ending is a moral triumph?

But to say this would be to take 'tragic' as if it were an absolute and must mean only what — largely because of those nineteenth-century changes in outlook — it means for us now: blank disaster and the unremitting gloom of loss, waste and meaninglessness. True, such things have figured in tragedy, but so over the ages has much else: stoic resig-nation and religious serenity, divine retribution and divine forgiveness, revolt against suffering and wisdom achieved through suffering. 'Tragic' is thus a relative term, and there is less point in arguing about whose plays deserve it than in understanding its changed reference in different ages. The aims and assumptions governing Schiller's use of the form we know as tragedy are separated from those of Büchner, or Kleist, or Hebbel, not just by a period of years but by a watershed in intellectual history. His drama and theory are rational not through personal whim or narrow sympathy but because they were the product of an age which believed in Man's reason as a fact and as a supreme value.

This raises the question how permanent a classic can be if its ethos can be so clearly dated — and consequently can 'date'. To this there are several answers. The first is that any student of literature who is not locked in the limiting beliefs or prejudices of his own age should be able, by an act of empathy, to appreciate the forms which the outlook of another day generated. The quality of a classic lies not in surface topicality but in the relation between materials and possibilities on the one hand and achievement on the other. Secondly, the ethos of Schiller's plays is far from the whole story. They keep their place, effortlessly, on the German stage because they are magnificent theatre. Sometimes they suffer severe adaptation – but so does Shakespeare; adaptations show that a work is too vital to be ignored, that it compels directors to come to terms with it rather than stage recent works more compliant with the spirit of the present. Thirdly, an ethos seldom dates totally. It may bear the stamp of a particular period, but it is not on that account dead. The history of literature and thought is a progression, but only to the naive is it necessarily progress. For the historically informed and aware mind, it makes up a range of choices which remain possible and need not exclude each other. The vision of, say, Samuel Beckett is not more essentially right because it stands later in time and speaks (when not reduced to silence altogether) in a language that comes home to us as more real. Schiller's language of moral heroism may seem suspect to us now, but beneath it there are issues of a kind that do not go away. Dilemmas still occur, moral decisions still demand to be made, the world of *Realpolitik* still needs to be confronted with a world of moral values. Drama which grasps these matters as supremely well as Schiller's stands out as a landmark and has a permanent worth.

Finally the sheer volume and consistency of those ten years' work remain impressive as a human achievement against odds akin to those of a Schiller drama. Only a narrow literary approach can shut out human considerations of this kind from the judgement of a poet's work. In one of his earliest letters to Goethe, Schiller doubted whether his illness would leave him time to master his creative problems by a complete 'Geistesrevolution'. But, he says, 'ich werde tun, was ich kann, und wenn endlich das Gebäude zusammenfällt, so habe ich doch vielleicht das Erhaltungswerte aus dem Brande geflüchtet'.[58] It is typical of Schiller that he here sees his own body as the expendable housing for an essential content. The intense effort to rescue this from the fire is, in its own way, as much a classic as the literary productions of that final decade.

Notes

1. *Dichtung und Wahrheit*, HA 9, 283.
2. To Karl August, 28 March 1788.
3. Ibid.
4. *Italienische Reise*, 1 March 1788, HA 11, 525.

5. Ibid., 30 March 1787, HA 11, 226. The note of 1 February 1788 (HA 11, 516) makes plain that the problems lie in the later sections of the work – 'ich kann weder so endigen noch alles wegwerfen'.

6. To Herder, 10 August 1789.

7. Hans M. Wolff's ingenious reconstruction in *Goethes Weg zur Humanität* (Berne, 1951), is not persuasive because it takes any human complexity or flaw in the characters at once as an inconsistency left from an earlier version. For fuller criticism see Wolfdietrich Rasch, *Goethes Torquato Tasso* (Stuttgart, 1954), pp. 65ff and 187f.

8. Cf. *Satyros*, Act III: 'Habt eures Ursprungs vergessen,/Euch zu Sklaven versessen,/Euch in Häuser gemauert,/Euch in Sitten vertrauert,/Kennt die goldnen Zeiten/Nur aus Märchen, von weiten' (HA 4, 194f).

9. Cf. above, pp. 31f. In particular, the poem satirising the Baron (*Theatralische Sendung* V, 8) plays off mother nature against noble father and is a comic version of Tasso's sentiments in II, 3 quoted above. Cf. also *Sendung* V, 13 on the 'Begriff des Wertes einer von der Natur allein ausgestatteten Menschheit' which the nobility has lost.

10. See WA III, 1, 113-24. Goethe has gained 'viel Terrain in der Welt', but feels like a captured bird; he has learned 'Ordnung' but lacks 'Erfahrenheit'. His struggles and hopes are summed up in the Latin words 'nemo coronatur nisi certaverit ante' – quoted aptly the day after the first mention of *Tasso*, which was to be concerned with crowns of oak and laurel and how they are merited.

11. Cf. Rasch, *Goethes Torquato Tasso*, pp. 125ff., on 'Tassos Wahn und die Wirklichkeit'.

12. E.M. Wilkinson's '*Torquato Tasso*. The Tragedy of the Poet', in Wilkinson and Willoughby, *Goethe, Poet and Thinker* (1972) isolates certain speeches as poetry within the verse, products of Tasso's gift.

13. Reported as Goethe's view in Caroline Herder's letter to her husband, mid-March 1789.

14. Cf. Rasch, *Goethes Torquato Tasso*, p. 44: 'ein schöpferishes Vermögen . . . ist ein . . . Stück reiner Natur . . . ein Fremdes in den Ordnungen des Lebens, die nicht mehr reine Natur sind, sondern vom Ursprung entfernt'.

15. This assumption (ibid., p. 34) seems as dubious as the equation on the same page of the Ferrara court and society in general.

16. Cf. the letter cited in note 13.

17. Hofmannsthal, *Ausgewählte Werke* (Frankfurt a.M., 1957), II, 433, 435.

18. Goethe to Karl August, 16 February 1788.

19. He certainly felt this when he reworked these scenes for the completed *Faust I*. Cf. Goethe to Schiller, 5 May 1798.

20. Schiller to Goethe, 29 November 1794 and the reply of 2 December.

21. See the five letters exchanged between 22 and 27 June 1797, esp. Schiller's of 23 June.

22. Some critics have argued that the Gretchen tragedy came first and was developed into a Faust play. This seems implausible. That Faust should become the male lead in a 'bürgerliches Trauerspiel' is odd enough; but that the male lead in such a play should demand to become a Faust figure is scarcely conceivable.

23. The scenes certainly written by 1775 are known from Luise von Göchhausen's transcript, discovered in 1887 and published as *Goethes Faust in ursprünglicher Gestalt*, now usually called *Urfaust*. It is in no sense a 'version', but a record of work-in-progress (or, more strictly, work-in-abeyance). It consists of Faust's opening monologues and the Erdgeist scene; Faust's conversation with Wagner; Mephisto's with the Freshman; Auerbachs Keller; a brief scene 'Landstrasse' (later excised); and virtually the whole Gretchen tragedy.

24. They occur in 'Trüber Tag. Feld' (an *Urfaust* scene) and in 'Wald und

Höhle' (a 1790 addition); perhaps also implicitly in the Erdgeist's words 'Du gleichst dem Geist, den du begreifst,/Nicht mir!'

25. The main inconsistency is between the God/Mephisto and the Erdgeist/ Mephisto conceptions. There is uncertainty whether Mephisto is *a* devil or *the* Devil. There is a contradiction between the Erdgeist scene and Faust's declaration in 'Wald und Höhle' that the apparition gave him the key to understanding Nature. The moving of 'Wald und Höhle' from its place in the Fragment (after Gretchen's seduction) to its place in *Faust I* (before) leaves some lines hard to explain, e.g. Faust's 'So tauml' ich von Begierde zu Genuss,/Und im Genuss verschmacht' ich nach Begierde' (11. 3249; cf. also 3295f. and 3345ff). There are many other details, down to the minutest texture of the poetry – e.g. ll. 626f: 'In jenem sel'gen Augenblicke,/Ich fühlte mich so gross, so klein', where Faust is speaking of the Erdgeist apparition of moments before and, as Staiger points out (*Goethe* 2, 335), 'das "Jenem" enthüllt, fast rührend naiv, die Ferne eines Vierteljahrhunderts'.

26. There is no clear evidence a plan existed earlier. Eudo Mason's view that 'the idea we should have of how such a poet as Goethe works' is that he all along 'knows what he is about' is an understandable reaction to the fragmentising conjectures of some textual critics, but remains a pious assumption. It does not correspond to the idea we do have of how Goethe worked, and it begs important questions with the vague words 'knows what he is about'. See Mason, *Goethes "Faust", its Genesis and Purport* (Berkeley and Los Angeles, 1967), p. 108; and pp. 176, 234, for ways the assumption is applied to particular problems. The most balanced approach to the problems and text of *Faust I* is Staiger's chapter mentioned in note 25.

27. The consistency applies at every known stage of the genesis: lines 1770-5, here quoted from the text of *Faust I*, already occur in the Fragment, in a scene (itself fragmentary) standing at the end of the 'grosse Lücke'. It is not of course sure how much of this consistency was intuitive, how much design.

28. Mason, *Goethes Faust*, p. 190.

29. Cf. Ibid., pp. 238ff., on Gretchen's Christian character.

30. Goethe to Eckermann, 6 June 1831.

31. Recorded in Crabb Robinson's diary for August 13, 1812. Schiller's earlier identification was not unconscious; its theory is stated in a letter to Reinwald of 14 April 1783.

32. To Goethe, 28 November 1796. For the same notion in *Über naive und sentimentalische Dichtung*, see above p. 89.

33. Schiller to Humboldt, 21 March 1796.

34. Schiller to Goethe, 28 November 1796.

35. *Werke* IV, 681f.

36. Ibid., 490f.

37. Ibid., 589, 592.

38. Ibid., 688.

39. Schiller to Körner, 25 May 1792. That the dramatist's intuition then comes close to the historical truth – as established by documents not known in Schiller's day – is persuasively argued by the historian Golo Mann, 'Schiller als Historiker', *Jahrbuch der Schiller-Gesellschaft* IV (1960).

40. Schiller to Cotta, 30 November 1796.

41. Staiger, *Schiller*, pp. 304f. 312, shows well how sympathy for Wallenstein is created against the balance of moral probability.

42. See Benno von Wiese, *Schiller* (Stuttgart, ³1963), pp. 655 and 676f., a concluding summary which particularly muddies the waters.

43. Goethe, 'Die Piccolomini. Wallensteins Erster Teil', WA 40, 43f. This was written with Schiller's cooperation, which makes its view the more authoritative.

44. See *Tod* III, 3: 'Der eignen Kraft nicht fröhlich mehr vertrauend,/Wandt' er sein Herz den dunklen Künsten zu'. In contrast Schiller's *Geschichte des Dreissigjährigen Kriegs* implies (*Werke* IV, 491) that the astrologer Seni's influence was of longer standing.

45. Schiller to Goethe, 5 January 1798.

46. *Uber das Erhabene, Werke* V, 792.

47. Don Cesar's words, far from being a dying speech, are followed by some 200 lines more of exchanges with his mother and still incestuously loved sister. He craves to know that she wants him to live, but once sure ('Die Träne sah ich, die auch mir geflossen') he cannot after all live, for fear the brother he has killed will be posthumously more cherished than he: all in all, not a simple 'moral' motivation for suicide.

48. Schiller to Goethe, 27 February 1798: 'Bei dieser Gelegenheit [viz., work on *Wallenstein*] habe ich aber recht gefühlt, wie leer das eigentlich Moralische ist . . .'

49. On pity as a social virtue, see Lessing to Nicolai, 13 November 1756; on tragedy and the divine plan, see *Hamburgische Dramaturgie*, 79. Stück.

50. *A Philosophical Enquiry into the Origin of our Ideas of the Sublime and Beautiful* ed. J.T. Boulton (1958), pp. 73, 51. The idea of the Sublime goes back it is true, to a Greek text of the 1st century AD ('Longinus', *On the Sublime*); but up to the eighteenth century 'sublimity' meant an elevated literary treatment, and only now came to refer to a class of natural objects which provoked a characteristic response.

51. *Beobachtungen über das Gefühl des Schönen und Erhabenen* (1764) merely distributes experiences into the two categories according as they evoke 'eine angenehme Empfindung, die aber fröhlich und lächelnd ist' or 'Wohlgefallen, aber mit Grausen'. Illuminatingly, blondes do the first, brunettes the second. *Werke* II, 246, 252.

52. *Kritik der Urteilskraft* para. 28, *Werke* V, 333f. This means that sublime objects should really now be called 'erhebend' rather than 'erhaben'. Schiller alone makes this point explicit, in his *Zerstreute Betrachtungen über verschiedene ästhetische Gegenstände, Werke* V, 550. Kant's and Schiller's subdivisions of the Sublime ('mathematisch'/'dynamisch', 'theoretisch'/'praktisch'; 'Fassung'/'Handlung') are less crucial.

53. *Uber den Grund des Vergnügens an tragischen Gegenständen* (1792), *Werke* V, 364.

54. *Uber die tragische Kunst* (1792), *Werke* V, 377.

55. Cf. *Vergnügen . . ., Werke* V, 369: ' . . . dem grossen Haufen als ein empörender Widerspruch erscheinen'.

56. Cf. *Tragische Kunst, Werke* V, 392.

57. Through the mouthpiece of Lenz, in the story of that name. See Büchner, *Werke*, Hamburger Ausgabe, I, 87.

58. To Goethe, 31 August 1794.

8

CLASSICS: (3) POETRY

I

Goethe's poetry of the classical decade is like a serene high plateau. Beyond it rise the higher peaks of his late lyrical and philosophical poems, but it is itself already a mature achievement. We have seen what made it possible. Italy gave him certainties, Christiane emotional security in physical love, Schiller added a sense of community, clarity and firmness of purpose; he offset the moods of discouragement and carried Goethe with him in the execution of a literary programme. Of this Goethe's poetry forms a part, just as much as do the collaborative projects, the *Horen* and *Xenien*.

It docs so in a general way by living up to the high regard Schiller expressed in *Über naive und sentimentalische Dichtung*, and specifically by meeting important challenges that essay contained. Schiller said apropos Haller and Klopstock that a didactic poem in which the thought itself was poetic had yet to be written; arguably Goethe achieved this in his poems on the metamorphosis of plants and of animals. Schiller's argument culminated in the idea of an idyll which, unlike traditional pastoral, would not avoid the conflict of real and ideal. The full conception is little short of a poetic millennium, but Goethe went some way towards it in his narrative poem *Hermann und Dorothea* which balances the idyllic country-town setting and characters against the upheavals and continuing threat of the French Revolution. If we add to these poetic 'solutions' the earlier *Römische Elegien* which Schiller's essay could already refer to as a touchstone of true decency in erotic writing, it is clear that Goethe's poetry was an exploration — in large measure a conscious exploration — of the problems and possibilities of modern poetry as such.

This does not fit the legend of an 'unconscious' Goethe, always the happy sleepwalker and god-given creator. But that legend will not fit what we know of Goethe after Italy: his observations and reflections on art and nature, his deliberate application of aesthetic principles to the completion of old works and the conception of new, his sophisticated concept of style as an artistic consummation which rests 'auf den tiefsten Grundfesten der Erkenntnis, auf dem Wesen der Dinge, insofern es uns erlaubt ist, es in sichtbaren und greiflichen Gestalten zu erkennen'.[1] He is no longer the self-absorbed, self-expressive poet (although *mutatis mutandis* his theories are still true to that original nature); he is now the conscious, rational legislator for and creator of a culture.[2]

Can this broad intention really apply to individual poems? For where drama or narrative allow sustained statement, poetry renders transitory feeling; the poet makes sallies, he does not conduct campaigns. But this limitation falls away when his single insights and inspirations arise from a view of life as coherently conceived as it is deeply felt. Individual poems, each a 'Gelegenheitsgedicht' in Goethe's sense, are then related points composing a pattern. Even the most private utterance has general implications, as the *Römische Elegien*, in celebrating individual happiness, also asserted a human norm. They were not crudely didactic, they were exemplary. That is a quality central to our idea of a classic, and the claim to be exemplary is an undertone of this decade's poetry. It is suggested by the forms Goethe now predominantly uses, the classical hexameter and elegiac couplet with their serene movement and seemingly effortless control; but it is also there in what is said.

It can be positively truculent, as in the elegy 'Hermann und Dorothea' which answers Goethe's critics by turning each of their charges — the sexual frankness of the *Elegien*, the aggressiveness of the *Xenien*, the rejection of dogma in his art and science and of hypocrisy in his personal life — into so many reasserted values. More often the exemplary note is unobtrusive, values are suggested in the characters and relationships portrayed — in 'Alexis und Dora' with its evocation of new love, or on a larger scale in the epic *Hermann und Dorothea* with its ideal environment 'wo sich nah der Natur menschlich der Mensch noch erzieht'.[3] In particular we hear it whenever man is set in nature, not merely as his background but as the order to which he belongs. Thus in 'Amyntas' the hero is lovesick but does not in the end wish to be cured — a common enough motif in love poetry, but here the reasons go deeper than usual. Everything in nature reveals laws, telling him that he too is 'unter das strenge Gesetz ehrner Gewalten gebeugt'; and 'nature' includes the ivy that sucks the strength from its host-tree just as love is sapping his strength: 'der gefährliche Gast, der geliebteste'. In the *Vier Jahreszeiten* cycle, a less dramatic love is shown growing with the seasons and putting down the powerful roots of human habit;[4] while in 'Die Metamorphose der Pflanzen', the poet explains plant morphology to his puzzled mistress and ends by reflecting how their love too has grown 'aus dem Keim der Bekanntschaft' to the stage of 'Blüten und Früchte'.

These are not mere decorative metaphors. Like the allusions to natural processes in *Wilhelm Meister*, they grow from the philosophy of nature Goethe had evolved since the mid-eighties. They express the emotions of a man who feels at home in a world he believes he has understood — and understood to be, in a quite non-theological sense, ultimately benevolent. Its unchanging laws establish beneath the flux of phenomena a resilient order, itself perceptible; there is beauty both in individual forms and in the ceaseless movement of nature's play with them. Nature was thus very like the ideal work of art as Goethe and Schiller conceived it: richness and control in a perfect balance. No wonder Goethe put his scientific vision into poetry — it would have been strange if he had not. In 1798 he planned a grand didactic poem in emulation of Lucretius's *De rerum natura*, but he wrote only two short pieces, on the morphology of plants and of animals. Here the exhilaration of Goethe's understanding, his pleasure in communicating it, the clarity and flow of the exposition and the intrinsic beauty of his conceptions together create a sober excitement and a far richer aesthetic satisfaction than is normally achieved by didactic poems. (Nor incidentally do we need to make allowances for an outmoded content, since the vision of nature as a flux of forms rather than a collection of objects makes Goethe a respectable forerunner of evolutionary biology.)

'Die Metamorphose der Pflanzen' reveals the 'geheimes Gesetz' that produced the immense variety of plant species. It recreates the cycle of a plant from the time the 'ruhiges Leben' locked in the seed first interacts with the 'milde Feuchte' of earth's tranquil womb. But this is no ordinary plant; its leaves vary richly in type — 'ausgedehnter, gekerbter, getrennter in Spitzen und Teile', shapes not compatible in any single real plant. They are the options of plant growth as such; what we are watching is nature's inner principle operating in a symbolic model, the 'Urpflanze'. Aptly nature herself is celebrated at the high-point, when leaf has been refined into stalk and crowned by the splendour of bloom:

Also prangt die Natur in hoher, voller Erscheinung.

With the forming of fruit, nature closes the 'Ring der ewigen Kräfte', and a new cycle is begun, another ring to be linked to the first in the chain of continuity.

'Metamorphose der Tiere' celebrates nature's mechanism of control and compensation. Each animal is a complex of needs and potentialities: if it develops this organ in response to its environment, it will not

develop that one, for it cannot evolve in all directions without limit. It
is a quantum contained in a 'heiligen Kreise lebendiger Bildung', under
a law of internal adaptation and redistribution:

> Diese Grenzen erweitert kein Gott, es ehrt die Natur sie:
> Denn nur also beschränkt war je das Vollkommene möglich.

Over-development or marked advantage in one area must mean corresponding deficiency elsewhere in the animal. Goethe calls this the key to
all morphology; it is a sophisticated concept of balance between 'Macht
und Schranken', 'Willkür und Gesetz', 'Freiheit und Mass', resulting in a
'bewegliche Ordnung'. The close returns to man, declaring that no
higher conception is attainable by moral thinker, man of action or poet
than this of nature's self-correcting system. Its authority applies in any
sphere; it is exemplary.

Some of its applications in Goethe's thinking are well known – e.g.
the sonnet 'Natur und Kunst' speaks of 'Beschränkung' and 'Gesetz' as
preconditions for artistic mastery. But the vital application is to man's
most basic understanding of himself and his place in nature. In some
form, clearly, he must accept the limitations placed on him as a certain
kind of creature, and the limited span of his existence as an individual.
This is hardly a new idea – it is a commonplace of Christian and other
religious orthodoxies – but the real meaning of an idea depends on the
way it is treated, on image, tone and emphasis.

Goethe came nearest to an orthodox treatment in his early Weimar
years. 'Grenzen der Menschheit' (1781) sees man's limits and the gulf
fixed between divine and human existence in the image of the gods
watching the stream that eternally flows past them, while we are raised
then swallowed by the individual wave. Or again:

> Ein kleiner Ring
> Begrenzt unser Leben,
> Und viele Geschlechter
> Reihen sie dauernd
> An ihres Daseins
> Unendliche Kette.

These two images actually conflict: in the first, the gods are detached
spectators of man's brief life; in the second, successive generations
somehow make up the life of the gods, perhaps already an obscure
intuition that any reality beyond man must be the larger order he helps,

however minutely, to compose.

The ring image returns in both 'Metamorphose' poems; a ring sets limits to an animal's development, and the ring of the natural cycle becomes a link in the chain of plant life. That the smaller unit is part of the larger now makes exact sense. And the tone is very different from the slightly forced solemnity of 'Grenzen der Menschheit'. It is calm, yet vigorous, almost eager (the opening of the second line) in its acceptance of an order which transcends individual phenomena but also depends on them for its inherent life:

Und hier schliesst die Natur den Ring der ewigen Kräfte;
Doch ein neuer sogleich fasset den vorigen an,
Dass die Kette sich fort durch alle Zeiten verlänge
Und das Ganze belebt, so wie das Einzelne, sei.

The Goethe who wrote this has come far – or gone back, to that feeling of oneness with nature so strong in the poems before Weimar, 'Herbstgefühl' or 'Auf dem See'. But to go back thus equipped with understanding is not just a happy return, it is a spiral movement upwards, or (to use one of his own favourite concepts) 'Steigerung'.

Of course, neither of the 'Metamorphose' poems spells out the implications for man of the limits on individual existence. But one other poem does face up to human transience, and makes this common but almost always melancholy poetic theme yield a conclusion that goes beyond resigned acceptance to full affirmation. 'Dauer im Wechsel' (*c*.1803) might almost have been called 'Metamorphose des Menschen'. True, it begins outside man as an elegy on the fleetingness of blossom and leaf and fruit in their natural cycle; but the elegiac mood nourishes a highly consequential argument that soon passes to man in search of something lasting. Here Heraclitus's saying that you never step twice into the same river leads to the subtler point that it is never the same 'you' that does it – no longer now the same Goethe who delighted in Roman monuments, in love-making, in clambering about 'auf und unter Bergen'[5]:

Du nun selbst! Was felsenfeste
Sich vor dir hervorgetan,
Mauern siehst du, siehst Paläste
Stets mit andern Augen an.
Weggeschwunden ist die Lippe,
Die im Kusse sonst genas,

Jener Fuss, der an der Klippe
Sich mit Gemsenfreche mass.

The body that we think 'is' ourselves is as fluid as Heraclitus's river, and
so the imagery of water is apt — once again, more precisely so than in
'Grenzen der Menschheit', where a wave of the allegorical river of time
took Man under while the gods looked on. Here, the stuff of the human
body *is* the wave:

Und was sich an jener Stelle
Nun mit deinem Namen nennt,
Kam herbei wie eine Welle,
Und so eilt's zum Element.

Like all of nature, Man is not an object but a movement.

At least, his material substance is. That can and must be given up as
it hastens past in the common cyclic sequence. But hastens past —
what? The pursuit of something not transient in the flux of matter
arrives at the mystery of identity despite cell-change, in particular at an
identity that can create something permanent in an order different
from (though ultimately dependent on) that of nature:

Danke, dass die Gunst der Musen
Unvergängliches verheisst,
Den Gehalt in deinem Busen
Und die Form in deinem Geist.

It is a poet's answer, since not everyone's thought and feeling can
achieve permanence in art; but if we look beyond the specific terms, it
can apply in some measure to any human activity that leaves an individual creative imprint on the world.

The argument has been beautifully fashioned out of experiences
which hover between the particular and the general, the reality of past
pleasures and bodily states balancing the reflective awareness that they
are now lost except to memory. Perhaps no poem on the theme of
transience gives so strong an impression of satisfaction with life, or
allows so little sadness to creep in — the repeated 'Ach' in stanzas 1
and 2 is only a rhetorical preliminary to the final emphatic acceptance.

Where the 'Metamorphosen' are science rendered in poetry, 'Dauer
im Wechsel' is poetry informed by science. All three rest, in the words
of 'Metamorphose der Tiere', on 'Schauen' not 'Schwärmen'; yet all

three are rich in an emotion responsive to what is observed. 'Science' here does not mean cold abstraction. Goethe's evocation of plant growth affects us differently from a series of computer models, which in information-content it resembles; his animal poem ends by invoking 'die liebliche volle Gewissheit'; 'Dauer im Wechsel' unforcedly befriends an austere truth. These poems both reveal and are products of the 'Grundfesten der Erkenntnis'.

Life so understood and understanding so matched by feeling; the calm pleasure of continuous scientific and poetic exploration; the satisfaction of communicating its results, privately to Schiller and artistically in works of mature achievement — all this made up, in spite of some conflicts with an incorrigible public in Germany and the nagging disquiet about events in France and their sequel, a decade of fulfilment. Goethe surely came close to realising the ideal he conjured up in his essay on Winckelmann at the end of this decade: 'Wenn die gesunde Natur des Menschen als ein Ganzes wirkt, wenn er sich in der Welt als in einem grossen, schönen, würdigen und werten Ganzen fühlt, wenn das harmonische Behagen ihm ein reines, freies Entzücken gewährt . . .' — if all this were fulfilled, he says, might not the universe cry out for joy at having reached its goal? What else is the point of all the expenditure of suns and moons and planets and milky ways, of worlds existing and worlds in the making, 'wenn sich nicht zuletzt ein glücklicher Mensch unbewusst seines Daseins erfreut?'[6] The description fits, barring the word 'unbewusst'. For consciousness completes a yet higher state, splendidly conveyed in the phrase 'harmonisches Behagen', which mingles the music of the spheres with the most earthly contentment;[7] and the poet's articulation of his happy state makes up for the actual silence of the universe. In all this he is, once more, exemplary. Not, however, in the sense of an example which can easily be followed and achieved again. That too is part of the meaning of a classic.

II

'Dass Euch mein Gedicht Freude machte, war mir sehr angenehm zu hören. Aber gegen Goethen bin ich und bleibe ich eben ein poetischer Lump'.[8] Schiller's response to praise from the Körners was not false modesty: his mind was settled about Goethe's superiority as a poet. But we should not simply take over (as has often happened) a verdict which was natural in him. A just comparison must first recognise that the two men wrote poetry of radically different kinds. A single notion of what 'lyrical poetry' is will not do as a basis for judgement. Indeed, Schiller hardly seems to have considered himself a lyrical poet. He could describe one of his poems as 'zu subjektiv *wahr*, um als eigentliche Poesie gelten zu können',[9] while earlier he had said that the lyrical genre was for him an exile, not a conquered province and called it 'das kleinlichste und undankbarste [Fach] unter allen'.[10] His attempts to legislate for it in the essays on Bürger and Matthisson were not very successful, and not even up to some insights of criticism in his own day.[11] It still perplexed him in theory long after he had accepted the authority of Goethe's poetry in practice; how could language, a medium of conceptual generality, render feelings and intuitions unique to one individual? Experience showed it could, yet by rights it ought to have been impossible.[12] As late as 1801 he is still seeking the inner necessity which must somehow lie behind the contingent elements of lyrical poetry.[13]

Clearly then we have to take Schiller's poetry on its own terms, not reject it for failing to be 'lyrical' in a way it never set out to be. It was frankly a poetry of ideas. Yet it must be insisted, against the background of eighteenth-century philosophical verse – Haller's austere reflections, say, or the popular didacticism of Tiedge's *Urania* – how much Schiller's was a *poetry* of ideas. Ideas were his element, and he responded to them poetically as other men respond to love and nature. Körner early noted that the richer the ideas, the more musical Schiller's verse became.[14] Certainly his rhythms and phrasing at their best have the characteristic of poetry, that they induce in the reader an emotion not explicable by the mere idea-content of the words. Thus, in 'Das Ideal und das Leben', the phrase describing the gods' eternal youthfulness – 'Wandellos im ewigen Ruin' – has as much verbal magic as any Romantic effect. The grandeur of its dramatic contrast may be rhetorical (as are many of Shakespeare's greatest effects) but the pathos of diction and cadence springs from an emotional response to an idea. Under the splendid words we feel the ache of mortality. Again, the line which ends the elegy 'Der Genius' – 'Einfach gehst du und still durch die eroberte Welt' – has a much more powerful and complex effect than the proposition that naive genius conquers all. That statement would inform us; Schiller's line enacts the process and moves us, turning the idea into an (aptly simple) movement. It opens emphatically yet unforcedly with the crucial word 'einfach', but by separating it from its companion-adverb 'still' it undoes any notion that genius systematically seeks effects; by the past participle 'erobert' it suggests an unquestioned *fait accompli* – genius passes serenely through its domain, unaware that it has conquered; and it so disposes words and concepts as to marry their sense with the potentially wistful rhythms of the classical pentameter.

There is similar matching of sound and movement to sense in some less familiar lines of the elegy 'Die Geschlechter':

> Tief verstummet die lärmende Jagd, des rauschenden Tages
> Tosen verhallt, und leis sinken die Sterne herab.

And where 'Das Lied von der Glocke' modulates into idyll, Schiller's picture of the herds returning at dusk uses the lightest of touches to evoke the animals' beauty and mass and domesticated strength:

> Und der Rinder
> Breitgestirnte, glatte Scharen
> Kommen brüllend,
> Die gewohnten Ställe füllend.[15]

Everything that is achieved in these examples is done by poetic means. Only their subordination to the larger strategy of a philosophical subject distinguishes them from the work of poets who deal in purely lyrical themes.

This shows what Schiller consciously strove to do. He knew ideas alone would not make poetry, any more than morals alone would make drama. He unashamedly valued ideas — when Wieland objected that 'Die Künstler' was not a poem, Schiller insisted that it was, and no worse a poem for having qualities that made it *more* than a poem.[16] Yet he could dismiss a major statement of his own ideas, 'Das Ideal und das Leben', as a 'blosses Lehrgedicht' by comparison with the elegy 'Der Spaziergang' where all his faculties had worked together 'als Eine Kraft', ideas had been kept at a constant poetic level, and — most important — he had achieved 'poetische Bewegung'.[17]

The idea of movement seems a fair criterion for the success of philosophical poetry as poetry. Ideas are essentially static, and to expound them is as mechanical and arid a task for poetry as describing a static object. Lessing had brilliantly explained in his *Laokoon* why it is that poetry, an art of succession in time, cannot and should not describe objects coexistent in space without translating their state into motion or effect — as Homer, with right instinct, had described the shield of Achilles in the making, and the beauty of Helen in its impact on the elders of Troy. Ideas similarly must be translated into situation, emotion, attitude, story; the poet must draw on myth, speak with other voices than his own, use dialogue — anything to avoid presenting ideas direct, as if preaching. For not only would this be at odds with the liberal nature of art, certainly of art as Goethe and Schiller saw it; it is also a fact of experience that without some such means to create movement, the poetic temperature remains low, language remains prosaic, lacking the friction with a material subject which will strike a spark.

Schiller's poems illustrate this, negatively and positively: 'Licht und Wärme', 'Hoffnung', 'Breite und Tiefe', 'Die Worte des Glaubens' and 'Die Worte des Wahns', all begin and end as straightforward statement, lacking inner tension or poetic concentration. Their only gesture is the wagging finger, relieved only by a dialectical relation between two of them, 'Die Worte des Glaubens' and 'Die Worte des Wahns'. The openings are bald assertion: 'Der bessre Mensch tritt in die Welt/Mit fröhlichem Vertrauen . . .'; 'Es reden und träumen die Menschen viel/ Von bessern künftigen Tagen . . .'; 'Es glanzen viele in der Welt,/Sie wissen von allem zu sagen . . .' And so on.

In contrast, 'Poesie des Lebens' opens with an emotional and intellectual attitude which is later countered by another; the words ' "Wer möchte sich mit Schattenbildern weiden . . ." ' is dramatic speech, and draws us into a situation. So does the single word of invitation that opens 'Der Tanz', making us the spectators of an unfolding pattern, not the readers of a disquisition:

> Siehe, wie schwebenden Schritts im Wellenschwung sich die Paare
> Drehen, den Boden berührt kaum der geflügelte Fuss.

Other openings — 'Ist der holde Lenz erschienen?' ('Klage der Ceres'), 'So willst du treulos von mir scheiden' ('Die Ideale'), 'Windet zum Kranze die goldenen Ähren' ('Das Eleusische Fest') — all use the same technique of propelling the reader *in medias res*. Sometimes the single speaking voice of the poet can create situational angle and raise the temperature of the language above prose by something like the same method: 'Selig, welchen die Götter, die gnädigen, vor der Geburt schon/Liebten . . .' ('Das Glück'); or 'Sagt, wo sind die Vortrefflichen hin . . .' ('Die Sänger der Vorwelt'). Even 'Das Ideal und das Leben', before it settles into sustained exposition and a long alternation of 'Wenn' and 'Aber' stanzas, manages to concentrate much of its argument in a first line which is placid yet charged with emotion: 'Ewigklar und spiegelrein und eben . . .'

'Poetic movement' means setting an idea in an emotional context or an imagined situation that the reader can participate in; the above ways of doing it are sometimes quite small, often traditional technical adjustments. Schiller also uses two larger-scale means. One is the ballad for which he is famous — justly so, for his narrative skill is supreme, and has only come to be underrated because his total mastery makes the thing look easy. The ballads, ostensibly at least, teach morality by historical or fictional example; we shall glance later at their place in Schiller's intellectual scheme. The other larger-scale means is to resolve an abstract idea into a real or imaginary movement through time. 'Die Künstler' takes the Enlightenment tenet that beauty is ultimately in harmony with reason and truth and shows the principle at work in history: savage, sensuous, pre-rational man was led along the right path by beauty, the work of artists. The rise of art is traced from crude beginnings to the pinnacle of man's rational maturity in a triumphantly celebrated present — 1789, almost the last moment of philosophical self-satisfaction before the French revolutionary Terror shook Enlightenment beliefs to their foundations. 'Die Götter Griechenlands' similarly creates depth of perspective, not by narrating conjectured history, but by referring constantly to two widely separated ages. It evokes now the mythology of Greece, now the modern beliefs which have replaced it, and laments the very different feeling for life these impose. Both are earlier poems, but the Classical decade has others of the kind to show — the walk through time and the stages of civilisation in 'Der Spaziergang'; a mythical version of the same theme with the goddess Ceres as the civiliser of Man in 'Das Eleusische Fest'; the conspectus of life's phases and the activities of social man in 'Das Lied von der Glocke'.

All this may make the creation of 'poetic movement' seem a purely technical matter: the poet is clear about what he wants to say and consciously shapes ideas into art. To some extent and in particular poems that may be true, but it is not the whole truth; the full picture makes Schiller's poetry more interesting and more moving. His ideas were more often *not* clear when he began to write, as he more than once insisted — e.g. apropos 'Die Künstler'. What he began with was emotion pressing for expression through a not yet determined material, and a vague sense of its right music: 'das Musikalische eines Gedichts schwebt mir weit öfter vor der Seele, als der klare Begriff von Inhalt, über den ich oft kaum mit mir einig bin'. Indeed, poetic creation itself had its roots in 'eine gewisse musikalische Stimmung'.[18] Körner's observation that rich ideas seemed to provoke Schiller's most musical verse perhaps touched on a different and deeper relation: the 'musical' element was not, or not only, a response to ideas, it could actually precede them in the poetic process and be the motive force behind their shaping. Far from putting clear-cut ideas into the receptacle of verse, Schiller was exploring ideas and their emotional feel through rhythm, image and the groping development of a poetic argument. Only when this was complete could it be matched against the initial mood and impulse; it might then accord with it or diverge from it totally.[19] Either way, clarity was more often the achievement of Schiller's poetry than its starting-point.

And even then it was a clarity of single poetic statements. Do they constitute a larger whole? Not by simple addition. Philosophical poetry originating, as Schiller's did, in inchoate emotions is a very different thing from philosophy itself. A changed mood will find expression in a new insight; one and the same problem will provoke varying, even conflicting, responses. 'Die Künstler' and 'Die Götter Griechenlands' are typical examples. In the first, beauty is an embodiment of truth, a vital stage in man's evolution as a rational creature, 'Frei durch Vernunft, stark durch Gesetze'. The pure white light of truth is refracted in the many forms of beauty, but the coloured rays finally reunite into one. The poem affirms all this as part of a 'weisen Weltenplane'. Yet 'Die Götter Griechenlands' says virtually the reverse. Truth is harsh. The poet yearns for the time when the beauty of mythic imaginings concealed it — 'Da der Dichtkunst malerische Hülle/Sich noch lieblich um die Wahrheit wand'. Every part of nature was then personalised as wood-nymph, stream-nymph, god; men saw Helios in his golden chariot where now 'Seelenlos ein Feuerball sich dreht'. Fate, necessity, death were blessedly wrapped in an anthropomorphic veil and were the more bearable for that. Now nature is empty and silent, 'die entgötterte Natur'; the old gods are no more use to a world that has put away childish things: 'Die, entwachsen ihrem Gängelbande,/Sich durch eignes Schweben hält'. This contrast of ancient and modern is only very partially the attack on Christianity it was seen as; it is just as much the lament of a scientifically literate agnostic who knows with his reason that the universe is in truth a cold place and that anything that gives it warmth and beauty is an illusion. The subject of the two poems is the same: the relation between appearance and truth. The attitudes and emotions they express are diametrically opposed.

Is this perhaps simple inconsistency, even artistic irresponsibility towards ideas?[20] Not at all. Each poem is true to a mood, and both moods are valid responses to experience as observed and reflected on; they are emotional interpretations of the world. That they diverge is not a flaw, but a characteristic of the poet. There is nothing remotely similar in Goethe's mature poetry — though his youthful 'Prometheus' and 'Ganymed' offer an analogy — because his temperament was now in harmony with itself and the world. Schiller's was not. The result is a poetry which, so far from being straightforwardly moral and didactic, proves to be profoundly dialectical, that is, it argues for and against, it asserts and doubts and re-asserts. If, when contrary statements are set side by side, the conflict can be resolved, then such poetry may come to have a 'system'. Schiller's does not; conflict persists and leaves only the equilibrium of tension.

To see this, we need only pursue the problem of truth and reason and their relation to the world of experience. In Schiller's positive moods, truth is an absolute good. In an early poem, 'Elysium', it is part of the paradisal state: 'Wahrheit reisst hier den Schleier entzwei'. This is the view 'Die Künstler' takes up. 'Die Macht des Gesanges' then makes truth the remover of all masks, an unquestionable value at least when set against deliberate deception: 'Und vor der Wahrheit mächtgem Siege/Verschwindet jedes Werk der Lüge'. And the poem 'An Goethe' affirms that art can delight us with its profound truth — 'Sie weiss durch tiefe Wahrheit zu entzücken'. But *is* truth delightful in itself? Can we live with it when we have it? The first speaker in 'Poesie des Lebens' scorns the false consolations of all 'Schein' and demands the naked truth, as a preparation for accepting the ideas of duty and necessity. But the second speaker pictures with horror a world from which all 'Schein' has been removed; without dream to veil it, 'Die Welt scheint was sie ist, ein Grab'. His examples of beneficent illusion are largely mythological figures — to that extent he is repeating the idea of 'Die Götter Griechenlands'; Schiller has gone beyond that poem in that 'Poesie des Lebens' brings together his conflicting attitudes to truth in one dialogue. Yet he still does not resolve the conflict. The second voice carries more weight by speaking last and longer, and is apparently the poet's own voice, but is not resoundingly the victor in the debate. On the idea that truth is like a basilisk eye — 'Ergreift dich die Versteinerung' — the poem dies away, as if the image had petrified the poet's own thought.

The question ramifies into ethics. Is there a moral truth, and how does it stand to reality? Is the world itself moral, or open to moral influence, so that noble actions are a right response to living in it? Schiller's ballads seem to say a resounding 'yes'. Art and nature, the power of drama and the return of the cranes, combine to reveal the murderers of Ibykus. The tyrant Dionysius in 'Die Bürgschaft' is moved and converted by an act of fidelity: ' "die Treue, sie ist doch kein leerer Wahn" '. A pious act by the Graf von Habsburg brings blessings, including election to the imperial throne, through 'das göttliche Walten'. The pious Fridolin is saved from a ghastly death: ' "Mit dem ist Gott und seine Scharen" ' ('Der Gang nach dem Eisenhammer'). The wilful knight in 'Der Kampf mit dem Drachen' adds humility to bravery, and is promptly rewarded. The answers are firm, even pat. The world seems readily malleable to moral acts. This, like the simplified boiling-down of the dramas, makes the 'popular' Schiller. And it is true that the discordant note which even the ballads contain is not obtrusive. Yet once heard, it tends to undo the confident assertions of the best-known ballads. The inexorable sea swallows Hero and Leander and finally 'giesst/Aus der unerschöpften Urne/Seinen Strom, der ewig fliesst'; Cassandra cries out 'Wer erfreute sich des Lebens,/Der in seine Tiefen blickt!'; 'Der Taucher' sees unspeakable horrors in the depths, to explore which is hubris; and it is the implacable depths that menacingly send back the ring Polykrates has sacrificed to them. A poet may speak truer, may be more profoundly himself, in the configurations and images he inclines to than in his reflective utterances. These images of water and dangerous depths join with others in the philosophical poems to make a pattern that belies the balladeer. 'Der spielende Knabe' pictures the baby on the safe island of its mother's lap yet starkly suggests the imminent reality of life:

Liebend halten die Arme der Mutter dich über dem Abgrund,
    Und in das flutende Grab lächelst du schuldlos hinab.

To know that reality, a grim descent is the only way. The second of the 'Sprüche des Konfuzius' allegorises the three dimensions of space and points down into the essence of things: 'Und im Abgrund wohnt die Wahrheit'. Hence the innocent in 'Der Genius' can say to his philosopher friend, 'du bist in diese Tiefen gestiegen,/Aus dem modrigten Grab kamst du erhalten zurück'. Such survival is not certain. The young would-be philosopher addressed in 'Einem jungen Freund' is told that, if he is not sure of his inner mission, he should flee 'den lockenden Rand, ehe der Schlund dich verschlingt'.

The ballads then, as usually read, are an optimistic façade. They are not the world as Schiller believes it to be, perhaps hardly the world as moral acts might collectively make it — the moral victories here are less hard-won than those of Iphigenie or of Schiller's own tragic heroes. Perhaps we should see the ballads as themselves a corpus of 'Schein', created to cover a truth that would not be bearable and to provide some encouragement. They were consciously popular works in design, redeemed by those regular unobtrusive signs that, if Schiller was whistling in the dark to keep people's spirits up, he never forgot how dark it was. We thus have an exoteric and an esoteric doctrine; for 'Die Worte des Wahns' expressly denies what the ballads suggest, namely that nobility can expect reward — 'dass das buhlende Glück/Sich dem Edeln vereinigen werde'. Does all this mean that we have settled the antinomy, and that the dark side is the real Schiller? Are we to read 'Die Ideale' as authoritative — Schiller's record of how he lost the ideals and beliefs of his youthful 'goldene Zeit' and now has only friendship to console him and work to occupy him when he asks the chilling question 'Wer folgt mir bis zum finstern Haus?' A reduced Schiller indeed, but the real Schiller nevertheless, if we are to judge by what he said of the poem's aptly flat close: 'Es ist das treue Bild des menschlichen Lebens, der Rhein der bei Leyden im Sande verloren geht'.[21]

It certainly is the 'real' Schiller in one sense: the Schiller who recognised what objective realities were and to whom the realist Goethe felt closest — 'Die Ideale' was Goethe's favourite among Schiller's poems to date.[22] It is the Schiller who wrote the equally disenchanted epigrams 'Erwartung und Erfüllung', 'Menschliches Wirken', 'Das gemeinsame Schicksal', where final wisdom is made up of remnants and resignation; the Schiller whose burgher bell has to proclaim 'dass nichts bestehet,/ Dass alles Irdische verhallt'; whose 'Punschlied' declares that 'Herb ist des Lebens/Innerster Kern'; and who concludes a poem on 'Die Gunst des Augenblicks', that theme so rich for lyrical poets and so endlessly generous to Goethe, with the grim quatrain:

> So ist jede schöne Gabe
> Flüchtig wie des Blitzes Schein,
> Schnell in ihrem düstern Grabe
> Schliesst die Nacht sie wieder ein.

Yet there is a Schiller even beyond this 'real' Schiller who has seen ideals and illusions crumble. It was precisely that pessimistic poem 'Die Ideale', that he said was too subjectively true to be real poetry, for in it 'das Individuum befriedigt . . . ein Bedürfnis, es erleichtert sich von einer Last'.[23] In other words, to let oneself be overwhelmed by recognised objective realities was for Schiller too *sub*jective, too much a defeat by one mood. Of course life was 'really' like that; any ideal — of hope, belief, moral principle — had to be created from one's inner resources. That was the definition of an ideal. The poems 'Die Hoffnung', and 'Die Worte des Glaubens' and 'des Wahns' insist on this:

> Es ist nicht draussen, da sucht es der Tor,
> Es ist *in* dir, du bringst es ewig hervor.

The reward must be inherent in the ideal itself and the mode of life it inspires, something Schiller knew and said before ever he read Kant. The pre-classical poem 'Resignation' puts it mercilessly:

> Du hast *gehofft*, dein Lohn ist abgetragen,
> Dein *Glaube* war dein zugewognes Glück.
> Du konntest deine Weisen fragen,
> Was man von der Minute ausgeschlagen
> Gibt keine Ewigkeit zurück.

Schiller's was thus the dialectic of a mind that constantly strives to affirm, and as constantly doubts; 'des Zweifels unsterbliche Hydra' was one of the facts of the spiritual life that the would-be philosopher had to be warned against ('Einem jungen Freund'). One might speak then of an initial idealism, of a clear-sightedness that dispelled illusion, of a new creative idealism beyond this, and of doubt lurking to question even that. But to think of it thus as a chronological sequence would be too simple, certainly in regard to the last three named. Rather, Schiller's poetic mind was equally open at different moments to changing moods, and gave each as eloquent an expression as his poetic means allowed. It is the continual oscillation that makes his poetry different from his philosophical system as expounded in his prose essays: however eloquent and poetic in phrasing these may be, they suppress the more volatile emotions in order to argue a consistent position. In the poetry, the emotions associated with thought are set free. Schiller is thus a poet of ideas, but also of the human strength and weakness that must sustain them. If we want an image in which to sum up this poetry, as Goethe's suggested a serene high plateau, it is provided by Schiller himself in 'Der Spaziergang'. The walker emerges from woods high on the mountainside, there is a view into the far distance and a dizzy height above and below him — all, in the eighteenth-century sense, sublime — and he has only a slender man-made security to carry him on his way:

Unabsehbar ergiesst sich vor meinen Blicken die Ferne,
Und ein blaues Gebirg endigt im Dufte die Welt.
Tief an des Berges Fuss, der gählings unter mir abstürzt,
Wallet des grünlichten Stroms fliessender Spiegel vorbei.
Endlos unter mir seh ich den Äther, über mir endlos,
Blicke mit Schwindeln hinauf, blicke mit Schaudern hinab.
Aber zwischen der ewigen Höh und der ewigen Tiefe
Trägt ein geländerter Steig sicher den Wandrer dahin.

If struggle and disharmony were Schiller's natural inheritance, we know how longingly he looked on at the harmony denied him. 'Das Glück' and 'Der Genius' are love-poems to a happier human type. His theory sets comedy above his own genre of tragedy because it can create in us the serene 'Zustand der Götter', where tragedy only makes suffering heroes.[24] Only if Schiller had realised the grand project for a 'sentimentalische Idylle' which he sketched to Humboldt[25] would all conflict have been removed from his own rendering of human experience. He planned to portray the marriage in Olympus between Hercules and Hebe — the human hero, raised now to the status of demi-god, and the goddess of beauty and youth. It was an apt conception: the labours of Hercules provided Schiller's poetry with images of struggle, essentially his own spiritual and intellectual struggle.[26] To have fully realised the apotheosis of Hercules in poetry would have transcended that struggle and his own poetic limitations.

Schiller never wrote the poem, nor have sketches for it survived. We do however have at the close of 'Das Ideal und das Leben', which is shaped by the contrast of human struggle and divine ease, a portrayal of Hercules crossing the line from mortal to immortal after his immense labours. This transition and transfiguration was the nearest Schiller could get to abandoning struggle and entering upon harmony. It is itself a moment of high poetic excitement, splendidly brought about by the way the penultimate stanza, most unusually in Schiller's poetry, is not end-stopped. Instead it opens out into the final one — an apt way to render the very point of transition — by a parallel construction. Labours have been heaped on the moral Hercules

Bis sein Lauf geendigt ist —

Bis der Gott, des Irdischen entkleidet,
Flammend sich vom Menschen scheidet
Und des Äthers leichte Lüfte trinkt.

Froh des neuen, ungewohnten Schwebens,
Fliesst er aufwärts, und des Erdenlebens
Schweres Traumbild sinkt und sinkt und sinkt.

Des Olympus Harmonien empfangen
Den Verklärten in Kronions Saal,
Und die Göttin mit den Rosenwangen
Reicht ihm lächelnd den Pokal.

These superb lines are a glimpse of the promised land to which so much of Schiller's poetry and critical thinking looks forward, but a glimpse only. What lay beyond the moment of transition was no longer Schiller.

III

Poetry at its best not only treats themes of perennial interest, it also gives a sense of what it was like to be alive, emotionally and intellectually alert, at a particular time and in a particular place — of how the world looked and felt to men, and of what it was then possible to believe, desire, and conjecture about experience. Goethe and Schiller, writing at a time when poetry had not yet withdrawn from the major areas of developing thought or secluded itself in private concerns and private language, make a conscious attempt in their great decade to penetrate and portray the world as it was and the ways it had become so, as these things were understood by the scientific, historical and philosophical thought of their day — in the forefront of which, it should be remembered, they themselves stood. Indeed, they were involved in it to a depth of specialisation which makes one admire their lucid poetic presentation the more. The grand intellectual survey their poetry contains is an important part of their joint programme. To the extent that poetry is a more immediate, less fictive projection of feeling than drama or the novel, it provides a bedrock of seriousness for a world of 'Spiel' and 'Schein'.

Yet at that depth, the poetry itself cannot be a collaborative venture. Goethe and Schiller might agree aesthetic principles, lay bare the laws of epic, make the novel respond to joint trial and reflection. They could compose satirical epigrams together and stimulate each other to produce ballads. But in the forms that reach down to the deeper poetic sensibility, every poet sees the world through different eyes — Goethe as a 'heiliges Rätsel' and a 'bewegliche Ordnung', Schiller as 'des Zufalls grausende Wunder'. However often we arc compelled to say the names together, Goethe and Schiller do not mingle and merge into one. They remain, despite all we have seen of a truly remarkable collaboration, each an unalterably individual voice.

Notes

1. *Einfache Nachahmung, Manier, Stil* (1789), HA 12, 32. The essay is devoted to the visual arts, but these had been from Goethe's 'Sturm und Drang' days (see the poems sectionalised in HA 1 as 'Künstlergedichte') the medium in which he discussed general questions of creation and criticism.

2. See the fine chapter of Gundolf's *Goethe* headed 'Klassizismus und Rationalismus', which sums up the work of this phase as 'Bildungspoesie höchster Art' (ed. cit., p.461).

3. The phrase is from the elegy 'Hermann und Dorothea', applied to the epic of the same name.

4. Cf. the epigrams 'Wie im Winter die Saat . . .' and 'Neigung besiegen ist schwer', especially the way, in the latter, form and sense pivot on the carefully placed word 'wurzelnd'.

5. Cf. Goethe to Jacobi, 9 June 1785: 'Hier bin ich auf und unter Bergen und suche das Göttliche in herbis et lapidibus'.

6. HA 12, 98.

7. Etymologically, 'Behagen' contains the idea of being protected and secure, and is thus close in feeling to the word 'geborgen' which we saw used in a crucial context in the *Römische Elegien* (above, p. 67).

8. Schiller to Körner, 27 June 1796, apropos 'Klage der Ceres'.

9. Schiller to Wilh. v. Humboldt, 7 September 1795, apropos 'Die Ideale'.

10. Schiller to Körner, 25 February 1789. Even the idea of a 'conquest', of which Schiller falls short, implies that a harmonious relation with lyric poetry was not conceivable.

11. Cf. Käte Hamburger, 'Schiller und die Lyrik', *Jahrbuch der deutschen Schiller-Gesellschaft*, XVI (1972).

12. To Goethe, 27 February 1798. This problem, first posed in *Kallias* (*Werke* V, 432; see above p. 113), is at its most acute in lyrical poetry.

13. To Goethe, 27 March 1801.

14. Körner to Schiller, 25 April 1788, apropos 'Die Götter Griechenlands'.

15. It is striking that as fine an interpreter of poetry as Emil Staiger can say of this passage: 'So ist es, unwiderruflich; oder: so soll es sein, so will es der Dichter, der im Namen der Menschheit spricht' (*Schiller*, p.184). Surely here a set attitude to Schiller, and a cliché one at that, prevents poetry getting a fair reading. Staiger does however allow (p.203) that Schiller wrote the finest single elegiac pentameter in German.

16. To Körner, 25 February and 9 March 1789.

17. Schiller to Körner, 21 September and 3 October 1795 and to Humboldt, 29 November 1795. Goethe told Schiller (6 October 1795) that 'die sonderbare Mischung von Anschauen und Abstraktion, die in Ihrer Natur liegt, zeigt sich jetzt [viz. in 'Der Spaziergang'] in vollkommenem Gleichgewicht'.

18. See to Körner, 25 February 1789 and 25 May 1792; and to Goethe, 18 March 1796.

19. Cf. to Körner, 25 May 1792, where Schiller says that what first drove him to write 'Die Künstler' was the very part cut out of the final text; and to Goethe, 27 March 1801 on the relation between 'die erste dunkle Totalidee' of a work and the 'vollendete Arbeit'.

20. Cf. Staiger, *Schiller* pp.160ff.
21. To Humboldt, 7 September 1795.
22. Ibid.
23. Ibid.
24. From a sketch in Schiller's Nachlass, 'Tragödie und Komödie', *Werke* V, 1018.
25. To Humboldt, 29/30 November 1795.
26. Hebe and Hercules appear in 'Die Götter Griechenlands' (first version, stanzas 9 and 18) as examples of the mythic imagination. 'Das Ideal und das Leben' builds up to its conclusion with allusions to some of Hercules' exploits — the fight with the Nemean lion and with the hydra. The poem 'Einem jungen Freund, als er sich der Weltweisheit widmete' then speaks, as we saw, of the courage needed 'mit des Zweifels unsterblicher Hydra zu ringen'; 'Würde der Frauen' uses the hydra image for man's unending conflict of wishes; and that other poem of doubt and re-assertion, 'Die Worte des Wahns', imagines the enemy of justice and good as the giant Antaeus whom Hercules had to strangle in mid-air because he got new strength each time he touched the earth:

> Und erstickst du ihn nicht in den Lüften frei,
> Stets wächst ihm die Kraft auf der Erde neu.

(The 'Lüfte'/'Erde' antithesis is very apt for the opposition between idealism and earthly evil.) Then in 'Dithyrambe' the poet pictures *himself* being taken up into Olympus and receiving the cup of nectar from Hebe, as Hercules does at the close of 'Das Ideal und das Leben'. If Chiron's celebration of Hercules in the second act of *Faust II* (lines 7381ff) is a cryptic allusion of Goethe's to Schiller, as Thomas Mann suggested in his Schiller essay (*Gesammelte Werke* 1960, IX, 938), it seems that Schiller may also have worked with the mythic identification himself — 'Dithyrambe', after all, was written after 'Das Ideal und das Leben' and can hardly have repeated its pattern unknowingly. Yet even here Schiller remains conscious of the limits of such identification: the last stanza of 'Dithyrambe' — 'Netz ihm die Augen mit himmlischem Taue,/Dass er den Styx, den verhassten, nicht schaue,/Einer der Unsern sich dünke zu sein' — and the poem's original title, 'Der Besuch', make clear that for him any apotheosis would be illusory, any escape temporary.

9

REALITIES ANCIENT AND MODERN: (1) REVOLUTION

The sense of a 'particular time and place' in Goethe's and Schiller's work may seem to stop short of politics. The years in which they prepared and created Classicism saw, after all, great upheavals in European society. The French Revolution, regicide and republic, began the destruction of absolutism and made every throne in Europe insecure; the Revolutionary Wars forged the French into a new kind of nation, and showed up correspondingly how incapable the Holy Roman Empire was of concerting diplomacy or war. Of all this there is little echo in the classics we have discussed, except *Hermann und Dorothea*. It used indeed to be held that withdrawal from contemporary realities into timeless art was the essence and achievement of Classicism, made possible and symbolised by the separate peace with France which Weimar, as a satellite of Prussia, enjoyed for precisely the decade of 'Hochklassik'. More recent criticism has perpetuated the view that Classicism was a withdrawal, but has decried this – on the principle that writers should be 'involved' – as escapism.

Neither view is tenable. Goethe and Schiller did not withdraw. Even while they concerned themselves with permanent questions of art and looked to antiquity for their ideals and inspirations, they followed events closely, strove to understand and come to terms with them. They did not welcome upheaval – why should they? If that makes them seem less than 'progressive', we must remember that it was not clear at the time whether the drift of history *was* progress. For Goethe, disturbed in his own creative progress, the Revolution seemed 'der Umsturz alles Vorhandenen ..., ohne dass die mindeste Ahnung zu ihm spräche, was denn Besseres, ja nur anderes daraus erfolgen solle'.[1] True, for many people the coming of the Revolution and its first phase, the work of the States General at Versailles, seemed set to realise Enlightenment ideals of freedom and reason. But the murderous partisan feuds of the Paris Convention, the execution of the King and the massacres of the Terror disillusioned them sharply. Klopstock's odes (e.g. 'Die Etats Généraux' and 'Kennet euch selbst' of 1789, and then 'Die Jakobiner' and 'Mein Irrtum' of 1792/3) show a pattern typical of many German writers.[2]

Goethe was sceptical from early on. Characteristically he looked to concrete particulars: had the Revolution benefitted those it purported to liberate, or merely given the people new tyrants? Were the 'apostles of freedom' not really after arbitrary power — 'Willkür', the mark of absolutism — for themselves? (*Venetian Epigrams* 54, 51) Goethe is not a mere cynic: in *Hermann und Dorothea* he does justice to the inspiring dawn of revolutionary freedom. But he is a realist, seeing high hopes fail through the fault of a 'verderbtes Geschlecht'.[3] He is not gentle towards the ancien régime either. The great, he notes, once looked down on anyone who could not speak 'der Franzen Sprache', but now they are alarmed that the people are speaking a new kind of French, the revolutionary 'Sprache der Franken'. Is that not, he asks with ironic *Schadenfreude*, what the great wanted? (*Venetian Epigrams* 59). These are examples not of withdrawal from politics, but of blunt speaking without prior commitment.

Similarly with the German invasion of France in 1792 on which Goethe went with Karl August. In his letters and his later account, he speaks as a participant but not a partisan. He suffers with the rest of the army from hunger, thirst, discomfort and the incessant rain; he tests himself by exposure to gunfire; he forages, organises, cheers his companions. Yet he remains essentially a 'müssiger Zuschauer'.[4] His graphic, detached observations anticipate Tolstoy's, especially those that capture war's confusion, its disproportion of effort and materials to anything achieved; or those that make contrasting patches of sense in the larger chaos, like the standard-bearer in a charge whose features remind him of happy moments spent with the boy's mother, a poignant link between war and peace.[5] Nothing is mitigated: the individual tragedies of the French populace; the shock to the army's wishful thinking when they were held at Valmy, which showed that the French were not a reluctant rabble but a nation in arms; the overall fiasco of the campaign, 'eine der unglücklichsten Unternehmungen in den Jahrbüchern der Welt'[6], all is presented plain and unvarnished. It meets the definition Goethe gives at the end of the *Campagne in Frankreich* when he contrasts partisan observers, who can take or leave what they observe or interpret it as suits their party line, with the poet who 'seiner Natur nach unparteiisch sein und bleiben muss', whose task it is 'sich von den Zuständen beider kämpfenden Teile zu durchdringen', and who, if conflict is irreconcilable, must resolve upon a tragic ending.[7]

Goethe's artistic works of the 1790s show a similar striving for objectivity. Among the refugee nobles in the framework narrative of the *Unterhaltungen deutscher Ausgewanderten* there is a champion of the Revolution as well as a spokesman of the old system. Criticism of French actions in Germany ('der Unterdrückungsgeist derer, die das

Wort Freiheit im Munde führten') is matched by criticism of complacent Germans who had cosseted themselves in the 'wenigen wohnbaren Zimmern des alten Gebäudes' — viz., the ancien régime. The charge of immature idealism in the young is met by that of corrupt conformism in the old; displaced aristocrats are described as taking everywhere with them all their arrogant pretensions and vanity, although the opening paragraph declines to blame them for their fundamental attitudes.[8] The plays inspired by the Revolution also look with disfavour on all parties. *Der Gross-Cophta* treats the necklace scandal that ruined Marie Antoinette's name, for Goethe the epitome of the decay and corruption in the French ruling classes which ultimately explained the Revolution. *Der Bürgergeneral* shows a village rogue getting what he can out of simple peasants by pretending Jacobin agents have chosen him to raise revolution locally; that it is only a pretence limits the fable's bite on real revolutionaries, but an innuendo remains that principles have sunk to the gutter and are a means for scoundrels to prosper. *Die Aufgeregten* brings the two culprits together, an aristocratic family which has long resisted a legal claim by local people, and a pompous revolutionary committed to verbiage and violence.

Such disenchantment with both sides balances out, leaving no impetus for basic change. Goethe is thus in practice conservative. He resolves conflict within the existing society: in the *Unterhaltungen*, where the Baroness insists that political disagreements be subordinated to the ideal of tolerance and good manners; in *Der Bürgergeneral*, where harmony is restored with the aid of a benevolent feudal lord; in *Die Aufgeregten*, where by rather trivial means the case is settled amicably. Goethe does not, that is, 'resolve upon a tragic ending'. Reconciliation is possible firstly because he does not treat the revolutionary impulse in Germany as real, but as something artificially and mischievously imported from France; and secondly because he is not a doctrinaire conservative, treating the status quo as an unquestionable norm, but a pragmatic conservative who supports the status quo until a better alternative is convincingly demonstrated and meanwhile envisages — indeed, insists on — piecemeal change. The Gräfin in *Die Aufgeregten* (III, 1) has seen in Paris the aftermath of oppression and is now resolved to commit no injustice and let none pass in silence, even though people may call her a democrat. This, Goethe later told Eckermann, was his own view; revolutions were the fault of governments that failed to give justice; timely reform was the proper policy, to everyone's benefit.[9]

Goethe thus put his trust in individual action, ethically inspired, in a situation of stability and manageable dimensions. Revolutionary change, by contrast, meant mass action, ideologically inspired, in a situation (as France increasingly showed) of disorder and unmanageable dimensions. In one work, *Die natürliche Tochter* of 1803, he tried to go beyond treating German outriders of revolutionary unrest, where things could be settled through comedy and compromise, and sketched an actual revolution, resolved at last on a tragic ending. He develops what was a hint in *Die Aufgeregten* and a perceptible theme in both framework and stories of the *Unterhaltungen*: the notion of moral self-control, even self-sacrifice, in contrast to selfishness and attachment to possessions. His heroine was to sacrifice herself at a crucial moment in the revolution, having been preserved and prepared for this much in the manner of Iphigenie: 'Im Verborgnen/Verwahr er mich, als reinen Talisman./Denn, wenn ein Wunder auf der Welt geschieht,/Geschieht's durch liebevolle, treue Herzen' (V, 9). The planned trilogy never got past the first, largely expository part; how cogent it would have been cannot be reconstructed from the very slight sketches for the continuation. It is hard to see how ethical initiative à la Iphigenie could effectively engage the large social turmoil the play sets forth. The failure of *Die natürliche Tochter* — both the failure to complete it, and the failure to find an appropriate poetic medium, for the characters are types and the dialogue stilted and wordy — points to a radical discrepancy between Goethe's individualist vision and the new world summed up in what Napoleon said to him at Erfurt in 1810: 'Was will man jetzt mit dem Schicksal, die Politik ist das Schicksal'.[10]

If mass movement and total upheaval were alien to Goethe, so was the new intellectual world of ideology. His reformism-from-above failed to recognise that people might aspire to enjoy inherent human rights: not just because he lacked the experience of a large, complex state in which the need for such constitutional protection becomes clear,[11] not simply because Weimar was not an oppressive princedom like Württemberg or Hessen, but because he was blind to claims of principle as such. Even freedom as a social principle was balanced by a pragmatic view of risks and results, a preference of the frying-pan to the fire. Thus he wrote of the 'Freiheitssinn' which arose among upper-class Germans in 1792: 'Man schien nicht zu fühlen, was alles erst zu verlieren sei, um zur irgendeiner Art zweideutigen Gewinnes zu gelangen'.[12] For Goethe, absorption in principle — he calls it 'Meinung', which makes it sound more relative and questionable — was the 'fever of the times', blinding men to their immediate relationships and true interests.[13]

Such pragmatism strikes some as merely the corrupt intellectual superstructure of German absolutism. But Goethe was not just anxiously defending the society that gave him settled working conditions. That his instinct for order went deeper than politics and was genuinely neutral is shown if we trace his most allegedly reactionary maxim — 'Es ist besser, dass Ungerechtigkeiten geschehen, als dass sie auf eine ungerechte Weise gehoben werden'[14] — to its origins. At the end of the siege of Mainz, when the French and their sympathisers left under a safe-conduct, a crowd made to take spontaneous revenge on a known collaborator. Goethe stopped them. It may be the man deserved punishment — Goethe calls local anger against German Jacobin collaboration 'höchst verzeihlich' — so that his intervention in a way impeded justice. But mob-justice is always disorder, and as he explained to a friend: 'Es liegt nun einmal in meiner Natur, ich will lieber eine Ungerechtigkeit begehen, als Unordnung ertragen'.[15] 'Injustice' meant rescuing a Jacobin; it would have been 'disorder' to break the conditions granted to revolutionaries (especially on Karl August's frontage). This is far from what the maxim is commonly assumed to mean. But to read it as hard-faced absolutism is, precisely, too narrow; ideological approaches may be as much out of touch with Goethe as he was out of touch with them.

Even so, his idea of order in politics does not match up to his conceptions in other spheres. The 'bewegliche Ordnung' of his science and philosophical poetry allows dynamism within a large and generous framework. Goethe had no framework to accommodate the movements in society which his age began to see on a grand scale; for him politics was not part of nature, its violence contradicted nature's mode of operation.

Nor did he find consolation or hope in the longer historical view. Others did. It was a common Enlightenment belief that Man was progressing towards a self-fulfilment which was his destiny ('Bestimmung'). That was history's purpose and meaning; the idea must be resisted that events were a random sequence, in Kant's words a 'trostloses Ungefähr', a 'planloses Aggregat'.[16] This teleological picture was a secular version of Christian theodicy, with the role of God taken over by Nature or an undoctrinal Providence; and it inherited theodicy's difficulties over the empirical evidence. Was Nature's 'hidden plan' visible at enough points to persuade men that the course of history was rational, and to encourage them to make it more so? Was a given event positive evidence? And what of events that were not — the defeat of a grand cause, say, or some manifestation of barbarism? Could these somehow be fitted into the great design or did they destroy it? It was easy at first to believe the Revolution was a positive sign, but hard during the Terror to maintain that belief. Many did not. Strikingly, for Kant himself — though in theory he held revolutions to be at all times unjust — the French Revolution and the sympathies it evoked in so many people proved a moral tendency in the race and the impossibility of total reversals in its progress.[17] But perhaps such undaunted confidence was possible only at a distance from the actuality of horror. Goethe's Gräfin saw 'wenig Erfreuliches' in Paris (*Die Aufgeregten* IV, 3); the Magister answers 'Wenngleich nicht für die Sinne, so doch für den Geist', a facile appeal to the 'long view' which is easier for those who were not there. Goethe, though never there himself, insisted on the realities. Once again, the particular challenged the general.

Nowhere more poignantly than in the case of an idealist who *was* there, Georg Forster, a man imbued with Kantian ideas who found himself in the thick of events in Mainz and Paris, was forced by his conscience to act and was tormented by his conscience when he saw the results, realising that he had lent his hand to certain evils in the pursuit of uncertain good. In his essay on *Staatskunst*, in the two books he was working on when he died in Paris in 1793, *Darstellung der Revolution in Mainz* and *Parisische Umrisse*, and in the letters of his last two years, we watch him struggling to represent the ultimate rightness of what he has seen and done. He watches at close quarters the sway of passion and self-interest, the new tyranny, the brutal measures, the violence of the Revolution which he likens to a volcano or a hurricane. Against this he argues that the Revolution has been set by Providence in exactly the right place in the great scheme; that it has gradually purified 'die allgemeine Vernunft' in France; that its eventual success is guaranteed by its moral origins, quite unlike those of selfish rebellions.[18] Yet, even more acutely than in Kant, we sense a *need* to believe, a fear of the alternative views which cannot be admitted 'wenn wir nicht auf dem Ozean der Teleologie den Kompass verlieren, uns einem blinden Ungefähr gänzlich preisgeben . . . wollen'.[19] Doubt and self-persuasion are plainer still in the letters. Here disillusionment often seems almost total, only to be lightened by a flicker of hope. Forster never avowedly abandons the optimistic long view. But the strain is clearly immense. Increasingly it pushes his Kantian expectations of moral progress towards a Hegelian acceptance of necessity. Human beings appear more helpless to affect their fate, individual or collective, and more expendable, 'eine Handvoll Mücken mehr oder weniger in dem Schwarm'.[20] The idea that Providence will make from men's conflicts of passion a result acceptable to the moralist turns into the idea that only a later outcome can decide which party was justified in its bloody vengeances on the other.[21] Men set in action by the Revolution may do things too terrible for posterity to grasp, but the standpoint of justice is too high for mortals: 'Was geschieht, *muss* geschehen'.[22] The 'thread of reason' is hard to see, only faith stands between the would-be optimist and Goethe's sceptical view of history as 'eigentlich nur ein Gewebe von Unsinn für den höheren Denker'.[23] The social radical was left conservatively reasserting an old rational schema, the political activist waiting passively for Providence to turn partial evil into universal good.

In 1789 Forster had rejoiced to see enlightenment translated into practice — 'was die Philosophie in den Köpfen gereift und dann im Staate zustande gebracht hat'.[24] Events showed that things were not that simple. Passions interposed between head and hand, as Forster abundantly saw. Yet dearth of feeling too could be just as harmful: he watched the rise of a tyranny of 'Vernunft ohne Gefühl', beside which the ravages of fire and flood were nothing.[25] And he saw other imbalances: men of insight who lacked courage and strength to act, men with ample physical energy which they harnessed to ignorance.[26] Man himself, the material of politics, was the problem.

But was it strictly a political problem? That is, was the mending of human imperfection a task that political theory or practice could handle? Forster, who had no deeper philosophical or psychological explanation for what he observed, could only hope it was: that the proper use of freedom would gradually be learned *in* freedom, failures being only the inevitable falls of children learning to walk.[27] This is the institutional view: first set society to rights, and it will make men better. But another view was possible, namely that we must first perfect the individuals who are to compose society; for any society devised or operated by imperfect men must itself be imperfect, and men will hardly grow perfect in it. Yet this view is just as open to objections, both logical — what agency within an imperfect society can perfect men? — and ideological: is the idea that men must be changed first not a conservative ruse to keep society the way it is for as long as possible?

This last objection, telling in the abstract, is less so in the particular situation of the nineties. A major attempt to reform society institutionally had been made and had seemingly failed, and the failure had been accompanied by gruesome excesses. These might be blamed on the ancien régime and the way it had repressed and distorted human nature[28], but attributing blame did nothing to cure the condition. It was natural to turn to the other approach and try to act on men rather than institutions. This is what Schiller did. Like Forster, he had held typically Enlightenment views, as witness two statements made on the very eve of the Revolution. His Jena inaugural lecture sketched the benevolent progress of Universal History down to a desirable present; and his poem 'Die Künstler' offered a vision of eighteenth-century man as rationally mature and in control of nature and himself. But by mid-1793, these ideas seemed fond illusions. The Revolution, which might have crowned that grand progress, had instead flung men back into barbarism: 'Der Moment war der günstigste, aber er fand eine verderbte Generation'.[29]

Despite Robespierre's grand claims that his nation was two thousand years in advance of the rest of humanity and virtually a new species,[30] such condemnation of the French was a commonplace. The judge in *Hermann und Dorothea* calls them a 'verderbtes Geschlecht' and Forster speaks of 'verderbten Zeitläuften'.[31] The revolutionaries were frequently called 'devils', largely because 1789 had raised such hopes of their virtue. For Schiller this commonplace was only the starting-point for investigating the imbalances between reason and feeling, knowledge and action, and ultimately philosophy and politics, which Forster recorded; and for reasserting, despite the revolutionary trauma, the Enlightenment idea of the perfectibility of man. In the *Briefe über die ästhetische Erziehung des Menschen*, Schiller argues his way out of the difficult circularities of the individual-society problem. To the question, what agency in an imperfect society can perfect Man, he answers: art. To the objection that periods of great art have often been periods of political and social decadence, he answers not by examples of the contrary (as Winckelmann might have done, who connected the greatness of Greek art with Greek democracy) but by an abstract argument, designed to show that at any historical juncture men need the right *kind* of art. He analyses Man into his rational and sensuous components, with corresponding impulses towards formal control and involvement in material reality; singles out aesthetic experience as the one area in which these impulses can interact harmoniously; establishes an ideal of beauty as the perfect equilibrium between them (to that extent his essay is his culminating contribution to aesthetics) but then prescribes ways in which art, by inclining more towards the 'formal' or the 'material' principle, can brace or relax whichever impulse needs treatment in any particular age. Crucially, he insists that the artist must be detached from his time: not, that is, from its problems, but from the influence of its prevailing character, for he could not correct this if he himself shared it. How is the artist to be independent of his times?

By communing with the greatest art of all, Greek art, which stands above all times and will help him find a pure self, the 'absolute unwandelbare Einheit seines Wesens' (Letter 9). And if Greek art sets the standard for the modern artist to emulate, Greek humanity becomes the standard of the human wholeness he aims to restore, for it showed an ideal 'Totalität des Charakters'. Such perfection was bound to pass, because the progress of mankind demanded specialisation, the division of labour and (however painful) alienation. But precisely art can give back the pristine balance for man to enjoy — and thus incidentally the basis for a fresh start in practical affairs. So art had a vital social function, but without yielding any of its freedom to the demands of particular philosophies or party lines.

Clearly Schiller was not 'withdrawing' into art or into a cult of antiquity. He was addressing burning problems of modern life. Art was to shape political character, antiquity was to guarantee the artist's independence and provide the ideals for him to work towards. Clearly, too, Schiller was not concerned, as is sometimes alleged, merely to produce a cultural elite.[32] His prescriptions (the word can be understood in the medical sense, given that he was treating the fundamental health of men and societies) cover both the 'wild' masses and the 'barbarous' nobility (Letter 4); he is not content with any partial improvements — 'am Ganzen wird dadurch nichts gebessert sein' (Letter 7); if he celebrates at the close of the work certain 'auserlesene Zirkel' which have attained his ideal (Letter 27), this is to show that realisation is possible. The function of art is now universal. Schiller's austere moral theory of tragedy, which presupposed a morally educated audience, now falls into place as meeting only one particular need. We have returned to that vision of art and its effects with which years before Schiller had ended his Mannheim address; only now it has been challenged, thought through in its full scope and minutest detail, and rigorously grounded.

It may still be wondered whether it is practicable. Admittedly, it is 'eine Aufgabe für mehr als ein Jahrhundert' (Letter 7). Its outcome is uncertain; but that is not just a polite way of saying that its failure is certain. It has been the spoken or unspoken faith of most artists. They may not have succeeded in making an ideal world, their efforts may seldom have been demonstrably decisive, but their work has been a large factor in social change. We can imagine if not exactly measure how much worse human affairs would have been without their influence. To that extent, the idea of aesthetic education in the broadest sense remains a tenable alternative to the idea of institutional change. Fashionable ideologies may dismiss it as passé; but fashions change. George Orwell remarks that the two views not only appeal to different people but probably also alternate through history; and as long as, in his words, 'the central problem — how to prevent power from being abused — remains unsolved',[33] neither view can be said to have proved itself to the exclusion of the other.

Schiller, then, is ideologically neither naive nor corrupt; he is neither an escapist nor an elitist. He is an individualist. Though he legislates for mankind, he thinks of it as an immense collection of individuals, none of whom should be compelled 'über irgendeinem Zwecke sich selbst zu versäumen' (Letter 6). In this, his response to politics is like Goethe's. Their obstinate attachment to human realities, rooted in their art and their thought about art, may seem dwarfed and mocked by the mass politics of their day and later. But what we know of this phenomenon suggests that theirs was an attachment without which a humane politics is not possible.

Notes

1. *Tag- und Jahreshefte* for 1793, HA 10, 438f.
2. For full surveys of German reactions to the Revolution, see G.P. Gooch, *Germany and the French Revolution* (1920); Alfred Stern, *Der Einfluss der Französischen Revolution auf das deutsche Geistesleben* (Stuttgart, 1928); Jacques Droz, *L'Allemagne et la Révolution Française* (Paris, 1949).
3. *Hermann und Dorothea*, canto VI, 'Klio. Das Zeitalter'. HA 2, 478ff.
4. To C.G. Voigt, 10 September 1792. Cf. also to Zelter, 8 August 1822: 'In solcher Tragödie den Grazioso zu spielen ist auch eine Rolle'.
5. *Campagne in Frankreich* (1822), HA 10, 231.
6. To C.G. Voigt, 15 October 1792.
7. *Campagne in Frankreich*, HA 10, 361.
8. *Unterhaltungen deutscher Ausgewanderten*, HA 6, 125-32. For the deliberate creation of balance, see Schiller to Goethe 29 November 1794 and Goethe's reply of 2 December.
9. To Eckermann, 4 January 1824. The answering speech of the Hofrat (balance again) defends the 'höheren Stand' even though people may call him an aristocrat, and may equally be taken as Goethe's own view. See F.J. Lamport, ' "Entfernten Weltgetöses Widerhall". Politics in Goethe's Plays', PEGS xliv (1973-4), p.56. Eckermann, 9 July 1827, describes a political conversation in which Goethe spoke 'wie immer als milder Aristokrat'.
10. *Unterredung mit Napoleon*, HA 10, 546.
11. As suggested by Wilhelm Mommsen, *Die politischen Anschauungen Goethes* (Stuttgart, 1948), pp.196ff. Mommsen's richly documented study tries to reconstruct the modes of thought of the times and to show their roots, while refraining from ideological criticism.
12. *Campagne in Frankreich*, HA 10, 317. Similarly in *Literarischer Sansculottismus*, though Goethe deplores the effects on literature of German

political divisions, he still says 'Wir wollen die Umwälzungen nicht wünschen, die in Deutschland klassische Werke vorbereiten könnten' (HA 12, 241).

13. See *Reise der Söhne Megaprazons*, a fragment in the manner of Voltaire's satirical *contes*, WA 18, 375f: 'Der Mensch misskennt seine wahrsten, seine klarsten Vorteile, er opfert alles, ja seine Neigungen und Leidenschaften einer Meinung auf'. Cf. *Unterhaltungen*, HA 6, 127, on the similar effects of Karl's passion for freedom.

14. *Maximen und Reflexionen* nr. 114, HA 12, 379.

15. *Belagerung von Mainz*, HA 10, 391.

16. Kant, *Idee zu einer allgemeinen Geschichte in weltbürgerlicher Absicht* (1784), Zweiter Satz and Neunter Satz in *Werke*, IV, 153, 164.

17. Kant, *Der Streit der Fakultäten*, Zweiter Abschnitt, 6 and 7, ed. cit., VII, 397-401.

18. *Parisische Umrisse*, Chapters 3 and 4, in Forster, *Werke* (Berlin and Weimar, 1968), I, 224 and 228f.

19. Ibid., p.231. Cf. *Über die Beziehung der Staatskunst auf das Glück der Menschheit*, ed. cit., I, 148f: '. . . wenn wir nicht den trostlosesten Fatalismus annehmen wollen, . . . so dürfen wir nicht zweifeln, dass die Wirkungen blinder, vernunftloser Kräfte im Plane des Ganzen . . . dergestalt hineinverwebt sind, dass ihre Misstöne sich im allgemeinen Zusammenklange verlieren'.

20. To Huber, 11 November 1793; to his wife Therese, 20 November 1793.

21. *Parisische Umrisse*, Ch. 5, *Werke* I, 248f.

22. To Therese, 27-9 December 1793.

23. Goethe, in conversation with Riemer and Kanzler Müller, 11 October 1824.

24. To Heyne, 30 July 1789.

25. To Therese, 16 April 1793.

26. To Therese, 8 April 1793.

27. *Darstellung der Revolution in Mainz*, Ch. 4, *Werke* 1, 209f. The 'deutsche Denker' Forster quotes for support in the footnote is Kant. Cf. *Die Religion innerhalb der Grenzen der blossen Vernunft*, IV, 4, *Werke* VI, 338.

28. Tom Paine said that the 'outrages [were] not the effect of the principles of the Revolution, but of the degraded mind that existed before the Revolution, and which the Revolution is calculated to reform'. Forster, *Werke* 1, 210, blames 'die lange Knechtschaft' and elsewhere (*Staatskunst*, 1, 135) the priests for any revolutionary failings.

29. To the Duke of Augustenburg, 13 July 1793, one of a set of letters which were the first version of the *Ästhetische Erziehung* of 1795.

30. Cf. Robespierre's speech to the National Convention of 18 floréal, year 2 (7 May, 1794): 'Le peuple français semble avoir devancé de deux mille ans le reste de l'espèce humaine; on serait tenté de le regarder au milieu d'elle comme une espèce différente'.

31. To Therese, 4 June 1793.

32. Cf. for example, Jost Hermand, *Von Mainz nach Weimar* (Stuttgart, 1969), pp. 46f. Hermand is, justifiably, concerned with ways in which the Classicists were (mis)readin the nineteenth century, yet himself describes the *Ästhetische Erziehung* as an attempt 'einen strengen Trennungsstrich zwischen Kunst und Politik zu ziehen' – the exact opposite of the truth.

33. George Orwell, 'Charles Dickens' in *Collected Essays, Journalism and Letters* (1968), vol. I, pp.427f. The dichotomy between moral and institutional reform is of course not absolute – the two might reasonably be seen as complementary. What Schiller was rejecting was a total transformation of society's institutions by men who were totally untransformed themselves.

10 DIVERGENCES

Literature develops by a mixture of continuity and change. We saw how a preoccupation with improving Man and society through art remained constant beneath the differing styles of Aufklärung, Sturm und Drang and Classicism; how the Weimar conception of art as an elevated and serious play with the realities of experience, liberating but also indirectly fruitful, grew from the Enlightenment principle of intellectual toleration; and, in the individual case, how Goethe's devotion to the external world in its richness and physical particularity underlay and unified his poetic evolution, putting its intellectual and stylistic phases into perspective as the deepening comprehension and fuller celebration of natural phenomena.

These are instances of growth-by-transformation, metamorphoses in Goethe's own sense. We must now ask what grew out of Weimar Classicism and how. Between 1794 and 1805 Weimar became the centre of German culture, Goethe and Schiller its arbiters. Their achievements over that short span were massive in every genre, and for every part of their practice there was an impressive grounding in theory. The millennium to which critics looked forward in the 1770s and 1780s had now arrived: Germany had native works, and a native Classicism, of European stature.

Viewed internally it thus had a literary Establishment; and reactions to an Establishment are always mixed. It attracts aspiring writers to its centre of power — Jean Paul, Hölderlin, Novalis, Tieck, the Schlegels, all came for some period in the 1790s to Weimar or Jena. It provokes admiration for its achievements but also envy of its status, a desire to imitate or emulate, but also an urge to rebel, supersede, do things differently. There is also a tendency to *be* different, for although a younger generation shares much of its elders' experience and is familiar with the same cultural materials and assumptions, it sees these things through different eyes. The dates in literary histories — Goethe b.1749, Schiller b.1759, Hölderlin b.1770, Friedrich Schlegel b.1772 — come alive if we remember what differences in age mean. For Goethe, who was forty when it began, the French Revolution threatened the order he had found or created in life; for Schiller, who was thirty, it challenged long-held views, forcing him to argue them more thoroughly (but not to change them). Neither man felt positively enough about the upheaval ever to have called it one of the 'greatest tendencies of the age', as

Friedrich Schlegel did, who was only seventeen when it happened.[1] To be really young 'in that dawn' meant growing up with a sense that any seeming permanence was provisional, change an open option, chaos always a — perhaps fruitful — possibility. In other words, the same calendar-years, the same events, will be quite different experiences for men at different stages of their lives. It is not the least remarkable thing about the Goethe-Schiller partnership that it overcame a ten-year age gap.

The Establishment, on its side, looks for recruits and support. In 1796 Goethe's first impression of Jean Paul was that with time he might well be 'zu den Unsrigen gerechnet', though this very soon yielded to the view that Jean Paul's imaginative world was insubstantial and a far cry from Classical health.[2] Jean Paul went his separate and peculiar literary way. In the same year Goethe judged that August Wilhelm Schlegel was in basic agreement with the Classical aesthetic — 'in ästhetischen Haupt- und Grundideen mit uns einig'.[3] And indeed, all questions of diplomacy apart — for there is much intrigue, calculation, and dissimulation of personal animus in the Schlegels' courting of the Classicists, on whom for a time they depended to further their literary careers[4] — there seemed to be much genuine agreement between them. Here lies the interest; the differences that are to constitute Romanticism arise unintended. A writer takes over an orthodoxy but suddenly realises it is not his whole, or deepest, conviction; a shift of emphasis in a restatement of familiar ideas opens the way to a new development; divergence gradually becomes radical opposition.

Thus Friedrich Schlegel's youthful essay *Über das Studium der griechischen Poesie*, written in 1795, sets up yet again the ideal of Greek literature for moderns to emulate: it has beauty, objectivity and an overall unity, whereas modern literature is a chaos of individual subjective expression, which he labels 'das Interessante'. Though he suggests at one point that Goethe has attained those high Greek qualities, his general view of modernity is stern and schoolmasterly; it will be a long, hard path back to the ideal.[5] Yet was he really at heart so devoted to antiquity and its standards? The year before, he had written to his brother that the problem of German poetry was how to *combine* the essence of modern and ancient[6] which implies a much more open mind. And in the passages of the essay which treat modern writers, especially Shakespeare, there is a tell-tale enthusiasm. Still, for purposes of the theoretical framework, tradition and orthodoxy have repressed these stirrings.

But before Schlegel could publish, he was helped to find his true preference by Schiller's *Über naive und sentimentalische Dichtung*, with its much deeper and more sympathetic feeling for the moderns' dilemma. Schlegel hastily added a preface to his treatise, begging friends of modern poetry not to take what it says as his final judgement. He pleads that his austere argument was necessary because only by setting up an absolute standard which seemed to allow modern poetry no value at all ('Ein Urteil, dem das Gefühl laut widerspricht!') was it possible to realise its totally disparate character, and be 'surprised and rewarded' by a 'brilliant justification' of the Moderns.[7] This rights the disharmony between the emphatic Classical principles of Schlegel's essay and his actual modern interests — at the price of confessing to an implausibly devious method of argument. The whole import of his theory decisively changes. Stress now falls not on the obligation of modern poetry to return to the norm of 'das Schöne', but on the necessity of 'das Interessante' as the medium through which this return is to occur. What the essay condemned, the preface calls 'ästhetisch erlaubt'; it has 'provisorischen ästhetischen Wert'. And since according to the theory (which overlooks Schlegel's own instancing of Goethe) the ideal can never be fully attained but only approached by an 'endlose Annäherung', it follows that modern subjective expression is going to enjoy its provisional status for some time.

This new pattern of ideas then becomes the Romantic programme, enshrined in the celebrated 116th Fragment which appeared the following year in the Schlegels' new journal, *Athenäum*.[8] That rhapsodic invocation (it can hardly be called a definition) hymns 'romantische Poesie' for its unfinishedness, its openness to any material or mood or mixture of genres, its capacity to accommodate every phenomenon of the age, its refusal of any final form ('das ist ihr eigentliches Wesen, dass sie ewig nur werden, nie vollendet sein kann') and of any law that would limit the poet's freedom. The sole remnant of Schlegel's former commitment to a Classical norm is his use of the word 'Klassizität'; but what he looks forward to is itself a 'grenzenlos wachsende Klassizität'. This is not so much a paradox as a contradiction; for the nature of the Classical is form, definition, limitation, it cannot 'grow boundlessly' and aspire to be a 'progressive Universalpoesie', embracing all that exists and deferring formal perfection indefinitely. From being more severely Classical than Schiller, Schlegel has gone to the extreme of permissive modernism.

Nor is the Fragment a chance aberration. Schlegel has by now openly repudiated his *Studium der griechischen Poesie* and declared that the Greeks are not a chosen people with a monopoly in poetry.[9]

Where his essay had spoken of modern poetry as a chaos waiting to be ordered, he will very soon speak of the chaos that waits for a harmonising touch as itself the highest order[10] — once more, a shift of emphasis that totally transforms an idea. What the harmonising touch would be, Schlegel does not make wholly clear. He speaks in both these passages of 'Liebe', and elsewhere of religion as the 'Zentrum aller Bildung',[11] which touches on the large problem of how culture and creativity are related to systems of belief. But the creation of order is not imminent — certainly there is nothing here in the way of a prescription for the literary craftsman. For practical purposes, the requirement of form in art, of any objective norm outside the mass of modern experiences and impulses themselves, has been abandoned. The only prerequisite is an ironic mind agile enough to manipulate these as materials — a development which goes far beyond Schiller's closely controlled principle of 'Spiel'.[12]

All this may seem of limited importance. Friedrich Schlegel was not artist enough to put his own ideas into execution; his novel *Lucinde* echoes rather than successfully embodies his theories.[13] August Wilhelm likewise was more critic and (brilliant) translator than primary poet. The brothers' journal, *Athenäum*, carried small amounts of creative writing in proportion to critical reflexion.[14] Arguably the ideas they put forward were too vague and grandiose to serve even a poet of genius as a positive programme. But they are still important as a negation, a sign that the Classical synthesis of Goethe and Schiller was not universally accepted, that its hold was being loosened before it was even properly established. The Romantics might admire Goethe and contribute to the growth of his individual reputation by their eulogies; and they might do this on a view of poetry and its historical development which stems ultimately from Schiller's theories. But in separating Goethe from Schiller in their judgements; in trying to drive a wedge between Goethe and Schiller by their intrigues; and above all in treating Goethe's poetry as only the dawn of a new age, insinuating themselves as his continuators[15] and suggesting that almost all was still to do, they were denying Classicism its status as a unified, coherent achievement of lasting value and authority.

Moreover, a similar sequence, agreement becoming divergence, recurs in the one undoubted poet of the Jena Romantic group, Novalis, and has direct poetic consequences. From admiring Goethe, and specifically *Wilhelm Meisters Lehrjahre*, he swings round to a total rejection of the novel; once again, this happens by gradual shifts within a constant pattern of ideas. In 1798, Novalis appreciates Goethe's tendency to perfect whatever he touches, his mastery of form ('Bildungskunst', 'Richtigkeit und Strenge') which is less only than that of the ancients, so that if he is to be surpassed, it must be in content ('Gehalt und Kraft, Mannigfaltigkeit und Tiefsinn' — very much what Schlegel summed up as 'das Interessante'). The modern content Goethe inevitably has, Novalis calls 'romantisch'. But by 1800 he has changed his mind. The content, in particular Wilhelm's social adjustment, the novel's tendency to return to a state of balance and see life through the eyes of good sense, strikes him as anti-poetic. Now formal qualities are only grudgingly conceded; the novel is 'undichterisch im höchsten Grade, was den Geist betrifft, so poetisch auch die Darstellung sei'. And later the same year Novalis's feeling for the form has been silenced altogether by Goethe's neglect of every kind of Romantic content — 'die Naturpoesie', 'das Wunderbare', 'der Mystizism' — in favour of merely 'gewöhnliche menschliche Dinge'. 'Artistic atheism' is declared to be the spirit of the book.[16] Goethe's novel clearly became the stimulus for a deliberate counter-statement, for while these feelings were bubbling up Novalis was working on his *Heinrich von Ofterdingen*, a work no one could accuse of lacking mysticism and marvels or of being concerned merely with ordinary human things.

Once again, the new is grafted on to the old; insofar as Novalis's novel is a 'Bildungsroman', its general idea owes something to Goethe's *Meister*, as did Tieck's artist novel *Franz Sternbalds Wanderungen* of 1798 (and even Schlegel's *Lucinde* declares itself to be an account of the 'Lehrjahre meiner Männlichkeit'[17]). But its interests and allegiances are strikingly different. Its hero is a poet with no touch of the hated prosaic in his experiences or destiny, and no doubts of the wholly self-sufficient value of art. Where Goethe, though not primarily a social realist, wrote within and about the world of his day, Novalis sets his story in (a highly idealised version of) the Middle Ages. The Middle Ages were to be the unifying interest of all the German Romantics, the first group in Jena and their successors in Heidelberg; medieval Europe was a source of motifs and inspiration, and a model for what society and culture should be like.[18] To that extent, it had the function antiquity had for the Classicists. But there is a fundamental difference. Where Goethe and Schiller used the society and literature of antiquity as a means to understand permanent conditions of man and art, and ultimately if indirectly to influence the realities of their own time, the Romantics used the Middle Ages — as they used certain staple forms, the *Märchen*, the *Volkslied* — to escape from modern life into a realm of the imagination where wonders need never cease.

Romanticism is thus such a different world, and it is quantitatively so rich, that it demands separate treatment.[19] But it is very much part of the present account to show how Romanticism grew out of and away from Classicism and what its simultaneous presence on the literary scene (something unique among European literatures) meant: namely that no sooner had the Classical balance been struck than it was disturbed. The Classical centre was occupied only briefly.

Romanticism was not the only challenge. It was perhaps the only one Goethe and Schiller saw as such: as a concerted movement it could not be overlooked. Other challenges came from single individuals, and thus hardly seemed sufficient to threaten the established poets' position; they were only felt uneasily to be signs of the times. But since the challengers were of the poetic stature of Kleist and Hölderlin, these now appear at least as important as Romanticism. They repeat the pattern of the Romantics' relation to Goethe and Schiller: admiration, dependence, the desire for encouragement and recognition — for, so to speak, a legitimate succession — mingle with resentment, self-assertion and an impulse to rebel and supplant. Kleist aspired to be his country's greatest poet and swore, it is reported,[20] to tear the laurel-wreath from Goethe's brow, though he passionately revered him. Hölderlin was as passionately devoted to Schiller, was influenced early on by Schiller's poetry and more lastingly by his ideas, accepted his sole authority on poetic and practical matters ('von Ihnen dependiere ich unüberwindlich').[21] Yet he also saw that this risked overwhelming his individuality. His gentle temperament and genuine humility shrank from the choice of surrender or revolt. Only when Goethe and Schiller failed to support his projected journal *Iduna* did he break out, in sudden certainty of his real worth, that they were afraid for their exclusive position if others should win fame: 'es scheint bei ihnen, die ich mir ungefähr als meinesgleichen denken darf, ein wenig Handwerksneid mitunter zu walten'.[22]

The new departures in Kleist's and Hölderlin's work show up most clearly where there seemed to be common ground with the Classicists. Kleist too treats themes from antiquity, but very differently. His *Amphitryon* struck Goethe as crypto-Christian, a twisting together ('Contorsion') of ancient and modern very far from an organic synthesis. His *Penthesilea* plainly shocked Goethe; Greek legend though she was, the Amazon queen who loves and slays Achilles seemed to Goethe something from a strange race, an alien region, the whole infinitely removed from the style and ethos of his own *Achilleis*, which by ironic coincidence came out in the same autumn of 1808 with the same publisher.[23] Hölderlin too was to be a poet of antiquity — perhaps *the* German poet of antiquity — and to evolve a vision of Greece markedly different from Goethe's and Schiller's. But that came later, when his contact with them was past. For the present, his common ground lay in the form, themes and language of his early poetry, all of which seem to echo Schiller. Yet it is precisely at the point where Hölderlin is moving beyond these to a new breadth of vision and calm grandeur of tone, in poems like 'Der Wanderer' and 'An den Aether', that Goethe and Schiller diagnose his apparently familiar case as Schiller's old problem of matching realities to his abstractions, agree that Hölderlin's is a dangerous subjectivity ('subjectivity' was the vice they anxiously observed in many rising writers) and try to coax Hölderlin down from his visionary heights to write small poems on idyllic subjects.[24]

It is common to berate them for failing to see Kleist's and Hölderlin's greatness and for not helping them more. Such criticism lacks a historical sense. They did a good deal, though they could have done more and no doubt would have if Kleist's and Hölderlin's tragic ends could have been foreknown. As *the* literary arbiters, they were under constant pressure to sympathise, patronise, assist and recommend. Sympathy was not always easy. When Kleist's *Zerbrochner Krug* failed on the Weimar stage, he wanted to challenge Goethe to a duel for allegedly sabotaging it with his adaptation. Though less drastic, Hölderlin's fixation on Schiller, his letters embarrassingly full of hero-worship and tortuous analyses of his devotion and its motives, hardly invited Schiller's further involvement. Still, Goethe did put Kleist's play on, did lend his name to support Kleist's journal *Phöbus*; Schiller did encourage Hölderlin, did publish his poems, did recommend his novel *Hyperion* for publication as having 'recht viel Genialisches'.[25] They both felt their responsibility to foster talent, though it was a 'desperate' business to discriminate among the teeming unknowns in a literary situation which only looks clear to us by benefit of hindsight.[26] But they also, inevitably, judged new work by the aesthetic principles that governed what they themselves produced. Anything wholly new that disturbed their synthesis was bound to get a cool reception; poets can seldom enter fully into other poets' experiments and solutions because they are too fully committed to their own. Wieland's sympathies with Kleist, as once before with the young Goethe, make him an exception.[27] There is an essential truth in Kleist's bitter jibe that for the Weimar stage Goethe would have set the howling of Penthesilea's pack to harmonious music.[28] And conversely, anything wholly acceptable to Goethe and Schiller could hardly be new, but only a pale repetition of their own achievements; hence Heine's later comment that Goethe's praise came to be a certificate of mediocrity.[29] Does this mean that the much-desired literary tradition creates as many problems as the total lack of tradition which the young Goethe and Schiller suffered from? Certainly, all achievement has the potential to inhibit. As Hölderlin wrote, it is more difficult to give proper expression to nature when there are masterpieces all about you than when the artist is alone with the living world.[30] Literary authority is always hard to administer liberally. But these factors were made unusually acute by the historically telescoped German situation: a long dearth had been suddenly ended by achievement on a grand scale, the more impressive for the contrast; and this belated Classicism was then questioned, not at two hundred years range as in France (where Racine and Victor Hugo never met) but while the Classical poets were still alive. The conclusion seems to be, not that there is no ideally stable condition for the growth of a national literature, but rather that an abnormal condition at some point in its history will cast a long shadow.

Notes

1. *Athenäumsfragmente* number 216 (published in 1798). See Schlegel, *Kritische Schriften* (Munich,[2] 1964), p.48.
2. See Goethe to Meyer, 20 June 1796, and the poem 'Der Chinese in Rom' of August 1796.
3. Goethe to Meyer, 20 May 1796.
4. August Wilhelm was a contributor to the prestigious *Horen* and wanted to remain one; Friedrich was not and wanted to become one; he waited impatiently for a 'Kopfnicken des Gnädigsten', i.e., Schiller. The sarcastic phrase (to August Wilhelm, 23 December 1795) is typical of the Romantics' calculating and hostile tone in private communications about the Classicists. For a detailed account of their relations, see Josef Körner, *Klassiker und Romantiker* (Berlin, 1924).
5. On what is 'interessant', see Schlegel, *Kritische Schriften*, pp.147f.: 'jedes originelle Individuum, welches ein grösseres Quantum von intellektuellem Gehalt oder ästhetischer Energie enthält'; on Goethe, pp.153ff.
6. To August Wilhelm, 27 February 1794.
7. Schlegel, *Kritische Schriften*, pp.115ff.
8. Ibid., p.38. For the sources and changing usage of the word 'romantisch', especially its early associations with the 'Roman', see Hans Eichner's essay in *'Romantic' and its Cognates. The European History of a Word* (Manchester, 1972).
9. See *Kritische Fragmente* (1797), numbers 7 and 91, in Schlegel's *Kritische Schriften*, pp.5, 18.
10. Compare *Studium der griechischen Poesie*, ibid., p.127, with *Gespräch über die Poesie* (1800), ibid., p.497.
11. *Ideen* (1800) number 14, ibid., p.90.

12. Cf. *Ideen* number 69, ibid., p.97: 'Ironie ist klares Bewusstsein der ewigen Agilität, des unendlich vollen Chaos'. On the divergence of Schlegel's ideas from Schiller's, see my essay 'Critical Consciousness and Creation: the Concept *Kritik* from Lessing to Hegel', in *Oxford German Studies 3* (1968).

13. Cf. the novel's opening section 'Julius an Lucinde', which speaks of 'Ordnung vernichten', 'reizende Verwirrung', 'unaufhaltsam progressiver Stoff', 'das schönste Chaos von erhabnen Harmonien und interessanten Genüssen'. Schiller criticised the book's formless and fragmentary character as 'der Gipfel moderner Unform and Unnatur' (to Goethe, 19 July 1799).

14. Of 1048 pages over a three year period, there were 40 of poetry and 60 of translations – at best one-tenth primary creative work.

15. Cf. August Wilhelm Schlegel on Goethe's discovery of a poetic language and Tieck's appropriation of the secret, in the essay 'Beiträge zur Kritik der neuesten Literatur', *Athenäum* I, pp.174f. In fact the evocation of Tieck's effects – 'die Sprache hat sich gleichsam alles Körperlichen begeben, und löst sich in einen geistigen Hauch auf . . . [es] spiegelt sich alle jugendliche Sehnsucht nach dem Unbekannten und Vergangenen' – shows how very far his poetry was from Goethe's, especially the Goethe of the 1790s.

16. Novalis's widely dispersed remarks on *Meister* are usefully brought together in Ewald Wasmuth's edition of the *Briefe und Werke* (Berlin, 1943), III, 271-80. The charge of 'artistic atheism' recalls Friedrich Schlegel's 'Goethe ist ohne Wort Gottes', quoted by Körner, *Klassiker und Romantiker*, p.91, from a notebook of 1797, i.e., before Schlegel's adulatory essay on *Meister* had appeared; once again, a striking gap between public position and private utterance.

17. Cf. the opening 'Julius an Lucinde', and a later section which has the phrase as its title.

18. Most programmatically in Novalis's *Die Christenheit oder Europe* (1799). Medievalism is already overwhelming in Wackenroder's rhapsodies on religious painting, the *Herzensergiessungen eines kunstliebenden Klosterbruders* (1796).

19. See volume 6 of this Literary History of Germany by A. Menhennet.

20. By his friend Ernst von Pfuel. See Helmut Sembdner (ed.), *Heinrich von Kleists Lebensspuren* (Munich, 1969), pp.88f.

21. Hölderlin to Schiller, 20 June 1797.

22. Draft of a letter to Susette Gontard, November 1799.

23. Goethe's judgements are assembled in Sembdner, *Heinrich von Kleists Lebensspuren*, pp.132f. and 224f. *Penthesilea* struck others as madness, although Fouqué came near its value – and its real affinity with the Greeks – when he wondered 'ist nicht vielmehr eine wirklich bacchantisch tolle Kraft in diesem Gewühl?' Sembdner, p.171.

24. Schiller to Goethe, 27 and 30 June, Goethe to Schiller 28 June 1797.

25. Schiller to his publisher Cotta, 9 March 1795.

26. Cf. Schiller to Goethe, 17 August 1797: 'Ich bin einmal in dem verzweifelten Fall, dass mir daran liegen muss, ob andere Leute etwas taugen, und ob etwas aus ihnen werden kann; daher werde ich diese Hölderlin und Schmid so spät als möglich aufgeben'. Schiller's trouble over his now forgotten 'Protégé' Siegfried Schmid is not so much a judgement on his critical flair as a reminder how many young hopefuls – often with little work yet to their name – he had to size up.

27 On Wieland and the young Goethe, see above p. 55. Of Kleist Wieland wrote, after hearing some scenes from the tragedy *Robert Guiskard*, that they promised something as great as Aeschylus, Sophocles and Shakespeare put together, and that Kleist was born to fill the gap in German literature which even Goethe and Schiller could not fill. See Wieland to Georg Wedekind, 10

April, 1804, in Sembdner, *Heinrich von Kleists Lebensspuren*, p.70.
28. See the epigram 'Der Theater-Bearbeiter der Penthesilea': 'Nur die Meute, fürcht' ich, die wird in W[eimar] mit Glück nicht/Heulen, Lieber; den Lärm setz' ich, vergönn, in Musik.'
29. Heine, *Die Romantische Schule* in *Sämtliche Werke* ed. Walzel (Leipzig, 1910), 7, 42.
30. Hölderlin to Schiller, 20 June, 1797.

11 REALITIES ANCIENT AND MODERN: (2) MYTHOLOGY

I

Weimar culture was wholly secular. Schiller's ethic has Christian analogues and perhaps ultimately, like much Aufklärung thinking, Protestant roots; Goethe could use the term 'pious' of his aspiration to know 'den ewig Ungenannten' in nature.[1] But their art is not subordinated to doctrine or cult. Gods appear in their work not as objects of belief but as chosen means, changing with the task in hand: 'Wir sind naturforschend Pantheisten, dichtend Polytheisten, sittlich Monotheisten', said Goethe.[2] Schiller was less serenely adaptable, more troubled (as 'Die Götter Griechenlands' shows) by the gap between such uses and real belief, but his position was substantially the same. The gods of Greece and Rome and occasionally, somewhat uneasily, of Christianity provided the Classicists with a language of the imagination.

This does not mean mere poetic decoration. For instance, in Goethe's elegy 'Euphrosyne', the dead woman's shadow-existence among legendary companions in the realm of Persephone, her apparition, the presence of Hermes to guide her back, make up a consistent medium in which to speak movingly of loss, mourning and remembrance. They create a serious mood, though they do not invite serious belief.

The Romantics were unhappy with such delicate distinctions. For them the separation of myth and belief was not a necessary feature of modernity, but an ill to be remedied if a true culture of community and conviction was to come about. They foresaw such a new birth from the pangs of revolution and war which Europe was suffering; revolution was to be, in Friedrich Schlegel's phrase, an 'Inzitament der Religion'.[3] They struggled back towards religion — a new one such as the young Schlegel dreamed of, or the old one to which numerous Romantics converted — as a binding force for the imagination. Sometimes they talked of creating a mythology — from modern physics, Indian philosophy, Shakespeare, Cervantes, Spinoza — but at root they wanted a system which they could *believe* in, which would lift the strain of freedom from the individual mind: 'das ist der eigentliche Punkt, dass wir uns wegen des Höchsten nicht so ganz allein auf unser Gemüt verlassen'.[4]

Such remedies show the paradox at the heart of Romanticism;

these were sophisticated men trying to outwit their own sophistication and put back the clock of consciousness to a true simplicity. But was it feasible, Hegel asked, for artists to take over beliefs *en bloc* 'um ihr Gemüt zu fixieren'?[5] Similarly Eichendorff, whose Catholicism ante-dated this cultural emergency, saw that his contemporaries had bor-rowed Christian mythology for the sake of its wonders and mysteries, and that essentially 'sie verfochten einen Glauben, den sie selber nicht hatten'.[6] As for a newly compounded mythology, how could such a deliberate measure produce the kind of common cultural language which men accept unthinkingly? Yet there seemed no alternative to these artificial procedures. For surely no modern could repeat the original process by which myths were created, 'sich unmittelbar anschliessend und anbildend an das Nächste, Lebendigste der sinnlichen Welt'.[7]

These opposed views, Classical and Romantic, of what culture should be are the background for judging what Hölderlin aspired to do and what he did. He has affinities with both sides. With Goethe and Schiller he shares the eighteenth-century devotion to Greek myths and poetic forms and the belief that the Greeks embodied an ideal humanity; with the Romantics, his more exact contemporaries, he shares the expecta-tion of a spiritual renewal which will grow from this time of the break-ing of nations. What sets him apart equally from the Classicists' non-belief and the Romantics' acute need to believe is a mode and intensity of feeling which draws myth and experience into intimate relation and has claims to be called primally religious. Certainly it transcends both the Classicists' use of antiquity and the Romantics' cerebral pro-grammes.[8] And the literary result is some of the most powerful and challenging poetry in the German language.

This did not grow instantly from youthful fervour. Hölderlin's feeling had first to be deepened by heart-breaking experience and matured (since in poetry 'feeling' cannot exist distinct from its form of expression) by trial-and-error, technical reflection and self-criticism. Still, his earliest poetry already contains constants, thematic threads that lead into his often labyrinthine world. There is poetic ambition ('Mein Vorsatz') and a Christian or Rousseauian criticism of society ('Die Ehrsucht', 'Auf einer Heide geschrieben'), later to combine in a strong sense of poetic mission; there is the desire for withdrawal into quietude and for a lost paradisal harmony; and occasionally, amid much conventional Christian acceptance of death and self-assurance of immortality, there are moments of intense, undoctrinal feeling:

Im Abendschimmer
Stand der Strom. Ein heiliges Gefühl
Bebte mir durchs Herz; und plötzlich scherzt' ich nimmer,
Plötzlich stand ich ernster auf vom Knabenspiel.

('Die Meinige')

Then in the early nineties comes emotional intensity of a problematic kind. He writes hymnic poems on the grand themes of friendship, love, freedom, harmony, humanity, beauty, youth, all familiar eighteenth-century ideals made newly topical by the Revolution. As the frequent personalisation in these poems hints, such ideals are secular gods and the service they demand is action. Hölderlin's ambition to win poetic immortality, which was already a transformation of Christian hopes, now changes by a further step into heroic activism. The poet aspires to sacrifice himself in the struggle for liberty. Reality seems unresistant, victory can be anticipated in the act of exhortation: the 'Hymne an die Menschheit' is dominated by the word 'schon', and ends in happy certainty − 'zur Vollendung geht die Menschheit ein'. Heroism becomes almost routine, as witness the phrase 'die traute Schreckensbahn' in the poem 'Melodie. An Lyda'. A simple myth serves to explain history: the original rule of love in the world was overthrown by 'Übermut', but has now been restored; the Revolution is the new 'Schöpfungsstunde' ('Hymne an die Freiheit'). The only uncertainty − see the two versions of that poem − is how long the destruction of tyranny will take; the process raises no other problems.

One must ask whether these are political poems, since recent critics have argued that Hölderlin was a jacobin.[9] The ideas are very naive, and also very general. The poet decries evil things, like tyranny, and lauds good things, like justice and freedom. This is unexceptionable, but not specific enough to be identified as jacobin or girondist. Here is a young man inspired by the most important event of modern times to declare his best feelings. The Revolution is the occasion of his poetry, politics is scarcely its subject. The hymns are first gropings towards a philo-sophical or religious (chiliastic) vision, which contemporary upheavals seemed to encourage, of the regeneration of man and society. When the Revolution failed of its promise, the vision persisted, developing in even less specifically political forms, albeit still loosely connected with the 'gärende Zeit' of the Napoleonic period.

But even as visionary generalisation these are not good poems. The hymnic genre imposed a rhetoric of exhortation, exclamation, invoca-tion, noble gesture and sacral language ('Heil!', 'heilig', 'hehr' and 'ha!')

and an unremitting sensationalism of verbs ('erglüht', 'schmettert', 'umschimmernd', 'bebend', 'höhnt'). The reader is meant to be carried away in idealistic intoxication, but is numbed by the monotony of means. Hölderlin was doubtless emulating his revered Schiller — the influence is a commonplace of literary history — but he reproduces only a narrow range of Schiller's effects. The rhetoric is more naked, the armature of developing thought weaker; and where Schiller varies movement and tone over a number of stanzas (e.g. the sequence beginning 'Schöne Welt, wo bist du?' in 'Die Götter Griechenlands'), making a public genre serve personal expression, Hölderlin's movement is stereotyped, his syntactic structures and phrasing dictated by the set stanza.[10]

For something more like the mature Hölderlin's voice we have, paradoxically, to go back to earlier poems such as 'Einst und Jetzt' and 'Ich duld' es nimmer' which do not attempt hymnic grandeur. The intricacy and variety of the alcaic stanza — one of the Greek metres Hölderlin was to make his own — already seem to liberate his more intimate feeling and render the subtler realities behind the bravado of the hymns; the strain of aspiration, the loneliness of sensitive youth, the bitterness of frustrated ambition. These are thus personal lyrics, and Hölderlin's mature poetry was to transcend the merely personal. But it did so by intensifying personal experience into paradigms of existence, not by ignoring it in favour of windy generalisation.

This turn begins around 1795, just before the fateful move to Frankfurt. The poem 'An die Natur' evokes lost childhood in fragments of recollected experience — the sky seen between branches, the scent of blossom, the brilliance of light, the bare heath, the rushing streams. 'Einst und Jetzt' too contrasted the happy child with the disconsolate youth walking 'einsam am Gestade hin'. But experience now becomes representative: the 'goldne Tage' suggest the Golden Age, the loss of happiness is the loss of nature itself, the 'Heimat' of the last stanza is both the poet's real home and Man's lost attachment to the tree from which, in the poem's opening image, he first grew. The immediate record found in 'Einst und Jetzt' has been replaced by a larger evocation of Man's 'sentimentalisch' condition. Yet it is not an overtly philosophical poem. It moves almost wholly in images, authenticated by experience though not merely registering it for its own sake.

This is the crucial shift from rhetorical expansion to poetic compression. Though 'An die Natur' uses the hymnic stanza, its voice is gentle and pensive, and the toning down of rhetorical volume allows symbolic resonances to be heard. Hölderlin is beginning to assemble the elements (in two senses — 'the constituents', but also 'primal things') for a vision: sky, air, light; streams that seek the ocean; flowers and harvest; childhood itself.

If Nature, as actuality and ideal, is one source of Hölderlin's thought and feeling, Greece is the other. The pre-Frankfurt poem, 'Griechenland', shows how much this is the world his mind inhabits. His enthusiasm for freedom and revolution was noticeably never embodied in poems on French places, people, events. Such particulars come only in his letters, and are then distressing ones; the tyranny of Marat and Robespierre, whose politically moderate victims Hölderlin pities and whose fall he welcomes with a most unjacobin relief.[11] But he evokes Greek places, landscape, customs, heroes and philosophers with strong elegiac emotion; Greece is another lost ideal. As Schiller taught, the ideal which contrasts so sharply with mere reality is also for its devotee the highest reality and demands to be restored. So Hölderlin is concerned not just to celebrate it in poignant phrase and image, like the lone crane sorrowing among the ruins as spring returns to a deserted Greek landscape, but also to bring about its return. In some moods — and his moods swung with the force and regularity of the tides, 'ewig Ebb und Flut'[12] — reality seemed too triumphantly oppressive; in others (witness the hymns already discussed) enthusiasm generated its own conviction. But these last were poetic 'highs' whose very vehemence ('Froh, als könnt' ich Schöpfungen beglücken,/Stolz, als huldigten die Sterne mir') guaranteed their transience. Something more was needed than subjective projections to sustain his vision and intent.

It was given in the person of Susette Gontard, to whose children Hölderlin became private tutor in Frankfurt. For him she was a revelation of beauty and goodness beyond anything he had known, giving him new faith when his heart had grown arid.[13] He again felt the peace of childhood — or rather he saw, in a poetic conceit recalling Goethe's 'Warum gabst du uns die tiefen Blicke?', that childhood had been an anticipation of her.[14] Aptly, he called her Diotima after the wise and beautiful woman in Plato's *Symposium* who teaches Socrates to see beauty as the symbol of all spiritual perfections. Her mere existence cast a different light on a 'geist- und ordnungsloses Jahrhundert'.[15] Love for this realised ideal transformed Hölderlin's poetry. Happiness released a flow of simple and beautiful images, composing visions that have serenity and substance where those of the idealistic hymns were hectic and flimsy. True, he was also striving consciously to do as Schiller had suggested and write a poetry more concrete, more balanced in the sense of the Classicists' theories.[16] But at most such craftsmanly intentions were in tune with emotional impulse; they cannot explain the new idyllic richness.

Hölderlin now celebrates a world in which he is at home. 'An den Aether' surveys all creatures that are nourished and embraced in their growth and diverse activities by the fatherly element of air. Plant and bird strive up into it, and for Man too, the restless wanderer about the earth, it is the direction of ultimate yearning. Yet even as the poet gazes up in strenuous aspiration, a quieter fulfilment falls unconstrained:

> Kommst du säuselnd herab von des Fruchtbaums blühenden
> Wipfeln,
> Vater Aether! und sänftigest selbst das strebende Herz mir,
>
> Und ich lebe nun gern, wie zuvor, mit den Blumen der Erde.

And 'Der Wandrer' (first version) imagines those restless wanderings of man, to polar ice and burning desert, only to evoke richly a return to the 'heimatliche Natur' of the Rhineland and an idyll of earth's friendliness. In this landscape things connect and embrace ('Wo die Ulme das alternde Hoftor/Übergrünt und den Zaun wilder Holunder umblüht'), the fruit grows as if to the poet's hand, the paths draw him on, he has returned as to his childhood, 'getreuer und weiser,/Friedlich zu werden und froh unter den Blumen zu ruhn'. These are already great poems, combining — but in a quite distinctive voice — Schiller's spiritual range and Goethe's sensuousness (cf. e.g. 'Herbstgefühl').

If Hölderlin can find such idyllic fulfilment, what has become of the conflict between good and evil which inspired his hymns? Other poems do continue to evoke a chaotic world where storms rage and Diotima's perfection is vulnerable 'wie die zarten Blüten im Winter'. Yet he holds on to the idea of the harmony that once emerged from chaos and (he can now hope) will again. He appeals to Venus Urania, who ordered the first chaos, to return and calm human struggles:

> Bis in der sterblichen Brust sich das Entzweite vereint,
> Bis der Menschen alte Natur, die ruhige, grosse,
> Aus der gärenden Zeit mächtig und heiter sich hebt.
>
> ('Komm und besänftige mir . . .')

The effect Diotima had upon him — 'sänftigen' or 'besänftigen' is her leitmotif, and she is sometimes herself likened to Venus Urania[17] — is here projected, in a transference typical of Hölderlin, on to the larger stage of human history. Chaos contains the promise of harmony, though the mechanism is obscure; but if there are historical processes that can thus be trusted, existence as a totality becomes acceptable.

This is strikingly put in 'Die Musse', where the poet sees, amid an idyllic landscape and the peace of town and villages, the signs of old strife, ruined temple-gates and pillars 'die einst der Furchtbare traf, der geheime/Geist der Unruh'. Yet this spirit of unrest is not an alien element in the eternal order, but a second son of nature, 'Mit dem Geiste der Ruh aus Einem Schosse geboren'. The operative forces of history are rooted in nature, all moves towards an ultimate desirable end. This conception looks back to Christian theodicy and perhaps gropes towards a dialectic of history such as Hölderlin's friend Hegel was to formulate. However we see it, it quenches activism. In a final vignette, the poet at home reading a newspaper — 'von menschlichem Leben/Ein erzählendes Blatt' — responds with the cry:

> Leben! Leben der Welt! du liegst wie ein heiliger Wald da,
> Sprech ich dann, und es nehme die Axt, wer will, dich zu ebnen,
> Glücklich wohn ich in dir.

The shorter concluding line seems to await, even defy, objections to such quietistic contentment. The poet has withdrawn from events into idyllic self-sufficiency.

Two related poems complete this picture precisely by being themselves fragmentary. 'Die Völker schwiegen, schlummerten . . .' evokes the wars raging all over Europe ('auf ungeheurer Walstatt . . . von dem blauen Rheine bis zur Tyber') which are the work of that same 'Geist der Unruh'. There is then a blank page followed by the isolated lines:

> Und blinken goldne Früchte wieder dir,
> Wie heitre holde Sterne, durch die kühle Nacht
> Der Pomeranzenwälder in Italien —

This, with its echoes of Goethe's 'Kennst du das Land', seems a sketch for an idyllic resolution. But how will the desired harmony arise from the turbulent present? The blank page cannot say. Hölderlin was perhaps seeking the answer and the essence of the struggle when he went on to attempt a poem about Napoleon, whose Italian campaign was then demonstrating his genius. But the poem admits defeat; this hero will not be contained in the traditional vessel of poetry:

> Der Dichter lass ihn unberührt wie den Geist der Natur,
> An solchem Stoffe wird zum Knaben der Meister.

> ('Buonaparte')

To apprehend him fully would have been, precisely, to penetrate that 'Geist der Natur' which in its sub-forms of 'Ruh' and 'Unruh' shapes history. This is close to Hegel's famous aperçu that Napoleon was the World Spirit on horseback. But Hegel also devised a theory relating the movement of history to the passions, intentions and actions of individual men; Hölderlin can only look on at events, waiting for some feature of the times to tally with his visionary expectations – as the Revolution had once seemed to, and as the Peace of Lunéville was to do in 1801, inspiring celebratory letters[18] and the poem 'Friedensfeier'.

The essence of Hölderlin's personal history and relation to his times is rendered in the novel *Hyperion*, which he completed in Frankfurt. By an original stroke – for none of the other German graecolaters gave much thought to the land of their dreams as it was now – he sets it in modern Greece. The scenes and ruins of antiquity make the loss of ancient greatness more keenly felt. Greece is desecrated by Turkish rule and Greeks bear it ignobly. Against this background, Hyperion suffers a series of inspirations and disillusionments. His friend Alabanda talks of rescuing the fatherland, of laurels and immortality, but has associates who speak the less heady language of revolutionary realism, which leads to a break with him. Hyperion withdraws into himself, and it is on emerging from this dark night of the soul that he meets Diotima. Like Susette Gontard, she is beauty and perfection and she understands his problems – the certainty that his idealism will meet repeated rebuffs, the risk that he may turn away from humanity and take refuge in their idyll. True to the teachings of Socrates' Diotima, she urges him to go beyond love of her particular beauty, to become a teacher, take the example of his refound wholeness among men, and restore 'die alte Wahrheit . . . in neu lebendiger Jugend'.[19] But he doubts the sufficiency of words and ideals and joins Alabanda in action. The situation mirrors the constant dilemma of intellectuals, not just in the eighteenth century: can poetry, thought, principle ever take effect without direct action? Hyperion tells Diotima: 'Der neue Geisterbund kann in der Luft nicht leben, die heilige Theokratie des Schönen muss in einem Freistaat wohnen, und der will Platz haben auf Erden und diesen Platz erobern wir gewiss'.[20] She replies that noble ends may be damaged and lost to sight in the effort to secure them by force, and this is drastically fulfilled when Hyperion's men murder and plunder indiscriminately.

Sickened, he reflects how vain was the hope 'durch eine Räuberbande mein Elysium zu pflanzen' (p.122). The problem of realising ideals and reforming the world has become no more tractable since that earlier robber-band of Karl Moor's.

The shamed Hyperion renounces Diotima, and she dies. In her last letter she dedicates him again to the prophetic role: 'Priester sollst du sein der göttlichen Natur, und die dichterischen Tage keimen dir schon' (p.155). He is tempted by a self-sacrificial death like that of the philosopher Empedokles, but feels unworthy of it. He travels — to Germany, which allows (at some cost to artistic unity) a direct statement of what the novel is meant to embody, namely that Hölderlin's German contemporaries are men without harmony and wholeness: 'ich kann kein Volk mir denken, das zerrissner wäre, wie die Deutschen. Handwerker siehst du, aber keine Menschen, Denker, aber keine Menschen, Priester, aber keine Menschen, Herrn und Knechte, Jungen und gesetzte Leute, aber keine Menschen — ist das nicht, wie ein Schlachtfeld, wo Hände und Arme und alle Glieder zerstückelt untereinander liegen, indessen das vergossne Lebensblut im Sande zerrinnt?' (p.160). Germans have no respect for 'die göttliche Natur' itself, which they profane and misuse. Genius lives in their midst like Ulysses reduced to beggar's disguise in his own house.

In this great diatribe the frustrations of Hölderlin's career become prophetic denunciation. This strikes familiar chords: the critique of fragmented modern existence in Schiller's *Ästhetische Briefe*, the complaints against German society in Goethe's *Literarischer Sansculottismus*, the record of rejection in Moritz's *Anton Reiser* here combine in a rhapsody of bitterness. Hölderlin's countervailing ideal is also close to Schiller. He envisages an education through beauty which will fit men for communal harmony: 'da, wo ein Volk das Schöne liebt, wo es den Genius in seinen Künstlern ehrt, da weht, wie Lebensluft, ein allgemeiner Geist, da öffnet sich der scheue Sinn, der Eigendünkel schmilzt, und fromm und gross sind alle Herzen und Helden gebiert die Begeisterung' (p.163). Even as a rebel leader, he had hoped his Greeks would be recognised not by a flag but by their changed inner nature. Now, disillusioned by action, he returns the more emphatically to the socio-aesthetic principle deeply engrained in eighteenth-century German writers.

Yet, typically of Hölderlin, there is a final stage after Hyperion's outburst when he rises above suffering and loss to an almost mystical reconciliation. If the heart can hold out through the midnight of sorrow, it learns 'dass . . . göttlich erst in tiefem Leid das Lebenslied der Welt uns tönt'. The world's dissonances are like a lovers' quarrel: 'Versöhnung ist mitten im Streit und alles Getrennte findet sich wieder'. He can feel Nature ecstatically as a unity, 'einiges, ewiges, glühendes Leben ist Alles' (p.164ff.). Blessed with this experience, Hyperion becomes — hence the sub-title — a hermit in Greece. Harmony proves itself once more an inner imperative, even when its absence in the outside world is most vehemently declared and the effort to achieve it has been resoundingly defeated.

To that extent the novel has fulfilled the aim stated in the foreword, to show the 'Auflösung der Dissonanzen in einem gewissen Charakter'. But the harmony achieved is not stable. No doubt the 'reconciliation' passage, set thus at the end of the book, was meant to have most emphasis. But there are points later in time (albeit earlier in the narrative sequence) when Hyperion swings from joy to dejection and back, finds his oneness with nature and loses it again, feels himself a god and an outcast.[21] It seems that Hölderlin's deepest governing principle is the psychic 'Ebb und Flut' which now brings the sense of harmony flooding over him, now bears it away beyond reach. This same pattern underlies his next major project, the tragedy *Der Tod des Empedokles* (three fragmentary versions, 1798-9).

The themes are once more nature-mysticism, prophecy and social renewal. Their outward form is the life of the Greek philosopher Empedocles — not an obvious dramatic subject, for no clear plot-line emerges from the sources. It is reported that he called himself a god; that he was a champion of freedom and equality; that he refused the kingship of Agrigentum; that he held a doctrine of the four elements and their union by the force of love; and that he died by plunging into the crater of Etna, perhaps to strengthen rumours that he had become a god. The difficulty of making these disconnected motifs cohere explains some of the weaknesses of Hölderlin's structure. Thus in the most elaborated version (E. I) Empedokles' claim to be a god outrages the people and he is outlawed, but the people follow and offer him the crown. This change of heart seems dictated by the need to connect the 'facts' of the source. The same applies to inconsistencies in Empedokles' own motives. He ascends Etna, implicitly, to atone for the hubris of calling himself a god; but when he has declined the crown and given the people his prophetic message of inner renewal and the casting off of old forms, his death becomes a self-sacrifice to exemplify it. Motivation is mixed further still by other ideas: that the prophet must not outstay his mission and risk being demeaned by earthly uses (this is part of Hölderlin's polemic against institutionalised religion which

'Heiliges wie ein Gewerbe treibt');[22] that it would be wrong to live on after his day of public disgrace; and that death is a 'return to nature' desirable in itself. This unresolved competition between themes suggests an unclear purpose. But there is a more interesting discrepancy yet, between outer action as such and Hölderlin's meaning. By the end of E. I, Empedokles' act of hubris is all but forgotten; its spiritual consequence, the desolation of losing his mystic harmony with nature, has been reversed and on Etna's heights he feels at one again with 'die allverzeihende Natur'. As if by a swing of mood, 'die schöne Zeit von meinem Leben' has returned and he approaches the mountain-top, where the gods' presence is stronger, with no sign of guilt. How can forgiveness be thus unearned? And how can nature forgive what was a sin against the gods?

The answer is that for Empedokles as for Hölderlin the reality behind 'the gods' *is* nature, 'die Allebendige', and the elements of air, earth, light with which Empedokles lived 'in einigem gegenwärtigem Olymp' (p.19). His 'fall' is not an outward dramatic act to be punished by the 'Rachegötter' the priest Hermokrates conceives of; it is an attitude of mind that somehow breaks the harmony with nature and is thereby its own punishment — just as, when it yields to a happier state, there can be a metaphorical 'forgiveness'. This is not a reductive interpretation — Hölderlin is not saying that the gods are *merely* nature. The movement is the other way: Empedokles reveres nature so deeply that it becomes divine, indeed it *constitutes* for him the idea of the divine. Still, it may well seem that Hölderlin is not dealing with tragic guilt at all, since the changes his protagonist undergoes are not willed or controllable. Pausanias duly suggests at one point, in an image Hölderlin often uses for movements of the spirit, that his master's spiritual aridity is part of a natural cycle like that of the seasons (p.20); and in E. II the outward 'claim to be a god' has faded from the plot, leaving only the inner state as dramatic subject.

Yet for Hölderlin that state was still the 'Ursünde'. He makes this comment on Empedokles' words to nature in E. I:

Verachtet hab ich dich und mich
Zum Herrn gesetzt, ein übermütiger
Barbar![23]

That man may thus lord it over nature is a spiritual peril Hölderlin was acutely aware of in these years. In two early sketches for *Hyperion* the hero confesses that in his youth he became 'tyrannisch gegen die

Natur'.[24] A letter written during work on *Empedokles* explains the idea fully. Man's consciousness separates him from nature, and his defining characteristic is an impulse to act upon it, 'den ewigen Vollendungsgang der Natur zu beschleunigen'. At its best this is a service rendered to nature, but at its worst it makes him think himself nature's lord and master. His free consciousness and all its works, the arts and activities of civilisation, are good only if he retains his reverence for the sources of life.[25] Otherwise he has usurped his power.

To Hölderlin such usurpation might well seem rife. Late eighteenth-century thought centred on man's consciousness, made it the condition of all his experiencing, preached it as a value, even — in Fichte — defined the world by reference to it as mere 'Nicht-Ich'.[26] To counter this, man needed reminding of his fundamental dependence on nature and her irreplaceable gifts. Only in such a frame of mind would his 'rule' be legitimate. The classic myth of usurpation — Jupiter supplant-ing his father Saturn as supreme god — helped Hölderlin to concentrate this insight in the ode 'Natur und Kunst oder Saturn und Jupiter'. Empedokles is expressly understood in the same terms, as a 'Sohn der gewaltigen Entgegensetzungen von Natur und Kunst'[27] and, in E. II, as a new more impertinent Jupiter reared by Saturn-nature (p.108). Thus behind the shifting moods and spiritual pitfalls of Hyperion and Empedokles there lies Hölderlin's prophetic concern with a modern original sin of which his protagonists are more the victims than the perpetrators. It is a hypertrophying consciousness which may promise, like the knowledge of good and evil in Genesis, to make men 'as gods' but in fact threatens to cut them off from their true roots.

Empedokles' role is, precisely, to remake the broken connection between Agrigentine society and nature. In E. I (pp.66ff.) we see him deliver his message, his 'Heiligtum', and receive — perhaps as poetic justice after Hyperion's failures and his own disgrace — due honour from men. The drama here becomes political, though it is a familiarly unideological, idealistic politics. Like Hyperion, Empedokles aims to change men from within. Externals are at issue only in that he is offered the crown and refuses it, which itself suggests that the essentials of society lie deeper than the possession of power. Even his words, 'Dies ist die Zeit der Könige nicht mehr', are not quite the revolutionary cry that is sometimes suggested. They are part of the Enlightenment's evolutionary view of progress: kings were appropriate once, but men must now take responsibility for themselves — 'euch ist nicht/Zu helfen, wenn ihr selber euch nicht helft'. Where Empedokles goes beyond this standard declaration of man's 'Mündigkeit', beyond even the nature-based liberalism of Posa's speech before King Philipp (see above, p.45f.), is in the intensity of his vision of nature as an all-giving source for social man. The Agrigentines are to abandon their old ways — 'Gesetz und Brauch, der alten Götter Namen' — and raise their eyes 'wie Neugeborne . . . zur göttlichen Natur'. Nature will inspire them to live in freedom, harmony and total equality, a true community can begin. The prophet, superfluous once nature's voice is listened to, can die leaving the people to their restored Golden Age — 'die glücklichen Saturnustage'. This is a revolution indeed, but one less of political forms than of men's deepest attitudes, a 'Revolution der Gesinnungen' such as Hölderlin still hoped for in the future when events in France were disillusioning.[28]

Familiar motifs recur in the later drafts. E. II ends with Empedokles' death seen as a mystical and historical necessity — 'es nährt/Das Leben vom Leide sich', and 'so musst es geschehn./So will es der Geist/Und die reifende Zeit,/Denn einmal bedurften/Wir Blinden des Wunders'. E. III brings a quite new figure, Manes the Egyptian, as a spiritual match for Empedokles, but its final recorded phrases again grope towards a future fulfilment — 'Neue Welt' and 'schon öffnet sich/die Flut über die Dürre'. But none of the three fragments will support a coherent interpretation, nor will all three taken together, since there is so much shift of emphasis within a general thematic pattern. For the same reason, Hölderlin's plans — the Frankfurt original, or the sketches for E. III — do not help. Nor does the essay 'Grund zum Empedokles', which purports to give the work's philosophic meaning but has (like most of Hölderlin's 'theoretical' writing) the cryptic density of private jottings rather than the clarity of formal exposition. And even if the essay did present some unifying conception, the fact remains (though it is often obscured by critics' reverence for the spirituality that produced the work or for the mission it treats) that Hölderlin failed to realise it in dramatic form. Indeed, there is little sign of a specifically dramatic grasp in any phase of the project.

But if *Empedokles* is a failed drama, it tells us much about Hölderlin and his aspirations. It voices the revulsion against orthodoxy which made him criticise his church and persistently avoid becoming a pastor;[29] it expresses the 'Verlangen nach Ewigem'[30] which was a constant of his experience; it celebrates the elements of life as hallowed entities, prime facts of existence which man too little appreciates; and it shows the impulse to resensitize men to these fundamentals by sheer intensity of vision.

Is this properly a religious vision? Not if 'religious' means talking about real gods that command and intervene, figures standing in a hierarchy laid down by doctrine. But it is precisely those limits Hölderlin's work goes beyond. For him the root of religion was man's 'Beziehung mit dem, was ihn umgibt'.[31] Hyperion is so overwhelmed by the richness of this world that he cannot conceive a god outside it; he declares that the wise man loves beauty, and only the people love the gods that are beauty's children.[32] Hölderlin can change 'der Götter Lob' to 'des Lebens Lob' without otherwise affecting the argument of an ode ('Ermunterung'). Nature is 'älter denn die Zeiten/Und über die Götter des Abends und Orients' ('Wie wenn am Feiertage . . .'). Praise of the earth is itself a religious act ('Germanien', final section), the earth a representative of the remote 'alte Vater' ('Der Mutter Erde',MS sketch). All this suggests an aesthetic pantheism or vitalism which does not so much preach as teach by example, that is, by the power of poetic speech to express the love and gratitude which man at his most sensitively aware feels for the stuff of life. It is hard to know what to call this if not 'religious'. It approaches that ideal of primal mythopoiesis which the Romantics could conceive but not realise, 'sich unmittelbar anschliessend und anbildend an das Nächste, Lebendigste der sinnlichen Welt' (see above, p. 195).

Some critics, assuming that 'Götter' in Hölderlin must mean what the word normally means, read his late poetry as religious in a quasi-orthodox sense and take the intense feeling and poetic power as a guarantee that there was 'something there'.[33] Yet the word 'gods' and other more specific ones — names of Greek deities, allusions to Christ, periphrases like 'Gott der Zeit' and 'Geist der Welt' — are a language of the imagination. Not, however, in quite the sense in which that phrase was used of Goethe and Schiller at the start of this chapter. They were choosing a medium deliberately and coolly, for historical and aesthetic reasons, to harmonise with what they had to say; and incidentally repaying a debt to antiquity for the deepened understanding of art it had given them. Both ancient source and modern use were consciously a matter of culture; and though they hoped culture would affect men profoundly for the better, it was not to be through cultic enthusiasm. In contrast, Hölderlin's is a primal projection of feeling into images and myths to which his emotions are wholly committed. He too may originally have aquired them as materials of culture, but his relation to them is more immediate; for him they do not just represent, they are totally identified with the natural world of which his poetry speaks.[34]

Modest though he was, he insisted on this profound difference between what he was striving to say and what other eighteenth-century poets had said. Were they not hypocrites to use divine names merely to decorate a world left dead by the understanding?

Ihr kalten Heuchler, sprecht von den Göttern nicht!
Ihr habt Verstand! ihr glaubt nicht an Helios,
   Noch an den Donnerer und Meergott;
      Tot ist die Erde, wer mag ihr danken?

('Die scheinheiligen Dichter')

What Schiller's 'Götter Griechenlands' elaborated in sorrow, Hölderlin here compresses in anger. The implication is clear; only when the earth is *not* a dead object of the understanding but awakens the basic religious response of gratitude – only when the poet is 'fromm, wie der Grieche war' ('An die jungen Dichter') – may he invoke divine names. This is uncompromising, and many eighteenth-century poets had lived on compromise. Since Klopstock's day sublime utterance had striven to survive the loss of belief in sublime beings and had delayed total secularisation by retaining the language of myth. Hölderlin is sometimes placed in this development, as a last flaring of the fire before it went out altogether.[35] But he stands rather in heroic isolation, denying value to that whole development, while he himself draws on deeper sources of emotion and refuses to separate poetic means and ends. Certainly no other eighteenth-century odes close the gap between idea and mythic symbol as his do. Even where a title suggests allegory – 'Natur und Kunst oder Saturn und Jupiter' – the myth is not the disposable package for an idea, nor is the apostrophe of Jupiter a decorative way of arguing about abstractions. From the first line we are drawn into an impassioned exchange with a basic force of life, myth matches imagination, imagination revivifies myth. The poet does not translate into, he thinks in mythic images in a way equalled only by Goethe in his 'Prometheus' or 'Ganymed'. Even where Hölderlin does not initially mention a divinity, he seems to grasp some fundamental reality, the archetype of some natural phenomenon – man's need for fire and shelter in winter, a river's breaking free from winter ice – and changes his titles accordingly, from 'Der Winter' to 'Vulkan' and from 'Der gefesselte Strom' to 'Ganymed'. The hand that has touched myth can scarcely any longer form mere literal statement, as is seen strikingly when he tries to write a 'kunstlos Lied' about a beautiful town, and every detail of the picture – the bridge, the river, its sources and banks, the storm-ravaged castle, the light, the gardens – transcends description and seems to touch the very shaping forces of life and fate ('Heidelberg').

Yet it does so without pointing onwards to 'higher' significances. This is not the mystic's book of nature which speaks of the unseen glories of god, these *are* the divine glories; things seized in their essence, set beside each other lucidly and lovingly. Even beyond this 'the gods' have another function in Hölderlin's late poetry. He looks forward to their return after long absence as the crown of a new age of human and social fulfilment – or, to take him less literally (and perhaps he himself did not distinguish clearly) the idea of a divine return is the supreme *symbol* for that fulfilment and the emotions it will arouse. At all events, he hopes it is imminent and that the present is, in the closing words of E. II, 'die reifende Zeit'.

II

Such hope needed support. Where could it come from? Perhaps, as ever, from the Greek example. So Hölderlin now looks back once more and evokes Greece with an unsurpassed beauty and richness of detail in what is arguably his greatest poem. 'Der Archipelagus' is intense in feeling yet measured and lucid in argument, grand in conception yet fully mastered and realised. It combines in its serene hexameters both lyric and epic–the keenest expression of Hölderlin's love for the Aegean island seascape, and a majestic retelling of episodes from the Persian Wars: the Greeks' initial defeat by Xerxes, their decisive victory at Salamis, the rebuilding of Athens. In particular Hölderlin celebrates the united Greek spirit which made triumph possible. From exemplary history he then moves on to prophecy, striving to carry over the ideal he has so fully actualised into an imagined near-future. Though the Greeks are gone, the forces by which their culture lived – the 'Kräfte der Höhe', the 'Himmlischen', the 'begeisternden Kräfte' – are still there, and seek hearts to dwell in:

Dass ein liebendes Volk in des Vaters Armen gesammelt,
Menschlich freudig, wie sonst, und Ein Geist allen gemein sei.

If the present falls lamentably short of this – 'es wandelt in Nacht, es wohnt, wie im Orkus,/Ohne Göttliches unser Geschlecht' – still the energies released by his vision of the past can raise him above it. With a 'Bis ... wieder' he rises to prophetic expectation, an enthusiastic 'schon' makes it a present certainty scarcely modified by a 'ferne' ('schon hör ich ferne des Festtags/Chorgesang'); the world, from being dark and godless, is suddenly 'voll göttlichen Sinns'. Yet the present tense is fragile hypothesis; in the closing lines the vision fades, a sobered voice admits that it may be long 'bis unsre Früchte beginnen', and the poet is once more struggling to keep above the waves of history and the 'Irrsal' of his personal fate.

This hints at the problems of prophetic poetry. It is doubly dependent on the past — for its inspiration, but also for its concreteness because a future perfection is hard to realise. (In much the same way, Schiller's 'sentimentalisch' poets turned back to old bucolic harmonies because a true 'sentimentalisch' idyll was almost impossible to achieve.) But the past refuses to connect convincingly with the future. There are analogies — between Persian and Napoleonic Wars, between the destruction of Athens and destruction in modern Europe, allowing hopes of a similar physical and spiritual reconstruction. Yet a gap remains which can only be fleetingly bridged by the visionary mood. Hölderlin saw this and strove to moderate his dependence on the past — 'Und rückwärts soll die Seele mir nicht fliehn/Zu euch, Vergangene! die zu lieb mir sind' ('Germanien') — for the understanding of modern times, strove to find his hopes wholly in the present.

Thus the late poetry is positive, even enthusiastic, about Germany and its future — surprisingly, when one remembers Hyperion's judgement on the Germans of his time. Yet even when Hölderlin was writing that, he could also predict a vital role for them in the longed-for 'Revolution der Gesinnungen'. No doubt this is a typical oscillation, 'ewig Ebb und Flut' again. But the way he rationalises his hopes is revealing. The Germans' very quiescence proves their future promise: 'je stiller ein Staat aufwächst, um so herrlicher wird er, wenn er zur Reife kömmt'.[36] This is his strategy against despair: a prophet seeking for signs must often read them by contraries. Personal experience had taught him that the gods moved in mysterious ways; they had never led him by straight paths ('Lebenslauf', stanza 3). It was bitter necessity to remember this now if he was still to believe in his mission, for nothing seemed to favour it. Cut off from the woman he loved, still not established as a writer, endlessly preparing himself for some vague future role, with no standing in society, his position appeared hopeless. Losing Diotima, who had first given him the strength 'Grosses zu sehn und die schweigenden Götter zu singen' ('Elegie'), might have been the final blow. So it had to become part of the pattern, a 'heiliges Leid' sent by the same gods who send inspiration ('Die Heimat'), a sacrifice demanded by this age of 'allentzweiende Hass' ('Der Abschied', first version). Suffering could then be a magical source of serenity — 'Wie so selig doch auch mitten im Leide mir ist' — and of belief in his task: 'Wer so/Liebte, gehet, er muss, gehet zu Göttern die Bahn' ('Menons

Klagen um Diotima', stanzas 2 and 9). This ancient mechanism of faith, seeing in adverse circumstance a paradoxical promise of fulfilment, is at the centre of all his prophecy.

The night of godlessness after the bright day of antiquity becomes itself a sign that a new day is about to dawn ('Brod und Wein'); the people's silence may presage their coming celebration of the divine ('An die Deutschen'); the limitations of human vision imply the grander perspectives we cannot see ('Rousseau'); more than once his own dejection becomes a hint that all will be well and shames him into a kind of certainty.

Then there are the positive signs that all is not lost; a pure personality is a 'sicheres Licht' ('An eine Fürstin von Dessau'); the soul of lovers is a refuge of true 'menschliches Leben', like the first signs of spring among the cold of winter ('Die Liebe'); the blossoming of earth and the blossoming of stars across the heavens are encouragement to a downcast heart ('Ermunterung'). Indeed, nature is a pervasive encouragement. What had earlier been glimpses of a perfection unconnected with larger events – the golden fruit at the end of 'Die Völker schwiegen, schlummerten ...', the roses and wine which are imagined bursting through the polar ice in 'Der Wanderer', the elements of personal idyll in 'An den Aether' and 'Die Musse' – now becomes systematic. The imagery of the turning year, of the growth of plant or child, of life's resilient fruitfulness, is called on to guarantee a larger idyll of peace and men's regeneration. After a dozen stanzas on war, peace can be made to seem sure by an appeal to earth's season:

> Du aber wandelst ruhig die sichre Bahn
> O Mutter Erd im Lichte. Dein Frühling blüht,
>   Melodischwechselnd gehn dir hin die
>   Wachsenden Zeiten, du Lebensreiche!

> ('Der Frieden')

(The serene movement of the verse, incidentally, shows how perfectly Hölderlin now fuses his thought with the Greek metres that are his staple form.) And in a greater 'year' still, the time-span in which cultures rise and fall, the glory of Greece is conceived moving north to Germany as surely as spring moves over the face of the globe: 'Wie der Frühling, wandelt der Genius/Von Land zu Land'; Germany, late but no less splendid for that, will be the 'reifeste Frucht der Zeit' ('Gesang des Deutschen').

This is the heart of Hölderlin's message and the last-named poem is the prophet at his most confident. Only the exact location of the 'höchstes Fest', the German Delos or Olympia, remains a secret of his constant muse, the chaos-ordering Venus Urania. But certainty is not the keynote of the late poetry. True, there are moments of total and triumphant conviction; nature comes marching to his prophetic drum, 'die Natur ist jetzt mit Waffenklang erwacht' ('Wie wenn am Feiertage ...'); there is to be a 'Brautfest der Menschen und Götter' ('Der Rhein'); the divine form has been shaken down like fruit from a tree — 'die langgesuchte,/Die goldne Frucht,/Uraltem Stamm/In schütternden Stürmen entfallen,/... Die Gestalt der Himmlischen ists' ('Friedensfeier'); Germany, in communion with nature and the gods it has long concealed, will hold festivals 'wo du Priesterin bist/Und wehrlos Rat gibst rings/Den Königen und den Völkern' ('Germanien'). Yet these are phases in a struggle for certainty. Nature itself only seems to support him because he chooses images that assimilate history to nature. This is self-persuasion, like all the prophet's strategies, and it needs constant renewal. Poem after poem swings between the tireless idealist and his flagging empirical self. 'An die Deutschen' promises bold assertion with its title, but records a sequence of expectancy, doubt, hope-against-hope, reaffirmation, and desolation at the prophet's homelessness in time. The poem is perfect — but as an expression of uncertainty. Precisely because he is uncertain, its phrases and images are pillaged for a new draft which reworks the issues in a new metre, starting this time from human limitations and ending with a strengthened faith that signs are the language of the gods and the prophet their warning eagle flying before the storm. Yet such confidence is only possible because the overt subject is now another seer, an undoubted prophet — Rousseau. In a similar alternation, 'Wie wenn am Feiertage ...', after carrying all before it, tails off in fears that he is a false prophet. And later, when a great hope has been fulfilled and peace is made, the poet can realise that he had given up believing in it, even though it was 'zuvorbestimmt': 'Versöhnender, der du *nimmergeglaubt*/Nun da bist ...'

Are we talking about a weakness or a strength in Hölderlin? That depends whether we mean the prophet or the poet, for they can and must now be separated. Prophecy as such does not guarantee poetry. It may be the occasion for it, generating and focussing the poet's emotion; but its content, the cultural apotheosis of Germany and the renewal of man and society, has no compelling quality in itself. It is not even very distinctive — as a reaction to German history, it has parallels in other, more concretely nationalistic minds like Fichte.[37] What moves us as poetry is the finely traced conflict between a delicate mind and a violent world, the ebb and flow of hope and desolation which virtually constitutes Hölderlin's poetic speech. Hölderlin aimed at sublimity, but what he achieves is poignancy, through the integrity with which he sets down a whole situation and his whole response. (The nearest analogy, though remote in time and genre, is the movement of Kafka's prose.)

Beyond this immediate textual effect, modern retrospect adds a further pathos even to the more triumphal assertions: because they were proved illusory by history; because they were mostly never even heard by Hölderlin's contemporaries; and because, as his mind breaks up, they are ever smaller islands of clarity in a sea of dark phrases and drifting fragments of argument. These three factors make Hölderlin a tragic figure. They also have implications which help us to place his work, its effects and its repute critically and historically.

Firstly the prophet's illusions. All prophecy is vulnerable to hindsight, and to say that Hölderlin was wrong would be trivial criticism, especially after arguing that the value of his poetry lies elsewhere. But juxtaposing his euphoric predictions and actual events, his inspired leap to conclusions and the slight justification for them, does show how tenuous is the grasp of the prophetic imagination on reality, in contrast to the modes of apprehension of soberer poets. Thus it only needed the (temporary) peace of 1801 to make Hölderlin see the epiphany of a god, the abolition of all illegitimate 'Herrschaft', the end of a thousand years of storms ('Friedensfeier'); the very 'Abend der Zeit' had come ('Versöhnender'). And in the most ambitious of all his visionary flights, he sees scripture explained by the course of history down to his immensely significant present moment: 'Die Taten der Erde bis itzt' ('Patmos'). Yet the moment passes and nothing changes: war returns, history continues its erring course, Germany is not singled out to give priestly counsel to the kings and peoples of Europe. These late intensifications of his hopes are an apocalypse of the imagination – not for nothing is their highpoint the vision on Patmos, the island of St. John's Revelation. Apocalypse is the logical conclusion of a poetry of yearning, need and aspiration which can find no corresponding reality. Certainly it is so for a mind whose reading of reality grows ever more obsessively selective; for if epochs of catastrophe to some extent invite such visions of history – the philosophy of Hegel, with whom the young Hölderlin had looked forward to a 'Reich Gottes',[38] has a similar leitmotif of historical culmination and the realising of an immanent spirit – it is also a typical symptom of the schizophrenia to which Hölderlin was succumbing to see deep significances at every turn.[39]

Secondly, the neglect by contemporaries. Central to Hölderlin's thinking is the idea of community. The prophet's life has meaning as service to his fellow-men. Only he can stand bare-headed in the storm,

Des Vaters Strahl . . . mit eigener Hand
Zu fassen und dem Volk ins Lied
Gehüllt die himmlische Gabe zu reichen

('Wie wenn am Feiertage')

And when this contact with the divine is established, he looks forward to a community of praise and social harmony. Both the prophet militant and the prophet triumphant are thus meaningless without community. Yet the greater part of this late poetry was not published in Hölderlin's lifetime, much of it never even finished but reworked time and again[40]. He was barely known except to a few friends, whose names − Conz, Storr, Sinclair − he wove into the text of his hymns as if to escape from total isolation. If the advocates of a national theatre in the 1770s, and Goethe and Schiller in their maturity, found it impossible to establish a German cultural community, how much harder was it for an obscure private tutor to create single-handed a new religious community. That is the measure of the gulf between ambition and actuality.

It is broadened by the third factor, the break-up of coherent discourse in the late poems and their drift into oracular obscurity. No community of readers in Hölderlin's day could have unravelled his meaning, and no audience since has been able to do so fully. The ingenuity of scholars has established no consensus about what the late Hölderlin means. When 'Friedensfeier' was discovered in 1954, his hymning of peace only brought new dissension. Of course, a general picture can be put together. He clearly still struggles to grasp what is going forward in (as he often called it) the 'workshop' of history. He creates new myths to link Asia, first source of the divine, with Europe ('Am Quell der Donau', 'Der Rhein'). He strives to reconcile love of Greece with love of homeland and faith in its appointed role ('Die Wanderung', 'Germanien'). He sees the Greek gods, especially Dionysus, and Christ as parts of a single history of divine manifestations ('Brod und Wein', 'Der Einzige'). He rises like an eagle above the geo-spiritual watersheds of time, in total freedom 'hinüberzugehn und wiederzukehren' ('Patmos'). What Greece has taught him must be applied to a native task, celebrating the national setting of a divine rebirth.

But to present all this as a 'system' is a different and easier matter than understanding the texts — indeed, it misrepresents them, insofar as the fine detail often has an unsystematic tentativeness that belies Hölderlin's programme of 'hohes und reines Frohlocken'.[41] More important, there is much in every text that is stubbornly cryptic. To stress this is not necessarily to use Hölderlin's madness as a pretext for rationing the receptive sympathy poetry needs. *Not* to stress it would be to evade the central experience of reading late Hölderlin. It is not just a matter of the crucial conundrums: who is the 'Fürst des Fests' in 'Friedensfeier'? what is meant by 'Gott der Zeit', 'Geist der Welt', 'Herr der Zeit', and how do they interrelate? is there identity or gradation at the close of 'Germanien' between 'das Ungesprochene', 'ein Wahres', and 'was vor Augen dir ist'? These are problems of a poetic indirectness which fails to be self-solving through context. But there is then the deeper difficulty that communication also fails when direct statement seems intended, and fails at the most basic level of organisation. The late hymns are articulated markedly round the adverbs and conjunctions of logical thought — 'denn', 'nämlich', 'aber', 'doch', 'drum'; yet all too often these are a skeleton of consequentiality from which the flesh of ordered thought is missing. Now it may be argued that poetry should not be read as discursive prose but understood by the imagination through symbol, association and subliminal hint. But where we find precisely those pointers of argument that are normally missing from poetry, we must accept that — as might be expected of a would-be prophet — a certain linear clarity was the aim, and we have to say that we seek it in vain. From *Empedokles* on, what Hölderlin had to say was complex intellectually and emotionally, intellectually *because* emotionally. In the odes, the set patterns of the Greek metres help to hold it to a course; there is vehement power, but there is also, for the most part, control. The late free-verse 'Gesänge', though they too show features of organisation in the often regular length and triadic grouping of their sections, increasingly lose that discipline. The minimal thread that we need tangles or breaks. To read the more difficult of them — 'Friedensfeier', 'Patmos', 'Der Einzige' — is to move from one uncertainty to another, trying desperately provisional keys to unlock a structure that is grandiose, very deliberately composed — each of these poems has at least three versions — yet never perspicuous. (Indeed, clarity seems to get less with each new version.) We are left eavesdropping on the self-communings of a poet who is not aware that he has retreated into a hermetic world.

At most he was aware that his language might seem unconventional

— in the preface to 'Friedensfeier' he begs indulgence if this should be so, and pleads: 'ich kann nicht anders'. His conscious intent remained to speak with a public voice, in 'grössere Gedichte', that is, the hymns, '[deren] Inhalt unmittelbar das Vaterland angehn soll oder die Zeit'.[42] This is obviously not a poet who intends hieratic obscurity for the sake of effect, but rather one who has drifted, as his letters surely confirm,[43] to the edge of the community of shareable meaning. The exegesis of late Hölderlin is a putting together of the pieces of a failed communicative act.

To recognise this is a necessary safeguard against getting so absorbed in teasing out the sense of the 'vaterländische Gesänge' that these come to loom larger than the fully achieved poems, the finest odes and 'Der Archipelagus'. Of course there is a fascination in the works which were to be the pinnacle Hölderlin's whole existence pointed towards; but they failed to be so, precisely, through the collapse of his powers. There is then a further temptation (even if we stop short of the modish assumption that madness is somehow more 'authentic' than sanity) to treat Hölderlin as a modern before his time rather than as a wholly untypical eighteenth-century poet. There may seem to be affinities: much modern poetry is obscure, its metaphors, experiences and allusions private, so that we must learn virtually a new language with each poet; there is no public mythology and only a thin remnant tradition of open communication; dark phrases fascinate with a self-sufficient beauty; for the poet to be lucid is to risk seeming banal. The result can sound very like Hölderlin, who certainly had what Gottfried Benn singled out as *the* lyric quality, the power 'das Wort faszinierend anzusetzen'.[44] But the choices and compulsions at work in Hölderlin's case are so different from those in modern poetry that to read him in this way — and, especially, to relish him in this way — is a grave anachronism. It is to accept as aesthetically normal what was a tragic accident.[45]

It can be a still more drastic anachronism when later history takes a poet up. After long neglect as a minor Romantic, Hölderlin's repute was refounded in the crisis years around the First World war. He was understood in the light first of heroic conflict, then of bitter defeat, as a source of some mysterious Germanic essence, a sibylline book with a dark yet vital message for his nation.[46] This line extends into the Nazi era. Obscure 'national' prophecy was easily appropriated by those who believed, or wanted others to believe, that they were realising the ideal it had pointed forward to; Hölderlin was pronounced 'arterhaltend, gemeinschaftbildend, willenstählend'.[47] Meanwhile the opposite political wing claimed him as a jacobin and alleged that the Marxian dialectic could be descried through the veil of mysticism in *Hyperion*.[48] That view continues into the present. A modern dramatist brings Marx himself to the mad Hölderlin's tower to declare it.[49] Commentators find encoded revolutionary meanings in everything from full works to the merest fragments of phrase.[50] A new critical edition is afoot, aimed at correcting the 'bourgeois' distortions of the standard text.[51] Hölderlin's, it is suggested, is the human community which 'the authorities' strive at all costs to prevent.[52]

It is pointless to ask which side is right in the struggle for Hölderlin's strangely prestigious figure. Both are wrong. Nationalists and Nazis thrust their crude meanings into the vacuum left by his poetic obscurity. Left-wing partisans, in reducing what Hölderlin wrote to a secret political code, disregard not just context and plausibility but the very nature of poetry. Hölderlin will not bear systematic political interpretation, and certainly not a revolutionary one. That the French Revolution was a central experience for him, as for all his generation, is undeniable (and has rarely been denied by 'bourgeois' editors and critics). But he grew noticeably more conservative and defensive in the face of events. For a south German and his family, these came close enough to show a very unideal face. Upheaval ceased to be a value. Hence, in the very midst of the Rastatt Congress from which he and Sinclair hoped for liberal reforms in South Germany, this practical reassurance to his mother: 'Und wenn die Bauern übermütig werden wollen, und gesetzlos, wie Sie fürchten, so wird man sie schon beim Kopf zu nehmen wissen'[53] — a most un-jacobin sentiment. Even on the plane of ideals, Hölderlin argued for the richness of poetry and of the community it might create as a desirable step beyond the schematic severity of politics.[54] He repeatedly warned Sinclair that implacable principle was all very well, 'aber einzig und allein von Stahl und Eisen zu sein, stehet uns nicht an, besonders bedanken sich die Poeten dafür'.[55] His planned journal, *Iduna*, consequently has a high aesthetic programme recalling Schiller's *Horen*,[56] while his ideal of human society is summed up in the phrase 'die ästhetische Kirche'.[57] It is not easy to believe all this is a cover, much less a code, for a smouldering revolutionary intent. And it is from this politically sobered outlook, or rather from the indestructible core of idealism which survived at its centre, that the grand but inchoate visions of the late poetry then arose.

Yet although the political claimants to Hölderlin's heritage have oversimplified him historically and poetically, they are an important symptom. It is not mere chance that they picked on this poet: his texts do speak glowingly of a community and a nation; he aspires to speak to, and eventually for, the collective. This conception goes far beyond what Goethe and Schiller conceived for their Classicism; it is an extreme form of the unity which (as we saw in Chapter 1) Classicisms as such can attain to, with the further addition of a religious enthusiasm no modern Classicism has embraced. Such social harmony and unity are among the highest of human ideals, yet they are ideals whose full realisation — paradoxically — would be ominous. 'Dass . . . Ein Geist allen gemein sei' is an aspiration that chimes uncomfortably with the aspirations of tyrants large and small, political and cultural. True, Hölderlin's imagined collective would have been pure and free, its reborn enthusiasm noble, its organisation something from which the State had withered away — 'Da Herrschaft nirgends ist zu sehn bei Geistern und Menschen' ('Friedensfeier'). But collectives and their enthusiasms are not commonly like that, and perhaps never were. To conceive them so is as unrealistic as was the noble view of Greek unity against the Persians in 'Der Archipelagus'[58], or the unsceptical view of the possibly charlatan Empedokles,[59] which exemplify respectively Hölderlin's social ideal and its prophet. Thus in the broadest social context — and no poet's work more obviously invites such consideration — Hölderlin's impulses and ideals are suspect, his basic conception of poet and audience anachronistic for a modern society where freedom depends on variety.

Hölderlin's tragic fate, the magic of his language, and the appeal of his unique personality tend to monopolise sympathy in any account which sets him beside his more fortunate contemporaries. He has indeed become himself almost a myth. Yet if we go beyond that emotional response, the culture Goethe and Schiller attempted must appear more acceptable for a late European, increasingly pluralist society. Their humanism, as far removed from the materialistic reduction of humanity as from atavistic collective feeling, their cautious nurturing of the unstable mixture which is individual man, was the only valid approach for their time. The secularism of their work and thought was not a cultural second-best, as the aspirations of Hölderlin and the Romantics might imply; it was a major part of their achievement.

Notes

1. 'Marienbader Elegie', stanza 14.
2. *Maximen und Reflexionen*, nr. 49, HA 12, 372.

3. Schlegel, *Kritische Schriften* (Munich² 1964), p.100.
4. Friedrich Schlegel, *Gespräch über die Poesie*, ibid., p.501.
5. Hegel, *Ästhetik*, ed. Friedrich Bassenge (²Frankfurt, n.d.), I, 579f.
6. Joseph von Eichendorff, *Zur Geschichte der neuern romantischen Poesie in Deutschland*, in Eichendorff, *Sämtliche Werke*, VII, 1, ed. W. Mauser (Regensburg, 1962), p.41.
7. Schlegel, *Gespräch über die Poesie*, ed. cit., p.497.
8. An analogous sketch known as 'Das älteste Systemprogramm des deutschen Idealismus' is included in editions of Hölderlin's works; but his part in it is not clear and his authorship, if only on stylistic grounds, less likely than Schelling's or Hegel's.
9. See below, p.217 and footnotes 48 to 51.
10. Beissner, in the Kleine Stuttgarter Ausgabe of Hölderlin calls the tone of these hymns 'härter, energischer, hymnischer' (II, 506) but without any substantiating analysis. Lawrence Ryan, *Hölderlin* (Stuttgart,² 1967), p.22, speaks more plausibly of the 'allzuleichtes Gelingen des hymnischen Aufschwungs, dem die Verbindung mit der realen Welt grossenteils abgeht'.
11. Letter no. 61, to his brother, July 1793; and letter 86, to his brother, 21 August 1794.
12. Letter 35, to Neuffer, 8 November 1790.
13. Letter 123, to Neuffer, 10 June 1796.
14. 'Diotima' ('Lange tot und tiefverschlossen') I, 218 etc.
15. Letter 136, to Neuffer, 16 February 1797.
16. Cf. letters 136, 144 (to Schiller, August 1797), 145 (to his brother, September 1797), and 167 (to Neuffer, 12 November 1798).
17. Cf. I, 133; I, 164f.; I, 224; for the full myth, see *Hyperion*, III, 66.
18. Letter 222, to his brother, (?) January 1801; letter 228, to his sister, 23 February 1801.
19. III, 92. Further *Hyperion* references in the text are to the pages of this volume.
20. III, 100. Hölderlin himself at times cast aside his plan of a long personal 'Bildung' leading to an eventual (poetic) 'Wirkung' on his contemporaries, and envisaged direct action. See letter 89, to Neuffer, November 1794; and the close of letter 172, to his brother, January 1799.
21. Hyperion's mystical reconciliation is described on the last page of the novel, but as something long past — it was this acceptance of his fate which, as the final stage of his story, made it possible for him to start telling it. Thus the opening letter, unusually for an epistolary novel, post-dates the close of the action; and so, therefore, does everything the letters say about their writer's present mood. E.g. the first two letters of the work show wildly swinging moods; while the second of volume 1, Book 2 (p.50) marks a highpoint of happiness but makes it plain that such moments are rare. We cannot be sure whether Hölderlin realised that this structure undid the climactic message of the novel's last pages.
22. IV, 24; cf. also IV, 62f. Further *Empedokles* references in the text are to the pages of this volume.
23. IV, 21f. The comment is a note in the margin of Hölderlin's manuscript.
24. III, 197 and 210.
25. Letter 179, to his brother, 4 June 1799.
26. Hölderlin heard Fichte lecture daily in Jena — see letter 89, to Neuffer, November 1794. He discusses Fichte's concepts of 'Ich' and 'Nicht-Ich' in letter 94, to Hegel, 26 January 1795.
27. *Grund zum Empedokles*, IV, 161. These 'Entgegensetzungen' correspond ultimately to the 'Trennungen, in denen wir denken und existieren' of letter 117, to Niethammer, 24 February 1796.

28. See letter 132, to Ebel, 10 January 1797.

29. Cf. letter 155, to his mother, 7 April 1798, on the 'Kanzel, die ich nicht betreten mag, weil sie zu himmelschreiend entweiht wird'.

30. Letter 41, to his mother, February 1791.

31. *Über Religion*, IV, 290. Hence Hyperion's low-points come from having 'gründlich mich unterscheiden gelernt von dem, was mich umgibt', III, 9.

32. III, 12 and 83.

33. Cf. Romano Guardini, *Hölderlins Weltbild und Frömmigkeit* (Munich, ²1955), p.278: 'Dass erlebt wird, bildet ein Zeichen dafür, dass es etwas gibt, was erlebt werden kann'; and Wolfgang Schadewaldt, *Hellas und Hesperien* (Stuttgart, 1960), p.661, on Hölderlin's 'Wiedergewinnung der Götter als der wirklich Lebendigen'.

34. In very much this sense, Karl Philipp Moritz called the Greek gods in Homer a 'Sprache der Phantasie' in his *Götterlehre oder mythologische Dichtungen der Alten* (Berlin, 1791), opening section.

35. Cf. Paul Böckmann, introduction to the anthology *Hymnische Dichtung im Umkreis Hölderlins* (Tübingen, 1965); Wolfdietrich Rasch, 'Ganymed. Über das mythische Symbol in der Dichtung der Goethezeit' in *Wirkendes Wort*, 2. Sonderheft, September 1954; and Wolfgang Binder, 'Grundformen der Säkularisation in den Werken Goethes, Schillers und Hölderlins', in *Zeitschrift für deutsche Philologie* (Sonderheft, 1964).

36. See note 28.

37. Fichte's *Reden an die deutsche Nation* of 1807/8 preach national regeneration and a community that is to arise – after Prussia's defeat by Napoleon in 1806 – from an age of egoism; they promise that Germany will be the 'Wiedergebärerin und Wiederherstellerin der Welt' (14.Rede, Philosophische Bibliothek, Leipzig 1944, p.233).

38. Letter 84, to Hegel, 10 July 1794.

39. This theme is explored with the necessary sensitivity (cf. below, note 43) by Martin Walser, *Hölderlin zu entsprechen* (Biberach, 1970).

40. Among the more or less finished odes not published are 'Gesang des Deutschen', 'An die Deutschen', 'Die Liebe', 'Der Abschied', 'Ermunterung', 'Natur und Kunst', 'An Eduard'; 'Der Frieden' and 'Rousseau' remained fragments. Among the elegies and hymns unpublished are 'Brod und Wein' (except the opening stanza), 'Am Quell der Donau', 'Germanien', 'Friedensfeier', 'Der Einzige'; 'Wie wenn am Feiertage . . .' remained a fragment.

41. For the programme, see letter 243, to Wilmans, December 1803. On Hölderlin's tentativeness as an expression of intellectual and poetic integrity, cf. David Constantine, 'The Meaning of a Hölderlin Poem', *Oxford German Studies* 9 (1978).

42. Letter 242, to Wilmans, December 1803.

43. Where mental break-up begins to show in the letters may not be easy to agree (though for obvious reasons less difficult than in the poetry) but the threshold might reasonably be set in 1802. To take documents of some complexity of content: letter 231, to his brother, (?) March 1801, presents familiar concerns of Hölderlin's in unusually dense form (see Adolf Beck's editorial elucidation of the 'schwierige Sinn', VI, 619); letter 236, to Böhlendorff, 4 December 1801, is more difficult still with its ellipses and allusiveness; while the further letter to Böhlendorff, nr. 240, (?)November 1802, has moved beyond ellipsis to passages of incoherence.

44. Benn, *Probleme der Lyrik*, in *Gesammelte Werke* ed Dieter Wellershoff (Wiesbaden, 1959), I, 510.

45. Throughout the nineteenth century, most of Hölderlin's late work was understood, i.e., disregarded, as the product of his madness. The turn came in

1914 when his first scholarly editor, Norbert von Hellingrath, in the Vorrede to volume 4 of his edition, called the late hymns 'Herz, Kern und Gipfel des . . . Werkes, das eigentliche Vermächtnis'. Yet Hellingrath also argued, in seeming contradiction, that by this stage Hölderlin had withdrawn into a private world ('sucht nicht mehr nach Äusserungsarten, durch die er wirken könnte, denkt nur noch ans Gedicht . . . da strömt es in ihm, da quillt die einsame Stimme, ist bloss sich selbst zur Freude'). This shows how much the new appreciation of Hölderlin owed to the modernist aesthetics – indeed, aestheticism – of the 1900s. From then on, instead of madness being a ground for ignoring Hölderlin's work, the dark fascinations of the late work became a ground for ignoring the madness – and ultimately for not fully facing the discrepancy between public intentions and incoherence. The assimilation of Hölderlin into 'modern' art then reaches its absurd conclusion in such writing as the following: 'As empty space is so expressly a part of modern painting and sculpture, as the silent intervals are so integral to a composition by Webern, so the void places in Hölderlin's poems, particularly in the late fragments, seem indispensable to the poetic act' (George Steiner, *Language and Silence*, 1967, p.67).

46. See 'Hölderlin' in Stefan George's *Blätter für die Kunst* (Elfte Folge, 1919), pp.11f.

47. W. Bartscher, *Hölderlin und die deutsche Nation* (Berlin, 1942), p.10. For a concise account of Hölderlin's reputation at German hands, see Robert Minder, 'Hölderlin unter den Deutschen' in Minder, *Dichter in der Gesellschaft* (Frankfurt, 1966).

48. Georg Lukács, 'Hölderlins *Hyperion*', in Lukács, *Goethe und seine Zeit* (Berne, 1947), p.121.

49. Peter Weiss, *Hölderlin* (Frankfurt, 1971), pp.174f.: 'Dass Sie/ein halbes Jahrhundert zuvor/die Umwälzung nicht/als wissenschaftlich begründete/ Notwendigkeit sondern/als mythologische Ahnung/beschrieben/ist Ihr Fehler nicht'. Where once the theologisers put Hölderlin's madness down to the overwhelming experience of the divine, it is now put down (p.180) to disappointment at the failed revolution.

50. Preeminently Pierre Bertaux, first in 'Hölderlin und die französische Revolution', *Hölderlin-Jahrbuch* (1967/8), then at greater length in a book of the same title (Frankfurt, 1969), and yet again 'War Hölderlin Jakobiner?' in Ingrid Riedel (ed.), *Hölderlin ohne Mythos* (Göttingen, 1973). (Cf. also Hans-Wolf Jäger's reading of 'Natur und Kunst' in the same essay-collection.) Bertaux works from simplistic assumptions via naive arguments to over-confident conclusions, commonly taking a hypothesis for a proof. The answers to Bertaux – e.g. Adolf Beck, 'Hölderlin als Republikaner', *Hölderlin-Jb* (1969), and Paul Böckmann, 'Die Französische Revolution und die Idee der ästhetischen Erziehung in Hölderlins Dichten', in W. Paulsen (ed.), *Der Dichter und seine Zeit* (Heidelberg, 1970), deploy noticeably more exact knowledge of the political background and argue more cautiously and cogently. Incidentally, just as the 'revolutionary' theory has Peter Weiss's drama, the biographically scrupulous Beck school now has its artistic version, Peter Härtling's novel *Hölderlin* (Darmstadt, 1976).

51. Friedrich Hölderlin, *Sämtliche Werke*, Frankfurter Ausgabe, edited by D.E. Sattler. Though Beissner's Stuttgarter Ausgabe leaves something to be desired (as any attempt to render the complexity of the Hölderlin texts is almost bound to) the much more elementary flaws of method and detail already apparent in the new edition make its usefulness questionable. See Sattler's *Probeband*, 1975; and, in the *Hölderlin-Jb* (1975-7), Sattler's presentation and the critical examinations by Binder, Uffhausen and Wellmann-Bretzigheimer.

52. See Walser, *Hölderlin zu entsprechen*, p.23.

53. Letter 155, to his mother, 7 April 1798.

54. Letter 172, to his brother, 1 January 1799.
55. Letter 188, to his sister, July 1799.
56. Letter 178, to Neuffer, 4 June 1799.
57. Letter 179, to his brother, 4 June 1799.
58. On Herodotus' showing (*Histories*, Books 7 and 8) Greek unity in the Persian Wars was a ragged affair, with the Argives, Corcyra, Thessaly and Thrace soon falling out, and many other groups remaining 'neutral in the war – which, to put it bluntly, is as good as saying that they were on the Persian side' (Penguin Classics edition, p.522). Cf. also R.B. Harrison, *Hölderlin and Greek Literature* (Oxford, 1975), p.94.
59. Hölderlin's source, Diogenes Laertius' *Lives of the Eminent Philosophers*, Book 8, also reports ample scepticism about Empedokles' actions, claims and motives – a very Greek element to which Brecht's poem 'Der Schuh des Empedokles' later does justice. It is not clear that Hölderlin's Greece was any more essentially right than that of other eighteenth-century graecolaters; at all events, the notion of some special innate affinity ('ihm ist Hellas a priori gegeben', as Gundolf wrote apropos 'Der Archipelagus') is to be taken with as much caution as other mystical notions about Hölderlin.

I

Shattered by Schiller's death in 1805, Goethe could see no way forward: 'Eigentlich sollte ich eine neue Lebensweise anfangen; aber dazu ist in meinen Jahren auch kein Weg mehr'.[1] He was already fifty-six. Schiller had been ten years younger and the more active element in their remarkable symbiosis — entrepreneur, combative spirit, aesthetic theorist, constructive critic and stimulator of grand undertakings, source of the 'Bewusstsein' needed alike for large-scale works and for carrying through a Classical programme. No wonder Goethe lost heart and cried out, in pathetic tribute to his friend's role, 'Wer reicht mir die Hand beim Versinken ins Reale?'[2]

Yet Goethe had twenty-seven years still to live and major works to create which amount to a new artistic 'Lebensweise'. Not that he altogether takes back his Classical achievements or denies the insights of Italy. Nor could he readily become pathological, exalted or mystical like Kleist, Hölderlin or the Romantics. But he did need change. Classicism, like any achieved programme, was in danger of becoming rigid and dogmatic, a constricting obligation rather than a source of energy. Goethe recognised this when he wrote, of historical change generally and literary movements in particular, that 'aus aller Ordnung entsteht zuletzt Pedanterie'.[3] Such pedantry shows in his minor works and activities: the excessively wrought style of *Die Natürliche Tochter*; the setting of themes from antiquity for the Weimar art-competitions,[4] which ignored Lessing's arguments in *Laokoon* against narrative painting; the *Achilleis* fragment which heavily takes up Homer's story in Homer's mode, where *Hermann und Dorothea* had transposed his spirit with a lighter touch to modern times — though even there, the notion of being a last contributor to the collective personality 'Homer' ('Doch Homeride zu sein, auch nur als letzter, ist schön') was an undue subservience and abdication of originality.[5] All these were departures from the essential insight of the *Römische Elegien* that 'the Classical' was a balanced mode of living and writing which could be achieved anew at any time.

Against these unhealthy symptoms there is one grand sign of health: *Faust*. Outwardly it was no subject for a Classicist, and in the first months of his conversion he had duly turned it to ridicule ('Hexenküche'), overridden its conflicts with poetic harmony ('Wald und Höhle'), cut its harrowing last scenes, and abandoned it as a fragment. He certainly had no business returning to it in mid-Classicism. Yet in 1797 return he did, restoring the cut scenes only partly toned down and creating rich new text at its nordic heart: Faust in his gothic study, the near-suicide, the Christian Easter choruses, the folk colour of 'Vor dem Tor', Mephisto's approaches, the pact scene. Goethe's (Classical) principle of finishing old projects is not enough to explain this sympathetic return to a non-Classical subject, nor is its fascination for him disproved by his calling it a mere casual stop-gap, a temporary sojourn on a 'Dunst- und Nebelweg', a 'barbaric production' for a 'nordic public'.[6] The truth lies farther back in the admission to Schiller that he dared not untie the packet that held Faust captive;[7] and it is told fully and movingly in the prefatory poem 'Zueignung' where the 'schwankende Gestalten' seen unclearly in his youth press in on the poet, arousing old un-Classical emotions, and his aesthetic certainties fade:

Was ich besitze, seh ich wie im Weiten,
Und was verschwand, wird mir zu Wirklichkeiten.

The completed *Faust I* duly transcends the Classical aesthetic, both by the absolute judgment that restored old scenes and the artistry that added new.

Yet returning to the *Faust* style was not simple regression; it was something larger, presaging the free creativity of the late work. 'Style', in the Classical Goethe's theory, was the pinnacle of a personal development[8] and in his Classical decade he might be thought to have attained this. But the idea of a once-for-all culmination, coinciding roughly with the artist's chronological maturity, hardly covers cases of exceptional longevity and creative vitality. Would these not create a perspective within which an achieved style and a theoretic commitment might be rounded off and become a past phase? Is there not a larger mastery yet in which, beyond the peak of a single style, there lies a whole range of styles? Whether one speaks of adaptability, catholicity, or virtuosity, the urge and ability to return to the *Faust* mode demonstrated that Goethe was acquiring it, and that neither art nor life had been finally caught in the confines of one programme. This is crucial: the work of the ageing and the old Goethe draws eclectically on a breadth of knowledge and practice which is more than the linear unfolding of a personal potential. And with this there goes an increasing historical consciousness, a tendency to think in great time-spans and to see himself in large contexts — 'sich selbst historisch werden'.[9] Experience, in this last phase, is more 'Erfahrung' than 'Erlebnis'. Or rather, the two interact, 'Erlebnis' challenges 'Erfahrung'. The larger awareness and the range of literary strategies are themselves responses to new crises and movements of the spirit, which secures the resulting works against the tediousness of parody and the frivolousness of mere play. Society, history and personal life still press for poetic answers, for example in *Die Wahlverwandtschaften* (1809), where a personal experience so painful that Goethe only ever made veiled reference to it posed a problem whose roots lay in the condition of society at a moment of historical change.

A background of secure social position and wealth sets off the moral uncertainties of four people whose attachments are rearranged by the chemistry of love. Are they no more free to decide their fate than those compounds which divide and cross-combine on meeting, by a compulsion chemists of the period called 'elective affinity'? Or is the idea of free choice — '*Wahl*verwandtschaft' — restored when the metaphor is brought back to the human sphere? And is it therefore moral effort, or lack of it, that will determine the outcome? This is a radical unease indeed. For the Classical Goethe Man was part of nature, but the laws governing him, albeit chemical,[10] were ultimately benevolent. Now, the relation of men and women to their natural being is presented as one of disharmony and conflict. The Classical synthesis of mind and senses, reason and nature, dissolves. It is as if the wild Mignon element, which *Wilhelm Meisters Lehrjahre* could accommodate within its overall harmony, were now a more real threat, unleashed by the simple act of bringing a husband's friend, a wife's niece, to the couple's country estate.

The working of the affinities puts them all to the test. Charlotte, cool and practical, subordinates feeling to the social code; so obediently, does her new 'partner', the Hauptmann. But Eduard is impatient of any self-denial, as the very shape of Goethe's phrase declares: 'Sich etwas zu versagen, war Eduard nicht gewohnt' (I, 1). For him desire is not to be resisted: 'er dachte, er überlegte, oder vielmehr er dachte, er überlegte nicht; er wünschte, er wollte nur. Er musste sie sehn, sie sprechen. Was daraus entstehen sollte, davon konnte die Rede nicht sein. Er widerstand nicht, er musste' (II, 16). What this sequence of verbs records is a choice to be compelled. In Eduard, nature is not just unrestrained but abetted, even egged on by his wilfulness.

Yet the affinity between his and Ottilie's natures is real. He may seize avidly any sign that they were meant for each other, but some are signs indeed: their mysteriously symmetrical headaches, the unwilled assimilation of her handwriting to his, their musical harmony despite his erratic dilettante playing. These reponses of Ottilie's highly sensitive organism, her mineral-divining, and especially the 'unerhörte Begebenheit' at the centre of the action — the loveless intercourse of Eduard and Charlotte which produces a child resembling the yearned-for absent partners — all belong to a realm Goethe had not explored before. Occasionally (and superbly) he had evoked sprites or ghosts — 'Erlkönig', 'Die Braut von Korinth'; but only the Romantics had probed far into the 'Nachtseite' of nature, revelling in it regardless of the moral problems it might raise. Goethe moves into this dark territory, not for the sake of literary novelty (though the mere appearance that this is so makes it a work he would not have approved of, much less written, a few years earlier) but to see what security can be found there. It is frankly an experiment.[11] Ottilie is Goethe's means, in that she is a character as much outside the social code by her naivety as Eduard is by his self-will. Her morality is a need for harmony with her inner self that makes her independent of, and at decisive moments able to oppose, what social *mores* require or allow. When the child dies and nothing stands in the way of divorce and remarriages, she alone refuses. She was to blame for the death, temporarily confused (or even invaded[12]) by Eduard's ruthless impulses. To the others the way seems clear for a happy ending; but she has lost her harmony and must regain it by 'Entsagung': 'ich bin aus meiner Bahn geschritten, ich habe meine Gesetze gebrochen ... Eduards werde ich nie! Auf eine schreckliche Weise hat Gott mir die Augen geöffnet, in welchem Verbrechen ich befangen bin' (II, 14). She speaks of laws and transgressions, her austere resolve accords with the strictest code, she becomes increasingly saintly, yet neither morality nor religion in any conventional sense is at work.[13] Her inspiration comes from deeper springs than reflection or principle. Only an impulse as strong as Eduard's can counter his (contrast her earlier, conventional decision to renounce him — II, 9 — which his presence easily overthrew). Nature is met by nature, spontaneous egotism in the Romantic mode by spontaneous asceticism. Goethe has 'waited patiently for the moral processes of nature'[14] to resolve his experiment.

That nature has moral processes is a paradox, and for most moralists and ages of moral consensus it would be a contradiction. But this society has no settled standards, only possibilities, ranging from the code Charlotte dutifully follows and the mindless attachment of Mittler to established institutions to the sophisticated freedom and talk about fixed-term marriages of the Graf and Baronesse. The characters must find their own way across uncertain terrain, and it is doubtful whether old maps can be used. Charlotte tries. In a significant though seemingly digressive conversation on fashions in landscape and architecture, she seeks reassurance that historical change can be undone: modern times have thrown off constraints – ' "an Kunst und Zwang soll nichts erinnern; wir wollen frei und unbedingt Atem schöpfen" ' – but is it not conceivable ' "das man aus diesem wieder in einen andern, in den vorigen Zustand zurückkehren könne?" ' (II, 8). The words echo her earlier hopes that, by taking thought, they can all be again as they were – 'in einen frühern, beschränktern Zustand könne man zurückkehren, ein gewaltsam Entbundenes lasse sich wieder ins Enge bringen'. But this is expressly called an illusion (I, 13). The connection between morals and other modes is not random, but central to the novel's meaning and to Goethe's aim 'soziale Verhältnisse und deren Konflikte symbolisch gefasst darzustellen'.[15] He was using problems of love and marriage, as Ibsen, Tolstoy and Fontane were to do in their more directly realistic way, to focus 'den ganzen Komplex des Lebens' (II, 12). It is not just a reflection *of*, but a reflection *on* society when at the outset we see how Eduard and Charlotte spend their idle time and money tinkering with the landscape. It implies an assumption of sovereignty over nature which is both illusion and hubris. For they prove powerless to control nature's forces – 'ein gewaltsam Entbundenes' – and the fate that results. There is no returning to the small order of their uneasy marriage, any more than to the larger order of a previous age. Only Ottilie achieves such a return – to her own personal order, and by intensely personal means. As a perceptive contemporary wrote, 'es kann heut zu Tage jeder seinen Gott nur in sich selbst finden'.[16] Even then it is only by extreme 'Entsagung' and a self-mortification that ends in death, restoring her own purity but nothing more. This is a tragic work, a fact which sufficiently indicates its distance from the Classical ethos.

Yet the manner is not tortured or expressive but detached, yielding little to those who wonder what the author 'really thinks'. This stylistic opacity, left intact by the sardonic, contradictory things Goethe said about the work, has been called aristocratic, laconic, Classical; it has given rise to the notion that there is a 'narrator' distinct from Goethe who even, according to one version, presents characters and actions in a way the reader is meant to reverse.[17] Less waywardly, one might see the stylistic restraint as a defence mechanism, pushed to the extreme because of the pain of Goethe's original experience;[18] or link the formality with his practice of dictating.[19] But those would be bio-graphical explanations. In terms of literary effect, the narrative manner, composed of familiar eighteenth-century conventions which Goethe slips easily into, evokes in kind the civilised surface of the lives the characters lead; while the real action proceeding beneath that surface is suggested by subtler, indirect means which are the novel's real achievement. Every casual-seeming word or act (the marital chess-moves of the opening chapters, the landscape works that are planned, done and undone), the settings through which the characters move (Ottilie and Eduard hastening ahead of Charlotte and the Hauptmann along untrodden paths in I, 7), the objects they possess (the moss-hut, Ottilie's locket), the dramatic events they participate in (Eduard letting off a firework display, alone with Ottilie, after and despite a near-catastrophe) all point into the decisive depths of motive, feeling and character. Where *Werther* treated intense emotion explicitly, this novel manipulates the world of objects and arrangements in which mature people's emotions are invested and through which they can consequently speak to, attract and hurt one another.

That the novel has these two modes or levels of communication springs directly from what it has to say. But this aptness is not a Classical effect (to call the work Classical for its style is to forget the reality this masks) because the modes are not in harmony, which follows from the disharmony they render. The Classical artistic synthesis breaks up because the Classical moral synthesis has broken up.

To see it in further disarray we need only glance on to *Wilhelm Meisters Wanderjahre*, the sequel to the *Lehrjahre* planned and written over the thirty years to 1829. It is many things though hardly in sum a novel. Outwardly it is a further instalment of 'Bildungsroman' — its framework narrative takes Wilhelm to the next phase of the apprenticeship metaphor, journeying. But it also moves on from this 'Wandern' to the idea of 'Auswandern', of emigration to America as one answer to the socio-economic problems of Europe, in particular the ruin of traditional trades by industrial mechanisation. This does not mean a turn to direct social realism; although Goethe builds into his text reports on the condition of weavers, he still approaches society via the morality of individuals. For through the sub-title, 'Die Entsagenden', the book also claims to be the coherent treatment of an ethical theme, commonly presumed to relate not just to the framework but to a series of inset Novellen which treat problems and entanglements of love (*Die Wahlverwandtschaften* began as one of these). Then there is the doctrine conveyed in the main narrative, especially by the Utopian episode in the 'pädagogische Provinz', of practical preparation for life in a community. The ideal is not now a full many-sided 'Bildung' for the whole man, but a specific training ('Ausbildung') which enables men to take their place as components of society. Finally there are massive transfusions of wisdom direct in two sets of formally unintegrated aphorisms.

The question is, how far all this matter and thought coheres or is held in aesthetic suspension. Iconoclastic criticism has seen the work as self-evidently formless and castigated the mass montage of aphorisms, or the leaving incomplete of an inset story, as disrespectful to the public and a failure to take art itself seriously.[20] More pious critics have tried to show the presence of form in the links between the aphorisms and the characters or action; or in the way the Novellen serve the theme by showing 'Entsagung' (or its failure). They argue that characters who appear in both inset story and main narrative 'graduate' morally from the one to the other, and that the whole is a 'cyclic' form apt for the portrayal of a range of ethical and religious positions.[21] They commonly concede that the *Wanderjahre* is not a novel, but claim that its symbols and connections make up an esoteric game of much greater sophistication than that simple genre.

This may be so. Yet to demonstrate it only in a sense strengthens the criticism that set the apologists going: for if the game is indeed played at the level they argue, there has been a withdrawal from literary form in the sense prose fiction normally entails, and certainly in the sense in which the Classical Goethe conceived and practised it. The *Lehrjahre* had intricacies enough, yet was wholly shaped narrative. But in the *Wanderjahre*, for all its symbolism (and the earliest iconoclast already saw it as 'one great arsenal of symbols')[22] reality and meaning, matter and thought do not fuse in an overall form. The reflective, the theoretical, and (especially) the manipulative preponderate. True, the inset-stories contain some of Goethe's finest narrative work, especially *Der Mann von fünfzig Jahren*, which displays the same mastery of deft suggestion as the *Wahlverwandtschaften* (and thus proves we are not dealing simply with powers in decline). Yet we are kept waiting for its close, as for that of *Das nussbraune Mädchen*, till a late stage of the main narrative. And if it can be alleged that characters graduate *morally* from story to framework, the intrinsic *narrative* interest of these interwoven rather than inset stories is downgraded by their dependence on the — duller — framework, with its own numerous insufficiently realised characters. The author is intent on keeping his head above the waters of narrative and his eye on a distant shore. He is expressly an 'editor', bringing together papers (III, 8), introducing the stories (II, 3), even discussing with the reader the division of the work into volumes (Zwischenrede at II, 8). He goes far beyond the functional necessity of the editor in *Werther*, without whom the death-scene and its aftermath could not have been told at all. Nor is this some super-subtle 'narrator-figure', since he so clearly shares Goethe's own past.[23]

Yet it is not that Goethe is failing to take art seriously; rather, he takes so seriously the purpose for which he is using art that he sometimes steps outside it, perhaps mistrusting art's capacity to communicate adequately. Prose narrative is by nature and origin the genre closest to discursive statement, from which it differentiates itself more subtly and gradually (within each given work as well as in the history of the genre) than poetry and dramatic text. It can consequently revert most easily to direct communication, the convention of addressing the reader can be taken literally, as when Goethe at a late stage writes: 'Hier aber wird die Pflicht des Mitteilens, Darstellens, Ausführens und Zusammenziehens immer schwieriger. Wer fühlt nicht, dass wir uns diesmal dem Ende nähern, wo die Furcht, in Umständlichkeiten zu verweilen, mit dem Wunsche, nichts völlig unerörtert zu lassen, uns in Zwiespalt versetzt' (III, 14). This is a frank expression of authorial anxiety in the face of what he calls 'das übernommene ernste Geschäft eines treuen Referenten'; he here frees himself from the narrative element in order to get, and give us, his bearings; and he draws together what he knows in the form of report, not artistic shape, just as, in mid-narrative in *Der Mann von funfzig Jahren*, he suddenly declared (and felt sure his readers would think him right) that he must now proceed 'nicht mehr darstellend, sondern erzählend und betrachtend' (II, 5). All this makes a consistent picture of withdrawal from the high Classical practice of art – matching, arguably, the withdrawal from the Classical ideal of 'Bildung' to the more modest one of 'Ausbildung'. Goethe has abandoned the principle which he still states as the first of the aphorisms 'Aus Makariens Archiv': 'Die Geheimnisse der Lebenspfade darf und kann man nicht offenbaren; es gibt Steine des Anstosses, über die ein jeder Wanderer stolpern muss. Der Poet aber deutet auf die Stelle hin'. That would be an apt critical comment on the *Wanderjahre*.[24]

The reasons for this double withdrawal are partly social. Since Schiller's death there had been turmoil: in 1806 the separate northern peace ended, Napoleon defeated Prussia, French troops flooding through Weimar brought home European realities. Classicism and its ideals seemed a distant memory. The old notion of 'Bildung' was shaken: 'alles von Jugend und Kindheit auf ward genötigt sich anders zu bilden, da es denn auch in einer tumultuarischen Zeit an Verbildung nicht fehlte'.[25] Tumult continued or, through the uneasy calm of the post-Napoleonic restoration and the Metternich era, seemed merely to have gone underground. Goethe worked on like a man living on the slopes of a volcano, more wary than hopeful. But society is far from all. The *Wanderjahre* also shows tendencies inherent in old age. Time presses, accumulated wisdom must be passed on; on the other hand, accumulated culture and mastered techniques tempt the artist into a play with arcane correspondences. Communicative and formal impulse, which once came together, are polarised. Art both falls short of and is in excess of what is needed.

Goethe's autobiographical project also springs from this. It sets out to communicate what art cannot – or what he feels his oeuvre so far has not; it aims to fill in the gaps between his individual works, providing *their* narrative framework. The dozen volumes of the 1806 *Werke*, outwardly 'ein Ganzes', remained 'zu wenig' and 'unzusammen-hängend',[26] chronology and causality, personal and historical, needed filling in. Each poetic work, Goethe felt, had treated one extreme of a nature given to extremes, and in that sense they were the fragments of a great confession 'welche vollständig zu machen dieses Büchlein [viz. *Dichtung und Wahrheit*] ein gewagter Versuch ist'.[27]

But this supplementary confession so long after the event (it gets no further than 1775 and the coming move to Weimar) is no sure guide to the state of mind at the time of sinning. In the amalgam – which all autobiography is – of an experienced past and an interpreting present, *Dichtung und Wahrheit* leans heavily towards the second. Goethe sees his young self at a distance, with tolerant irony; he does not recreate that self with the immediate felt life and idiosyncratic angle to the universe that are so strong in Montaigne's *Essays* or Rousseau's *Confessions*. It is a success story in which the problems and discomforts of existence are toned down: the turbulence of Goethe's youth, richly documented in letters and poems and his friends' reports, is understated by a generous margin. There are flashes of colour in the evocation of background (the old Frankfurt of his childhood) or event (an Imperial coronation), and some good portraits – Herder, Merck, Jung Stilling. But even these are more judicious than vivid. Wisdom and the higher view predominate. The measured, even staid, tones tell us more about the old than the young Goethe. It is once more the withdrawal from immediacy, a product of the 'Zeit der Resultate und Résumés.'[28]

Not so the *Italienische Reise* to which, skipping the first Weimar decade, Goethe turned next. Here he was once more an editor, but of supremely fresh and vigorous documents: the letters and diaries of that in every sense vital journey are printed largely unchanged. Their immediacy shows up the pallor of mere results: 'Die früheren Eindrücke verlöschen, die Resultate bleiben freilich, das ist denn auch wohl der Zweck, aber früher war das Leben'.[29] The book reconstitutes 'Leben', and becomes Classical not just in treating that historic rebirth, but by presenting the theoretical conclusions as they grew from the richness of experience.

The *Italienische Reise* also has topical life. For the Classical vision was worlds away from what German art had since become. Romanticism had all along made sensuous reality a mere vehicle for allegorical 'higher' meanings. Its early rhapsodies and theories[30] had now been followed by artists, in particular the christianising Nazarene school which was based, ironically, in Rome. Now Goethe by the 1810s had broadened his sympathies, he strove to see Romantic writing and painting positively, or at least to value individual achievements even when suspicious of the tendency they implied.[31] He gave his blessing to Sulpiz Boisserée's restoration and promulgation of German medieval art and published essays on it, by himself and others, in his journal *Kunst und Altertum*. But there were limits. For him medieval art was decidedly a stage in human culture. If there were many mansions in the house of art, the middle ages were the dark cellar, primitive, past, and not to be imitated. He swung between hopes that Romantic medievalism heralded a new advance, and impatience with the failure of form and 'Gestaltung' that for him typified all Romantic art. His highest ideal even now remained Greek form; and he found little wrong with the views his old Italian papers contained.[32] Perhaps going through these brought the matter to a head. He and Meyer published the long overdue onslaught on the excesses and fundamental falsity of Romantic art *Neudeutsch-religios-patriotische Kunst*; and the *Italienische Reise* became the positive counterpart to this polemic, a grand reiteration of all that Classicism was and meant. It dwarfs Romanticism and the Romantics. With its embracing vision of nature, culture, society and man, it shows how solidly founded was the edifice of Goethe's poetic work in his now remote Classical decade — in the days, that is, when he was still a poet.

II

For in the decade after Schiller died, he hardly seemed one. Age does not favour lyrical writing: old men are less likely to fall in love, to feel each new spring as a revelation, or in general to suffer the sharp emotions that stimulate lyric. We have seen that Goethe now kept experience at arm's length. He felt he had enough of it still needing to be processed, indeed he actually feared new 'Einwirkungen und Aufregungen'.[33] To collect and record a past self, gather scattered writings, develop lines of scientific enquiry he had long opened up, push forward the autobiography lest his life be written by some lesser spirit when he was dead — these seemed the proper occupations of age.

Yet there were stirrings. New emotion inspired the *Wahlverwandtschaften*. A parallel set of sonnets also faces the reality of this unexpected upheaval. The choice of so deliberate and artificial a form is not chance: the sonnet is the opposite extreme and necessary counterpoise to the force Goethe now begins to call 'dämonisch', and their interplay yields 'ein neues Leben' (Sonnet 1). Was love perhaps, as Ottilie's diary said (II, 4), an old man's only means to rejuvenation? It was certainly an important one for Goethe, suffered rather than sought, but poetically fruitful. It is at the heart of the *West-Östlicher Divan*, the great poem-cycle begun in 1814 whose longest section sings yet another new beloved, Marianne Willemer.

This poetry is not however brought on by love alone. It is in full flood before ever the poet meets his new partner; one poem, 'Phänomen', actually foretells a new love, so that it almost seems as if the usual assumed process was reversed and love was stimulated by poetry. Indeed, in one sense this was so. For the rejuvenation that made possible both love and the *Divan* sprang from the work of another poet. In 1812 a translation appeared of the fourteenth-century Persian poet Hafiz and in him Goethe found a startling reflection of his own life and work. Honoured by princes, especially the Shah Sedshan (read: Karl August), Hafiz led in Shiraz (read: Weimar) a life of study and pleasure through one of the stormiest periods of Asian (read: European) history. Dynastic wars culminated in the campaigns of Timur, as the French Revolutionary Wars had culminated in the campaigns of Napoleon. Hafiz met Timur in person, as Goethe had met Napoleon at Erfurt in 1808. Both conquerors came to grief in winter wars, Timur in China, Napoleon in Russia. But political upheavals did not touch Hafiz' serenity — it was no good waiting for peace before singing immortal songs of nature, love and wine. This is a pre-echo not so much of Goethe's Classical practice as of his refusal to join in the anti-French jingoism which seized young poets in the 'Wars of Liberation' in 1813.

Goethe's turn to Persia was thus only half an escape. He called it a hegira after Mohamed's historic flight, and the first poem of the *Divan*, duly titled 'Hegire', evokes a universal collapse from which the poet flees, eastwards and backwards in time, 'in des Ursprungs Tiefe'. Yet that depth only reflected a similar strife and chaos. Rather than escaping from history's discomforts, Goethe was exploring again its patterns of recurrence. Small consolation, perhaps, in itself. But he was also thereby finding refuge and reassurance in his great predecessor. Hafiz confirmed him in his whole way of being and inspired new poetry in defiance of surrounding disorder. A tone heard once before, when Rome and her poets gave him confirmation of himself, returns: in poem-titles like 'Freisinn', 'Dreistigkeit', 'Derb und Tüchtig', in openings like 'Dichten ist ein Übermut' or 'Lasst mich nur auf meinem Sattel gelten'. This is the 'Buch des Sängers' which, with the 'Buch Hafiz', celebrates poetry and the return to poetry in a champagne mood that remains characteristic of most of the *Divan*.[34] Goethe revels in the new-found eastern mode. He can recall the delights of Greek style, the firm lines produced by the energetic shaping hand:

> Mag der Grieche seinen Ton
> Zu Gestalten drücken,
> An der eignen Hände Sohn
> Steigern sein Entzücken;

but now there is the bliss of taking to a freer element:

> Aber uns ist wonnereich,
> In den Euphrat greifen
> Und im flüssgen Element
> Hin und wieder schweifen.

The poetic result is magically beyond doubt:

> Löscht ich so der Seele Brand,
> Lied, es wird erschallen;
> Schöpft des Dichters reine Hand,
> Wasser wird sich ballen.

> ('Lied und Gebilde')

These lines already typify the *Divan*. Despite what Goethe says in the poem 'Nachbildung', he hardly imitates Hafiz's Persian forms — and he does not need to imitate his spirit, since it comes as a reminder of his true self. The form is short lines, simple rhymed quatrains, mostly short poems – nothing could be less pretentious, more apparently lightweight. The style is casual, off-hand, the syntax loose ('Lied, es wird erschallen'), there is a strong sense of a voice speaking, relaxed and colloquial. Yet this is partly illusion, the art that conceals art, for the language is finely wrought. No mere speaking voice attains such delicacy and unforced concision, such a supple familiarity with delight as this:

> Ros und Lilie morgentaulich
> Blüht im Garten meiner Nähe;
> Hinten an, bebuscht und traulich,
> Steigt der Felsen in die Höhe . . .
>
> ('Im Gegenwärtigen Vergangenes')

The easy tone and simple form have immense reserves. They are ideal for the playful sensuousness of the 'Buch der Liebe' ('Ja, die Augen . . .', 'Versunken'), for the humour of the 'Buch des Paradieses', where the poet imagines himself in the Moslem heaven and hears the plaints of the much-tried houris, or for the vinous rhapsodies of the 'Schenkenbuch'. But they also accommodate a near-mystic seriousness by the same daring yet unobtrusive ellipsis and compression:

> In der Liebesnächte Kühlung,
> Die dich zeugte, wo du zeugtest,
> Überfällt dich fremde Fühlung,
> Wenn die stille Kerze leuchtet.
>
> ('Selige Sehnsucht')

Again and again Goethe achieves what the poem 'Segenspfänder' calls 'höchsten Sinn im engsten Raum'. Where his autobiographical records surveyed the façades of experience, describing them in leisurely formulation under no beneficent pressure, in the *Divan* his thought and language once more take the poetic shortcut to the centre of things. The poet has triumphantly survived within the ageing writer. He achieves profound and poignant insight within a single stanza:

> Ist's möglich, dass ich, Liebchen, dich kose,
> Vernehme der göttlichen Stimme Schall!
> Unmöglich scheint immer die Rose,
> Unbegreiflich die Nachtigall.

Or again:

> Der Spiegel sagt mir, ich bin schön!
> Ihr sagt: zu altern sei auch mein Geschick.
> Vor Gott muss alles ewig stehn,
> In mir liebt ihn, für diesen Augenblick.
>
> ('Suleika spricht')

In these two exquisite miniatures one can see why Goethe spoke of reflection as the dominant feature of the *Divan*:[35] the one makes beauty transparent for its larger meaning; the other captures the delight of love, unbelievable but real. Yet this is not the distant wisdom of maxim and retrospect, not an abstraction apart from the renewed experience of loving. It is part of the response of an old man in love again, part of his perception itself.

For the *Divan* is distinctively about love in age. If love was a recurrent theme for Goethe, it was never the same twice — not, as popular legend would have it, an identical force repeatedly switching on an identical poetry. In his youth, the beloved was hardly perceived as a reality distinct from his emotions, his poems were shaped by the excitement of loving itself or by the pain of love's complications ('Maifest', 'Willkommen und Abschied', 'Auf dem See', 'Neue Liebe, neues Leben'). In his maturity he knows a real woman, but their enjoyment is also for him a crowning moment where history, culture and nature meet and enhance each other in conscious fulfilment (*Römische Elegien*). The *Divan* too mingles nature with culture. Knowledge and awareness — of love, of legendary past lovers, of himself as once more a lover, living the role of an Eastern love-poet, Hatem to Marianne's Suleika — once again enhance pleasure: 'Freude des Daseins ist gross,/Grösser die Freud am Dasein' ('Die schön geschriebenen . . .'). He feels unease too, at having so little to offer in return for her youth and beauty: 'zu erwidern hab ich nichts'. But he does have feeling, intense enough to make no hyperbole too bold:

> Nur dies Herz, es ist von Dauer,
> Schwillt in jugendlichstem Flor;
> Unter Schnee und Nebelschauer
> Rast ein Ätna dir hervor.
>
> ('Locken, haltet mich . . .')

The lover, like the poet, is alive within, only hidden by the craggy grey exterior. This essential or rediscovered youthfulness is attested by recurrent motifs of fire, freedom, consumption, generosity, happy poverty, enjoyment of the present. The fire set going by the spark of Hafiz' example ('In deine Reimart . . .', 'Wo hast du das genommen?'), the fire that transforms the questing moth ('Selige Sehnsucht'), the fire that consumes Hatem or that burns petals to an essence of perfume ('Dir mit Wohlgeruch zu kosen'); the giving of cities ('Hätt' ich irgend wohl Bedenken . . .?') and the giving of alms ('Und was im *Pend-Nameh* steht'); the poverty of the man whose heart has been stolen, and the riches he can share in return ('Nicht Gelegenheit macht Diebe' and 'Hochbeglückt in deiner Liebe') – all this is in clear contrast to the anxious storing and tidying, documenting and recapitulating of the autobiographical project. The moral is read from the image of alms-giving:

> Reiche froh den Pfennig hin,
> Häufe nicht ein Gold-Vermächtnis,
> Eile freudig vorzuziehn
> Gegenwart vor dem Gedächtnis.

And yet this present was unrealisable, the woman already married, the poet-lover just as unfree in his public eminence. The eastern roles the couple played offered total freedom, but only in the imagination; reality required 'Entsagung', fulfilment was restricted to poetry. Such as it was, it was at least a double fulfilment, with Marianne's own poems – 'Hochbeglückt . . .', 'Ach, um deine feuchten Schwingen', 'Was bedeutet die Bewegung' and possibly others – answering and equalling Goethe's, a far greater wonder than the mere assimilation of Ottilie's handwriting to Eduard's. And at least, too, it was not a sub-limation of erotic feeling into something different, but a celebration of desire and delight as the very substance of spiritual life:

> Denn das Leben ist die Liebe,
> Und des Lebens Leben Geist.
>
> ('Nimmer will ich . . .')

The *Divan* is a renewal of poetic inspiration amid the prosaic dili-gence of age. But if Goethe was to complete his major life's work, *Faust*, he needed both of these. He had to obey the Director's behest from the 'Vorspiel auf dem Theater' and write poetry to order. He had done it once, to complete Part I of *Faust*; Part II was a task of another order of magnitude. But it was now or never; in his late seventies he could no longer complacently rely on 'Wiedermorgen und Immermorgen'.[36] Under this pressure he achieved, in a way not clear to himself, a wholly conscious creativity which was yet unrepeatable and the equivalent of the true poetic madness.[37] It was a classic riposte to the mysticising Romantic view of poetic composition, especially since the resulting poetry validated (and validates) itself.

It is the poetry of *Faust II*, in the broadest sense — the brilliant play of words and of an inexhaustibly fertile imagination — that most impresses. This remains true even if one feels confident that the work has dramatic unity. For Goethe's 'completion' expanded far beyond the functional minimum needed to resolve the plot (which he finally does in Act V in almost laconic form) and is a rich — often chaotically rich — elaboration of imaginary situations and adventures, allegories and symbols, across whose epic breadth and passages of lyrical intensity the dramatist lays a trail of salient moments. These do constitute a plot but can hardly compete for attention with the poetic play which is the work's driving force and is given free rein to take the poet where it will. Aptly, Goethe spoke of the finished 'Klassische Walpurgisnacht' as 'zustande gekommen, oder vielmehr ins Grenzenlose ausgelaufen'.[38]

That episode preludes Faust's possession of Helen; yet it cannot easily be reduced to that simple dramatic function. Insofar as it is not a wholly self-sufficient game with Greek myths and monsters and early theories of the earth's genesis, a poetic bestiary and a new *De rerum natura*, it is a journey through the symbolic night of these primitive shapes and shaping forces into the clear daylight of Classical Greek beauty which Helen just as symbolically represents. And though she is linked into the main dramatic theme, in that possessing her beauty makes Faust declare his contentment with the moment (unnoticed by Mephisto, who seemingly must wait, literal-minded, for the actual words 'Verweile doch' to be spoken), although Helen thus does become part of the plot, with all her cultural connotations she is as much in excess of its direct requirements as Faust himself was in excess of the requirements of Gretchen's tragedy with all his legendary ones. If Helen nevertheless is essential, it is not to the drama as such, but to the nexus of symbolic associations which the Faust figure, the Faust action, and indeed the very act of writing *Faust* had acquired for Goethe. Through her and Faust's relation to her he can speak symbolically of the qualities he revered in the ancient world, portray a marriage of the uneasy Northern mind with that alien yet longed-for serenity and perfection, sketch a reconciliation of Classical and Romantic. (The episode was indeed for a time a half-separate work with the title 'Helena. Klassisch-romantische Phantasmagorie. Zwischenspiel zu Faust'.) Such extra dimensions athwart the purposive line of drama are one aspect of a general change that characterises Part II. The work now moves on a different plane and to wholly different effect from Part I. That was an action within the normal confines of drama, often markedly naturalistic despite its magic content; Part II knows no such confines, the imagination is the limit, and magic is not just its content but its precondition. Part I ends with the harrowing immediacy of Gretchen's cell before her execution; Part II begins with Ariel soothing Faust's conscience, turning him away from that harrowing past and towards new ventures within a quite un-naturalistic reality. Faust himself is no longer so much a real dramatic character as a focus for Goethe's ranging fantasy. The stance and style of the poetry change accordingly: from the Erdgeist dialogue with its urgent exchanges in stabbing irregularly patterned rhyme to the detached reflections in orderly terza rima pentameters of Faust's monologue at sunrise ('Anmutige Gegend'); from his excited glimpse of sensuous beauty in the witch's mirror to the high aesthetic rhetoric of his praise of Helen's image ('Rittersaal'). These are essentially parallel passages, perhaps deliberately so — there are many correspondences between scenes, motifs and episodes of Part I and Part II.[39] But they are as much contrasts as links. In the two pairs of scenes named, analogous experiences are met in fundamentally different ways; there is a shift from the immediate rendering of dramatic emotion to statements of feeling mediated through a reflective faculty which is not just that of the speaking character.

There is similar detachment in the presentation of the mythic figures. When the Sphinxes plead their ignorance of Helen to the questing Faust — 'Wir reichen nicht hinauf zu ihren Tagen,/Die letztesten hat Herkules erschlagen' (ll.7197f); or when Helen introduces herself — 'Bewundert viel und viel gescholten, Helena' (ll.8488), or looks back on the tragic effects of her beauty (ll.9246ff); or when Nereus recalls how he warned Paris of the disaster his sexual adventure would bring on Troy: 'Die Lüfte qualmend, überströmend rot,/Gebälke glühend, unten Mord und Tod:/Trojas Gerichtstag, rhythmisch festgebannt,/ Jahrtausenden so schrecklich als gekannt' (ll.8114ff) — in all these instances, the speakers are at once in time and outside it, primitive but also looking back on the primitive, Greek yet also aware of the centrality of Greek myth, legend and art in Western life. Personal and cultural consciousness fuse. As Helen says, 'Ich scheine mir verlebt und doch so neu' (ll.9415). Any urgency in Helen's or Nereus's words is not the urgency of stage-drama but of historical and ethical perspective, springing from tragic recognition of the timelessness of temptation and attraction and their nemesis.

Finally there is the detachment that allows the characters an awareness of the very poetic forms in which they are conceived. When Helen is intrigued by the rhymed verse of Faust's Northerners, he teaches her to speak in it — and to join him in very nearly saying the fateful words of the pact:

> *Faust.*   Nun schaut der Geist nicht vorwärts, nicht zurück,
> Die Gegenwart allein —
> *Helena.*   Ist unser Glück.
>
> (ll.9381f)

In all this, a very different hand is at work from the one which shaped Part I. In almost every literary respect, there is more separating the two parts than joining them.[40]

Reviewing these cultural materials and symbolic meanings of *Faust* II may make it sound portentous and forbidding. Against this we need to remember Goethe's frequent insistence that these were 'ernste *Scherze*', and the impatience with the German search for profundity which made him cry out: 'Ei, so habt doch die Courage, euch ergetzen zu lassen, euch rühren zu lassen, euch erheben zu lassen'.[41] To be sure, they were '*ernste* Scherze', and his impatience was something of an over-reaction, since *Faust* II is not without its profundity. But what he was insisting on was surely the delight poetic work is meant to give: it must be read in a mood of play and release. So among many possibilities the 'Klassische Walpurgisnacht' can be read as burlesque, and the masquerade of Act I ('Weitläufiger Saal') has been well called a 'dichterisch kommentierte Revue'.[42] The court scenes in Acts I, II and IV are rich in social, political and anti-clerical satire. And with Mephistopheles there is always a down-to-earth humour and sardonic wit. This in fact makes him one of the play's strongest unifying factors, stronger even than Faust himself. Though his humour grows from what in the play's ethics are limitations, aesthetically it holds it together: at whatever far reach of the mythic or poetic imagination we find ourselves, Mephisto provides a familiar point of reference, a cynical landmark in a fantastic scene. Thus when all are agog at the beauty of Helen's apparition, she proves to be simply not his type:

Das wär sie denn! Vor dieser hätt' ich Ruh';
Hübsch ist sie wohl, doch sagt sie mir nicht zu.

(ll.6479f)

And as the scientific excitement mounts of creating a homunculus by
crystallisation, there is this blasé comment from one who has seen it all,
Lot's wife included:

Wer lange lebt, hat viel erfahren,
Nichts Neues kann für ihn auf dieser Welt geschehn.
Ich habe schon in meinen Wanderjahren
Kristallisiertes Menschenvolk gesehn.

(ll.6861ff)

Above all to offset solemnity there is the pleasure of Goethe's
exuberant virtuosity in every kind of verse, Greek and modern, rhymed
and unrhymed, pentameter, trimeter, Alexandrine, *Knittelvers*,
Madrigalvers, couplets, quatrains, terza rima; and his range of tone from
the solemn, tragic and mysterious to the easy colloquial, often in
successive lines, as when Mephisto evokes the Mütter, the realm of
eternal shapes from which Faust must bring back the real Helen, in a
tone that moves from the nonchalantly chatty to the sublime:

Bei [diesem] Schein wirst du die Mütter sehn,
Die einen sitzen, andre stehn und gehn,
Wie's eben kommt. Gestaltung, Umgestaltung,
Des ewigen Sinnes ewige Unterhaltung.

(ll.6285f)

All this creates a glittering play of moods and textures which matches
the often bewildering succession of subjects and figures, subtly embodying their values and characteristics.[43] It is the grand poetic performance
for which in retrospect the *Divan* — by any other poet's standard itself
a magnum opus — turns out to have been a five-finger exercise. In its
richness and range, its sovereign imaginative play and its unsurpassed
virtuosity of technique, *Faust II* is a work only an old poet (and no
other old poet) could have written.[44]

   Nor could any other poet have found quite the means Goethe finds
to save Faust, means which derive from the very philosophy and
practice of poetry itself. Behind the dramatic issue and Goethe's poetry
there lies one and the same problem: where in the flux of time and

individual life is value to be located? Absolute religions and philosophies locate it in some final static condition (salvation, nirvana, oneness with the Ideal) and assign value to ordinary experience, if at all, only as the medium through which or the means by which that condition can be reached. They conceive man as a fixed essence, only temporarily doomed to exist in a world of change. The original Faust of legend belonged to such a religious view, but he sinfully abandoned an orthodox absolute in favour of some obvious substitutes − power, pleasure, lust. He was merely an evil-doer within the religious system. Goethe's Faust from the first is halfway out of that system, for he recognises no absolutes that would devalue human experience (and he is much too sophisticated to settle for his predecessor's crude delights). But nor does he believe that experience could ever satisfy him. Yet the very bitterness with which he denies this, the very energy with which he strives (albeit away from the limitations of all experience rather than towards any goal) betrays a nostalgia for absolutes. Man has been fed on absolutes for so long that he goes on seeking them, even in inappropriate places, and is disillusioned when they cannot be found. Nietzsche was to term this phenomenon 'religious after-pains'.[45]

But when Faust finally does affirm the moment, it is not an absolute, not an experience to end all experiences, but a vision of continuity; it looks forward to an endless sequence of activity whose value lies in being congruent with man's true nature. For he is not an essence but a process, and it is not his temporary misfortune but his very definition and dignity to change and develop within a world that is equally in flux. There is no such thing as 'Zustand', all is 'Bewegung'.[46] And poetry is men's means to know and live with that ever-moving reality, it arises when one flux glimpses the other − inevitably not in its totality, but in single particulars which momentarily reveal and represent it before they pass: 'Das ist die wahre Symbolik, wo das Besondere das Allgemeinere repräsentiert, nicht als Traum und Schatten, sondern als lebendig-augenblickliche Offenbarung des Unerforschlichen'.[47] In seeing things thus, Faust achieves his author's poetic relation to experience − and thereby rises clear of Mephisto's grasp, even though he does speak the formula of the wager. He has learned to live symbolically. This is to see all experiences as relative but not as valueless. No single moment can achieve the absolute, but each has a symbolic potential; and their value taken together lies in the sequence they compose, the larger patterns of nature into which they flow, and the participation in these larger patterns that they allow men.

The sense of such participation through moments of heightened insight is everywhere in the late poetry. It is already present in the love poems of the *Divan*. Suleika's 'In mir liebt ihn, für diesen Augenblick' opens a window on permanence, at the furthest possible remove from the traditional lyric exhortation to 'gather rosebuds while ye may': love is a contact with the divine. That does not make it a mere allegory of religion, or vice versa: to take either as a mere vehicle for the other is to miss the interpenetration of the two. Love is the most intense way of knowing beauty, the physical world, the divine, which are not separable. Nor are they in another *Divan* poem where the beloved is known and named in every form of the natural world, just as Allah is named in a hundred ways by the Moslem believer:

> In tausend Formen magst du dich verstecken,
> Doch, Allerliebste, gleich erkenn ich dich.

She is present to the poet's senses in the shapes and qualities of wind, water, cloud, plant, sunrise. She is his path to all knowledge:

> Was ich mit äussrem Sinn, mit innerm kenne,
> Du Allbelehrende, kenn ich durch dich.

All this is not a matter of definable beliefs, but of knowing and venerating reality and resisting its reduction to the monotony of doctrine. 'Das Mannigfaltige glaubt man nicht, man erkennt es' — Goethe transcends the expedient narrowness of dogma with these words, and in the same spirit balances the holy Koran with the splendours of a peacock feather.[48] Such a hallowing of experience sets him apart equally from poets who merely capture the moment for its beauty and poignancy, and from those others who draw from it or impose on it doctrinal meanings. Deeper than the first, freer than the second, he is a 'mystic without religion'.[49]

But the known reality the old poet evokes is not just the immediate experience of his senses, the lover's symbolic perceptions. He also rises to a higher plane and in a handful of poems gives a quintessential view of the universe as science and reflection had brought him to see it. This is a unique philosophical poetry, unlike the pale abstractions of eighteenth-century philosophical verse and a more intense utterance than he himself had earlier achieved. With their strong, memorable rhythms within firm stanza patterns and their compressed phrasing, the grandiose generalisations in these poems have a sensuousness of their own — for when generalisation is born of a lifetime of observing and reflecting, it can be not a reduction but a concentrate of reality.[50]

It can begin quietly, unpretentiously, from a seeming conversational reminiscence about the poet's scientific work:

> Freudig war, vor vielen Jahren,
> Eifrig so der Geist bestrebt,
> Zu erforschen, zu erfahren,
> Wie Natur im Schaffen lebt . . .

The poetic temperature rises with this unprosaic formula; it hits off Goethe's concern with nature-as-process rather than with objects and awakens echoes of his 'Metamorphose' poems — one of the intertextual effects that are at their richest in the late poems, where so much can be present to the mind's ear. The conversational tone yields as a simple 'Und' sums up the years spent patiently pursuing the single force that lives in so many forms; and there follows a series of grand propositions on the workings of nature:

> . . . Und es ist das ewig Eine,
> Das sich vielfach offenbart;
> Klein das Grosse, gross das Kleine,
> Alles nach der eignen Art.
> Immer wechselnd, fest sich haltend,
> Nah und fern und fern und nah;
> So gestaltend, umgestaltend —
> Zum Erstaunen bin ich da.

Each of these short lines succinctly states a large conception — of proportion, specification, relationship, process. But they transcend mere statement by the play of contrast, chiasmus, repetition and paradox, and become poetic incantation, embodying the endless movement that cannot be exhaustively described. At the close, a universe of changing forms opens out before the mind, impossible to contain, forcing the recognition that wonder is the only resort — and the poet's true function. To this he resigns himself in a mood of reverent exhilaration.

If this is a poetry of wisdom, it is a modest wisdom that looks on 'mit bescheidnem Blick' at the intricate handiwork of the 'ewige Weberin', Nature. Weaving is an old image in Goethe — the Erdgeist laboured 'am sausenden Webstuhl der Zeit' to fashion 'der Gottheit lebendiges Kleid' — and it recurs again and again throughout his life

whenever he is most excited or humbled by the sense of nature's inter-
locking complexities, 'Wo Ein Tritt tausend Fäden regt . . . Ein Schlag
tausend Verbindungen schlägt' ('Antepirrhema').[51] Yet, though modest,
these remarkable statements also have great authority. It is as if the
poet has seen into the workings of the universe at some central axis,
has been initiated, and is now reporting calmly and without presumption
how things really are:

Wenn im Unendlichen dasselbe
Sich wiederholend ewig fliesst,
Das tausendfältige Gewölbe
Sich kräftig ineinander schliesst,
Strömt Lebenslust aus allen Dingen,
Dem kleinsten wie dem grössten Stern,
Und alles Drängen, alles Ringen
Ist ewige Ruh in Gott dem Herrn.

('Wenn im Unendlichen . . .')

Here once more is the paradoxical harmony of the infinite and the
constant pattern, of flux and closed form, of a ceaseless activity and
the overarching calm that it composes.

These late poems are not in an ordinary sense 'nature description',
nor are they vehicles for particular philosophical or scientific doctrines.
Yet not for nothing did Goethe print them first in his scientific journals.[52] For their deceptively simple and seemingly abstract language also
vividly suggests the highest complexity and concreteness, so that it is
easy to give his images the specific content of modern scientific theories
which resolve static phenomena into patterns of movement, change and
interaction: plate tectonics, ecological systems, animal ethology, evolutionary adaptation. The principles of life and the physical universe seem
to move before our eyes, the inexhaustible productiveness of nature,
'jenes Meer . . ., Das flutend strömt gesteigerte Gestalten' ('Im ernsten
Beinhaus . . .'). This is a god's eye view of creation, recalling Goethe's
comment that it was the ultimate triumph of all poetry 'dass man selber
zum Seher, das heisst: Gott ähnlich wird'.[53]

But having seen, how does one act? How does the grand vision affect
the individual? In 'Urworte. Orphisch', Goethe views the forces that
shape a human destiny — Daimon, the personal principle; Tyche, the
random influences of one's surroundings; Eros, the power of passion;
Ananke, external compulsion; and Elpis, ever-resilient hope — and
epitomises each in a massive, lapidary stanza: 'poetisch, kompendios,

lakonisch'.[54] In other late poems, 'Prooemion', 'Eins und Alles', 'Vermächtnis', he becomes expressly didactic. An ethical position has grown, gradually and unforcedly, from his long scientific and poetic reflection. As the anticipations of phrase and idea in these poems hint, it is in large part the ethos contained in *Faust*, a philosophy of activity, of human limitation transcended by real or symbolic participation in the grand movement of life, and — once this has been achieved — of acceptance.

'Acceptance' normally means conformism, quietism, resignation. Much criticism in recent years has slated Goethe for these socially harmful qualities, for failing to be the spearhead of protest and change which writers, it is conceived, ought to be. Certainly, if we look outside the poetry, this charge seems to hold good. We find a self-styled liberal who is in practice grown very conservative, even reactionary;[55] an acknowledged great man of his nation who, in sharp contrast to the ideals of his partnership with Schiller, no longer believes he can have any direct influence on his society;[56] a figure of immense prestige, indeed a cultural monument ritually visited by travellers from all over the civilised world, yet in touch only by letter with what is going forward in the decisive centres of European affairs — with Zelter in Berlin, with the Franco-German diplomat Reinhard; a tirelessly active writer whose world has shrunk, even as his vision widened and took in the whole universe, to the monastic isolation of a Weimar workroom: 'Klein das Grosse, gross das Kleine'.

But what matters, and asks to be judged, is the work done in that room. Something may be demanded of writers as men, but what they can achieve directly in society is unlikely to be much — Goethe, certainly, was never in a position of power anything like commensurate with his reputation, least of all in the Metternich era. In his work by contrast the writer, however conservative in practical matters age has made him, can hold to and propagate notions that are at odds with any outward conformism. For the act of acceptance is not conformist when it is an acceptance of change, of dynamism, of 'Stirb und werde', a philosophy of constant renewal through the motion that never ceases inside phenomena because it constitutes their life. True, the radical idea that 'Alles muss in Nichts zerfallen,/Wenn es im Sein beharren will' ('Eins und Alles') is balanced in a directly answering poem by a faith in constancy and continuity of being ('Vermächtnis'). But these are themselves dynamic: 'Das Ew'ge regt sich fort in allen', even within its conserving framework of laws. So that if Goethe is not a revolutionary, he is a profoundly evolutionary thinker, worlds away from the conformism both outer *and* inner of the Biedermeier period in which these last years of his life fall; worlds away from (say) Mörike, who keeps his gaze limited to the eventless countryside of Swabia, or Stifter, who will not look beyond the precariously ordered rose-garden of *Der Nachsommer*.

Thus the difference between Goethe's spirit and that of Biedermeier art stares us in the face, unless – impermissibly – we ignore what he wrote and look only at the static dignity of the old court poet. Goethe deserves at least the kind of rehabilitation that Heine gave to Hegel, whose conscious conservatism was belied by a dynamism inherent in his dialectical system, out of which revolutionary doctrines could later arise.[57] That Heine himself with the political half of his mind dismissed Goethe's achievement as superseded with the term 'Kunstperiode' was a crude injustice to Goethe, and more particularly a failure to recognise that the seeds of life can lie in art.[58] And if it is objected that the seeds so obviously present in Goethe's poetry never took root and grew, as Hegel's for better and worse did in Marx, the fault does not lie in their author. Only in the extremes of politicised criticism are all the sins of the children visited upon the father.

Change is the centre of Goethe's poetic conception, and to the end of his own life and poetry change is at work 'umzuschaffen das Geschaffne'. At seventy-four, he broke his world and remade it by falling in love yet again, this time with a girl of seventeen whom he seriously wished to marry. It was a situation fit, as he realised, for an Iffland comedy,[59] but from it he made a tragic poem and one of his greatest.

The 'Marienbader Elegie' gainsays almost everything he had achieved and become. He was an essentially conciliatory, untragic nature,[60] and the poem is unrelievedly bitter. He had distilled experience into a mature self-knowledge, and his wisdom cannot cope with this new upheaval.[61] He had made himself profoundly at home in a world he understood and accepted, he was a favourite of the gods, and he is now cast out. He had his own unique piety, yet it dissolves when he is not with her; his own philosophy of activity, which he cannot follow after losing her, even though in imagination he hears Ulrike exhort him to it. He was linked to the world by a tireless response to its beauty and a deep fascination with its inner workings, and suddenly these lost all meaning. Age had brought him serenity and detachment, and he is now overcome by raw feeling, helpless 'Sehnen', tears, sufferings that his enfeebled will cannot master. In short, a culture has broken down.

The poetry makes this clear. Not by incoherence – the 'Elegie' is

one of the most lucid, compelling lyrical poems in existence, as its
compulsive composition in the coach from Marienbad is one of the
most remarkable documented cases of poetic inspiration. But its very
qualities show up dramatically what has suddenly fallen away. Since
the days of High Classicism Goethe's poetic speech had been double-
stranded, personal utterance and traditional reference in one; since at
least the *Divan* he had grown accustomed to manipulating elaborate
conventions, speaking through a mask, giving even passionate feeling
the balancing element of conscious play. Now all that is lost, leaving a
direct, almost bald language to chronicle emotional disaster:

> Der Kuss, der letzte, grausam süss, zerschneidend
> Ein herrliches Geflecht verschlungner Minnen.
> Nun eilt, nun stockt der Fuss, die Schwelle meidend,
> Als trieb' ein Cherub flammend ihn von hinnen;
> Das Auge starrt auf düstrem Pfad verdrossen,
> Es blickt zurück, die Pforte steht verschlossen.

True, this has the verbal intensity and compression, as well as the
stanzaic grandeur, of these late years; but the immediacy is that of
Goethe's early great lyrics. This is the voice not of culture, but once
again of nature.

There are, to be sure, cultural allusions — movingly to Man's first
exclusion from Paradise, and later to Pandora's box — but they are not
enough to create a protective role or ironic distance, they are not even
consoling recollections. Nor is there much consolation in Goethe's use
of the culture he had created himself:|of the poem 'An Werther' as a
prologue, or of a *Tasso* quotation as epigraph to the Elegy. Thoughts on
Werther's fate only lead to a bitter conclusion: 'Zum Bleiben ich, zum
Scheiden du erkoren,/Gingst du voran — und hast nicht viel verloren'.
And the *Tasso* reminiscence only serves to bring out how precisely
Goethe's real desolation repeats the pattern of the earlier imagined one,
down to the characteristic motions of a mind in search of comfort.
Tasso's 'Ist alles denn verloren?' with its despairing answer 'Nein, es ist
alles da, und ich bin nichts,/Ich bin mir selbst entwandt, sie ist es mir',
is echoed by the old Goethe's 'Ist denn die Welt nicht übrig?' and his
despair at a more total loss still: 'Mir ist das All, ich bin mir selbst
verloren'. Indeed, the Tasso parallel makes the Elegy that much more
shattering. It reminds us that it is not now an archetypal figure of
poetic hypersensitivity who has lost his grip, but one of the most
balanced and perfected minds known to us, a 'self' as rich, complex

and controlled as was the 'All' he had grasped — both lost for a girl's glance, for a fulfilment the gods seemed to offer but then withdrew:

Sie drängten mich zum gabeseligen Munde,
Sie trennen mich, und richten mich zugrunde.

No other Goethe poem ends this darkly, this uncompromisingly. There is no final harmony (the poem 'Aussöhnung', added to make up a trilogy, was not only of earlier composition but intrinsically too light to outweigh the Elegy's own close), no natural or moral resolution, least of all any deliberate act of 'Entsagung'. There is only the pain of an enforced 'Entbehren'.[62] Having learned to live symbolically, Goethe had fallen back into desire for a fulfilled real present, staked all on it as a gambler stakes high on a single card, and lost.[63]

Yet to renew feeling, even painful feeling, is to renew life. Goethe had travelled to Bohemia in search of 'sinnliche Anregung' (though doubtless not of quite this kind) so as not to lose himself in abstractions and absolutes.[64] The Marienbad crisis had a strangely invigorating effect on his physical and mental health, a 'gesunde Heiterkeit' is evident.[65] Balance is regained, serenity returns, activity resumes. It would of course be foolish to assert that serenity was then constant in his last years. There are dark moods as well. Age, in his own words, is a 'stufenweises Zurücktreten aus der Erscheinung'.[66] Death nears, contemporaries vanish, the 'dark catafalque' looms behind all happier thoughts.[67] It needs an effort to abandon what age takes as 'entbehrlich' and to appreciate its positive gifts.[68] Yet against this he has new thoughts which it would be worth living a second time to pursue,[69] and a feeling of inexhaustible creative potential which forces him to envisage, as for Faust, an afterlife of continuing activity.[70] Creativity is an unquestioned value. And there continue to be moments, for example in Dornburg in the weeks after Karl August died, when existence comes together in symbolic concentration and is simply accepted: 'Da wollen und müssen wir denn alles gelten lassen'.[71]

We must not get lost in biography. The acceptance and serenity that matter are those of the last poems; the mysterious 'Der Bräutigam', with its closing gesture 'Wie es auch sei, das Leben, es ist gut'; the genial ease and intense perceptions of the 'Chinesisch-deutsche Jahreszeiten', renewed cultural play in the mask of an old mandarin; and the poems written in Dornburg. In all these, there are images of deprivation (the lost bride) or darkness — 'Schwarzvertiefte Finsternisse/Widerspiegelnd ruht der See' — but they are balanced by images of beauty and light.

Sunrise and moonrise embody hope and unspoken expectation, sunset itself a last glory and a mysterious assurance. These poems are about the simplest phenomena but unobtrusively speak the poet's deepest feelings. The self is transcended yet pervades the pictured world with its own concerns, in the paradoxical mixture that symbol for Goethe was: 'die höchste Anmassung und die höchste Bescheidenheit'.[72] His last Dornburg poem evokes a single day from early to late, its varied beauty, its changing moods and tempo, and captures through its rise and fall the whole course of natural life:

> Früh, wenn Tal, Gebirg und Garten
> Nebelschleiern sich enthüllen,
> Und dem sehnlichsten Erwarten
> Blumenkelche bunt sich füllen,
>
> Wenn der Äther, Wolken tragend,
> Mit dem klaren Tage streitet,
> Und ein Ostwind, sie verjagend,
> Blaue Sonnenbahn bereitet,
>
> Dankst du dann, am Blick dich weidend,
> Reiner Brust der Grossen, Holden,
> Wird die Sonne, rötlich scheidend,
> Rings den Horizont vergolden.

But counterpointing the rise and fall, there is another movement, the gently rising tension of the single sentence which moves to a climax in the main clause it saves to the end. For though the three quiet stanzas are full of real things seen, felt, appreciated, these are not merely described. They are the conditions and means for a consummation: if each phenomenon is met with a grateful heart, then sunset will transfigure the day's dying moments. The literal sense is too simple not to mean more. It hints at the final acceptance by nature of a man who has tirelessly sought and loved her in her wholeness and her every detail.

A consummation, but not a curtain line. It is still only 1828, there are four more years of life, endless work to do, a last collected edition to work at, *Faust* to complete — 'immer höhere und reinere Tätigkeit bis ans Ende'.[73]

Notes

1. To Zelter, 1 June 1805.
2. In the sketch for 'Schillers Totenfeier', WA 16, 567.
3. *Maximen und Reflexionen* nr. 138, HA 12, 383.
4. Cf. Walther Scheidig, *Goethes Preisaufgaben für Bildende Künstler* (Weimar, 1958).
5. See the objections of the contemporary sculptor Schadow, quoted in Scheidig p.141; and Schiller's tactful letter of 18 May 1798 restraining Goethe from too antiquarian a treatment of the Achilles subject.
6. See to Schiller, 22 and 27 June 1797 and 28 April 1798.
7. To Schiller, 2 December 1794.
8. Cf. *Einfache Nachahmung der Natur, Manier, Stil* (1789), HA 12, 30ff.
9. Cf. HA 8, 465; and the letter to C.H. Schlosser of 25 November 1814.
10. See to Schiller, 23 October 1799.
11. The narrative tone, as set by the detached opening words 'Eduard – so nennen wir einen reichen Baron im besten Mannesalter . . .', can be thought of in this light. Eduard's words to Charlotte in I, 2: ' "in Gottes Namen sei der Versuch gemacht" ' are then a calculated *double entendre*. It is noteworthy that the description of Eduard's and Ottilie's first embrace – 'Wer das andere zuerst ergriffen, wäre nicht zu unterscheiden gewesen' (I, 12) – not only echoes the description of chemical recombinations in I, 4 but subtly assimilates human agents to chemicals by using 'das andere' rather than the possible 'den anderen'.
12. A striking suggestion by Paul Stöcklein, *Wege zum späten Goethe* (Hamburg, [2]1960), p.48.
13. Cf. Goethe to Charlotte von Schiller, 5 May 1810, looking back to Ottilie as an 'irdische Heilige'. Stöcklein's arguments, *Wege zum späten Goethe*, on the *Wahlverwandtschaften*, like Flitner's on the 'Alterswerk' as a whole (*Goethe im Spätwerk*, Bremen, [2]1957) tend to assimilate Goethe too substantially to Christian traditions where he was at most using Christian terms and imagery.
14. George Eliot, 'The Morality of *Wilhelm Meister*' in *The Essays of George Eliot* ed. Pinney (New York,[2]1967), p.147.
15. Goethe in conversation with Riemer, 28 August 1808.
16. K.W.F. Solger in a letter-essay on the *Wahlverwandtschaften* (repr. HA 6, 635).
17. The 'narrator' notion was originally no more than a witty conceit dropped *en passant* by Stöcklein, *Wege zum späten Goethe*, pp.11f. It was taken to great lengths by H.G. Barnes, *Goethe's Die Wahlverwandtschaften* (Oxford, 1967). Later criticism (e.g. G. Marahrens in *Festschrift Hallamore*, Toronto 1968) assumes the hypothesis but does nothing to substantiate it. That there is a narrative *manner* is a quite different thing. This simply underlines the story's artificiality (see above, note 11) and the absence of any implied claim to direct realism. It thus has links with the story's origin as a Novelle. Cf. Walter Benjamin, *Goethes Wahlverwandtschaften* in Benjamin, *Gesammelte Schriften*, I, 1 (Frankfurt, 1974), pp.167f.
18. Goethe said that no one could fail to recognise in the novel a 'tief leidenschaftliche Wunde' (HA 10, 505). This is scarcely true, so effectively has the formality of his style overlaid it.
19. Cf. above, Chapter 6, note 48; and Wilhelm to Jacob Grimm, 24 November 1809, quoted HA 6, 641.
20. Cf. G.H. Lewes, *Life and Works of Goethe* (Everyman edn.), pp.525, 549. Such objections are not just Anglo-Saxon-commonsensical. See e.g. Riemann's article *Wilhelm Meister* in the *Goethe-Handbuch* ed. Zeitler, vol. 2

(Stuttgart, 1917). True, Lewes's indignation arose partly from Eckermann's report (*Gespräche mit Goethe*, 15 May 1831) on the composition and publication of the *Wanderjahre*, and this has been shown to be inaccurate by Wilhelm Wundt, *Goethes Wilhelm Meister und die Entstehung des modernen Lebensideals* (Berlin, 1913), appendix pp.493-509. Yet it is striking that Goethe himself made no claim to have created a unifying form, even when this was suggested to him. See to Boisserée, 2 September 1829. On the contrary, he admitted the book's 'collective' character and was content that readers should appropriate piecemeal whatever they enjoyed. See to Rochlitz, 28 July 1829.

21. The earliest efforts in this direction already in Wundt, *Goethes Wilhelm Meister*. Cf. also Erich Trunz's commentary in HA 8; H.J. Schrimpf, *Das Weltbild des späten Goethe*, (Stuttgart 1956); A. Henkel, *Entsagung. Eine Studie zu Goethes Altersroman*, (Tübingen, 1954); W. Emrich, 'Das Problem der Symbolinterpretation', *DVjs* 26 (1952).

22. Lewes, *Life and Works of Goethe*, p.542.

23. Cf. II, 8 (HA 8, 258) where the editor, faced with the rejection of theatre by the Pädagogische Provinz, is loath to admit that all the time and effort he spent on it was wasted.

24. Cf. also the enclosure in a letter to Zelter, 26 November 1825 (printed as *Über das Lehrgedicht*, WA 41^2 225-7): 'Alle Poesie soll belehrend sein, aber unmerklich, sie soll den Menschen aufmerksam machen, wovon sich zu belehren wert wäre; er muss die Lehre selbst daraus ziehen, wie aus dem Leben'.

25. To Knebel, 24 December 1824.

26. HA 9, 7ff.

27. HA 9, 283. The autobiography was first conceived in 1809. Books 1 to 15 appeared in 1814 as *Aus meinem Leben. Dichtung und Wahrheit*. The final Part, Books 16 to 20, was only completed after *Faust* II in 1831 and appeared posthumously.

28. To S.S. von Uwarow, 27 February 1811. Cf. also to King Ludwig I of Bavaria, 17 December 1829.

29. To Sulpiz Boisserée, 16 December 1816.

30. See above, p. 192,on Wackenroder's *Herzensergiessungen eines kunstliebenden Klosterbruders*; and cf. Friedrich Schlegel, *Aufforderung an die Maler der jetzigen Zeit* (1805) in *Schriften*, pp.584ff.

31. Cf. the somewhat backhanded compliments in letters to the painter Runge, 2 June 1806, and to the writer Arnim, 14 November 1808.

32. *Romanticism a stage*: cf. to Reinhard, 14 May and 22 July 1810; *the 'dark cellar'*: to Jacobi, 7 March 1808; *a new advance?*: to Reinhard, 7 October 1810; *failed 'Gestaltung'*: to Zelter, 30 October 1808; *the Greeks*: to Knebel, 9 November 1814; *his papers*: to Boisserée, 9 November 1814. The late letter to Iken, 27 September 1827, may stand as an epitome of Goethe's attitude: he there says it is time for a reconciliation between Classical and Romantic — and in the next breath rejects 'falsche Muster' and celebrates the (Classical) Renaissance as a victory over 'mönchische Barbarei'.

33. To Zelter, 15 September 1807.

34. Cf. Kommerell, *Gedanken über Gedichte*, p.269: 'Das Gedicht schäumt auf, man hat noch den Knall des Champagnerpfropfens im Ohr'.

35. To Zelter, 29 October 1815.

36. To Sulpiz Boisserée, 22 October 1826.

37 To Wilhelm von Humboldt, 1 December 1831. See also to Humboldt, 17 March 1832. Goethe's emphasis on consciousness is the more striking because he now leaned generally to a Romantic view of poetic creation as part of the 'Nachtseite' of nature, a kind of 'Wachschlaf', 'traumartig'. See to Nees von Esenbeck, 23 July 1820.

38. Letter to Eckermann, 9 August 1830.
39. Cf. to K.J.L. Iken, 23 September 1827, on the principle of 'einander gegenübergestellte und sich gleichsam ineinander abspiegelnde Gebilde'.
40. Cf. Goethe's comments to Boisserée (Boisserée's diary, 3 August 1815, quoted HA 3, 430) and to Eckermann, 17 February 1831. Also the letter to F.A. Stapfer, 4 April 1827.
41. To Eckermann, 6 May 1827.
42. Staiger, *Goethe* III, 294.
43. See the excellent brief survey by Erich Trunz, HA 3, 483ff., esp. 489f.
44. Cf. Gottfried Benn's arabesques on *Faust* II in *Altern als Problem für Künstler*: 'Sicher das geheimnisvollste Geschenk Deutschlands an die Völker der Erde . . . Wo kommt das alles eigentlich her, das schwebt doch völlig im Imaginären, das ist ja Tischrücken, Telepathie, Schrulligkeiten, da steht einer auf einem Balkon, irreal und unbeweglich, und bläst hell oder dunkel gefärbte Seifenblasen, immer neue Tonpfeifen und Strohhalme zaubert er hervor, die bunten Kugeln abzublasen – ein grossartiger Balkongott, Antike und Barock noch implantiert, Wunder und Geheimnisse um seine Schösse'. Benn *Werke* 1, 577.
45. Nietzsche, *Menschliches, Allzumenschliches* para 131, 'Religiöse Nachwehen' in *Werke* ed. Schlechta I, 530f.
46. Cf. explicitly to Niebuhr, 23 November 1812: 'Zustand ist ein albernes Wort; weil nichts steht und alles beweglich ist'.
47. *Maximen und Reflexionen* nr. 752, HA 12, 471.
48. See in the *Divan* the section 'Mahomet' in the *Noten und Abhandlungen*, HA 2, 143, and the poem 'Ich sah mit Staunen und Vergnügen'.
49. Cf. Grete Schaeder, *Gott und Welt. Drei Kapitel Goethescher Weltanschauung* (Hameln, 1947), p.82.
50. See the excellent discussion of 'Altersstil' in Max Kommerell, *Geist und Buchstabe der Dichtung* (Frankfurt, ⁵1962), pp.11ff.
51. E.g. Faust viewing the sign of the macrocosm: 'Wie alles sich zum Ganzen webt,/Eins in dem andern wirkt und lebt' (ll.447f). Faust's profession of faith to Gretchen: 'Und drängt nicht alles/Nach Haupt und Herzen dir,/Und webt in ewigem Geheimnis/Unsichtbar sichtbar neben dir?' (ll.3447ff). Faust on the Brocken: 'Der Frühling webt schon in den Birken' (3845). One of Werther's profoundest reflections on nature – the letter of 18 August in Book 1 – ends: 'Himmel und Erde und ihre webenden Kräfte um mich her: ich sehe nichts als ein ewig verschlingendes, ewig wiederkäuendes Ungeheuer' (HA 6, 53). The opening of *Des Epimenides Erwachen* speaks of Fate '[das] brausend webt, zerstört und knirschend waltet' (HA 5, 366). And in Goethe's very last conversation with Eckermann, 17 March 1832, he speaks of 'die zeugende Kraft Gottes, wodurch allein wir leben, weben und sind'. Common too is the directly related image of the warp and weft ('Zettel und Einschlag') in which Goethe seeks to capture complex, especially dialectic processes: the relation of conscious to unconscious in musical composition, letter to W. von Humboldt, 17 March 1832; the interplay of different types of men in history, *Maximen und Reflexionen* nr. 1103, HA 12, 519; and, most celebrated, the interaction of 'das Dämonische' and the world order in the last book of *Dichtung und Wahrheit*, HA 10, 177. The whole image-complex probably has roots in mystical tradition.
52. 'Prooemion', 'Eins und Alles' in *Zur Naturwissenschaft überhaupt*; 'Parabase', 'Epirrhema', 'Antepirrhema', and 'Urworte. Orphisch' in *Zur Morphologie*.
53. To Wilhelm von Humboldt, 1 September 1816. Sure enough, the weaving image is once more on hand ('das Gewebe dieses Urteppichs'), as is the notion of time being gathered into a symbolic moment ('Vergangenheit, Gegenwart und Zukunft . . . in eins geschlungen'). The work in question is not a lyrical poem, but

the *Agamemnon* of Aeschylus.
54. HA 1, 403.
55. Soret noted in his *Conversations* under 19 September 1830: 'Goethe est libéral d'une manière abstraite, mais dans la pratique il penche pour les principes ultra'. Goethe certainly believed in leaving politics to the experts (to Bucholtz, 14 February 1814) and was deferentially impressed when he met Metternich ('... Männer, die das ungeheure Ganze leiten' (to Gräfin O'Donell, 30 October 1813). He was hostile to the freedom of the press (to Karl August, 5 October 1816 and to Voigt, 27 January 1818), and it seems likely that he supported the reactionary Karlsbad decrees (to Karl August, 3 September 1819). In both these cases, Goethe was markedly less liberal than Karl August himself.
56. E.g. to Zelter, 12 January 1830.
57. In the appendix to *Lutetia* entitled 'Kommunismus, Philosophie und Klerisei' (Paris, 15 June 1843). *Sämtliche Werke* ed. Walzel, 9, 359f.
58. In his review of Menzel's *Die deutsche Literatur*, 1828, 5, 351; later and more influentially in *Die Romantische Schule*, 7, 49. Against Heine's view should be set Matthew Arnold's comment on 'Goethe's profound imperturbable naturalism', namely that 'nothing could be more really subversive of the foundations on which the old European order rested' and that 'no persons are so radically detached from this order, no persons so thoroughly modern, as those who have felt Goethe's influence most deeply'. Arnold, 'Heinrich Heine', in *Essays in Criticism*, First Series, ed. R.H. Super, Michigan 1962, p.110.
59. To Kanzler von Müller in conversation, 2 October 1823.
60. Cf. the famous statement in the letter to Zelter of 31 October 1831.
61. Cf. especially the line 'Nur wer sich kennt, der hat das Recht zu lieben', in the fragment 'Denn freilich sind's . . .' which is almost certainly a paralipomenon to the Elegy.
62. The distinction is worth insisting on, since it is central to the whole ethical and poetic issue. Staiger in his edition of the poems (II, 377) speaks, perhaps inadvertently, of 'der ganze Schmerz einer unwiderruflichen Entsagung', which is misleading.
63. Goethe's own simile. See to Eckermann, 15 November 1823.
64. To Schultz, 8 July 1823.
65. To Amalie von Levetzow, Ulrike's mother, 9 September 1823. Cf. also to Zelter, 24 August and to August von Goethe, 30 August 1823.
66. *Maximen und Reflexionen*, nr. 748, HA 12, 470.
67. To Zelter, 26 July 1828.
68. To Marianne von Willemer, 12 January 1832.
69. To Zelter, 29 April 1830.
70. To Zelter, 19 March 1827.
71. To Zelter, 9 August 1828.
72. To Schubarth, 2 April 1818.
73. Goethe to Eckermann, 6 June 1831, of the aged Faust.

13 EPILOGUE

In a long historical perspective, we can see Goethe's work and thought as a fleeting point in a process of transition, a temporary balance between two conditions of disequilibrium – in this respect too a centre. It was the culmination of an eighteenth-century development in which spiritual systems, whether of abstract rationality or religion, approached the formerly discredited world of earthly phenomena and sense experience and achieved a measure of integration with them. We saw this most clearly in the case of aesthetic theory,[1] but Goethe's poetry too rests on the same principle. In it, the spirit is not in contradiction with the physical reality of the world, on the contrary it grows from it, the two can be seen as essentially one: 'Der Geist des Wirklichen ist das wahre Ideelle'.[2] Hence in Goethe's own ordering of his poetry, the great scientific and philosophical poems of the Classical years and after bear the collective title 'Gott und Welt' and the word 'Gott', though not Christian in sense, is not a meaningless formality.

If this synthesis between material and spiritual had not been so fully achieved and found such perfect expression in Goethe, the moment of transition from a world dominated by Christian spirituality and philosophical schematism would not have been so clearly marked. Because it did find such expression, it stands out as the kind of highpoint which Hegel in his *Ästhetik* conceived Classicism as being: preceded by an excess of spirit over matter, succeeded by an excess of matter over spirit, a moment when the two were fused. Hegel of course, as a child of his time, located such Classical perfection in antiquity, labelled all the art of modern, i.e., post-Christian, times 'Romantic', and – again as a child of his time – accepted, even welcomed, the break-up of that synthesis and the supersession of art itself by his own métier, philosophy. As a contemporary, standing too close for perspective, he did not see how exactly Goethe and the best achievements of his age fitted into a similar historical pattern.

Sure enough, just as the Classical synthesis in Hegel's account is untenable and dissolves, Goethe's synthesis did not last. We saw something of how it was questioned and undermined when it was barely established.[3] This could hardly be otherwise, given the lateness of Germany's Classicism in relation to European developments. So from the watershed of the Goethezeit we descend to the disharmonies of the nineteenth century – to the necessary disharmonies of the social and political sphere, but also to the more fundamental disharmonies between spirit and matter in art and thought.

In Hegel's system, for long the dominant influence in the intellectual world, spirit — indeed, 'Spirit' — is restored to pride of place, while matter, whether the substance of physical phenomena, historical events, or works of art, is Its realisation, Its way of coming to consciousness of Itself. Yet even here the true underlying trend is towards materialism. That mystical entity, 'the Spirit', often turns out on sceptical examination to be only a hypostatisation, an analytic term, a grand label attached to material things and processes in order to give them the consecration of the unquestionable. In clearer, franker men — innovative artists like Büchner and Heine, revolutionary thinkers like Marx and Nietzsche — supremacy is openly given to the necessities of the material world. It is at most nostalgia for the harmony of a Goethean vision that makes Büchner still seek in science, beyond the harsh realities of social and personal existence, the dimly sensed 'Gesetz der Schönheit' of nature;[4] just as Heine's aspiration to a Grecian health is a desperate attempt to recapitulate the *Roman Elegies*. Büchner's return to religion in his brief dying words, and Heine's over the eight years of his fatal illness, confirm the split between material concerns and the spiritual realm, which is now inhabited only in defeat. Nor is there anything in Marx's analysis of the world, or in Nietzsche's monistic account of man and his culture (which again looks wistfully back towards Goethe as the ideal) to contradict this trend. And for three of these four thinkers, the missing harmony is less a personal thing than an aspiration for men within society, as material units in an area determined by material forces.

Such demands were foreign to Goethe. When in his late years he looked at European society, he was persuaded of its intractability to cultural influence, convinced that his power and competence lay only in the cultural field. The rest had grown beyond the individual grasp. Such disconnection was inherent in his situation from early on. Art in his youth lacked an adequate social base. He built his oeuvre without support from the conditions Classicisms normally arise from. It had to borrow its strength from elsewhere, from personal impulses, from scientific ideas, from ancient sources:

Gabe von obenher ist, was wir Schönes in Künsten besitzen,
　　Wahrlich, von unten herauf bringt es der Grund nicht hervor.[5]

Yet the art he and Schiller produced *implies* a society — implies, that is, a level of thought and feeling, of ethical and aesthetic discrimination, of aspiration and compassion — which never arose to match it. Much of the bitterness directed at German Classicism in recent times springs from the disappointment of politically aware critics at the failure of a national society ever to come up to the standards of an art which, throughout the nineteenth century, it was so ostentatiously proud to own. 'Der deutschen Klassik ist keine klassische deutsche Politik gefolgt'.[6] What did follow instead was 'grosse Politik', to use the term with which Nietzsche scorned Bismarck and his Reich.[7] And even before that stage, what had followed was the abrogation of liberal principles — of integrity as the Schiller of *Wallenstein* or the Goethe of *Iphigenie* understood that quality — by liberal men who opted in 1848 for a nation of external power rather than a nation of internal freedom.[8] For this, and for the subsequent catastrophes of German history, more relevant and substantial culprits are needed (and available) than two great poets who did not raise the call to revolution in one pocket-duchy amid the chaos of German principalities. 'There is something hard and ungrateful', an actual revolutionary of the day wrote, 'in the destructive instinct which so often forgets what *has* been done by the great men who preceded us, to demand of them merely an account of what more *might* have been done'; and 'it would be idle to speak of social art at all, or of the comprehension of humanity, if we could not raise altars to the new gods without overthrowing the old'.[9]

In the end, however socially aware our literary criticism and historiography are (and this study has tried to show the social influences which helped shape works of art and to suggest the influences these then exerted), it has to be recognised that literature is not merely one branch of ideology, left or right; that it has a distinctive nature, without which it would lose value and interest for most of its readers, and a distinctive way of communicating which is not that of simpler documents; that the criteria by which we judge it must begin by being internal to literature, its aims, conventions, and developments; and that the prime criterion is what a man *made*.

In Goethe's case, there is no questioning the grandeur of the things made, or of the processes of their making. And he made more than just single works. It was not much of an exaggeration when Byron addressed him as 'first of existing writers, who has created the literature of his own country and illustrated that of Europe'.[10] He was born into a country lacking, by European standards, a literature; by his death, and in large part through his efforts, German literature was admired and influential all over Europe, emulated even in France, an acknowledged major component of that 'Weltliteratur' the conception of which was coined by the old Goethe.

Even without that fulfilment of a 'literarische Sendung', Goethe is one of the handful of writers whose substance is something richer than any work or the sum of all their works: 'nicht nur ein guter und grosser Mensch, sondern eine Kultur'.[11]

Notes

1. See above, pp.71ff.
2. To Leopoldine Grustner von Grusdorf, 30 March 1827.
3. See above, Ch. 10.
4. *Über Schädelnerven*, in Büchner, *Werke* (Hamburger Ausgabe), II, 292.
5. Goethe and Schiller, *Tabulae votivae*, nr. 50, 'Deutsche Kunst'.
6. Karl Robert Mandelkow, 'Wandlungen des Klassikbildes in Deutschland im Lichte gegenwärtiger Klassikkritik', in Karl Otto Conrady (ed.), *Deutsche Literatur zur Zeit der Klassik* (Stuttgart, 1977), p.435.
7. Nietzsche, *Jenseits von Gut und Böse*, 'Völker und Vaterländer', para. 241, in *Werke* ed. Schlechta, II, 706f.
8. See Sir Lewis Namier's essay 'Nationality and Liberty', in Namier, *Vanished Supremacies* (1958).
9. Giuseppe Mazzini, 'Byron and Goethe', in Mazzini, *Essays* (The Scott Library edition, n.d.), pp.103f.
10. Dedication to the second edition of *Sardanapalus* (1823).
11. Nietzsche, *Menschliches, Allzumenschliches*, vol. 2, 'Der Wanderer und sein Schatten', para. 125, in *Werke*, ed. Schlechta, II, 928.

Secondary references have been kept to a minimum. Only the more helpful, challenging or historically distinctive critical literature is quoted or referred to in text and notes. The following is a check-list of these items, augmented by a few further titles (marked with an asterisk) which are likely to be useful to students of the period.

Auerbach, E. *Mimesis. Dargestellte Wirklichkeit in der abendländischen Literatur* (Berne, 1947)

Barnes, H.G. *Goethe's 'Die Wahlverwandtschaften* (Oxford, 1967)

*Barth, I.M. *Literarisches Weimar* (Stuttgart, 1971)

Bartscher, W. *Hölderlin und die deutsche Nation* (Berlin, 1942)

Beck, A. 'Hölderlin als Republikaner', *Hölderlin-Jahrbuch* 1969

*—— *Hölderlin : Eine Chronik in Bild und Dokument* (Frankfurt, 1970)

Benjamin, W. *Goethes Wahlverwandtschaften*, in Benjamin, *Gesammelte Schriften*, I, 1 (Frankfurt, 1974)

Benn, G. *Altern als Problem für Künstler*, in Benn, *Gesammelte Werke*, ed. D. Wellershoff, vol. 1 (Wiesbaden, 1959)

—— *Probleme der Lyrik*. Ibid.

Bertaux, P. 'Hölderlin und die französische Revolution', *Hölderlin-Jahrbuch* (1967/8)

—— *Hölderlin und die französische Revolution* (Frankfurt, 1969)

—— 'War Hölderlin Jakobiner?', in Riedel (ed.), q.v.

Bettex, A. *Der Kampf um das klassische Weimar* (Zurich 1935)

Binder, W. 'Grundformen der Säkularisation in den Werken Goethes, Schillers und Hölderlins' *ZfdPh*, Sonderheft (1964)

*—— (ed.) *Über Hölderlin* (Frankfurt, 1970)

—— 'Votum zur Diskussion der Frankfurter Hölderlin-Ausgabe.' *Hölderlin-Jahrbuch* (1975/7|)

*Blackall, E. *The Emergence of German as a Literary Language* (Cambridge, 1959)

Boas, E. *Schiller und Goethe im Xenienkampf* (Stuttgart, 1851)

Böckmann, P. *Hymnische Dichtung im Umkreis Hölderlins* (Tübingen, 1965)

—— 'Die französische Revolution und die Idee der ästhetischen Erziehung im Dichten Hölderlins', in W. Paulsen (ed.) *Der Dichter und seine Zeit* (Heidelberg, 1970)

*— *Schillers Don Karlos. Edition der ursprünglichen Fassung und entstehungsgeschichtlicher Kommentar* (Stuttgart, 1974)

Bruford, W.H. *Theatre, Drama and Audience in Goethe's Germany* London, [2]1957)

*— *Germany in the Eighteenth Century. The Social Background of the Literary Revival* (Cambridge, 1935)

— *Culture and Society in Classical Weimar* (Cambridge, 1962)

Burger, H.O. (ed.) *Begriffsbestimmung der Klassik und des Klassischen* (Darmstadt, 1972)

*Burschell, F. *Schiller* (Reinbek bei Hamburg, 1968)

*Cassirer, E. *Die Philosophie der Aufklärung* (Tübingen, 1932)

— *Freiheit und Form* (Darmstadt, [3]1961)

Conrady, K.O. (ed.) *Deutsche Literatur zur Zeit der Klassik*. Stuttgart 1977

Constantine, D. 'The Meaning of a Hölderlin Poem'. *Oxford German Studies* 9 (1978)

Curtius, E.R. *Europäische Literatur und lateinisches Mittelalter* (Berne, 1948)

Droz, J. *L'Allemagne et la Révolution Francaise* (Paris, 1949)

Durzak, M. *Poesie und Ratio* (Bad Homburg, 1970)

*Eichner, H. *Friedrich Schlegel* (New York, 1970)

— (ed.) *'Romantic' and its cognates. The European History of a Word* (Manchester, 1972)

Elschenbroich, A. (ed.) *Deutsche Dichtung im achtzehnten Jahrhundert* (Munich, 1960)

Emrich, W. 'Das Problem der Symbolinterpretation'. *DVjs* 26 (1952)

Fairley, B. *A Study of Goethe* (Oxford 1947)

*— *Goethe's Faust. Six Essays* (Oxford 1953)

Fambach, O. (ed.) *Schiller und sein Kreis. Ein Jahrhundert deutscher Literaturkritik*, vol. II (Berlin 1957)

Fauchier-Magnan, A. *The Small German Courts in the Eighteenth Century* (London, 1958)

Flitner, W. *Goethe im Spätwerk* (Bremen, [2]1957)

Garland, H.B. *Schiller the Dramatic Writer. A Study of Style in the Plays* (Oxford, 1969)

Gerhard, M. *Der deutsche Entwicklungsroman* (Halle, 1926)

Gooch, G.P. *Germany and the French Revolution* (London, 1920)

Guardini, R. *Hölderlins Weltbild und Frömmigkeit* (Munich, [2]1955)

Gundolf, F. *Goethe* (Berlin, [9]1916)

Hamburger, K. 'Schiller und die Lyrik'. *Jahrbuch der deutschen Schiller-Gesellschaft* XVI (1972)

Harrison, R.B. *Hölderlin and Greek Literature* (Oxford 1975)

Heller, E. 'Goethe and the Avoidance of Tragedy', in Heller, *The Disinherited Mind* (Cambridge, ³1971)

Henkel, A. *Entsagung. Eine Studie zu Goethes Altersroman* (Tübingen, 1954)

Hermand, J. *Von deutscher Republik* (Frankfurt, 1968)

— *Von Mainz nach Weimar* (Stuttgart, 1969)

Hofmannsthal, H. von *Wilhelm Meister in der Urform*, in Hofmannsthal, *Ausgewählte Werke* vol. 2 Frankfurt 1957

— *Unterhaltung über den Tasso von Goethe*. Ibid.

Houben, H.H. *Verbotene Literatur* (Berlin, 1924)

*Jacobs, J. *Wilhelm Meister und seine Brüder. Untersuchungen zum deutschen Bildungsroman* (Munich, 1972)

Jäger, H.W. 'Zur Frage des 'Mythischen' bei Hölderlin. In : Riedel (ed.) q.v.

*Kaiser, G. *Von der Aufklärung bis zum Sturm und Drang 1730-1785* (Gütersloh, 1966)

*Kelletat, A. *Hölderlin. Beiträge zu seinem Verständnis in unserem Jahrhundert* (Stuttgart, 1967)

Klaiber, T. *Die deutsche Selbstbiographie* (Stuttgart, 1921)

Klotz, V. *Die erzählte Stadt* (Munich, 1969)

Kommerell, M. *Gedanken über Gedichte* (Frankfurt, ²1956)

— *Geist und Buchstabe der Dichtung* (Frankfurt, ⁵1962)

Körner, J. *Klassiker und Romantiker* (Berlin, 1924)

Lewes, G.H. *The Life and Works of Goethe* (Everyman Edition, ⁵1938)

Lovejoy, A.O. *The Great Chain of Being* (Harvard 1936)

*Lüders, D. (ed.) *Hölderlin. Sämtliche Gedichte* Text und Kommentar 2 vols. (Bad Homburg, 1970)

Lukacs, G. *Die Theorie des Romans* (Berlin, 1920)

— *Goethe und seine Zeit* (Berne, 1947)

Mandelkow, K.R. 'Wandlungen des Klassikbildes in Deutschland im Lichte gegenwärtiger Klassikkritik', in Conrady (ed.) q.v.

Mann, G. 'Schiller als Historiker', *Jahrbuch der deutschen Schiller-Gesellschaft* IV (1960)

Mason, E.C. *Goethe's 'Faust'. Its Genesis and Purport* (Berkeley and Los Angeles, 1967)

Mazzini, G. 'Byron and Goethe'. In : Mazzini, *Essays* (n.d.)

Meyer, F. *Friedrich Nicolai* (Leipzig, 1938)

Minder, R. 'Hölderlin unter den Deutschen', in Minder, *Dichter in der Gesellschaft* (Frankfurt, 1966)

Mommsen, W. *Die politischen Anschauungen Goethes* (Stuttgart, 1948)

Namier, L. *Vanished Supremacies* (London, 1958)

Nisbet, H.B. *Goethe and the Scientific Tradition* (London, 1972)

*Peacock, R. *Hölderlin* (Manchester, 1938)

Pyritz, H. 'Der Bund zwischen Goethe and Schiller', *PEGS* XXI 1950-1

Raabe, P. *Die Horen. Einführung und Kommentar*. Darmstadt 1959

Rasch, W. 'Die klassische Erzählkunst Goethes', in Burger (ed.) q.v.

—— 'Ganymed. Über das mythische Symbol in der Dichtung der Goethezeit', in *Wirkendes Wort*. Sonderheft (September 1954)

—— *Torquato Tasso. Die Tragödie des Dichters* (Stuttgart 1954)

*—— *Goethes 'Iphigenie auf Tauris' als Drama der Autonomie* (Munich 1979)

Reed, T.J. 'Critical Consciousness and Creation. The Concept "Kritik" from Lessing to Hegel'. *Oxford German Studies* 3 (1968)

*—— 'The Goethezeit and its Aftermath', in Pasley (ed.) *Germany. A Companion to German Studies* (London, 1972)

*Reeves, N. and Dewhurst, K. *Friedrich Schiller : Medicine, Psychology, Literature* (Oxford 1978)

*Reiss, H.S. *Goethe's Novels* (London, 1969)

*Rickert, H. *Goethes Faust. Die dramatische Einheit der Dichtung* (Tübingen, 1932)

Riedel, I. (ed.) *Hölderlin ohne Mythos* (Göttingen 1973)

Riemann, R. 'Wilhelm Meister', in Zeitler (ed.) *Goethe-Handbuch* (Stuttgart, 1917)

Roberts, J.M. *The Mythology of the Secret Societies* (London, 1972)

Ryan, L. *Hölderlin* (Stuttgart, ²1967)

Sartre, J.P. *Qu'est-ce que la littérature?* repr. (Paris, 1964)

Sattler, D.E. 'Editionsprinzipien und Editionsmodell'. *Hölderlin-Jahrbuch* (1975/7)

Schadewaldt, W. *Hellas und Hesperien* (Stuttgart, 1960)

Schaeder, G. *Gott und Welt. Drei Kapitel Goethescher Weltanschauung* (Hamlin, 1947)

Schaefer, A. *Goethe und seine grossen Zeitgenossen* (Munich, 1968)

Scheidig, W. *Goethes Preisaufgaben für bildende Künstler* (Weimar, 1958)

Schmidt, A. *Nachrichten von Büchern und Menschen* (Frankfurt, 1971)

Schmidt, E. *Lessing* (Berlin, 1899)

—— and Suphan B. *Xenien 1796* (Weimar, 1893)

*Schöffler, H. *Deutscher Geist im 18.Jahrhundert* (Göttingen, 1956)

Schrimpf, H.J. *Das Weltbild des späten Goethe* (Stuttgart, 1956)

Schulz, G. *Schillers Horen. Politik und Erziehung* (Heidelberg 1960)

Sengle, F. *Wieland* (Stuttgart, 1949)

Sommerfeld, M. *Goethe in Umwelt und Folgezeit* (Leiden, 1935)

Stahl, E.L. *Die religiöse und die humanitätsphilosophische Bildungsidee und die Entstehung des deutschen Bildungsromans im 18.Jahrhundert* (Berne, 1934)

*— *Schillers Drama. Theory and Practice* (Oxford, 1954)

Staiger, E. *Goethe* (Zurich, [3]1960-3)

— *Schiller* (Zurich, 1967)

— 'Fruchtbare Missverständnisse Goethes und Schillers', in Schaefer (ed.) q.v.

Steiner, J. *Sprache und Stilwandel in Wilhelm Meister* (Zurich, 1959)

Steiner, G. *Language and Silence* (1967)

Stern, A. *Der Einfluss der Französischen Revolution auf das deutsche Geistesleben* (Stuttgart, 1928)

Stöcklein, P. *Wege zum späten Goethe* (Hamburg, [2]1960)

Szondi, P. *Lektüren und Lektionen* (Frankfurt, 1973)

Trilling, L. *The Liberal Imagination* repr. (New York, 1964)

Uffhausen, D. 'Anmerkungen zum Erstling der Frankfurter Hölderlin-Ausgabe'. *Hölderlin-Jahrbuch* (1975/7)

Walser, M. *Hölderlin zu entsprechen* (Biberach, 1970)

Ward, A. *Book Production, Fiction and the German Reading Public 1740-1800* (Oxford, 1974)

Watt, I. *The Rise of the Novel*, repr. (Peregrine Books, 1963)

Wellman-Bretzigheimer, G. 'Zur editorischen Praxis im Einleitungsband der Frankfurter Hölderlin-Ausgabe.' *Hölderlin-Jahrbuch* (1975/7)

Wiese, B. von *Schiller* (Stuttgart, [3]1963)

Wilkinson, E.M. 'Reflections on translating Schiller's "Aesthetic Letters"', in F. Norman (ed.) *Schiller Bicentenary Lectures* (London, 1960)

— and Willoughby, L.A. *Goethe Poet and Thinker* (London, 1962)

Wolff, H.M. *Goethes Weg zur Humanität* (Berne, 1951)

Wundt, W. *Goethes Wilhelm Meister und die Entstehung des modernen Lebensideals* (Berlin, 1913)

*Wuthenow, R.R. *Das erinnerte Ich. Europäische Autobiographie und Selbstdarstellung im 18.Jahrhundert* (Munich, 1974)

INDEX

Fictional characters, authors of secondary literature, and correspondents whose names figure only in the notes are not included. The alphabetical ordering discounts umlauted vowels.